DEFLATIONISM AND PARADOX

Deflationism and Paradox

Edited by
JC BEALL
and
BRADLEY ARMOUR-GARB

CLARENDON PRESS · OXFORD

OXFORD
UNIVERSITY PRESS

Great Clarendon Street, Oxford OX2 6DP

Oxford University Press is a department of the University of Oxford.
It furthers the University's objective of excellence in research, scholarship,
and education by publishing worldwide in

Oxford New York

Auckland Cape Town Dar es Salaam Hong Kong Karachi
Kuala Lumpur Madrid Melbourne Mexico City Nairobi
New Delhi Shanghai Taipei Toronto

With offices in

Argentina Austria Brazil Chile Czech Republic France Greece
Guatemala Hungary Italy Japan Poland Portugal Singapore
South Korea Switzerland Thailand Turkey Ukraine Vietnam

Published in the United States
by Oxford University Press Inc., New York

First published 2005

British Library Cataloguing in Publication Data
Data available

Library of Congress Cataloging in Publication Data
Data available

Typeset by SPI Publisher Services, Pondicherry, India
Printed in Great Britain
on acid-free paper by
Biddles Ltd., King's Lynn, Norfolk

ISBN 0–19–928711–2 978–0–19–928711–6

Contents

List of Contributors

BRADLEY ARMOUR-GARB is Assistant Professor of Philosophy, the State University of New York at Albany, and was a fellow of Wolfson College, Oxford. He works primarily on philosophical logic, the philosophy of language, and metaphysics, and has published articles on a constellation of issues, including truth, meaning, the paradoxes, and the like. He is coeditor, with JC Beall, of *Deflationary Truth* (Open Court Press, 2005) and *Deflationism and Paradox* (Oxford University Press, 2005).

JODY AZZOUNI is Professor of Philosophy, Tufts University. His books include *Metaphysical Myths, Mathematical Practice: The Ontology and Epistemology of the Exact Sciences, Knowledge and Reference in Empirical Science*, and *Deflating Existential Commitment: A Case for Nominalism.*

JC BEALL is Associate Professor of Philosophy, University of Connecticut, and Research Associate at the AHRC Arché Centre for the philosophy of logic, language, mathematics, and mind, at the University of St Andrews. In addition to papers on truth-related topics and paradox, Beall is the editor of *Liars and Heaps* (Oxford University Press, 2003), coauthor, with Bas C. van Fraassen, of *Possibilities and Paradox: An Introduction to Modal and Many-Valued Logic* (Oxford University Press, 2003), and coauthor, with Greg Restall, of *Logical Pluralism* (Oxford University Press, in press). Beall is currently finishing a monograph on truth and paradox (Oxford University Press, forthcoming).

HARTRY FIELD is Professor of Philosophy, New York University. His books include *Science Without Numbers* (Princeton University Press, 1980), *Realism, Mathematics and Modality* (Blackwell, 1989), and *Truth and The Absence of Fact* (Oxford University Press, 2001). Field's main research areas include metaphysics, epistemology, philosophy of logic, philosophy of mathematics, philosophy of science, and philosophical logic; he has published on those topics in *the Journal of Philosophy, Mind, Noûs, Philosophical Quarterly, Philosophical Review, Journal of Philosophical Logic*, and others.

CHRISTOPHER GAUKER is Professor of Philosophy, University of Cincinnati. He is the author of *Thinking Out Loud: An Essay on the Relation between Thought and Language* (Princeton University Press, 1994), *Words without Meaning* (MIT Press, 2003) and *Conditionals in Context* (MIT Press, forthcoming). He is hoping for a renaissance in philosophy.

MICHAEL GLANZBERG is Associate Professor of Philosophy, University of California at Davis. He works mainly on logic and the philosophy of language. He has published articles on truth, paradox, the semantics/pragmatics boundary, presupposition, and demonstratives.

Dorothy Grover is Adjunct Professor of Philosophy, Canterbury, and Professor Emeritus at the University of Illinois at Chicago. She has published extensively in philosophical logic, formal logic and is the originator of the prosentential theory of truth. She is the author of *A Prosentential Theory of Truth* (Princeton University Press).

Anil Gupta is Distinguished Professor of Philosophy, University of Pittsburgh. His research interests lie in logic, epistemology, and metaphysics. His publications on the concept of truth include 'Truth and Paradox', 'A Critique of Deflationism', and *The Revision Theory of Truth* (written with Nuel Belnap).

Volker Halbach is Fellow of New College and Lecturer, University of Oxford. His research interests include logic, philosophy of language, epistemology and philosophy of mathematics. In particular, he has worked on axiomatic theories of truth. He is the author of *Axiomatische Wahrheitstheorien* and articles in *Mind*, the *Journal of Symbolic Logic*, the *Notre Dame Journal of Formal Logic*, the *Journal of Philosophical Logic*, *Erkenntnis*, *Synthese*, and other journals.

Leon Horsten is Professor of Philosophy, University of Leuven. His main research area is philosophical logic: truth and paradox, the paradox of the knower, and that of provability. He has published on these subjects in journals including *Journal of Philosophical Logic*, *Notre Dame Journal of Formal Logic*, *Journal of Symbolic Logic*, *Synthese*, and *Erkenntnis*. Together with Volker Halbach, he has published *Principles of Truth* (Ontos Verlag, 2004). He also works on problems in metaphysics, epistemology, and philosophy of mathematics.

Paul Horwich is Professor of Philosophy, New York University. His recent publications include *From a Deflationary Point of View* (Oxford University Press, 2004) and *Reflections on Meaning* (Oxford University Press, 2005).

Graham Priest is Boyce Gibson Professor of Philosophy, University of Melbourne, and Arché Professorial Fellow, Department of Logic and Metaphysics, University of St Andrews. His books include *In Contradiction, Beyond the Limits of Thought, Introduction to Non-Classical Logic* and *Towards Non-Being* (forthcoming).

Greg Restall is Associate Professor of Philosophy, University of Melbourne, and Fellow of the Australian Academy of Humanities. His main research interests are in logic, both formal and philosophical, and he has published papers in those areas. His books include *An Introduction to Substructural Logics* (Routledge), *Logic* (Routledge), and *Logical Pluralism* (Oxford University Press, 2005). He is currently working in proof theory and its connections to meaning theory.

Alan Weir is Senior Lecturer, Queen's University Belfast, Northern Ireland. He has also taught at the Universities of Edinburgh and Birmingham and at Balliol College, Oxford. He has published articles on logic and philosophy of mathematics in a number of journals including *Mind*, *Philosophia Mathematica*, *Notre Dame Journal of Formal Logic*, and *Grazer Philosophische Studien*, and contributed chapters in a number of volumes published by Oxford University Press.

A Short Introduction

JC Beall and Bradley Armour-Garb

Typical introductory essays aim to do one of two things (or both): either provide a synopsis of the individual essays or provide sufficient background material for the essays. This introductory essay is atypical. The essays in this volume are self-contained, for the most part, and the relevant background material is covered elsewhere. Accordingly, our modest aim in this introduction, aside from providing references for background material (see §4), is to give a brief sketch of the motivation: why a volume devoted to the narrow topic of *deflationism and paradox*?

1. DEFLATIONARY THEORIES IN ONE BROAD STROKE

Deflationary theories of truth (and semantic notions, generally) are generally characterised negatively, in terms of a contrast with more substantial theories of truth (and, again, of other semantic notions), which they aim to *deflate*. For present purposes, we may characterise a deflationary theory of truth as embracing the *fundamental equivalence* of $\mathsf{True}(\mathcal{A})$ and $\mathcal{A}$.

What does 'equivalence' mean here? Different answers yield different versions of deflationism, and we will not here survey the field; however, at the very least, $\mathsf{True}(\mathcal{A})$ and $\mathcal{A}$ are taken to be materially equivalent – each enjoying the same 'semantic status'.[1]

The given equivalences are 'fundamental' in that they are both conceptually and explanatorily basic. To say that they are *conceptually basic* is to say that there are no 'deeper facts' about the given notion (truth, denotation), in terms of which it can be defined or in terms of which the given equivalences themselves can be explained.

Conceptually, such equivalences are brute. The upshot of such conceptual fundamentality is that the equivalences are more or less analytic, as well as being necessary and a priori. To say that they are *explanatorily basic* is to say that our 'truth'-talk is

[1] The same applies to other basic semantic notions, like *denotation*, where Denotes (b, c) is 'equivalent' to True (b = c). The given equivalence with respect to 'denotation' may—and often will—be qualified with an antecedent condition concerning existence, or perhaps some 'free' version, employing a free logic, will be given. The details are irrelevant, for this introduction, as the individual essays contained in this volume adequately elaborate, when relevant.

explained, where explanation is required, by nothing 'deeper' than such equivalences—or by the inference rules (e.g., true-in, true-out) that yield them. The deflationist thus predicts, and is required to establish, that the explanatory role of truth is exhaustively explained by the equivalences, which equivalences are thus the fundamental explainers of all cases of 'truth'-talk.[2] Thus, both conceptually and explanatorily, the equivalences are taken by the deflationist to be *bedrock*.[3]

2. WHY DEFLATIONISM AND PARADOX?

Over the last few decades, deflationary theories (concerning semantic notions) have encountered numerous objections but, for the most part, they have held up well. That said, and leaving aside the objections to deflationism that have been discussed, one—*foundational*—topic has been ignored: semantic paradoxes. That is surprising, given that, on the surface, semantic paradoxes seem to be more problematic for deflationism than rival 'inflationary' theories.

Consider a caricature (but a suggestive one, we hope) that regards variants of the Liar Paradox.[4] There seem to be sentences that can be used to attribute falsity (or lack of truth) to themselves and that are understandable (in one's own idiolect or language, in general) and, thus, meaningful. Example:

> The first displayed sentence in §2 is not true.

By the 'fundamental equivalence' governing 'is true', the first displayed sentence in §2 is equivalent to *'The first displayed sentence in §2 is not true' is true*. Assuming a detachable conditional for which Identity holds—i.e., a detachable conditional $\rightarrow$ such that $A \rightarrow A$ is (logically) true—we have it that the first displayed sentence is not true if true, and that it is true if not true. Assuming that the first displayed sentence in §2 is either true or not true, we quickly get that it is both, which is, by most lights, either impossible or, at any rate, a very bad result.

That much (familiar Liar paradoxes) is familiar. But why is *that* any more problematic for deflationary theories than for rival 'inflationary' theories? At least on the surface (but, we admit, possibly no deeper than that), there are several reasons for thinking that semantic paradoxes appear to be more problematic for deflationists than for 'robust' theorists.

First, inflationary (sometimes called 'substantive') theories can (and, in general, will) rely on an *inflated* theory of meaning, in order to avoid such paradoxes. 'Inflationists' will thus marshal such theories, in order to insist that there simply is

[2] One important consequence of the construal of the equivalences as explanatorily basic is that *truth-conditions* play no substantial role in explaining either meaning or content, on pain of (vicious) circularity.

[3] There is much more to this framework, and many more details, but (again) the more may be picked up elsewhere [2] (and see §4). For present purposes, we intend only a simple sketch that motivates the volume, letting individual chapters provide further details.

[4] The same caricature, suitably amended, applies to the paradoxes of denotation and the like, as we hope is obvious.

no (paradox-generating) proposition, appearances to the contrary notwithstanding. But deflationists, as in §1, cannot obviously follow a similar path, since the constraints on a theory of meaning are severe.[5]

Second, inflationary theorists can simply claim that, for reasons of brute metaphysical fact, the relevant equivalence of True($\mathcal{A}$) and $\mathcal{A}$ does not in general hold; or they can claim that the T-schema does not generally hold, for paradox-riddled sentences like the one displayed in §2. Such claims may—and almost certainly will—appear to be ad hoc. That said, it seems that inflationary theories have room to rely on brute facts that, despite appearance, break the 'fundamental equivalence' to which *deflationists* are committed—though (we should warn) on pain of abandoning one of the precious few common features that tie deflationists and inflationists together![6]

Third, inflationary theories can fairly easily invoke 'truth-value gaps', and thereby reject Bivalence, perhaps along the lines of the 'polarity view'—situation-theoretic parts of the world, along the lines of van Fraassen [8], or Barwise and Perry [3].[7] But *deflationists* cannot obviously go down that road.

To see why, assume, as we (with many deflationists) do, that falsity is truth of negation, that is, that False($\mathcal{A}$) is 'equivalent' (in a deflationist's preferred sense) to True($\neg\mathcal{A}$). To say that $\mathcal{A}$ is neither true nor false is thus to say something of the form $\neg(\mathcal{A}\vee\neg\mathcal{A})$, which itself is either inconsistent (depending on the logic) or, at least, not obviously true. If, for example, $\neg$ behaves along so-called Strong Kleene lines (gap-in, gap-out), then $\neg(\mathcal{A}\vee\neg\mathcal{A})$ is itself not true if $\mathcal{A}$ is not true. So, how does the deflationist (truly) assert that $\mathcal{A}$ is not true if it is neither true nor false? One *might* invoke 'exclusion negation', which takes 'gaps' to 'truths' and is otherwise classical. The problem is that an 'exclusion'-liar will then be foisted, as an apparent inconsistency-generator, which is something most deflationists will try to avoid.

For the foregoing reasons, deflationists appear—at least on the surface—to face a tougher time either accommodating or responding to semantic paradoxes than do their 'robust' rivals. But even if such appearances go no deeper than the surface, the paradoxes still pose a pressing issue for the eventual prospects of semantically driven deflationary theories of truth. If the deflationist requires that her theory of truth be consistent, then she must give an account of how such consistency is achieved in the face of apparent paradox. That much, of course, is common to any theorist—robust or otherwise. What constrains the deflationist—though not the inflationist—is that the deflationist's account of the paradoxes must satisfy (at least) the following two requirements:

[5] This is not to say that deflationists cannot invoke propositions. They can; but if they do, they will not be able to invoke terribly high standards regarding the conditions under which a sentence is said to *express* a proposition. Perhaps more to the point, the deflationist can invoke propositions, provided the relevant *expression-relation* is suitably deflated. See [5, 7] for discussion.

[6] We do not like the term 'deflationist', due to the wildly divergent uses. That said, the term is now fairly entrenched (within philosophical circles) as a catch-all for the actual theories—minimalism, disquotationalism, pro-sententialism, and the like—that are at issue in this volume.

[7] The idea is to model 'gap-makers' by adding an appropriate 'polarity', much in the way that one gets 'negative facts' [4].

1. Deflationistically kosher: The account must not invoke more of truth (or denotation, or content, or semantic notions, in general) than is available, given the (conceptual and explanatory) fundamentality of the equivalences.
2. Respect the target role: The *role* of truth (or denotation, etc.) must not be compromised.

We (briefly) review the requirements.

The 'kosher' requirement is obvious, though (again) it highlights a difference between inflationary and deflationary constraints. The 'respect the role' requirement is likewise straightforward. One might ask why we have a truth predicate if, as deflationists agree, it is not in the language to pick out some salient feature of the world (e.g., in the way that, say, 'is a cat' does), and especially if, as deflationists agree, True($\mathcal{A}$) is simply equivalent to $\mathcal{A}$ (in some sense of 'equivalence' or other).

Deflationists, of any stripe, maintain that the *raison d'être* of (deflationary) truth—the sole reason for its being in the language in the first place—is to serve a *practically* important expressive role. In particular, 'is true' affords generalisations that, for practical purposes, we could not otherwise make. Typical examples involve so-called 'blind ascriptions', as when Wrigley said to Field 'Nothing that you said in Chicago is true', despite Wrigley's inability to remember exactly what Field said. Other examples involve 'big' theoretical generalisations, where, for reasons of time or space, we cannot state every individual claim; instead, one simply asserts that the given (possibly infinite) set of claims is true, or that one of a (possibly infinite) set of claims is true. Thus, deflationists—despite differences of detail on other points—are committed to there being an important expressive role associated with 'is true' and the other semantic predicates, in general. What the 'respect the target role' requirement amounts to, then, is simply this: Any 'solution' to the liar paradox (and variants), to be adequate, must not compromise the expressive role for which the target predicate was introduced.

3. CLOSING REMARKS

There has been a great deal of discussion about the prospects of deflationism but very little—until this volume—about how (if at all) deflationists can accommodate paradox. The extent to which such paradoxes arrest deflationism's progress is a wide open question. By all lights, the paradoxes are challenging—even with as much wiggle-room as robust theorists enjoy. The challenge is all the more acute when the constraints are tightened.

The purpose of this volume is to explore the extent to which either deflationism can accommodate paradox (as some of the contributors argue) or the extent to which paradox undermines deflationism (as others argue). The result, we hope, will serve to both sharpen the ongoing debate about deflationary theories, and perhaps, along the way, make progress on paradox, in general.

4. BACKGROUND READING

As above, the chapters of this volume are fairly self-standing, and the authors (in our opinion) have done a nice job of achieving a 'user-friendly' discussion. That said, most of the chapters presuppose familiarity with a lot of basic notions, too many to lay out in this essay. While we expect that most readers will be familiar with the requisite basics, there may be those (very few, we expect) who lack the basics in one area or other. The following list is for such readers.

There are three salient areas of background reading—basic logical notions, deflationism, and paradox, In addition to references given in individual chapters, we here list a few works that are intended for 'advanced undergraduates'.

1. Basic logical notions:
   a. JC Beall and Bas van Fraassen, *Possibilities and Paradox: An Introduction to Modal and Many-Valued Logic* (Oxford: Oxford University Press, 2003).
   b. Graham Priest, *An Introduction to Non-Classical Logic* (Cambridge: Cambridge University Press, 2001).
2. Deflationism:
   a. Marian David, *Correspondence and Disquotation* (Oxford: Oxford University Press, 1994).
   b. Bradley Armour Garb and JC Beall, *Deflationary Truth* (Chicago: Open Court Press, 2004). The introductory essay surveys the main deflationary positions and the volume contains papers covering representative objections and replies.
3. Paradox:
   a. Robert L. Martin, editor, *Recent Essays on Truth and The Liar Paradox* (Oxford: Oxford University Press, 1984). [A collection of earlier seminal work on semantic paradox.]
   b. Anil Gupta, 'Truth', in Lou Goble (ed.) *The Blackwell Guide to Philosophical Logic* (Oxford: Blackwell, 2001). [A concise discussion of standard theories of truth that purport to accommodate paradox.]
   c. JC Beall, 'Semantic and Logical Paradoxes', in Dale Jacquette (ed.) *Philosophy of Logic* (Dordrecht: Kluwer, forthcoming), in the forthcoming multi-volume series *Philosophy of Science* under the general editorship of Dov Gabbay. [This is a 60–90 page survey, concentrating on contemporary work on the Liar.]

REFERENCES

[1] Alan Ross Anderson and Nuel D. Belnap. *Entailment: The Logic of Relevance and Necessity*, vol. 1. Princeton University Press, Princeton, 1975.

[2] Bradley Armour-Garb and JC Beall. 'Varieties of Deflationism'. In Bradley Armour-Garb and JC Beall, eds, *Deflationary Truth*. Open Court Press, Chicago, 2004. In press.

[3] Jon Barwise and John Perry. *Situations and Attitudes.* MIT Press, Bradford Books, 1983.

[4] JC Beall. 'On Truthmakers for Negative Truths'. *Australasian Journal of Philosophy,* 78: 264–268, 2000.

[5] Hartry Field. 'Deflationist Views of Meaning and Content'. *Mind,* 103: 249–285, 1994. Reprinted in [6].

[6] —— *Truth and the Absence of Fact.* Oxford University Press, Oxford, 2001.

[7] Paul Horwich. *Meaning.* Oxford University Press, 1998.

[8] Bas C. van Fraassen. 'Facts and Tautological Entailments'. *Journal of Philosophy,* 66: 477–487, 1969. Reprinted in *Entailment* vol. 1 [1].

1

Transparent Disquotationalism

JC Beall

I. BACKGROUND

God could use only the T-free fragment of English to uniquely specify our world. We are unlike God in that respect; we need a device that enables us to overcome finite constraints in our effort to describe the world. That device is 'true' or, for clarity, 'dtrue', a device introduced via rules of intersubstitution: that $\mathsf{dT}\langle\mathcal{A}\rangle$ and $\mathcal{A}$ are intersubstitutible in all (transparent) contexts.[1] The sole role of dtruth—the reason behind its introduction into the language—is to enable generalisations that, given our finite constraints, we couldn't otherwise express.

So goes a common metaphor that guides many deflationary theories of truth. What distinguishes deflationists from non-deflationists is that the former take dtruth to be fundamental: if there are other truth predicates in the language, they are derivative, deriving from 'dtrue' and other connectives. In a slogan: all that need be explained about truth is explicable in terms of dtruth (and other logical tools).

With Hartry Field [13] I embrace deflationism—indeed, disquotationalism—as a methodological stance. The basic argument for 'methodological deflationism' invokes Ockham: if, as it (so far) appears, our truth-talk can be explained (or, in some cases, explained away) in terms of dtruth, then we ought to recognise only dtruth and its derivatives; positing more than dtruth would be postulation without profit. Moreover, it is a sound methodological strategy, as Field notes, to pursue disquotationalism as far (and earnestly) as we can; for in doing so—and, plausibly, only in doing so—we will either see where it breaks down (where, for example, more than mere dtruth is required) or we will see its vindication. Either way, we will learn the dtruth about truth.

I am grateful to Hartry Field and Graham Priest for ongoing discussion, and also for comments and suggestions on an earlier draft. I am also grateful to Michael Lynch, Daniel Nolan, Greg Restall, Dave Ripley, Stewart Shapiro and, most recently, Lionel Shapiro. All of these philosophers have raised important issues for transparent disquotationalism, issues that can only be—and will be—taken up elsewhere.

[1] Throughout, I will use 'dT' to represent our expressive device—'is dtrue'—and the angle-brackets as some sort of naming-device (where appropriate). (For the most part, I let context settle use-mention.)

2. SEMANTIC PARADOX

The guiding metaphor, as above, has us introducing 'dtrue' not to name some property in the world but, rather, to enable generalisations about the world and its features. The simplest way to achieve such a device is as above: that, for any (declarative) sentence $\mathcal{A}$, $\mathsf{dT}\langle\mathcal{A}\rangle$ and $\mathcal{A}$ are intersubstitutible in all (transparent) contexts. But 'dtrue' is a predicate, and introducing it into the grammar of English yields spandrels, unintended by-products of the device. Some of those spandrels are paradoxical:

The first displayed sentence in §2 is not dtrue.

The task is to figure out what to do with such sentences.

I agree with Field [16] that the game is over if, in the face of such paradoxes, the fundamental intersubstitutivity of $\mathsf{dT}\langle\mathcal{A}\rangle$ and $\mathcal{A}$ is abandoned. Another desideratum (also shared with Field) is the validity of the T-schema. Such desiderata are not jointly achievable in a classical framework. A non-classical route is needed.

Field's recent work—under the program of 'pure disquotationalism'—appears to achieve the given desiderata while retaining a *consistent* expressive device, a consistent dtruth theory.[2] While his work, by my lights, is the most promising approach within the constraints of a consistent dtruth-theory, I will not discuss Field's theory in this paper.[3] My aim in this paper is merely to sketch an alternative approach: 'transparent disquotationalism', a version of 'dialetheic deflationism' that achieves the (above) desiderata by accepting that dtruth is an inconsistent device (given via an inconsistent theory). I believe that transparent disquotationalism sits well with the guiding deflationary metaphor and, more importantly, appears to be simpler than Field's position. Whether I am right about those (alleged) virtues is for debate to tell. For present purposes, my aim is simply to sketch the basic position and answer a few objections.[4]

3. GAPS, GLUTS, AND 'NOT'S: A BASIC FRAMEWORK

With Field I agree that there are gaps in the language, that some (meaningful) sentences are 'indeterminate'—that neither language (its rules, etc.) nor the world determines that such sentences are dtrue or dfalse. Semantic paradoxes themselves, I believe, give no good reason to think that there are gaps. Rather, the appearance of gaps arises from reflection on vagueness, non-denoting terms, and other such familiar phenomena.[5] For present purposes, I will not argue for gaps but, rather, recognise

[2] See Field's chs 2 and 4 of this volume, and references therein.

[3] See Priest's chapter (ch. 3) for discussion.

[4] This is part of a larger (monograph) project, which takes up many of the philosophical and logical issues that, for space considerations, are suppressed here.

[5] I am *not* suggesting that gaps are *forced* upon us by the pressures of rational reflection. I claim only that the appearance of gaps is an initially strong one, one that, by my lights, we have no pressing reason to reject.

them as a logical option for sentences. Some sentences are such that they may (logically) be neither dtrue nor dfalse; they are 'gappy', neither the world nor language determining their dtruth.

Recognising gaps calls for some account of how we can consistently express that $\mathcal{A}$ is gappy (assuming, as I do, that we can consistently express as much). For such purposes Field introduces a 'definitely' operator.[6] I prefer to recognise a device that is already commonly recognised—exclusion negation (or pseudo-exclusion, as I will explain below). When Agnes says that the king of France doesn't exist, presumably, Agnes is employing exclusion.[7] When Max says of a borderline sentence that it is not dtrue, presumably, Max is employing exclusion. And it does no harm to say the same about *'this sentence is dfalse' is not dtrue*: exclusion is at work.[8]

The idea, in short, is that dfalsity is dtruth of (let us say) choice-negation $\sim$, and to say that $\mathcal{A}$ is neither dtrue nor dfalse is to say something of the form $\neg(\mathcal{A} \vee \sim\mathcal{A})$, where $\neg$ is exclusion.[9]

The apparent trouble with exclusion, of course, is that (due to paradoxical spandrels) it yields apparent gluts—sentences that are both dtrue and dfalse.[10] But since the current proposal allows for gluts, such apparent trouble is no trouble.

3.1 A Formal Picture: FDE*

The idea can be modelled using a four-valued language along the lines of Anderson and Belnap's FDE [1, 2].[11] Our semantic values $\mathcal{V} = \{1, \mathsf{b}, \mathsf{n}, 0\}$ are ordered thus:

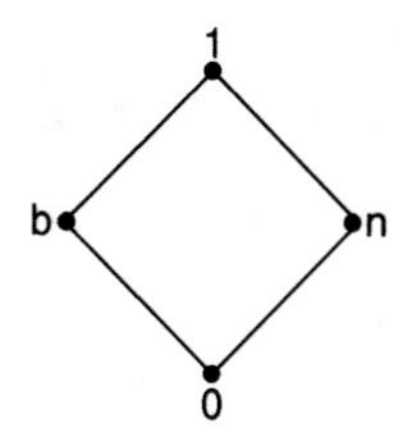

Intuitively, 1 models sentences that are dtrue but not dfalse, 0 sentences that are dfalse but not dtrue, b sentences that are both dtrue and dfalse, and n sentences that are neither. The designated values $\mathcal{D}$ are 1 and b, the idea being that dtrue sentences are designated (even when they are also dfalse).

[6] See Field's work (and references therein) in this volume.

[7] I am not suggesting that that conclusion is forced upon us, but only that it is a natural go.

[8] Note that if we didn't recognise more than one negation, then the apparent distinction between 'simple' and 'strengthened' liar-sentences collapses in a deflationary framework—or, at least, in a pure/transparent disquotational framework.

[9] Exactly how to model these negations is taken up in §3.1.

[10] The terminology of 'gaps' and 'gluts' stems, I believe, from Kit Fine's work [17].

[11] The name 'FDE' is now common for the following framework; however, it is perhaps unfortunately so named, since there are various accounts of 'first degree entailment'. But I shall follow what now seems to be common practice.

Interpretations are functions v from sentences into $\mathcal{V}$ such that $v(\mathcal{A} \wedge \mathcal{B})$ and $v(\mathcal{A} \vee \mathcal{B})$ are the glb and lub of $v(\mathcal{A})$ and $v(\mathcal{B})$, respectively.[12]

In FDE we have only (what I shall call) 'choice negation' $\sim$, which toggles 1 and 0 and is fixed at both b and n. We add another negation, pseudo-exclusion $\neg$, which toggles 1 and 0, is fixed at b, but takes n (gaps) to 1. The result is (what I shall call) FDE*.[13] Accordingly, FDE*-interpretations 'obey' the following diagrams with respect to negation:

$\sim$	$\mathcal{A}$	$\neg$	$\mathcal{A}$
1	0	1	0
n	n	1	n
b	b	b	b
0	1	0	1

Notice that dfalsity, following standard thinking, remains dtruth of negation—dtruth of *choice* negation, as opposed to pseudo-exclusion (henceforth, exclusion).

A *model* of $\mathcal{A}$ is an FDE*-interpretation that designates $\mathcal{A}$, that is, an interpretation v such that $v(\mathcal{A}) \in \mathcal{D}$. And a model of $\Gamma = \{\mathcal{A}_1, \ldots, \mathcal{A}_n\}$ is a model of $\mathcal{A}_i$, for each $1 \leq i \leq n$.

Consequence $\Vdash$ is defined thus: $\Gamma \Vdash \mathcal{A}$ iff every model of Γ is a model of $\mathcal{A}$. Valid sentences are consequences of $\emptyset$.

3.2 Remarks

As expected, excluded middle fails for choice negation but holds for exclusion: $\nVdash \mathcal{A} \vee \sim \mathcal{A}$ but $\Vdash \mathcal{A} \vee \neg \mathcal{A}$. Moreover, both negations exhibit standard double-negation behaviour, at least in terms of 'inferences'. For example: $\mathcal{A} \dashV\Vdash \sim\sim\mathcal{A}$ and $\mathcal{A} \dashV\Vdash \neg\neg\mathcal{A}$.[14]

Standard de Morgan laws hold for choice: $\sim(\mathcal{A} \vee \mathcal{B})$ is equivalent to $\sim\mathcal{A} \wedge \sim\mathcal{B}$ (and similarly for the other laws). But exclusion is different; de Morgan laws will generally hold in one direction but not both. Of particular importance—given the role of exclusion in the notion of 'gaps'—is that we have

$$\neg(\mathcal{A} \vee \mathcal{B}) \Vdash \neg\mathcal{A} \wedge \neg\mathcal{B}$$

but we do not have equivalence; in fact,

$$\neg\mathcal{A} \wedge \neg\mathcal{B} \nVdash \neg(\mathcal{A} \vee \mathcal{B})$$

12 For present purposes I lay out the propositional semantics; the predicate extension—including the resulting dtruth-theory—is straightforward. For general options see Priest [29].

13 This is not the best name, as it might suggest an approach to FDE using the Routely star, but I trust that no confusion will ensue.

14 Note, however, that in the double-exclusion case, this is only bi-consequence, not equivalence in the strong sense of 'same value' (which does hold in the choice case). What we have in the exclusion case is co-designation: $\mathcal{A}$ and $\neg\neg\mathcal{A}$ are both designated or both undesignated on any FDE*-interpretation.

A counterexample: $v(\mathcal{A}) = \mathsf{n}$ and $v(\mathcal{B}) = \mathsf{b}$. In that case, $v(\neg\mathcal{A}) = 1$ and $v(\neg\mathcal{B}) = \mathsf{b}$, and so $v(\neg\mathcal{A} \wedge \neg\mathcal{B}) = \mathsf{b}$. But, then, $v(\mathcal{A} \vee \mathcal{B}) = 1$, and so $v(\neg(\mathcal{A} \vee \mathcal{B})) = 0$.[15]

Is the 'non-standard' behaviour of exclusion—failure of some de Morgan principles—a problem? I see no reason to think as much, in general. Presumably, choice is our 'default' negation; we employ exclusion when we need to talk about failures of choice. Our 'intuitions' about de Morgan, in turn, are presumably based on choice—or, at least, based on 'normal cases', 'determinate cases', and so on. That some such (de Morgan) principles should fail for exclusion seems, as said, not to be a problem, in general.

On the other hand, one might worry that such de Morgan 'failures' pose a problem for the role of exclusion in the notion of gaps. Gappy sentences, I've said, are neither dtrue nor dfalse. But that, one would think, ought to be *equivalent* to saying that such sentences are (exclusion-) not dtrue and (exclusion-) not dfalse. The worry is that such equivalence fails, given that, as above, $\neg(\mathcal{A} \vee \mathcal{B})$ and $\neg\mathcal{A} \wedge \neg\mathcal{B}$ are not equivalent, in general.

Fortunately, the worry isn't serious: $\neg(\mathcal{A} \vee \mathcal{B})$ and $\neg\mathcal{A} \wedge \neg\mathcal{B}$ *are* equivalent in the special case where $\mathcal{B}$ is $\sim\mathcal{A}$, which is precisely the case involved in saying that $\mathcal{A}$ is neither dtrue nor dfalse. Accordingly, the general failure of de Morgan (for exclusion) seems not to be a particular problem for the notion of gaps.

One advantage of the two negations is that they may be combined to yield a stronger notion of truth, one that Dummett [12] highlighted in an argument (from gaps) against deflationism. Dummett pointed out that if $\mathcal{A}$ is gappy then calling $\mathcal{A}$ 'true' appears to be false. But, then, since dtruth requires that $\mathsf{dT}\langle\mathcal{A}\rangle$ and $\mathcal{A}$ be equivalent, gaps thereby seem to undermine dtruth. But that is the wrong lesson to draw. What Dummett's argument shows is that there is a stronger notion of truth than dtruth—one according to which an ascription of 'truth' to $\mathcal{A}$ is false if $\mathcal{A}$ is gappy. Such a notion is definable in terms of our two negations and dtruth [7]. In particular, define our 'robustly true' predicate rT thus: $\mathsf{rT}\langle\mathcal{A}\rangle$ iff $\mathsf{dT}\langle\sim\neg\mathcal{A}\rangle$.[16]

It is also worth noting that the law of non-contradiction, in the form

$$\neg(\mathcal{A} \wedge \neg\mathcal{A})$$

or, equivalently (given dtruth),

$$\neg(\mathsf{dT}\langle\mathcal{A}\rangle \wedge \neg\mathsf{dT}\langle\mathcal{A}\rangle)$$

holds for exclusion,[17] even though it is logically possible—and, indeed, according to transparent disquotationalism, actual—that some sentence $\mathcal{A}$ is such that $\mathsf{dT}\langle\mathcal{A}\rangle \wedge \neg\mathsf{dT}\langle\mathcal{A}\rangle$ is dtrue. A 'transparent disquotationalist' takes Liar-sentences *not* to undermine the dtruth of non-contradiction; such sentences indicate only that the law (so given) is also dfalse.

[15] The given 'inference' holds if our values are linearly ordered thus: $1 \succ \mathsf{b} \succ \mathsf{n} \succ 0$. But in that case, de Morgan will break down for choice.

[16] Note that Field [15] makes the same response to Dummett in terms of his 'definitely' operator. As above, I think that recognising exclusion is more natural (and ultimately simpler) than Field's 'definitely', but debate will tell.

[17] Of course, non-contradiction does not hold for choice, as there are no valid choice-negations.

4. A SUITABLE CONDITIONAL

Most theories of dtruth emphasise the importance of the T-schema (or 'dtrue'-schema). I also take the T-schema seriously, but its status is derivative: if we have a conditional $\looparrowright$ that satisfies Identity (i.e., $\Vdash \mathcal{A} \looparrowright \mathcal{A}$), then the T-schema falls out of the fundamental intersubstitutivity of $\mathsf{dT}\langle\mathcal{A}\rangle$ and $\mathcal{A}$. One desideratum, then, is that our conditional satisfy Identity. Another desideratum is that it detaches—that some suitable version of Modus Ponens holds.[18]

Beyond such basic desiderata (e.g., Identity, Detachment), which, presumably, are desiderata common to most disquotational theories, other issues emerge for the current (paraconsistent) proposal. If, as I propose, we simply accept that our expressive device is inconsistent (that there are 'dtrue'-ful gluts), we need to rethink contraction-principles and contraposition.[19]

Contraction. Consider common versions of contraction (where $\looparrowright$ is some detachable conditional):

» $\mathcal{A} \wedge (\mathcal{A} \looparrowright \mathcal{B}) \looparrowright \mathcal{B}$

» $(\mathcal{A} \looparrowright (\mathcal{A} \looparrowright \mathcal{B})) \looparrowright (\mathcal{A} \looparrowright \mathcal{B})$

» $\mathcal{A} \looparrowright (\mathcal{A} \looparrowright \mathcal{B}) \Vdash \mathcal{A} \looparrowright \mathcal{B}$

Such principles give rise to triviality (everything being dtrue) in virtue of Curry's paradox [4, 11, 22, 23]. Spandrels such as 'If this sentence is dtrue, then every sentence is dtrue' pose a problem if the given conditional detaches, satisfies Identity (yielding the T-schema), and also contracts. For example, where dT is our expressive device (dtruth predicate), let $\mathcal{C}$ be of the form $\mathsf{dT}\langle\mathcal{C}\rangle \looparrowright \bot$, where $\bot$ is an explosive sentence (like 'everything is true'), and $\looparrowright$ satisfies both Identity and Modus Ponens. Then explosive Curry is cooked thus:

$\mathsf{dT}\langle\mathcal{C}\rangle \looparrowright (\mathsf{dT}\langle\mathcal{C}\rangle \looparrowright \bot)$	T-schema (Simplification)
$\mathsf{dT}\langle\mathcal{C}\rangle \looparrowright \bot$	Contraction for $\looparrowright$
$(\mathsf{dT}\langle\mathcal{C}\rangle \looparrowright \bot) \looparrowright \mathsf{dT}\langle\mathcal{C}\rangle$	T-schema (Simplification)
$\mathsf{dT}\langle\mathcal{C}\rangle$	Modus Ponens for $\looparrowright$
$\bot$	Modus Ponens for $\looparrowright$

The other contraction-principles similarly yield triviality. So, a suitable conditional needs to avoid such contraction.[20]

[18] We already have two 'material conditionals' deriving from disjunction and the two negations. One of those (viz., choice) will fail to satisfy Identity; the other (exclusion) will satisfy Identity, since it satisfies excluded middle. But neither 'conditional' is suitable since neither detaches in any respect. (Disjunctive Syllogism is invalid in FDE*.)

[19] Of course, as Field and others have noted, *everybody* ought to rethink contraction, but it is particularly pressing in a strong paraconsistent setting such as transparent disquotationalism.

[20] If there are other conditionals in the language (as there may well be), the language—expanded to the predicate level—must be 'robustly contraction-free', to use Restall's terminology [32]. For extensive discussion of contraction in paraconsistent settings, see Restall [33, 34].

Contraposition, in the form

$$\mathcal{A} \looparrowright \mathcal{B} \vdash \dagger\mathcal{B} \looparrowright \dagger\mathcal{A}$$

(where $\dagger$ is a negation), seems to be motivated by the thought that gluts are logically impossible. Given such (alleged) impossibility, it stands to reason that if $\mathcal{B}$ is dfalse and $\mathcal{A} \looparrowright \mathcal{B}$ dtrue (where $\looparrowright$ is detachable) then $\mathcal{A}$ too is dfalse (or gappy, and so its exclusion-negation dtrue). But reason doesn't so stand if we take gluts seriously; after all, $\mathcal{B}$ itself may be both dtrue and dfalse.[21]

4.1 Proposal

For purposes of a conditional (not necessarily the only conditional in the language, or even a conditional expressing *entailment*), we expand the language along modal lines—invoking points of evaluation. Exactly how this is done is not pressing, for present purposes.[22] I will assume that our interpretations are now expanded so that each sentence $\mathcal{A}$ is given a value at each point x, the value being $v_x(\mathcal{A})$.

Our set of points $\mathcal{W}$ is the union of two sets, $\mathcal{N}$ (normal points) and $\mathcal{NN}$ (non-normal points),[23] with a distinguished element $@ \in \mathcal{N}$ (the actual point) and $\mathcal{N} \cap \mathcal{NN} = \emptyset$. In addition, $\mathcal{W}$ is ordered by a heredity relation $\sqsubseteq$, intuitively, $x \sqsubseteq y$ iff everything dtrue at x is dtrue at y.

Finally, interpretations come equipped with an 'arbitrary evaluator' γ the task of which is to assign values to $\rightarrow$-claims at non-normal points: γ takes claims of the form $\mathcal{A} \rightarrow \mathcal{B}$ and yields elements of $\mathcal{V}$ at non-normal points.

With the foregoing in hand, our conditional $\rightarrow$ is given as follows

Where $x \in \mathcal{N}$:

» $\mathcal{A} \rightarrow \mathcal{B}$ is dtrue at x iff for every $y \in \mathcal{W}$ such that $x \sqsubseteq y$, if $\mathcal{A}$ is dtrue at y then $\mathcal{B}$ is dtrue at y.

» $\mathcal{A} \rightarrow \mathcal{B}$ is dfalse at x iff $\mathcal{A}$ is dtrue at x and $\mathcal{B}$ dfalse at x.

Where $x \in \mathcal{NN}$:

$v_x(\mathcal{A} \rightarrow \mathcal{B}) = \gamma(\mathcal{A} \rightarrow \mathcal{B}, x)$

CONSTRAINT: If, for any $x \in \mathcal{NN}$, $\gamma(\mathcal{A} \rightarrow \mathcal{B}, x)$ and $\gamma(\mathcal{B} \rightarrow \mathcal{A}, x)$ are designated, then $\gamma(\mathcal{C}(\mathcal{A}) \rightarrow \mathcal{C}(\mathcal{B}), x)$ and $\gamma(\mathcal{C}(\mathcal{B}) \rightarrow \mathcal{C}(\mathcal{A}), x)$ are designated, for any context $\mathcal{C}$.[24]

[21] Moreover, triviality ensues if, for example, $\looparrowright$ contraposes and that all $\mathcal{A}$s are $\mathcal{B}$s entails the dtruth of $\mathcal{A} \looparrowright \mathcal{B}$.

[22] For common options consult any of Beall and van Fraassen [9], Chellas [10], Hughes and Cresswell [18], Priest [29, 31], Restall [34], or other texts that discuss intensional frameworks.

[23] Non-normal points were first invoked by Kripke [20] to model Lewis systems weaker than S4 (systems in which Necessitation fails). Routley and Meyer [36] and Routley and Loparic [35] invoked such points for purposes closer to the current project, as have Priest [25] and Mares [21]. I will briefly return to the philosophical import of non-normal points in §6.

[24] Without the constraint, substitutivity of equivalents, if it is expressed via $\rightarrow$, will easily fail. Some might think the constraint ad hoc, but I think it not so. All that we are doing is finding that (proper) subset of 'arbitrary evaluators' that respect what we take conditionals to do—viz., satisfy substitutivity of equivalents. (That said, an alternative approach that delivers such substitutivity

Consequence is now given in terms of 'dtruth-preservation' over all base points (of any interpretation). So long as there is no interpretation that designates all $\mathcal{A}_i$ at @ but fails to designate $\mathcal{B}$ at @, then $\mathcal{A}_1, \ldots, \mathcal{A}_n \Vdash \mathcal{B}$. Similarly, valid sentences are those that are designated at all base points of all interpretations.

4.2 Virtues of the Conditional

The target desiderata are achieved:[25]

DETACHMENT: While we don't have *all-points detachment* ('dtruth-preservation' over all points), we do have it at all *base-points* (at @ for any given interpretation). To get a counterexample to

$$\mathcal{A}, \mathcal{A} \rightarrow \mathcal{B} \Vdash \mathcal{B}$$

we would need $v_@(\mathcal{A}) \in \mathcal{D}$, $v_@(\mathcal{A} \rightarrow \mathcal{B}) \in \mathcal{D}$ and $v_@(\mathcal{B}) \in \{\mathsf{n}, \mathsf{0}\}$. But if $v_@(\mathcal{A} \rightarrow \mathcal{B}) \in \mathcal{D}$, then there is no point y such that $@ \sqsubseteq y$ and $v_y(\mathcal{A}) \in \mathcal{D}$ but $v_y(\mathcal{B}) \in \{\mathsf{n}, \mathsf{0}\}$. Accordingly, Modus Ponens (at the 'actual world') holds.

IDENTITY: We have the validity of $\mathcal{A} \rightarrow \mathcal{A}$, and hence (in the full predicate extension) the T-schema, given the fundamental (intersubstitutivity) rules governing 'dtrue'.[26]

NO CONTRACTION: Counterexamples to the given contraction principles emerge in virtue of non-normal worlds. Consider, for example, a 2-point interpretation in which $v_@(\mathcal{A}) = \mathsf{n} = v_@(\mathcal{B})$ and, where $w \in \mathcal{NN}$, $v_w(\mathcal{A}) = \mathsf{b}$, $v_w(\mathcal{B}) = \mathsf{n} = \gamma(\mathcal{A} \rightarrow \mathcal{B}, w)$, and, for all other $\rightarrow$-claims at w, let $\gamma(\mathcal{C} \rightarrow \mathcal{D}, w) = \mathsf{b}$.[27] Then

$$v_@(\mathcal{A} \rightarrow \mathcal{B}) = \mathsf{n} = v_@(\mathcal{A} \rightarrow (\mathcal{A} \rightarrow \mathcal{B}))$$

and, in turn, since $@ \sqsubseteq w$ and $\gamma(\mathcal{A} \rightarrow (\mathcal{A} \rightarrow \mathcal{B}), w) = \mathsf{b}$,

$$v_@((\mathcal{A} \rightarrow (\mathcal{A} \rightarrow \mathcal{B})) \rightarrow (\mathcal{A} \rightarrow \mathcal{B})) = \mathsf{n}$$

and hence $\nVdash (\mathcal{A} \rightarrow (\mathcal{A} \rightarrow \mathcal{B})) \rightarrow (\mathcal{A} \rightarrow \mathcal{B})$. Similar models serve to invalidate the other contraction principles.

NO CONTRAPOSITION: We have two versions of contraposition, one for exclusion and one for choice. Each version fails. Consider, for example, a 2-point interpretation

without explicitly invoking a constraint such as above, is Priest's framework in [25]. For discussion of Priest's framework that equally applies to the current proposal, see Mares [21]—though note that Mares is concerned with 'relevant conditionals' and →, as here given, is not relevant in the technical sense.)

[25] It is worth comparing the virtues of this conditional with Field's (see chs 2 and 4). Both conditionals seem to yield target desiderata, the difference being that this one does it in an apparently simpler fashion and, pending further discussion, it is not implausible that this one—unlike Field's—models some genuine conditional in natural language (though I'm not yet prepared to press that point). But, as with other issues concerning the two positions, debate will tell. (And see §6 for some discussion.)

[26] But see §6 for further discussion.

[27] Letting γ assign b to all other $\rightarrow$-claims at w ensures heredity—i.e., $@ \sqsubseteq w$.

according to which $v_{@}(\mathcal{A}) = 1 = v_{@}(\mathcal{B}) = v_w(\mathcal{A})$ and $v_w(\mathcal{B}) = \mathsf{b}$. In that case, $v_{@}(\mathcal{A} \rightarrow \mathcal{B}) = 1$ and, since w is a point such that $@ \sqsubseteq w$ and $\sim\mathcal{B}$ is designated but $\sim\mathcal{A}$ undesignated, $v_{@}(\sim\mathcal{B} \rightarrow \sim\mathcal{A}) = \mathsf{n}$. (Again, to ensure heredity, just let γ assign b to all the target conditionals.) Accordingly, we have

$$\mathcal{A} \rightarrow \mathcal{B} \nVdash \sim\mathcal{B} \rightarrow \sim\mathcal{A}$$

The same counterexample invalidates the exclusion-version of contraposition; hence, $\mathcal{A} \rightarrow \mathcal{B} \nVdash \neg\mathcal{B} \rightarrow \neg\mathcal{A}$.

Substitutivity of Equivalents: This is ensured via the constraint on 'arbitrary evaluators' γ. We have, for any context $\mathcal{C}$, that $\mathcal{A} \leftrightarrow \mathcal{B} \Vdash \mathcal{C}(\mathcal{A}) \leftrightarrow \mathcal{C}(\mathcal{B})$.

There are other virtues but, for present purposes, I briefly turn to the emerging philosophical picture.[28]

5. THE PHILOSOPHICAL PICTURE: TRANSPARENT DISQUOTATIONALISM

The philosophical picture is straightforward. Dtruth (or 'dtrue') is a device that we introduce solely for purposes of generalisations—generalisations that we couldn't otherwise express. The device is not introduced to name some important property or, in general, to generate 'new claims' about the world; it is introduced to be *transparent*, to 'reveal' claims that—given our finite situation—we couldn't otherwise express. But, of course, some 'new claims' are inevitable—those such that 'dtrue' cannot be eliminated via the fundamental rules of intersubstitutivity. Consider, for example, the first displayed sentence in §2. The (non-linguistic) world leaves the matter open, leaving the language (if anything) to settle the matter. The status of the first displayed sentence in §2 turns on whether 'not' is choice or exclusion. Transparent disquotationalism is open to various (logical) options. In the choice case, the given sentence is gappy; in the exclusion case, glutty. But there is no reason to squirm at either result. Our device is doing its work in a simple way.[29]

I should also make plain that there is no reason to recognise gluts beyond the 'merely semantic' fragment of the language. The 'dtrue'-free fragment, I believe, is glut-free.[30] The position is that our expressive device (dtruth), introduced into the grammatical environment of English (in which we have two different negations),

[28] The proposed conditional is a variant of techniques used in 'relevant' literature; it arose from my failed attempts to enlist the services of a 'Melbourne restricted quantification' conditional [8], with which the current proposal has many common features. (I should also point out that I am tempted by a linear-ordering of $\mathcal{V}$, instead of the more standard ordering given here. There are various virtues of a linear-ordering, but also many oddities. For purposes of sketching the general position—transparent disquotationalism—I avoid discussion of the differences engendered by a linear-ordering.)

[29] See §6 for a bit more discussion on taking choice-Liars to be gappy (versus glutty).

[30] This sort of 'simply semantic inconsistency' can be modelled along Kripke/Woodruff lines, although there are difficulties bringing in pseudo-exclusion. I have (and continue to) work on this [6], but I will skip it here. One early attempt at 'simply semantic inconsistency' is Woodruff [37] (though, again, monotonicity is lost if pseudo-exclusion is brought in, and Woodruff's framework also lacks a suitable conditional).

earns its keep in a way that—incidentally (by way of 'spandrels')—renders it inconsistent at various 'fixed points' in the semantic fragment of the language. But, again, so long as such inconsistency doesn't interfere with the job of 'dtrue' or our inquiries, in general, then it needn't be shunned. Moreover, as Priest [23, 27] has argued for some time, there seem to be no non-question-begging arguments for thinking that truth—or, in the current case, dtruth—must be consistent. And for a deflationist of any stripe, who cannot invoke some 'robustly consistent nature of truth', the point is even more to the point: that there seems to be no good reason not to accept the apparent inconsistency of dtruth.[31]

Transparent disquotationalism takes the transparency of 'dtrue' seriously and allows at least the logical possibility of both gaps and gluts. In the end, the main argument for transparent disquotationalism is one of simplicity and naturalness: compare it with its rivals. The point of this paper is to put the general framework on the table for such comparison.[32] For now, I briefly answer a few objections.

6. A FEW OBJECTIONS AND REPLIES

OBJECTION. JUST DTRUE T-CONDITIONALS: While $\rightarrow$, as given above, satisfies the desideratum of Identity—and thereby yields the T-schema (via the fundamental intersubstitutivity governing dtruth)—it fails to achieve another desideratum: namely, that instances of the T-scheme never be dfalse. After all, if $\mathcal{A}$ is both dtrue and dfalse (at @), then $\mathcal{A} \rightarrow \mathcal{A}$ will likewise be dtrue *and dfalse*, and hence $\mathsf{dT}\langle\mathcal{A}\rangle \rightarrow \mathcal{A}$ will be dtrue *and dfalse*. But we want not only that such T-conditionals always be dtrue; we want that they never be dfalse. Transparent disquotationalism, at least with the conditional so given, fails to deliver the latter desideratum.[33]

REPLY: Two replies.

First, unless one is objecting to gluts, in general, it isn't clear why the alleged desideratum is a desideratum. After all, suppose that we allow that some sentence $\mathcal{A}$ is both dtrue and dfalse, that is, that $\mathcal{A}$ and $\sim\mathcal{A}$ are dtrue. Then $\mathcal{A}$ is a dtrue sentence that is equivalent to a dfalse sentence, and hence $\mathsf{dT}\langle\mathcal{A}\rangle \rightarrow \mathcal{A}$ is a conditional with a dtrue antecedent and a dfalse consequent. Why shouldn't the given T-conditional be dfalse? As far as I can see, the only reason for imposing the alleged desideratum stems from a prior complaint against gluts, something that—as far as the objection explicitly goes—is not at issue.[34]

[31] Note that I am *not* arguing that rational reflection forces an inconsistent dtruth-theory upon us! I believe that, qua disquotationalist (or deflationist, in general), an inconsistent dtruth-theory is the simplest and most natural, but I know of no knock-down arguments for the position.

[32] This paper is part of a monograph. The paper is included in this volume not to discuss all the details but, rather, simply to set the general approach beside the represented rivals.

[33] This objection is due to conversation with Hartry Field.

[34] As Daniel Nolan noted (in conversation), one might also expect that T-conditionals be dtrue *and dfalse* especially if, as in the current case, the proposed theory of dtruth is openly inconsistent. Given the fairly important status of T-conditionals in a theory of dtruth, an explicitly inconsistent theory of dtruth ought (in some sense) to have dfalse (and dtrue) instances of the T-scheme. While I think there is something to Nolan's suggestion, I will not pursue the point here.

Second reply. Suppose that, against the first reply, the alleged desideratum is imposed, that T-conditionals are never to be dfalse. As the objection points out, that desideratum is not achieved for $\rightarrow$ as currently given; however, one can—if need be—achieve the desired result by stipulating different 'dfalsity conditions' for @ and any point $y \neq @$. In particular,

$\mathcal{A} \rightarrow \mathcal{B}$ is never dfalse at @;

For any normal $x \neq @$, $\mathcal{A} \rightarrow \mathcal{B}$ is dfalse at x iff $\mathcal{A}$ is dtrue at x and $\mathcal{B}$ dfalse at x.

The virtues of $\rightarrow$ still hold under this set-up, but there will be no interpretation v such that $v_{@}(\sim(\mathcal{A} \rightarrow \mathcal{A}))$ is designated. (I should point out that, pending some motivation, I am not attracted to this second reply. I give it only as an option, should good reason to endorse the current objection emerge.)

Simplicity lost: Perhaps transparent disquotationalism affords a very simple framework for dtruth, but only in that there are no restrictions placed on the predicate and no apparent revenge problems. But surely the resulting system is more complicated 'in daily life', since it undermines much of our usual reasoning—for example, Disjunctive Syllogism (DS).

Reply: The general thrust of this objection has been sufficiently answered by Priest [23], but it is important to emphasise two points. The first is that, although not developed here, transparent disquotationalism, as here proposed, recognises inconsistency—sentences that are both dtrue and dfalse—only at the semantic level; there is no suggestion that such inconsistency emerges in semantic-free sentences (sentences that do not use one or more of our expressive devices). Accordingly, there is a straightforward sense in which DS is perfectly reliable when its instances are restricted to sentences in which (for example) 'dtrue' is eliminable—'grounded sentences', along Kripkean lines.

Second point. While the logic developed here—that is, the logic that results from the semantic framework discussed in this paper—is monotonic, the position may be filled out along the 'adaptive' lines of Batens [3]. An adaptive paraconsistent logic is a non-monotonic logic that serves to model the idea that for a large fragment of the language, instances of (for example) DS are 'dtruth-preserving'; it is just that when $\mathcal{A}$ and $\sim\mathcal{A}$ are dtrue, a weaker paraconsistent base kicks in.[35] Accordingly, the alleged complications involved in 'losing' DS are not nearly as clear as the objection suggests.

Uniformity of Solutions: Priest [30] argues that a virtue of dialetheism is that it gives uniform solutions to both the semantic and logical paradoxes (and, in fact, that Ramsey's very 'distinction' is thereby not genuine). Transparent disquotationalism is far from uniform in the same respect, as not all paradoxical claims—even within the same family (e.g., Liars)—are treated alike. Choice Liars—and Curry sentences—are taken to be gappy while exclusion Liars are glutty. This gives a speckled theory that fails to respect the obvious uniformity of the phenomena.

[35] For an adaptive version of FDE, see the appendix in Beall [5], which can easily be expanded to yield an adaptive logic of FDE*. (The version in [5] is a more general version of Priest's gap-free 'minimally inconsistent LP'. Priest discusses the philosophical import of such a non-monotonic framework in [24].)

Reply: There is a plain sense in which I agree with Priest's arguments against Ramsey's 'distinction', that both families of paradox are treated alike: such phenomena are either gluts or gaps.[36] On the other hand, the objection is correct that, unlike Priest's uniform solution, I do not accept that all Liars (or the like) are gluts. But that is more to the 'transparent' point of disquotationalism. If neither language nor the world determines that 'this sentence is dfalse' is dtrue or dfalse (or both), then such is the status of that Liar: it is simply underdetermined, neither dtrue nor dfalse. But language does determine the dtruth (and dfalsity) of some Liars—for example, exclusion-Liars. The resulting picture is indeed speckled compared with Priest's uniformity of gluts, but it is not clear why such speckles should be a blot against the theory. Why not accept that language and world call for a speckled theory (in the given sense)? No obvious reason is forthcoming.[37]

Of course, as far as FDE* goes, one could (logically) treat 'simple Liars'—choice-Liars—as gluts, as opposed to gaps. But, methodologically, I'm inclined to accept the principle that if neither the world nor language determines the dtruth or dfalsity of $\mathcal{A}$, then there is no good reason to accept that $\mathcal{A}$ is both dtrue and dfalse. And since excluded middle fails for choice, there's no obvious reason to think that choice-Liars are gluts. Similarly with respect to standard truth-tellers: logically—as far as FDE* is concerned—one can treat them as gaps, gluts, or classically evaluable; however, since language and world fail to determine their dtruth or dfalsity, I leave them at that, as 'undetermined', simply gappy.

Field Uniformity: Field's 'pure disquotationalism', with his 'definitely' and conditional (see this volume), appears to give a unified solution to all (relevant) paradoxes—semantic, 'extensions' (properties), and even soritical paradox.[38] And, it seems, he does as much consistently. Transparent disquotationalism, as developed here, is inconsistent (due to exclusion instead of Field's 'definitely') yet seems not to yield a unified approach to paradox in Field's sense. Why not, then, just go with Field's approach?

Reply: Again, there is a plain sense in which I too give a unified response to both semantic and soritical paradox: the phenomena are either glutty or gappy. Moreover, I agree that, in some sense, both phenomena arise from indeterminacy in the language. The difference is that the indeterminacy yields—on my picture—overdeterminacy (gluts) in some (purely semantic) cases. Still, the objection is correct that Field's theory treats the relevant phenomena exactly alike, whereas I do not. Part of the trouble in assessing the current objection is that, by my lights, we remain without a

[36] I should note that I do not accept Priest's arguments about *mathematical sets*, but I will not pursue the issue here. (I *do* accept that semantic *extension*-theory is inconsistent, but the identification of mathematical sets—whatever the set-theory—and semantic extension-theory is something that I reject. But, again, this is for elsewhere.)

[37] I should point out that the related expressive device 'denotes' is not easily treated along Priest's 'uniform gluts' line. It seems to me that *some* paradoxes of denotation call for gluts, and some for gaps, although some of this will turn on how one decides to treat cases of denotation-failure. I leave this for discussion elsewhere, but see Priest [26, 28] for some of the issues.

[38] Actually, I do have some worries about whether Field's approach resolves the paradoxes of denotation, but I will not pursue those worries here.

general account of *vagueness*. (We have many responses to the sorites, but that is different from having a clear account of vagueness itself.) Pending such an account, it is hard to tell—and, perhaps, premature—to judge whether vagueness-related paradox and semantic paradox are, at root, the same basic phenomenon calling for a unified theory along Fieldian lines. For now, I leave the ultimate weight of the current objection open. As above, the merits of transparent disquotationalism over Field's alternative will need to be weighed on standard pragmatic virtues. The question, I believe, is whether achieving a consistent dtruth-device is worth the apparent complexity involved.[39]

DTRUTH AT A POINT: *Dtruth at a point* is essential to your account of the given conditional. How can this be cashed out in terms of dtruth? How, that is, is this compatible with disquotationalism?

REPLY: One option is to go 'fictionalist' with respect to such points, and take 'dtrue at a point' along the lines of 'according to the story'. On such an approach, all the 'truth' involved in 'dtrue at a point' is dtruth: we have an operator α_x (intuitively, 'according to story *x*') and dT, and the fundamental intersubstitutivity of dtruth needn't fail in the context of α_x—for example, one may go from $\alpha_x \mathsf{dT}\langle \mathcal{A} \rangle$ to $\alpha_x \mathcal{A}$ and back. Accordingly, no threat to disquotationalism arises.

Some such fictionalist line also sits well with a promising account of 'non-normal worlds' due to Priest [25].[40] Non-normal points, on this proposal, are simply points (fictions) according to which conditionals behave in rather bizarre patterns. If we are already prepared to recognise 'points of evaluation' in our semantics (e.g., in standard 'possible worlds' accounts), there seems to be no a priori reason that we shouldn't recognise different sorts of such 'points'. In particular, there's no a priori reason against points—'worlds'—at which actual logical laws fail. And that, in the end, is all that the non-normal points—our fictions—amount to. For present purposes, I will leave the matter there (and take up a fuller discussion elsewhere).

I think that there are other options (including something along Lewisian realist lines, but with an absolute, primitive notion of actuality); however, the fictionalist route is sufficient to show that there are options available.[41]

SUPERVENIENCE TRANSGRESSED: Many philosophers have the intuition that truth—dtruth or otherwise—*supervenes* on the 'non-semantic facts'.[42] The current proposal bucks the supervenience constraint: some sentences—e.g., the exclusion

[39] I should emphasise that while, as I have said, I do not think that Field's approach is as natural or simple as the current proposal, I do believe that it is the best of the current 'consistentist' disquotational options.

[40] Note that, unlike the current proposal, Priest does not subscribe to a fictionalist account of such points (or 'worlds'). Priest treats the 'nature' of normal and non-normal points the same; it is just that the latter are points at which logical fictions 'take place' or are 'made true'. The suggestion sits well with the current proposal, on which the points themselves be treated along fictionalist lines.

[41] Another option is take such 'points' and 'dtruth at a point' at face value, as merely mathematical models that happen to be useful in getting a grip on the language. Such a line requires, of course, a fuller story about mathematics, in addition to explaining (away) standard objections to instrumentalist approaches to such points. But I think such a route might also be available.

[42] Kripke himself suggests such a feature, but see Michael Kremer [19] for discussion on that point.

version of the first displayed sentence in §2—do not supervene on non-semantic facts (that is precisely why they're 'merely semantic') but, according to transparent disquotationalism, they are none the less dtrue. This is a defect of the position.

REPLY: While supervenience is not maintained globally (over the whole language) in FDE*, the intuition is none the less respected over all 'non-essentially semantic' (grounded) sentences.[43] And that is important. After all, it is precisely the non-paradoxical fragment—the 'grounded' fragment—on which our intuitions about 'supervenience' are built. That the (unexpected) 'spandrels' serve as (the only) exceptions to supervenience seems not unreasonable.[44]

7. CLOSING REMARKS

Transparent disquotationalism is a (strong) paraconsistent approach to dtruth, recognising both gaps and gluts as logical options for dtruth-ascriptions. Any argument for the position will turn on pragmatic virtues of 'naturalness' and 'simplicity' in comparison with rival theories. I have not made the case for the position in this paper; that is for a larger project. The aim of this paper is to put the general position on the table, letting readers begin the comparative analysis against other approaches represented in this volume.

REFERENCES

[1] ALAN ROSS ANDERSON AND NUEL D. BELNAP. *Entailment: The Logic of Relevance and Necessity*, vol. 1. Princeton University Press, Princeton, 1975.

[2] ALAN ROSS ANDERSON, NUEL D. BELNAP, AND J. MICHAEL DUNN. *Entailment: The Logic of Relevance and Necessity*, vol. 2. Princeton University Press, Princeton, 1992.

[3] DIDERIK BATENS. 'A Survey of Inconsistency-Adaptive Logics'. In D. BATENS, C. MORTENSEN, G. PRIEST, AND J-P VAN BENDEGEM, eds, *Frontiers of Paraconsistency*, pp 49–73. Research Studies Press, King's College Publications, Baldock, 2000.

[4] JC BEALL. 'Curry's Paradox'. In EDWARD N. ZALTA, ed., *Stanford Encyclopedia of Philosophy*. CSLI, Stanford University, 2001 (January).

[5] ——. 'True and False—As If'. In GRAHAM PRIEST ET AL., ed., *The Law of Non-Contradiction*. Oxford University Press, Oxford, 2003. In press.

[43] This is not obvious from the presentation in this paper, but in the fuller framework, a constraint yielding 'simply semantic inconsistency' is imposed. (In effect, one defines models in such a way that, for example, $v(\mathcal{A}) \in \{1, \mathsf{n}, 0\}$ for any $\mathcal{A}$ in the dT-free (and, in general, semantic-free) fragment—and, in turn, given the constraints of intersubstitutivity on dT, similarly for any ascription of dT to such $\mathcal{A}$. This is filled out in [6].)

[44] Another (very tentative) reply is this: The supervenience of dtruth on the 'non-semantic facts' seems itself to be inconsistent, at least on the surface. After all, the supervenience intuition requires that a sentence is not dtrue if not 'grounded'. Consider, then, a dtruth-teller: 'this sentence is dtrue' (call it τ). Supervenience demands that τ be not dtrue. But, then, to claim of τ that it is dtrue is to claim something dfalse—at least if the supervenience principle (or relation) itself is a sufficiently non-semantic 'grounder'. Hence, τ itself says something dfalse, and so is dfalse. But that is inconsistent with the dictates of the supervenience principle.

[6] ——. 'Simply semantic inconsistency'. To appear in *Australasian Journal of Logic*, 2004.
[7] ——. 'Deflationism and gaps: untying 'not's in the debate'. *Analysis*, 62(4), October 2002.
[8] ——. ROSS BRADY, ALAN HAZEN, GRAHAM PRIEST, AND GREG RESTALL. 'Relevant Restricted Quantification'. *Journal of Philosophical Logic*, forthcoming. Partially funded by a University of Melbourne small grant, 2004.
[9] —— AND BAS C. VAN FRAASSEN. *Possibilities and Paradox: An Introduction to Modal and Many-Valued Logic*. Oxford University Press, Oxford, 2003.
[10] BRIAN F. CHELLAS. *Modal Logic: An Introduction*. Cambridge University Press, Cambridge, 1980.
[11] HASKELL B. CURRY. 'The Inconsistency of Certain Formal Logics'. *Journal of Symbolic Logic*, 7: 115–17, 1942.
[12] MICHAEL DUMMETT. 'Truth'. In M. DUMMETT, ed., *Truth and Other Enigmas*. Duckworth, London, 1978.
[13] HARTRY FIELD. 'Deflationist Views of Meaning and Content'. *Mind*, 103: 249–85, 1994. Reprinted in [14].
[14] ——. *Truth and the Absence of Fact*. Oxford University Press, Oxford, 2001.
[15] ——. 'No Fact of the Matter'. *Australasian Journal of Philosophy*, 81: 457–80, 2003.
[16] ——. 'The Semantic Paradoxes and the Paradoxes of Vagueness'. In JC BEALL, ed., *Liars and Heaps: New Essays on Paradox*. Oxford University Press, Oxford, 2003.
[17] KIT FINE. 'Models for Entailment'. *Journal of Philosophical Logic*, 3: 347–72, 1974.
[18] G. HUGHES AND M. CRESSWELL. *A New Introduction to Modal Logic*. Routledge, London, 1996.
[19] MICHAEL KREMER. 'Kripke and the Logic of Truth'. *Journal of Philosophical Logic*, 17: 225–78, 1988.
[20] SAUL A. KRIPKE. 'Semantical Analysis of Modal Logic II: Non-Normal Modal Propositional Calculi'. In ADDISON ET AL., ed., *The Theory of Models*, pp 206–20. North-Holland Publishing Co, 1965.
[21] EDWIN D. MARES, ed. *Relevant Logic: A Philosophical Interpretation*. Cambridge University Press, Cambridge, 2004.
[22] ROBERT K. MEYER, RICHARD ROUTLEY, AND J. MICHAEL DUNN. 'Curry's Paradox'. *Analysis*, 39: 124–8, 1979.
[23] GRAHAM PRIEST. *In Contradiction: A Study of the Transconsistent*. Martinus Nijhoff, The Hague, 1987.
[24] ——. 'Minimally Inconsistent LP'. *Studia Logica*, 50: 321–31, 1991.
[25] ——. 'What is a Non-Normal World?'. *Logique et Analyse*, 35: 291–302, 1992.
[26] ——. 'On a Paradox of Hilbert and Bernays'. *Journal of Philosophical Logic*, 26: 45–56, 1997.
[27] ——. 'What Is So Bad About Contradictions?'. *Journal of Philosophy*, XCV(8): 410–26, 1998.
[28] ——. 'Semantic Closure, Descriptions and Triviality'. *Journal of Philosophical Logic*, 28: 549–58, 1999.
[29] ——. 'Paraconsistent Logic'. In DOV M. GABBAY AND FRANZ GÜNTHNER, eds, *Handbook of Philosophical Logic* (*2nd edn*), vol. 6. D. Reidel, Dordrecht, 2000. In press.
[30] ——. *Beyond the Limits of Thought* (*expanded, revised edn*). Oxford University Press, Oxford, 2001.
[31] ——. *An Introduction to Non-Classical Logic*. Cambridge University Press, Cambridge, 2001.

[32] Greg Restall. 'How to be *Really* Contraction-Free'. *Studia Logica*, 52: 381–91, 1993.
[33] ——. *On Logics Without Contraction*. PhD thesis, The University of Queensland, January 1994.
[34] ——. *An Introduction to Substructural Logics*. New York: Routledge, 2000.
[35] Richard Routley and A. Loparic. 'Semantical Analyses of Arruda-da Costa *P*-systems and Adjacent Non-Replacement Systems'. *Studia Logica*, 37: 301–20, 1978.
[36] ——, Val Plumwood, Robert K. Meyer, and Ross T. Brady. *Relevant Logics and their Rivals*. Ridgeview, 1982.
[37] P. Woodruff. 'Paradox, Truth, and Logic'. *Journal of Philosophical Logic*, 13: 213–52, 1984.

2

Is the Liar Sentence Both True and False?

Hartry Field

"Will no one rid me of this accursed Priest?"

Henry II

1. DIALETHEISM

There are many reasons why one might be tempted to reject certain instances of the law of excluded middle. And it is initially natural to take 'reject' to mean 'accept the negation of'. But if we accept the negation of a disjunction, we certainly ought to accept the negation of each disjunct (since the disjunction is weaker[1] than the disjuncts). So accepting $\neg(A \lor \neg A)$ should lead us to accept both $\neg A$ and $\neg\neg A$. But to accept both a sentence ($\neg A$) and its negation is, in at least one sense of the phrase, to accept a contradiction.

So accepting $\neg(A \lor \neg A)$ would be intolerable if contradictions implied everything: we would be logically committed to every imaginable absurdity. But there are "paraconsistent logics" where contradictions in the above sense (pairs consisting of B and $\neg B$, for some B) do not entail everything.

It is not especially controversial that paraconsistent logics might be useful for certain purposes, e.g. analyzing certain notions of "relevant implication" and/or "what a possibly inconsistent theory should be taken as directly committed to". But I am interested in the issue of a particular kind of use, the one motivated above: a use of paraconsistent logic to license the simultaneous literal belief in both B and $\neg B$, in full knowledge that we believe both, and where such knowledge gives no pressure to revise one of the beliefs. In short, where the beliefs, though "contradicting" each other, are not in any serious sense in *conflict*. I will adapt Graham Priest's term 'dialetheism'

Thanks to JC Beall and Graham Priest for useful comments on earlier drafts.

And lest the epigraph of this paper mislead, I would like to say that Graham Priest was extremely encouraging about my earliest attempt at a non-dialetheic solution to the semantic paradoxes; I might not have pursued the matter were it not for this encouragement, and I have found his open-minded attitude in discussing these topics admirable. So I am not calling for the remedy that Henry II was calling for!

[1] Not necessarily strictly.

for the doctrine that we should fully accept certain sentences while also accepting their negations. This is not quite Priest's usage, as we'll see. Nonetheless, Priest is an advocate of dialetheism in this sense; in fact, its most prominent advocate.

The argument with which I began shows that if we want to disbelieve instances of excluded middle (in the sense of, believe their negations) then we should be dialetheists (not merely that we should accept paraconsistent logics for some purposes). And as Priest has often urged (e.g. [13]), the most familiar arguments against the coherence of dialetheism are seriously faulty, a result of a refusal to take the doctrine seriously.

I have two terminological quibbles with Priest. The more minor one concerns the use of the term 'contradiction'. Priest revels in saying that we should accept contradictions. Here 'contradiction' is used either in the sense indicated above (a pair of a sentence and its negation) or in the sense of a sentence of form $B \wedge \neg B$; since Priest and I both advocate the use of logics in which any two sentences imply their conjunction and in which a conjunction implies each conjunct, there is no interesting distinction between accepting a contradiction in one of these senses and accepting it in the other, so I will henceforth not bother to make this distinction. Talk of accepting contradictions shows a flair for the dramatic, but I think it tends to put people off for bad reasons. Given the kind of logic Priest advocates, I think a better use of the term 'contradiction' would be: sentence that implies every other. On this alternative usage, the way to put Priest's view is that sentences of form $B \wedge \neg B$ (or pairs $\{B, \neg B\}$) aren't in general contradictory: they don't imply everything. The issue of course is purely verbal; but because of the possibility of confusion, I will from now on avoid the term 'contradiction'.

A somewhat more important terminological issue concerns the term 'dialetheism'. Priest explains dialetheism as the doctrine

(D) Certain sentences are both true and false;

where 'false' means 'has a true negation'. There is no doubt that a dialetheist should accept (D); nonetheless, (D) seems to me an unfortunate way to define the term.

To see why, let me anticipate what is to follow, by saying that one of the main prima facie benefits of dialetheism in my sense is that it allows us, despite the semantic paradoxes, to maintain the complete intersubstitutivity of $True(\langle A \rangle)$ with A (in contexts not involving quotation marks, propositional attitudes, etc.). Since $False(\langle A \rangle)$ means $True(\langle \neg A \rangle)$, this means that *$False(\langle A \rangle)$ will be completely intersubstitutable with $\neg A$, and hence with $\neg True(\langle A \rangle)$.*

If we agree to these properties of 'True', then believing $A \wedge \neg A$ should be equivalent to believing $True(\langle A \rangle) \wedge False(\langle A \rangle)$. So if Priest were to have put dialetheism as the view that we should fully believe of some sentences that they are both true and false, I could have no complaint: it would be effectively the same as my own 'true'-free formulation. But a problem with defining dialetheism as the doctrine (D) that certain sentences *are* both true and false is that while a dialetheist should certainly believe

(i) $True(\langle A \rangle) \wedge False(\langle A \rangle)$

for certain A (e.g. the Liar sentence), he should believe the opposite as well. For the dialetheist accepts both $True(\langle A \rangle)$ and $False(\langle A \rangle)$. But from $False(\langle A \rangle)$ we get $\neg True(\langle A \rangle)$, by the italicized claim in the last paragraph; so

(ii) $False(\langle A \rangle) \wedge \neg True(\langle A \rangle)$,

which surely entails the negation of (i). If we assume that A entails $\neg\neg A$ (as nearly everyone would, including Priest), then from $True(\langle A \rangle)$ we get $\neg\neg True(\langle A \rangle)$, which yields $\neg False(\langle A \rangle)$ by the same italicized principle; so we also get

(iii) $True(\langle A \rangle) \wedge \neg False(\langle A \rangle)$

and

(iv) $\neg True(\langle A \rangle) \wedge \neg False(\langle A \rangle)$,

each of which also entails the negation of (i). The situation for the existential generalization (D) is a bit more complicated, but here too I think Priest needs to disbelieve it (believe its negation) as well as believing it; hence, given the equivalence, regard it as false as well as true.

Of course, it is a consequence of dialetheism that some sentences are both true and false, and there is no particular problem in the fact that the particular sentence (D) is among them. But what is odd is to take as the doctrine that *defines* dialetheism something that the dialetheist holds to be false as well as true. And it is misleading to characterize the dialetheist's attitude toward, say, the Liar sentence as the view (i) that it is both true and false, when one could equally well have characterized it as the view (iv) that it is neither true nor false, or as the view (ii) that it is false and not true, or the view (iii) that it is true and not false. On the alternative characterization of dialetheism in terms of acceptance, there are no such oddities: a dialetheist will say that we should accept both A and $\neg A$, for the relevant A, and has no reason to say the opposite.

Priest could resist my complaint, on the grounds that he himself does not accept the full intersubstitutivity of $True(\langle A \rangle)$ with A: he takes them not to be intersubstitutable in negation contexts ([12], secs. 4.9 and 5.4), and that destroys the equivalence between 'false' and 'not true'. Nonetheless, I do not think he ought to resist: the alternative characterization I have suggested ought to be acceptable to him, and has the advantage of not ruling out the intersubstitutability of $True(\langle A \rangle)$ with A. One of the advantages of dialetheism, in either sense, is that it makes possible the full intersubstitutivity of $True(\langle A \rangle)$ with A; it would be a shame to adopt a definition of dialetheism that is badly behaved when this possibility is realized.

Enough of terminological quibbles, and on to more serious issues.

2. REJECTION

I have said that it is tempting to reject certain instances of excluded middle, and initially tempting to take this to involve accepting the negation of those instances. And I have noted that succumbing to this second temptation leads to dialetheism. But in fact it is worse than this. For not only should accepting $\neg[A \vee \neg A]$ lead to accepting both $\neg A$ and $\neg\neg A$, that in turn should lead to accepting $A \vee \neg A$. Indeed, this last inference is immediate: $\neg A$ surely implies $A \vee \neg A$.[2] So if to *reject B* is to have an attitude that precludes accepting it, then *accepting the negation of* instances of excluded middle is not a way of rejecting those instances, and indeed *is incompatible with* rejecting them! If we want to *reject* a given instance of excluded middle, we had better *not* accept its negation. (I have not ruled out rejecting some instances without accepting their negations, and accepting the negations of others without rejecting them. But for any given instance of excluded middle, we cannot both reject it and accept its negation.)

How should we understand rejection? As a propositional attitude, on par with acceptance.[3] To a first approximation anyway, accepting A is having a high degree of belief in it; say a degree of belief over a certain threshold T, which may depend on context but must be greater than $\frac{1}{2}$. (Degrees of belief are assumed to be real numbers in the interval [0, 1].) To the same degree of approximation, rejecting A is having a low degree of belief in it: one lower than the co-threshold $1 - T$. This has the desired result that rejection precludes acceptance. (And it allows, as of course we should, for sentences that we are uncertain enough about to neither accept nor reject.)

Now, if degrees of belief obeyed the laws of classical probability, then rejecting A would have to be the same as accepting its negation. For in classical probability theory, $P(A) + P(\neg A)$ is always 1; so $P(A) < 1 - T$ (rejection) iff $1 - P(\neg A) < 1 - T$ iff $P(\neg A) > T$ (acceptance of negation). But if $P(A) + P(\neg A)$ could be greater than 1, then we could accept the negation of A without rejecting it; indeed if it could be sufficiently greater than 1, we could accept both A and $\neg A$ and therefore reject neither. And if $P(A) + P(\neg A)$ could be less than 1, we could reject A without accepting its negation; if it could be sufficiently less than 1, we could reject both A and $\neg A$. It is clear that a dialetheist ought to allow that $P(A) + P(\neg A)$ can be significantly greater than 1 (perhaps as high as 2): if you accept A and accept $\neg A$, you give both high probabilities (perhaps as high as 1); and you do not reject either since rejection precludes acceptance. Similarly, someone who rejects an instance $A \vee \neg A$ of excluded middle (not necessarily a dialetheist) will reject both A and $\neg A$, hence for that person $P(A) + P(\neg A)$ will be substantially less than 1 (perhaps as low as 0).

The upshot is that there is no problem distinguishing rejection from acceptance of the negation, in nonclassical logics that either do not include certain instances of excluded middle or include the negations of certain instances of it.

Where there *may* be a difficulty for dialetheism, though, is in conducting debates about what to reject. Suppose I reject the existence of God, and offer to my theistic friend compelling arguments against it. I expect my friend to try to rebut my arguments, or at least be worried about them (or, more optimistically, to recant his belief); but to my chagrin my friend turns out to be a dialetheist, and though he

[2] $\neg\neg A$ implies it too, in any logic where $\neg\neg A$ implies A; and the logics that Priest and I are interested in mostly have this feature. Indeed, in the future I will for simplicity assume that $\neg\neg A$ is equivalent to A.

[3] This proposal is not new: see for instance [11]. (The characterization to follow, in terms of degrees of belief, is not to be found in [11], but seems in keeping with the spirit of it.)

accepts my arguments and agrees with me about the nonexistence of God, he also believes in the existence of God. What I really want to do is alter his attitudes: get him to *reject* the existence of God, not merely *disbelieve* it. How can I proceed? Well, perhaps I can show him that the existence of God together with other things he accepts entails some other claim Q that I assume he'll reject; say, one for which I already know he accepts its negation. But if he's willing to carry his dialetheism far enough, he may be "dialetheist with respect to Q" as well as "dialetheist with respect to the existence of God": he may accept Q along with its negation. Perhaps there are certain sentences that he truly rejects, rather than merely accepts their negations; but these may not provide a sufficient basis to allow any argument that he should reject the existence of God, *even when he can be convinced to accept the non-existence of God.*

The worry, then, is that if the acceptance of $\neg A$ doesn't suffice for the rejection of A, it is unobvious how debates about rejection are to be conducted. I take it to be an important *challenge* to dialetheism to answer this, but I don't mean to say that it is obvious that the dialetheist can't meet the challenge.[4] Indeed, I'm increasingly inclined to think that it can be met, by working out a view according to which rational discourse is governed by rules that are strongly biased against the taking of a dialetheic attitude toward any given sentence; only very strong conceptual pressure can overcome the bias. There may also need to be a separate bias against the taking of a dialetheic attitude toward *too many* sentences.

3. TRUTH PARADOXES (I)

But is there any serious motivation for adopting a dialetheist position and therefore having to meet challenges like the one just mentioned? I am skeptical. Obviously there is no way of completely ruling out in advance that there might be some problem solvable better by dialetheist means than by non-dialetheist, but I do not think there is *any reason whatever* to believe that this will be the case. Indeed, I think it very likely that any problem that can be solved by dialetheism can be solved without it, and that when the best solutions of each sort are set side-by-side the non-dialetheic solution will always seem more attractive; in which case dialetheism is a position that we do not need.

I am going to spend the rest of this paper illustrating this conjecture with a single example, but it is the example widely viewed as the dialetheist's best case: the semantic paradoxes.

The naive theory of truth presupposes a background syntactic theory, which can be formalized in arithmetic. In addition to this, it has at least two components. The first is the Tarski axioms:

(T): $\quad True(\langle A \rangle)$ if and only if A.

[4] Note also that the person who advocates restricting the law of excluded middle faces a somewhat analogous challenge: for on such a view we should sometimes reject A without accepting $\neg A$, and an account is needed of how to carry out debates about when this is to be done. In this case the question is how to deal with a view that rejects both 'there is a God' and its negation, perhaps on verificationist grounds, because it refuses to accept the corresponding instance of excluded middle.

For another observation on behalf of the dialetheist, see note 21.

The second is the principle mentioned already: *True*($\langle A \rangle$) should be everywhere intersubstitutable for A (in a language free of quotational contexts, intentional contexts, and so forth); that is, if B and C are two sentences alike except that one has *True*($\langle A \rangle$) in one or more places where the other has A, then B implies C and conversely. It may seem redundant to list these components separately, for they are equivalent in classical logic. But as we will see, there are non-classical logics in which they are not equivalent. (Either direction of implication might fail.) Myself, I am interested mostly in logics "classical enough" for the equivalence to hold; but we need to bear in mind the possibility of logics that are not "classical enough".

In classical logic itself, each component of naive truth theory is inconsistent, given the background syntactic theory. For the syntactic theory allows us to construct a Liar sentence Q_0 which is interderivable with $\neg True(\langle Q_0 \rangle)$; so the second component of the naive theory would make Q_0 interderivable with $\neg Q_0$. That would make Q_0 and $\neg Q_0$ each inconsistent, so their disjunction would be inconsistent; but their disjunction is an instance of excluded middle and hence classically valid. So the second component of the naive theory is classically inconsistent; and since the first component is classically equivalent to it, it is classically inconsistent as well.

Kripke ([8]) shows that we can consistently retain *one component of* the naive theory of truth, by weakening classical logic to the logic K_3 obtained from the strong Kleene 3-valued truth tables by taking only the "highest" of the three values as "designated". More exactly, let the three semantic values be 1, $\frac{1}{2}$, and 0, thinking of 1 as "best" and 0 as "worst". Let an *assignment function* s be a function that assigns objects to variables, and let a *valuation* be a function that assigns semantic values to pairs of atomic formulas and assignment functions. Extend the valuation to complex formulas by the "strong Kleene rules"

$$\| \neg A \|_s = 1 - \| A \|_s$$
$$\| A \wedge B \|_s = min\{ \| A \|_s, \| B \|_s \}$$
$$\| A \vee B \|_s = max\{ \| A \|_s, \| B \|_s \}$$
$$\| A \supset B \|_s = max\{1 - \| A \|_s, \ \| B \|_s \}$$
$$\| \forall x A \|_s = min\{ \| A \|_{s^*} \, | s^* \text{is just like } s \text{ except possibly in what it assigns to } x\}$$
$$\| \exists x A \|_s = max\{ \| A \|_{s^*} \, | s^* \text{is just like } s \text{ except possibly in what it assigns to } x\}.$$

Finally, regard an inference as *valid* iff in every valuation in which the premises all get value 1, so does the conclusion; and regard a sentence as valid iff in all valuations it gets value 1. Clearly the inference from $\{A, \neg A\}$ to any sentence B is valid; similarly for the inference from $\neg(A \vee \neg A)$ to anything. So this is not a logic for dialetheists, or, virtually equivalently, for deniers of excluded middle; but it is a logic that allows *rejecting* some instances of excluded middle, since excluded middle is not valid.[5] (Of course, no inference that is not classically valid can be K_3-valid.)

It is natural to take a logic not only to include a set of validities, but also to include rules for establishing some validities from others (relevant for when one expands the logic). One such rule, correct under the strong Kleene semantics, is disjunction

[5] Indeed, no sentence (as opposed to inference) is valid in the logic as it stands. However, we will soon consider extensions of the logic in which this is not so.

elimination: if A implies C and B implies C, then $A \vee B$ implies C. I will henceforth understand K_3 to include this meta-rule (and the analogous rule of $\exists$-elimination).

Kripke's "fixed point argument" shows that if we weaken classical logic to K_3, then it is consistent to assume the second component of the naive truth theory: the intersubstitutivity of $True(\langle A \rangle)$ with A.[6] But we do *not* get either direction of the Tarski schema (taking 'if... then' to be represented by '$\supset$', which seems the only *remotely* reasonable way to interpret it in K_3): for given the intersubstitutivity property of 'True', each direction of the Tarski schema is equivalent to $A \supset A$, but that is not valid in K_3 (it is equivalent to an instance of excluded middle).

Truth theory in K_3 is not a very satisfactory theory.[7] Not only do we not get the full naive theory of truth, the logic is in many ways simply too weak to comfortably reason in. (The absence of a conditional obeying the law 'if A then A' is a symptom of this.) And this fact could seem a motivation for dialetheism.

For there is a minor variant of the logic—Priest's LP—that can easily seem more satisfactory. As a semantics for LP we can assign semantic values in just the same way as for K_3; we simply redefine validity. In particular, we take an inference to be valid just in case in all valuations where the premises all get values *other than 0*, so does the conclusion; and we take a sentence to be valid just in case it does not get value 0 in any valuation. The Kripke fixed point proof then shows that it is consistent to assume the intersubstitutivity property in this logic too; and this logic does validate $A \supset A$, so the truth schema is validated as well. We have the naive theory of truth in its entirety; the only cost is dialetheism, for the Liar sentence and its negation will both be consequences of the truth theory.

But I do not think this is really much of an improvement over the situation with K_3.[8] For the main problem with K_3 wasn't the inability to get the Tarski schema, it was the fact that the logic is too weak to reason with in a natural way, as indicated by the absence of a reasonable conditional. That is true for LP as well: '$\supset$' is in some ways even worse as a candidate for the conditional in LP than it is in K_3, because it doesn't even validate Modus Ponens.

Moreover, though in LP we can validate the Tarski axioms, we do so in a disappointing way: we validate some of their negations along with them. It does not seem to me much of a "save" of the Tarski schema if many of its instances come out not as "simply true" but as having the same dialetheic status as the Liar sentence itself has.

So far, then, we do not have a satisfactory resolution of the paradoxes, either non-dialetheic or dialetheic.

[6] Indeed, we get what I will call "strong consistency": roughly speaking, it is "consistent with any starting model that has standard syntax".

[7] Indeed, it isn't completely clear that Kripke's own discussion of a truth theory based on the strong Kleene tables is intended to motivate a theory based on the logic K_3: it might be intended to motivate a theory, later formalized by Feferman ([1]), based entirely on classical logic. Of course, since it is based on classical logic, the "Kripke–Feferman theory" does not satisfy either component of the naive truth theory. (In particular, in the Kripke–Feferman theory we can assert that the Liar sentence is not true; hence we can assert the Liar sentence, but cannot assert that it is true.)

[8] Here I retract an ill-thought-out suggestion in [2], p. 145.

4. TRUTH PARADOXES (II)

A natural response to the difficulties with using K_3 and LP as the logic for truth theory is to try to supplement one of them with a new conditional. Doing so requires great care: it is not easy to find a set of laws for the conditional that have reasonable strength and do not themselves lead to paradox given naive truth theory. For instance, the Curry paradox shows that (assuming naive truth theory), if our conditional satisfies Modus Ponens then it cannot validate any of the following inferences:

Importation: $A \to (B \to C) \vdash A \wedge B \to C$
$\to$-Introduction: From $A \vdash B$, infer $\vdash A \to B$
Contraction: $A \to (A \to B) \vdash A \to B$.

(The argument against Importation requires the inference from $A \wedge A \to C$ to $A \to C$, but I take it that that inference is totally uncontroversial.)[9] Moreover, there seems to be no low-cost restriction of Modus Ponens that would improve the situation. For instance, it might initially seem that we could obtain a satisfactory logic by restricting the Modus Ponens rule $A, A \to B \vdash B$ to the case where A does not itself contain an $\to$; that would block the derivation of the Contraction form of the Curry paradox in the previous note.[10] A minor difficulty is that such a restricted

[9] First version of Curry paradox: For any sentence B, no matter how absurd, let C_B say "$True(\langle C_B \rangle) \to B$". We now "prove" B, using Modus Ponens, Contraction, and naive truth theory, as follows. (I also use $\wedge$-elimination, but this could be avoided simply by replacing each Tarski axiom in biconditional form by two conditionals.)

1. $True(\langle C_B \rangle) \leftrightarrow (True(\langle C_B \rangle) \to B)$	(Tarski axiom for C_B)
2. $True(\langle C_B \rangle) \to (True(\langle C_B \rangle) \to B)$	(1, defn of $\leftrightarrow$, and $\wedge$-elimination)
3. $True(\langle C_B \rangle) \to B$	(2, Contraction)
4. $(True(\langle C_B \rangle) \to B) \to True(\langle C_B \rangle)$	(1, defn of $\leftrightarrow$, and $\wedge$-elimination)
5. $True(\langle C_B \rangle)$	(3, 4, Modus Ponens)
6. B	(3, 5, Modus Ponens)

That establishes the claim for Contraction. As noted later in the text, this implies the claim for Importation and for a slightly stronger form of $\to$-Introduction, viz. the inference from $\Gamma, A \vdash B$ to $\Gamma \vdash A \to B$.

A second (and more famous) proof of the Curry paradox works even for the weaker form of $\to$-Introduction. (But unlike the proof for the stronger form of $\to$-Introduction, this one assumes that Modus Ponens can be used even in hypothetical arguments; that is, this one assumes the full rule $A, A \to B \vdash B$, rather than the weaker rule used in the first proof that from $\vdash A$ and $\vdash A \to B$ we can infer $\vdash B$). The proof:

1. $True(\langle C_B \rangle) \vdash True(\langle C_B \rangle) \to B$	[Intersubstitutivity property of 'True']
2. $True(\langle C_B \rangle), True(\langle C_B \rangle) \to B \vdash B$	[Modus Ponens]
3. $True(\langle C_B \rangle) \vdash B$	[1,2]
4. $\vdash True(\langle C_B \rangle) \to B$	[3, $\to$-Introduction]
5. $True(\langle C_B \rangle) \to B \vdash True(\langle C_B \rangle)$	[Intersubstitutivity property of 'True']
6. $\vdash True(\langle C_B \rangle)$	[4,5]
7. $\vdash B$	[3,6]

[10] A further restriction to block the use of Modus Ponens in hypothetical proofs would block the second derivation; alternatively, someone might be tempted by the view that we should give up $\to$-Introduction but not Contraction, making only the first derivation threatening.

Modus Ponens would be awkward to employ: we would need to keep track of which sentences that we are representing with sentence letters have an $\rightarrow$ hidden inside them. A more serious difficulty is that since the goal is to keep the equivalence of $True(\langle A \rangle)$ to A, we would need to also rule out applying Modus Ponens when A contains a predication of 'True' to a sentence with an $\rightarrow$. And we would need to rule out application of the rule when the premise applies 'True' to all members of a class that may contain sentences with an '$\rightarrow$', e.g. 'All sentences on the blackboard are true'. Not only would it be a bit tricky to formulate the rule with all these added restrictions, but the resulting rule would be so restricted that our reasoning would be crippled.

So the only serious recourse, given that we want the naive theory of truth, is to adopt a logic that does not validate either Importation, $\rightarrow$-Introduction, or Contraction. Most people find the loss of Contraction surprising, but in fact the only obvious arguments for Contraction (in the sense in which I am using the term)[11] presuppose one of the other two principles. For instance, Importation would get us from $A \rightarrow (A \rightarrow C)$ to $A \wedge A \rightarrow C$; from there, the further inference to $A \rightarrow C$ is totally compelling. Alternatively, we might note that from $A \rightarrow (A \rightarrow C)$ and A, we can infer C by two applications of Modus Ponens; so with a slightly stronger version of $\rightarrow$-Introduction (allowing a side premise), we can get from $A \rightarrow (A \rightarrow C)$ to $A \rightarrow C$. I think that these reflections on the assumptions underlying the obvious arguments for Contraction make it less surprising that Contraction might be given up.

There is in fact a well-known logic in which Importation, $\rightarrow$-Introduction and Contraction all fail: "fuzzy logic", *aka* Lukasiewicz continuum-valued logic (with 1 as sole designated value). It is an extension of K_3, and it is commonly taken as a good logic for reasoning with vague concepts, so it does seem to meet the criterion of usability. Unfortunately, it will not do for naive truth theory: although it evades many of the paradoxical arguments, naive truth theory is still inconsistent in it. (See [7].)[12]

But a few years ago I began thinking seriously about the program of extending Kleene logic with a new conditional that does allow for the naive theory of truth (including substitutivity of $True(\langle A \rangle)$ with A *even within the scope of the new conditional*), and have obtained some positive results. The first attempt ([3]) was actually a rather mixed success: though naive truth theory is consistent in it (indeed, "strongly consistent" in it, in the sense of note 6), still the $\rightarrow$ of the logic does not reduce to the ordinary $\supset$ when excluded middle is assumed for the antecedent and consequent; this leads to some counterintuitive results. My second attempt ([4]) solved these problems: I called the logic LCC. I am not sure it is the best possible logic for saving naive truth theory, but it seems more than adequate.

Let me clarify something: when I speak of a logic "for naive truth theory", I do not mean to suggest that we use a different logic here than elsewhere. My view is that LCC

[11] The term 'Contraction' is sometimes used not for the inference rule I've stated but for a structural rule. Giving up contraction in *that* sense would involve supposing that a sentence B might be "a consequence of A taken twice" without being a consequence of A *simpliciter*. I am certainly *not* giving up contraction as a structural rule. (Doing so would seem to me to do serious violence to any normal notion of consequence.)

[12] Restall [14] obtained an earlier result, slightly short of this but enough to show that this logic will not do for truth theory.

is a good candidate for our basic, all-purpose logic. Might regarding LCC as a general logic cripple our reasoning in physics, mathematics, etc.? No: we can add all instances of excluded middle in the language of pure mathematics and pure physics as non-logical axioms. We might want to resist adding excluded middle when some of the terms are vague: that is a separate issue I do not want to get into here. (Let me just say that as far as I can see, LCC handles vague notions at least as well as "fuzzy logic" does—in some ways better.) And of course if one thinks that certain parts of the language of basic physics or even basic mathematics (such as quantification over all ordinals) are vague, then abandoning excluded middle for vague terms will lead to abandoning it for those parts of physics and mathematics. But the point is that nothing in my account *requires* that it be abandoned outside of the special case of the use of 'True' in "self-referential" contexts.

I do not want to get into the details of how LCC works, but I'll say something to indicate its general flavor. As remarked, it is an extension of the Kleene logic K_3 (including the meta-rules of disjunction elimination and $\exists$-elimination). In my presentation of it in [4] I used only the three semantic values of K_3, viz. $1, \frac{1}{2}$ and 0. In such a presentation, $\rightarrow$ cannot be value-functional: the value of $A \rightarrow B$ (relative to an assignment s) is not determined by the values of A and of B (relative to s). All we get is the following table of possible values:

$\rightarrow$	B = 1	B = $\frac{1}{2}$	B = 0
A = 1	1	$\frac{1}{2}$,0	0
A = $\frac{1}{2}$	1	1,$\frac{1}{2}$	$\frac{1}{2}$,0
A = 0	1	1	1

Which values we do get for given A and B is determined in the theory, but not just by the semantic values assigned to A and to B.

There is, though, a way of subdividing the value $\frac{1}{2}$ into infinitely many distinct semantic values, in a way that will make all the connectives value-functional; indeed, the consistency proof offered in [4] could be rewritten in these terms. To describe the space of such "fine-grained semantic values", consider any initial ordinal Π greater than ω, and let F^{Π} be the set of functions from $\{\alpha | \alpha < \Pi\}$ into $\{1, \frac{1}{2}, 0\}$. Call a member f of F^{Π} *cyclic* if there is a ρ_f such that $0 < \rho_f < \Pi$ and for all β and σ, $f(\rho_f \cdot \beta + \sigma) = f(\sigma)$ (when these are defined, i.e. when $\rho_f \cdot \beta + \sigma < \Pi$). Call a member f of F^{Π} *regular* if (i) it is cyclic and (ii) either it is a constant function or else $f(0) = \frac{1}{2}$. (Note that given (i), (ii) implies that if f is not constantly 1 or constantly 0 then for some ρ_f in the interval $(0, \Pi)$, f assumes the value $\frac{1}{2}$ at each right-multiple of ρ_f. It is this consequence that gives (ii) its importance.) Let V^{Π} be the set of regular members of F^{Π}. For a sufficiently large Π, V^{Π} will serve as the space of semantic values.

V^{Π} has a natural partial ordering: $f \preceq g$ if and only if $(\forall \alpha < \Pi)(f(\alpha) \leq g(\alpha))$. The partial order has a largest element **1**, viz. the function that assigns everything the value 1, and a smallest element **0**, viz. the function that assigns everything 0. And the partial order is symmetric around a middle point $\frac{1}{2}$, the function that assigns everything value $\frac{1}{2}$; this will be the value of the Liar sentence. (If f has both the values 0 and 1 in its range it will be incomparable with $\frac{1}{2}$; if its range includes $\frac{1}{2}$ and 1 but not 0 it will be strictly between $\frac{1}{2}$ and **1**; and if it includes $\frac{1}{2}$ and 0 but not 1 it will be strictly between $\frac{1}{2}$ and **0**. The earlier 3-valued semantics eliminated any distinctions among values that weren't **1** and **0**, which is why the conditional could not be represented value-functionally within it.)

For each of the sentential connectives, I will now describe an operation on V^{Π}. The operation $\curlywedge$ corresponding to conjunction is simply pointwise minimum: $(f \curlywedge g)(\alpha)$ is $min\{f(\alpha), g(\alpha)\}$. Similarly for disjunction: $(f \curlyvee g)(\alpha)$ is $max\{f(\alpha), g(\alpha)\}$. It needs to be verified that these are regular if f and g are, but that is easy: for cyclicity, simply let $\rho_{f\wedge g}$ and $\rho_{f\vee g}$ be a non-zero common right-multiple of ρ_f and ρ_g that precedes Π;[13] and the satisfaction of requirement (ii) on regularity is obvious. Negation is also handled pointwise: $(f^{*})(\alpha)$ is $1 - f(\alpha)$. Here the preservation of regularity is even more evident, for ρ_{f^*} can be taken to simply be ρ_f. Far more interesting is the operation $\Longrightarrow$ corresponding to the conditional; $(f \Longrightarrow g)$ (0) will be

$$1 \text{ if } (\exists\beta < \Pi)(\forall\gamma \in [\beta, \Pi))[f(\gamma) \leq g(\gamma)];$$
$$0 \text{ if } (\exists\beta < \Pi)(\forall\gamma \in [\beta, \Pi))[f(\gamma) > g(\gamma)];$$
$$\frac{1}{2} \text{ otherwise;}$$

and when $\alpha > 0$, $(f \Rightarrow g)(\alpha)$ will be

$$1 \text{ if } (\exists\beta < \alpha)(\forall\gamma \in [\beta, \alpha))[f(\gamma) \leq g(\gamma)];$$
$$0 \text{ if } (\exists\beta < \alpha)(\forall\gamma \in [\beta, \alpha))[f(\gamma) > g(\gamma)];$$
$$\frac{1}{2} \text{ otherwise.}$$

This too preserves regularity: this time, take $\rho_{f\Rightarrow g}$ to be of form $\gamma \cdot \omega$, where γ is a common right-multiple of ρ_f and ρ_g that precedes Π. (We could use the least such $\gamma \cdot \omega$, in place of Π in the clause for $(f \Rightarrow g)$ (0).)

It is easily seen that the space V^{Π} is a deMorgan algebra with respect to the operations $\curlywedge, \curlyvee$ and *, and that for any f and g, $f \curlywedge f^{*} \preceq \frac{1}{2} \preceq g \curlyvee g^{*}$; this implies that if validity is defined in terms of preserving value **1** in all valuations in this space, we obtain at least the sentential part of the logic K_3, in the narrow sense of K_3 that does not include the disjunction-elimination rule. The disjunction-elimination rule requires an additional fact, that **1** be "join-irreducible", i.e. that there be no values f and g for which $f \curlyvee g = \mathbf{1}$ even though neither of f and g is **1**. But we have that too, by the regularity requirement: for if $f \curlyvee g = \mathbf{1}$ and neither f nor g is **1**, then neither f nor g is **0** either, and so $f(0) = g(0) = \frac{1}{2}$; so $(f \curlyvee g)(0) = \frac{1}{2}$, so $f \curlyvee g \neq \mathbf{1}$.

The other important feature of this algebra is that it is complete with respect to cardinalities smaller than II: that is, for any subset S of V^{Π} with cardinality less than

[13] There is such a predecessor of Π, given that Π is an initial ordinal.

that of Π, the functions min(S) and max(S) that give their pointwise minimum and maximum are in V^{Π}. (To verify the cyclicity of these functions, simply let ρ_S be the smallest non-zero common right-multiple of all the ρ_f for f in S; it must be less than Π, by the cardinality restriction on S.) Because of this completeness property of the algebra, there will be no problem of treating quantifiers in a model whose domain has cardinality less than Π. (We will need to use a larger space of semantic values for dealing with models of large cardinality than for dealing with models of small cardinality, but this creates no problems.) In fact, max(S) is **1** if and only if $\mathbf{1} \in S$; so we get not only the K_3-valid inferences involving $\exists$, but also the meta-rule of $\exists$-elimination.

The point of a valuation space V^{Π} is to form V^{Π}-valued models. A *V^{Π}-valued model* W for a language (without function symbols) consists of a domain U of cardinality smaller than Π, an assignment of an object in U to each individual constant, and an assignment, to each n-ary predicate p of the language, of a function p_W from U^n to V^{Π}; given such a model, we obtain a value $|||A|||$ in V^{Π} for any sentence A of the language (and for any formula of the language relative to any assignment of objects in U to the free variables), by using the operations described above. (I use the triple bars to indicate these fine-grained values, in contrast to the double bars used earlier for the coarse-grained values in $\{0, \frac{1}{2}, 1\}$.) A V^{Π}-valued model *treats p classically* if it assigns it a function whose range is a subset of $\{\mathbf{0}, \mathbf{1}\}$. For each V^{Π}-valued model W of a language, there is a corresponding classical model W^- *on the $\rightarrow$-free sublanguage built from the atomic predicates that the V^{Π}-valued model treats classically*:[14] the classical model and the V^{Π}-valued model have the same domains, and $\langle u_1, \ldots, u_n \rangle$ is in the extension of p in W^- when $p_W(u_1, \ldots, u_n)$ is **1**, and fails to be in the extension of p in W^- when $p_W(u_1, \ldots, u_n)$ is **0**. I'll call W^- the *classical reduct* of W.

What do we do with these V^{Π}-valued models? Suppose we are given any decent classical model M for a base language L without 'True' or '$\rightarrow$'; where by a *decent* classical model, I simply mean one that contains within it a standard model of arithmetic. (The reason for so restricting is so that the model will contain within it a standard model for the syntax of the language L^+ obtained by adding 'True' and '$\rightarrow$' to L; that seems a minimal prerequisite to even raising the question of the semantics of 'True'.) What we want is to be able to find a Π and a V^{Π}-valued model M^+ of the full language L^+ such that

(i) M^+ has M as its classical reduct (so that M^+ has the same domain as M and in effect gives the same classical extension to predicates of L that M gives them)
(ii) M^+ validates the naive theory of truth.

For (ii), the main requirement is

(iia) if u is any sentence A in the full language, $True_{M^+}(u) = |||A|||$ (and therefore $|||True(\langle A \rangle)||| = ||A|||$).

[14] Indeed, there is really no need to go to the $\rightarrow$-free part of the language; we could instead interpret the $\rightarrow$ as $\supset$ in the classical valuation.

In addition, we require

(iib) for any u in *dom (M)* ($= dom(M^+)$) that is not a sentence of L^+, $True_{M^+}(u)$ is 0.

Then the import of the Fundamental Theorem of [4] is that there is a way of obtaining such an M^+, for any decent classical model M.[15]

I take this to be an adequate resolution of the paradoxes of truth, in a non-dialetheic logic.

5. OTHER PARADOXES

How about semantic paradoxes involving notions other than truth? Not a problem: the construction generalizes straightforwardly to satisfaction; and other semantic notions (denotation, definability) are explainable from that.[16]

We also get a consistent theory of properties and (non-extensional) relations with naive comprehension in biconditional form. (Instead of 'properties and relations'

[15] To immunize against a confusion, I should point out that while the sequence of values $|A|_\alpha$ discussed in that paper is related to the semantic value f_A of A discussed here, they are not the same. For typically, the function assigning $|A|_\alpha$ to α will not have the regularity requirements needed for inclusion in V^Π. What we do have (by the Fundamental Theorem of the other paper) is that there is a unique member f of V^Π and an ordinal β less than Π such that $(\forall\alpha \geq \beta)(|A|_\alpha = f(\alpha))$, and that f is what I am here taking to be the semantic value of A.

[16] How does this fit with the Appendix to ch. 1 of [12], which appears to show that the Berry paradox (for the naive theory of denotation) arises without assuming excluded middle? The answer is that the proof there uses a principle about the least number operator μ that is tantamount to excluded middle or to a restricted version of it: viz.,

(*) $\exists x A(x) \rightarrow \exists y[y = \mu x A(x)]$

(where the quantification is over numbers, and where $A(x)$ is allowed to contain vocabulary that leads to breakdowns of excluded middle). To see that (*) is really a (possibly restricted) form of excluded middle, let B be any sentence, and let $A(x)$ be

$[x = 1] \vee [x = 0 \wedge B]$.

Then $\vdash A(1)$; so $\vdash \exists x A(x)$ and $\vdash \forall y[y = \mu x A(x) \rightarrow (y = 0 \vee y = 1)]$, and so (*) implies

(**) $[0 = \mu x A(x)] \vee [1 = \mu x A(x)]$.

At this point the discussion divides. (I) On the most natural reading of the least number operator, $0 = \mu x A(x)$ is equivalent to $A(0)$ and hence to B, and $1 = \mu x A(x)$ is equivalent to $A(1) \wedge \neg A(0)$ and hence to $\neg B$, so (**) is in effect $B \vee \neg B$, and so (*) implies a general form of excluded middle. (II) There is also an alternative construal of the least number operator, on which $0 = \mu x A(x)$ is equivalent to $Det[A(0)]$ and hence to $Det[B]$, where *Det* is an operator meaning "it is determinately the case that", and $1 = \mu x A(x)$ is equivalent to $Det[A(1)] \wedge \neg Det[A(0)]$ and hence to $\neg Det[B]$; in that case, (**) is in effect $Det[B] \vee \neg Det[B]$, so (*) implies only excluded middle restricted to determinateness claims. But that restricted excluded middle is enough to breed paradox all by itself, without the least number operator, via sentences that assert of themselves that they are not determinately true. Any treatment of the paradoxes of truth that accords with the naive truth schema will thus have to avoid excluded middle for determinateness claims, and so again cannot accept (*). (The semantics outlined in this paper does allow for determinateness operators in the language, but these operators do not obey excluded middle: see sections 5 and 6 of [4], and sections 6–8 of [5].)

I will just say relations, since properties can be conceived as 1-place relations.) This is most naturally shown *in analogy with* the semantic case, by starting with a given domain for a given language L (adequate to talking about natural numbers and finite sequences), and going to a larger language with the binary predicate '$Rel(z, n)$' (meaning "z is an n-place relation") and the binary predicate '$\Delta(s, z)$' (meaning "for some n, z is an n-place relation and s is an n-place sequence that instantiates z"). Then we inductively expand the domain by adding new entities: for each formula and choice of a finite set of distinguished variables (say $\Theta(x_1, \ldots, x_n, u_1, \ldots, u_k)$, with the x_is distinguished), and any entities $o_1, \ldots, o_k$ that are either in the ground model or have previously been added, we add a new entity $\lambda x_1, \ldots, x_n\Theta(x_1, \ldots, x_n, o_1, \ldots, o_k)$. Given this background, we can construct a valuation for the instantiation predicate Δ which validates the naive comprehension schema

$$\forall u_1 \ldots \forall u_k \exists z[Rel(n, z) \wedge \forall x_1 \ldots \forall x_n[\langle x_1 \ldots x_n\rangle \Delta z \\ \leftrightarrow \Theta(x_1, \ldots, x_n, u_1, \ldots, u_k)]],$$

by proceeding in complete analogy with the treatment of satisfaction. (Call this the autonomous approach; it is set out in more detail in [6].) Alternatively, one can *reduce* the property case to the semantic case, by modelling n-place relations as "objectified formulas", that is, as pairs $\langle A, s\rangle$ where A is a formula that may contain the satisfaction predicate and s is a function that assigns objects to all variables in A other than the particular variables $v_1, \ldots, v_n$. Then $\langle o_1, \ldots, o_k\rangle$ instantiates $\langle A, s\rangle$ iff "the combination of $\langle o_1, \ldots, o_k\rangle$ with s" satisfies A.[17] In either case, the model is one where all properties and relations are definable from the ground model, but that is just for getting a consistency proof; not all models of the naive theory of relations will have this form (as is completely evident on the autonomous approach).

Of course, excluded middle cannot be assumed for instantiation claims generally: for instance, if R is the property of not instantiating itself (on the reductive approach this would be $\langle$'$\neg Sat(x_1, x_1)$', $\emptyset\rangle$, where $\emptyset$ is the null assignment function), then the assumption that R either instantiates itself or does not leads to contradiction. All we can say in general is that '$\langle o_1, \ldots, o_k\rangle$ instantiates $\langle A, s\rangle$' will get a semantic value in the space V^{Π} (and that it gets precisely the same value as A gets with respect to the combination of $\langle o_1, \ldots, o_k\rangle$ with s). In contrast, the modelling just given shows that we *can* consistently assume of anything that it either is a relation or is not, and assume of any two relations that they either are the same or they are not: we can give a value in $\{\mathbf{0}, \mathbf{1}\}$ to any claim not involving the instantiation relation, even if it is about properties and relations.

Can we also get a consistent theory of extensions (relations-in-extension, including classes as the $n = 1$ case), with naive comprehension in biconditional form? I'm

[17] This reductive approach will not work as it stands if the naive theory of relations explicitly asserts that relations are not linguistic—or rather, that they are not pairs whose first member is linguistic. We could handle this by adding "duplicates" of the objectified formulas to the ground model, and use these duplicates as the properties and relations in the model (still allowing them to apply to themselves, of course); though it is probably easier to take the autonomous approach.

I have not thought about whether there is any problem getting the naive semantics and the naive theory of relations together, when relations are explicitly declared non-linguistic. I doubt that there is a problem, but for here I restrict myself to the claim that each of these theories is individually obtainable.

not sure: there do seem to be complications in modifying the construction so as to ensure extensionality, while also getting the other desired laws such as substitutivity rules for identity.[18] But even if we cannot, I am not sure that this is particularly worrisome. In the case of sets we have a perfectly good *non-naive* theory, the theory of iterative sets (e.g. Zermelo-Fraenkel set theory), and I do not see any obvious reason to demand more. That theory has no analog that is satisfactory for the semantic paradoxes (since the analog of the fact that the Russell set doesn't exist would have to be that the predicate 'is not true of itself' doesn't exist, which is absurd). Nor does it have a satisfactory analog for properties in the sense of the term that has application in semantics, for the point of having properties in that sense demands that there be a property corresponding to every predicate. (Similarly for relations more generally.) It is because iterative set theory has no satisfactory analog in these cases that the naive theories of truth and satisfaction and of properties and relations are so important. If there is an analogous need of a naive theory of sets (or extensional relations more generally), it is quite unobvious what it is.

I should add that the naive theory of non-extensional relations could be used to make iterative set-theory more attractive: we can use naive properties and relations for most of the purposes that "proper classes" have traditionally been put, for the extensionality of proper classes plays little role. Thus we avoid well-known puzzles about "how the proper classes differ from another level of sets". This idea of proper classes as entities of a very different nature than iterative sets was well articulated by Parsons in [10]; the view being suggested in this paragraph is a slight variant, in which we allow proper class-surrogates to "belong to" proper class-surrogates, and indeed accept naive comprehension for them.[19] Moreover, though the law of excluded

[18] It is worth mentioning that to have any hope of getting

(EXT) $\forall s(s \in y \leftrightarrow s \in z) \leftrightarrow y = z$,

we must abandon the assumption of excluded middle for identity claims. To see why, let K be the "Curry set" $\{w | w \in w \rightarrow \bot\}$; let o_z be $\{w | w \neq w\}$, and o_y be $\{w | w = w \wedge K \in K\}$. By (EXT), $o_y = o_z \leftrightarrow (K \in K \rightarrow \bot)$; so by the definition of K and naive comprehension, $o_y = o_z \leftrightarrow K \in K$. But on the semantics in the text, excluded middle cannot be assumed for $K \in K$. (Note that if the Russell set were used in place of the Curry set, we would not have a counterexample to excluded middle: the claim corresponding to $o_y = o_z$ would then have value **0**.) The situation is in marked contrast to the non-extensional case, where excluded middle for identity claims was unproblematic.

Moreover, while we can hope to get transitivity and substitutivity in the form of pairs of rules (e.g. for transitivity, the rules $x = y \models y = z \rightarrow x = z$ and $\neg(y = z \rightarrow x = z) \models x \neq y$), the conditional forms $x = y \wedge y = z \rightarrow x = z$ and $x = y \rightarrow (y = z \rightarrow x = z)$ inevitably fail if we adhere to (EXT). (Let o_y and o_z be as above, and let o_x be $\{w | w = w\}$.) But this really isn't surprising: a failure of those forms of transitivity seems pretty much inevitable when "indeterminate identity" (failure of excluded middle for identity claims) is allowed.

The real problem with adhering to any form of extentionality is securing the validity of the rule $\forall w(w \in x \leftrightarrow w \in y) \models x \in z \leftrightarrow y \in z$, a rule which is independent of how identity is treated. (If this can be secured while retaining comprehension, then to retain substitutivity rules for identity we might need to weaken (EXT) a bit, e.g. by replacing the left to right conditional by the two rules $\forall s(s \in y \leftrightarrow s \in z) \models y = z$ and $\neg(y = z) \models \neg\forall s(s \in y \leftrightarrow s \in z)$.)

[19] The idea of a theory that abandons excluded middle to allow proper classes to belong to themselves has also been suggested previously, e.g. in [9]. But that was in the context of a logic that does not contain a reasonable conditional and does not allow naive comprehension in biconditional

middle cannot be assumed generally, it can be assumed for sentences in which quantifiers are suitably restricted, e.g. to the iterative sets, or to those and the proper class-surrogates that apply only to iterative sets, or to various larger subuniverses. Excluded middle is only abandoned in connection with certain things (such as class of all *classes* that don't belong to themselves) which don't exist in any of the classical theories. I don't claim that this view of proper classes has huge advantages over Parsons', though I do think it has some;[20] my main point here is that with *any* view that postulates class-like entities with a fundamentally different character from iterative sets, an awkwardness in the iterative theory is removed, thus undermining one argument one might have had for a naive account of *extensional* entities like sets.

My claim then is that we have a unified account of all the paradoxes that are really in the same ballpark as the paradoxes of truth, in a non-paraconsistent logic.

6. DIALETHEIC VARIANTS

Can the dialetheist do as well? I am not sure. An obvious thought is that just as the dialetheist can "dualize" K_3 to obtain LP, so too he can dualize LCC to obtain "Dual LCC". Dual LCC has just the same semantics as LCC, but in the 3-valued formulation its designated values are 1 and $\frac{1}{2}$ rather than just 1, and in the infinite-valued (fine-grained) formulation its designated values are all values other than **0**.

Dual LCC does avoid the second of the difficulties I raised for LP: the negation of the instances of the Tarski schema get value **0** in Dual LCC as in LCC, and hence they are not assertible; so the truth schema is saved in a more serious sense than in LP. But the first difficulty that I raised for LP arises here too: Dual LCC, like LP, does not validate Modus Ponens. The exceptions to Modus Ponens will be somewhat fewer than in the case of LP, since in the 3-valued formulation of the semantics of Dual LCC, $A \rightarrow B$ sometimes takes the undesignated value 0 when A has the designated value $\frac{1}{2}$ and B has the undesignated value 0; but sometimes $A \rightarrow B$ has value $\frac{1}{2}$ when A has $\frac{1}{2}$ and B has 0, and that is enough to ensure a violation of Modus Ponens in Dual LCC. An example is the standard Curry sentence $C_\perp$, provably equivalent to $True(\langle C_\perp \rangle) \rightarrow \perp$ and hence to $C_\perp \rightarrow \perp$ in naive truth theory; where $\perp$ is any sentence with semantic value **0**. So $|||C_\perp|||$ is the same as $|||C_\perp \rightarrow \perp|||$. This value is not **0** (in

form, which severely limits the utility of the theory. For instance, without such a conditional, one cannot assert that each class x is a subclass of itself (in the sense that for all z, if z belongs to x then z belongs to x); nor can one assert that if x belongs to the class of those z such that $\Phi(z)$, then $\Phi(x)$.

[20] Parsons' own view did not allow impredicatively defined classes of sets; the alternative suggested here does, and I do take that to be a fairly clear advantage. Parsons could of course have allowed impredicatively defined classes without allowing proper classes as members. I believe he didn't because it would have made classes look too much like "just another level of sets". But on my view that worry doesn't arise: the "classes" are just properties, and they obey completely different laws: for instance, self-instantiation is allowed.

Parsons' view might be thought to have an advantage over the one suggested here, in that he can define identity for classes so that the axiom of extensionality holds. But in fact I could adopt the same definition of "identity": it is just that outside of Parsons' restriction to classes *of sets*, the defined notion does not behave in the way one would expect a definition of identity to behave.

fact, its value is the function that assigns $\frac{1}{2}$ to 0 and to limits, 0 to odd ordinals, and 1 to even successors). But then the inference from $C_\perp$ and $C_\perp \rightarrow \perp$ to $\perp$ is a counterexample to modus ponens.[21]

We can avoid this problem by shifting to "Almost-Dual LCC", where the designated values are those f such that $\frac{1}{2} \preceq f$; in other words, those functions that after a certain point never contain the value 0. Almost-Dual LCC does validate Modus Ponens (Modus Ponens for $\rightarrow$, not for $\supset$); and as with Dual LCC, it has the virtue that negations of instances of the truth schema never come out designated. But it has a different defect: the disjunction $C_\perp \vee \neg C_\perp$ is designated even though neither $C_\perp$ nor $\neg C_\perp$ is; as a result, this logic would lead to a solution of the Curry paradox with a supervaluationist flavor, in that you could assert that the Curry sentence is either true or false but would not be allowed to say which. Relatedly, we would have a failure of disjunction elimination: $C_\perp$ implies $\neg C_\perp$ (since it implies $\perp$, given Modus Ponens), and $\neg C_\perp$ implies $\neg C_\perp$, but $C_\perp \vee \neg C_\perp$ doesn't imply $\neg C_\perp$.

To avoid these problems, one would need to find an acceptable set of designated values which either excludes $C_\perp \vee \neg C_\perp$ or includes $\neg C_\perp$. (It cannot include $C_\perp$ if it is closed under Modus Ponens.) But it cannot exclude $C_\perp \vee \neg C_\perp$ if it is to include the Liar sentence, since the semantic value of $C_\perp \vee \neg C_\perp$ is strictly bigger than that of the Liar. Indeed, given the reasonable additional demand that the theory validate $\wedge$-Introduction, then the set of designated values cannot exclude the value of $C_\perp \vee \neg C_\perp$ as long as it contains *any* pair of form $\{f, f^*\}$: for if f and f^* are designated, then $\wedge$-Introduction requires that $f \curlywedge f^*$ be designated too; but $f \curlywedge f^* \preceq \frac{1}{2} \preceq [C_\perp \vee \neg C_\perp]$, so the Liar sentence and $C_\perp \vee \neg C_\perp$ must receive designated values too.

In short, the only alternative, for a dialetheist who wants a theory based on the algebra V^{II} and that validates reasonable rules, is to include the value of $\neg C_\perp$ but not that of $C_\perp$ among the designated values. But the semantic value of $\neg C_\perp$ is so similar in

[21] Despite the inadequacy of Dual LCC, it may be interesting to contemplate: in particular, I think it helps undermine the general worry about dialetheism contemplated at the end of Section 2. The worry was that if the acceptance of $\neg A$ does not suffice for the rejection of A, how are arguments for the rejection of A to be conducted? Dual LCC is relevant to this because it contains a sequence of stronger and stronger "negation-like" operators. Let DA abbreviate $A \wedge (\top \rightarrow A)$, where $\top$ is any sentence of form $B \rightarrow B$; and let $N_0 A$ be $\neg A$, and for each k let $N_{k+1}A$ be $DN_k A$. (We could extend this a long way into the transfinite, by using the truth predicate to get the effect of infinite conjunctions at limits.) For each k—or each ordinal α, on the transfinite extension—$|||N_\alpha A \wedge A|||$ will have a value other than **0** when A has as its value a function in which $\frac{1}{2}$ and α-length sequences of 0's both appear arbitrarily late. So there is no α for which accepting $N_\alpha A$ quite suffices for rejecting A. None the less, it requires very special assumptions about A to accept even $N_1 A \wedge A$; accepting $N_1 A$ thus makes it ***harder*** not to reject A than does the mere acceptance of $\neg A$. And as α increases, it becomes harder and harder not to reject A while accepting $N_\alpha A$. Indeed for nearly any choice of semantic value that A might have, it is possible to find a sufficiently big $\sigma[A]$ such that $|||N_{\sigma[A]} A \wedge A|||$ is 0. My thought is, then, that this battery of stronger and stronger negations might serve the dialetheist's needs in arguing for rejecting undesirable claims.

If it were possible to "conjoin all the N_{α}'s" into a "supernegation operator" N for which accepting NA compelled rejecting A, this would lead to the objection that we have made dialetheism uninteresting: perhaps N is what we should have called negation (and the truth of NA is what we should have called the falsity of A), and it is only because we have made an alternative choice that the logic is "dialetheic". But whatever the merits of this objection, it does not arise if it is impossible to conjoin all the N_α; and that *is* impossible in Dual LCC.

structure to that of $C_\perp$ (in both, 0 and 1 alternate at successors, with $\frac{1}{2}$ at all limits) that it is hard to see how there can be a natural choice for the set of designated values that includes $\neg C_\perp$ but not $C_\perp$.

(This is less than an impossibility proof: technically, the question is whether the algebra contains any prime filters that are both closed under "Modus Ponens for $\Longrightarrow$" and contain some sentence and its negation, and I have not investigated this beyond the observations just made.)

Of course a dialetheist is not restricted to theories based on the algebra V^{II}, and there may well be some way for a dialetheist to do better than Dual LCC and Almost-Dual LCC: not only preserving the naive truth theory and making negations of instances of the truth schema undesignated (so that the instances of the truth schema come out "*solely* true"), but also making both Modus Ponens and disjunction elimination valid. That would certainly be of interest. Still, I doubt that it would make a strong case for dialetheism. In the case of LP and K_3, there was at least a prima facie advantage of the dialetheic logic over the non-dialetheic (inadequate though both were): despite its inadequacies from lack of a decent conditional, LP gave the full naive theory of truth (albeit in a somewhat disappointing way), whereas K_3 did not. But in the present case, we already get the naive theory of truth with the non-dialetheic logic, so there seems to be no special motivation for going dialetheic. The main case for dialetheism has disappeared.

REFERENCES

[1] Solomon Feferman. Toward useful type-free theories, I. *Journal of Symbolic Logic*, 49: 75–111, 1984.

[2] Hartry Field. *Truth and the Absence of Fact*. Oxford University Press, Oxford, 2001.

[3] ——. Saving the truth schema from paradox. *Journal of Philosophical Logic*, 31: 1–27, 2002.

[4] ——A revenge-immune solution to the semantic paradoxes. *Journal of Philosophical Logic*, 32: 139–77, 2003.

[5] ——. The semantic paradoxes and the paradoxes of vagueness. In JC Beall, ed., *Liars and Heaps*. Oxford University Press, 2003.

[6] ——. The consistency of the naive theory of properties. *Philosophical Quarterly*, 54, 2004.

[7] Petr Hajek, Jeff Paris, and John Shepherdson. The liar paradox and fuzzy logic. *The Journal of Symbolic Logic*, 65: 339–46, 2000.

[8] Saul Kripke. Outline of a theory of truth. *Journal of Philosophy*, 72: 690–716, 1975.

[9] Penelope Maddy. Proper classes. *Journal of Symbolic Logic*, 48: 113–39, 1983.

[10] Charles Parsons. Sets and classes. In Charles Parsons, ed., *Mathematics in Philosophy*. Cornell University, 1983.

[11] Terence Parsons. True contradictions. *Canadian Journal of Philosophy*, 20: 335–83, 1990.

[12] Graham Priest. *In Contradiction*. Martinus Nijhoff, Dordrecht, 1987.

[13] ——. What is so bad about contradictions? *Journal of Philosophy*, 95: 410–26, 1998.

[14] Greg Restall. Arithmetic and truth in Lukasiewicz's infinitely valued logic. *Logique et Analyse*, 139–40: 303–12, 1992.

3

Spiking the Field-Artillery

Graham Priest

I submit my cause to the judgment of Rome.
But if you kill me, I shall rise from my tomb
To submit my cause before God's throne.

Thomas Becket[1]

1. INTRODUCTION

Deflationism about truth centres upon the idea that, in some sense, there is no more (or less) to the claim that $\langle A \rangle$ is true than there is to A itself. (Angle brackets indicate some appropriate name-forming device here.) Clearly, it is difficult to hear this view in a way that does not endorse Tarski's T-schema in full generality. But if one does this, then, in the natural course of events, contradiction arises in the form of the Liar and similar paradoxes. Deflationists have often prevaricated over this matter, suggesting the imposition of ad hoc restrictions on the T-schema.[2] The unsatisfactoriness of this is clear, however. It is much more natural to accept the full T-schema and the contradictions to which this gives rise, but to use a paraconsistent logic which isolates the paradoxical contradictions.[3]

In 'Is the Liar Both True and False?'[4] Field provides another way in which the T-schema may be accommodated, but this time consistently. He does this by proposing a logic with a novel sort of conditional, to be employed in formulating the T-schema, but without the Law of Excluded Middle (LEM). Field takes it that his construction provides a better solution to paradoxes such as the Liar than any consistent proposal currently on the market. Here I agree. He also argues that it is better than a dialetheic

[1] T. S. Elliot, *Murder in the Cathedral,* II: 198–200.
[2] See, e.g., Horwich (1990), p. 41.
[3] See Beall and Armour-Garb (2003) and Beall (2004). Not that dialethism about the paradoxes is committed to deflationism about truth: dialetheism goes with any theory of truth. See Priest (2000).
[4] Field (2005). In what follows, page and section references refer to this unless otherwise indicated. All italics in quotations are original.

solution. Indeed, he suggests that his construction entirely undercuts dialetheism. Here I disagree. This paper explains why.[5]

2. PRELIMINARY MATTERS

Field's paper starts with a number of worries about dialetheism—or at least the way that I have formulated it—and though they are not central to the thrust of his criticism, they are not completely unconnected either, so let me start by taking them up.

Let $\bot$ be a logical constant such that, for all A, $\bot \vdash A$.[6] Classically, $\bot$ is equivalent to $B \wedge \neg B$ (for any B). Field thinks that should these two notions come apart (though he does not, himself, think that they do), it is preferable to use the term 'contradiction' for something equivalent to the former; I use it for the latter. As he points out, this is a terminological matter, and nothing hangs on it. For my part, I simply note that history is on my side in this usage. Traditionally, negation has been thought of as a contradictory-forming functor, so that A and $\neg A$ are contradictories, and pairs of the form A and $\neg A$ a contradiction. (The conjunction is not an issue here, as Field points out.) Moreover, authorities from Aristotle to Hegel, *none of whom subscribed to Explosion*, called them this.

Next, a dialetheist holds that the liar sentence, L, is both true and false (i.e., has a true negation): $T\langle L\rangle \wedge T\langle \neg L\rangle$. If one subscribes to the principle:

$$(^*)\, T\langle \neg A\rangle \leftrightarrow \neg T\langle A\rangle$$

it also follows that L is not true and not false: $\neg T\langle L\rangle$ and $\neg T\langle \neg L\rangle$. Thus we have, $T\langle L\rangle \wedge T\langle \neg L\rangle \wedge \neg T\langle L\rangle \wedge \neg T\langle \neg L\rangle$. It seems 'misleading', says Field, to characterise the status of the Liar simply by the first two conjuncts. Moreover, given that $\neg(A \wedge \neg A)$ as well, it also follows by a bit of juggling that, for any A, $\neg(T\langle A\rangle \wedge T\langle \neg A\rangle)$. This is the negation of dialetheism, the view that some contradictories are both true. If one is a dialetheist, this does not prevent dialetheism being true too; but, thinks Field, it is better to define dialetheism in such a way that the view is not an inherently contradictory one.

Now, as a matter of fact, I do not subscribe to (*);[7] but even if I did, I do not feel the force of the objection that Field feels. It seems to me to be perfectly natural to characterise the Liar as both true and false, since—given (*)—this entails its other properties. And it would be most misleading to characterise it by some other pair of conjuncts with the same property. Thus, for example, given that there are consistent truth-value gap solutions to the Liar, to describe it as neither true nor false would be *most* misleading. As for dialetheism itself being inconsistent, my aim has never been to avoid inconsistency, but to tame it. I do not think that the contradictory nature of dialetheism is worse than any of the other contradictions I subscribe to.[8]

[5] I am grateful to a number of people for illuminating discussions concerning the matters in this paper; principally to Hartry Field himself, but also to JC Beall, Bradley Armour-Garb, Allen Hazen, and Greg Restall.

[6] See Priest (1987), 8.5. [7] See Priest (1987), 4.9. [8] See Priest (1987), p. 91.

Field then raises a more substantial objection to dialetheism. The point is a familiar one. How can criticism of a view be possible if it is open to a person simply to accept their view together with the content of any objection that is put to it? The answer, however, is simple. Accepting A and $\neg A$ is always a move in *logical* space. This is so even if one accepts classical logic. After all, the person who accepts everything accepts classical logic. This does not mean that it can be done *rationally*. In a nutshell, it is rational to accept a view if it comes out better than any rival on the weighted sum of good-making criteria—such as ontological leanness, simplicity, non-(ad hocness), maybe even consistency, etc. It is rational to reject it if a rival comes out better.[9] In particular, the view of a person who accepts something or other *plus* the content of an objection put to it may well fail this test.[10]

3. REVENGE IS SWEET

With these preliminary points out of the way, let us now turn to the heart of Field's paper: his attempt to solve the semantic paradoxes of self-reference. In passing, let us note that the paradoxes of self-reference are but one reason for being a dialetheist. There are many other arguments to this effect: arguments concerning Gödel's incompleteness theorem, motion, inconsistent laws and similar things, arguments concerning the limits of thought.[11] Field says (p. 27): 'I don't think there is *any reason whatever* to believe that [there might be some problem solvable better by dialetheist means than by non-dialetheist means]'. Now, it may or may not be the case that the paradoxes of self-reference provide the strongest argument for dialetheism, but these other arguments are not a nothing, and Field has done nothing whatever to show where they fail.

But let us stick with the semantic paradoxes. Field thinks that to accommodate the T-schema one needs a non-classical and detachable conditional (i.e., one that satisfies Modus Ponens). In this we are in full agreement. Such a conditional is given in *In Contradiction*.[12] There is also a wide variety of relevant conditionals that will do the job. (In fact, I now prefer one of these, a depth-relevant logic somewhere in the vicinity of B.[13]) One may even have relevant conditionals in a logic without the LEM, and in which the T-schema is demonstrably consistent.[14] We have, then, a multitude of possibilities, and we need to address the question of which is the best. I will turn to

[9] This is discussed in Priest (1987), 7.5, and in greater detail in Priest (2001a).

[10] In fn. 19, Field moots the possibility of a family of operators, N_α, such that it gets 'harder and harder' to accept $A \wedge N_\alpha A$ as α increases. Now, even without Field's construction, there is an operator, N, such that accepting A and NA is really hard—irrational, in fact. Let NA be $A \rightarrow \bot$. Then one who accepts A and NA is committed to everything. For further discussion of N and its relationship to negation, see Priest (1999), esp. sect. 8.

[11] These are detailed in Priest (1987) and (1995).

[12] Priest (1987), ch. 6. In fact, a couple of options are given there, depending on whether or not one wants to endorse contraposition.

[13] See Priest (2001b), chs. 9, 10. One may show the non-triviality of the T-schema based on such logics by drawing on the work of Brady (1989). See Priest (2002), 8.2.

[14] See, e.g., Brady (1983).

this in due course, but first let us see whether Field's construction really does solve the paradoxes.

A standard objection to proposed consistent solutions to the semantic paradoxes is that they all seem vulnerable to 'revenge' paradoxes. There is a certain notion the intelligibility of which the theorist presupposes which, if it is included in the language in question, can be used to refashion the paradox. Hence consistency can be maintained only at the cost of incompleteness—which naturally gives rise to a hierarchy of metalanguages, and so to familiar problems of the same kind.[15] Field claims that his theory is immune from this problem. Is it? The fullest treatment of the point is in Field (2003). In this section and the next I follow his exposition and discussion there. (Though I make no attempt to summarise the technical details of his construction.)

Field's semantics is based on a three-valued logic, where the values are 1, 1/2 and 0. It also employs a (double) transfinite recursion. In terms of this, we may define the ultimate semantic value of a formula, A, $\| A \|$, which is one of these three values. (Ultimate value is value at *acceptable* levels of the hierarchy.) Validity is defined in terms of the preservation of ultimate value 1. For any A, $\| T\langle A\rangle \| = \| A \|$; and given the recursive truth conditions for $\rightarrow$, this ensures that the T-scheme holds in the form of a biconditional. Having ultimate semantic value 1 is to be understood as determinate truth—or at least, something like it; the reason for the hedging will become clear in due course—ultimate value 0 is determinate falsity, and ultimate value 1/2 is indeterminacy. All three notions can, in fact, be defined in terms of determinate truth. $\| A \| = 0$ iff $\| \neg A \| = 1$, and $\| A \| = 1/2$ iff $\| A \| \neq 0$ and $\| A \| \neq 1$. It is, at any rate, the notion of determinate truth and its cognates which threaten revenge paradoxes for Field.

In terms of $\rightarrow$, Field shows how to define a family of operators, D^σ (for a certain family of countable ordinals, σ) each of which may be taken to express determinate truth, in some sense. Each predicate in the family applies to some of the sentences that have ultimate value 1, but not others. And each of the standard sentences that are indeterminate, A, such as the Liar sentence, the Curry sentence, various extended paradoxes employing the D^σ themselves, and so on, can have their semantic status expressed in terms of some D^σ in the family—in the sense that $\neg D^\sigma A \wedge \neg D^\sigma \neg A$ has ultimate value 1. All these sentences may therefore have their indeterminacy expressed, in some sense. A natural question at this point is whether every indeterminate sentence, B, satisfies $\neg D^\sigma B \wedge \neg D^\sigma \neg B$, for some D^σ, and so can have its status expressed in this way. The answer to this is currently unknown.[16] If this is not the case, then the language is clearly expressively incomplete, since there are indeterminate sentences whose status cannot be expressed. But even if it is, it is not clear that the construction is an advance on the Tarskian one in this respect. In the Tarski hierarchy, each sentence can have its semantic status expressed by some sentence in the hierarchy. Field, it is true, has a single language, not a hierarchy. But this is a superficial difference. One can always think of a hierarchy of languages as a single language.

[15] See Priest (1987), ch. 1 and Priest (1995), Conclusion.

[16] Field (in correspondence) has conjectured that this is, in fact, the case.

The expressibility of the status of particular sentences in the language is not the major worry, however. None of the D^σ predicates expresses determinate truth *in general*; and it is this that gives rise to the paradigm revenge problem. Suppose that there were a predicate, D, in the language, such that $D\langle A\rangle$ has ultimate value 1 if A does, and ultimate value 0 otherwise. We then have an extended paradox of the usual kind. By the usual self-referential moves, we could construct the sentence, F, of the form $\neg D\langle F\rangle$. Substituting in the T-schema gives us that $T\langle F\rangle \leftrightarrow \neg D\langle F\rangle$. Now if F is has ultimate value 1, so does $T\langle F\rangle$, and so, therefore, does $\neg D\langle F\rangle$ (the T-schema preserving ultimate truth values); hence F does not have ultimate value 1; conversely, if F does not have ultimate value 1 then $\neg D\langle F\rangle$ does, as, therefore, does F. Deploying the Law of Excluded Middle, we are back with the usual contradiction.

There is a possible move here, with which Field shows some sympathy. Let D express genuine determinate truth; we may add this to the language if necessary. Why must we suppose that it satisfies the LEM? If it does not, the paradox is broken. We still have a revenge problem with us, however. Let F be as before. Suppose that its status is determinate. Then we have Excluded Middle for F, $F \vee \neg F$, and so a contradiction. On pain of contradiction, F cannot be determinate. But its status cannot be expressed by $\neg D\langle F\rangle \wedge \neg D\langle \neg F\rangle$. For this, after all, entails $\neg D\langle F\rangle$, that is, F, and so $F \vee \neg F$; in which case we have a contradiction. Consistency is purchased, as ever, at the expense of expressive incompleteness.

4. ENTER ZF

But wait. Field's construction is a set-theoretic one, and the language of set-theory can be taken to be a part of Field's object language. The metatheory is therefore expressible in the object language. But this means that ultimate truth value can be defined in the object language—and in such a way that it satisfies the Law of Excluded Middle. And the semantics shows that the theory is consistent. What has gone wrong here?

The answer is that, despite initial appearances, appropriate metatheoretic reasoning *cannot* be performed in the object theory. In one sense, the language may be expressive enough; but in another, and more important, sense, it is not. As Field himself points out, though one can define a predicate 'has ultimate value 1' in the language, this has to be interpreted with respect to the ground model of ZF which kicks off the transfinite construction. And for the usual reason, this model can contain only an initial segment of the ordinals. 'Ultimate value 1', then, means only determinate truth with respect to this initial segment of ordinals, not absolute determinate truth. Field's metatheory cannot be expressed in the object language any more than that of ZF can be expressed in ZF, and for exactly the same reason. If it could be, the theory would be able to establish its own consistency, which is impossible, by Gödel's second incompleteness theorem.[17] Consistency, then, is maintained only by the usual trade-off with expressiveness.

[17] In particular, if $B(x)$ is a proof predicate for the theory—or at least, an appropriate axiomatic fragment of it—one cannot prove $\forall x(B(x) \rightarrow Tx)$, or a consistency proof would be forthcoming.

It is worth noting, at this point, that this failure of ability on the part of *ZF* is effectively its own revenge problem. If *ZF* could express all that one would expect, it would collapse into inconsistency. Specifically, the inability of *ZF* to express its own semantic notions (is one of the things that) keeps it consistent. If it were able to show the existence of a universal set, and hence of an interpretation (in the model-theoretic sense) of its own language, inconsistency, in the shape of Gödel's (second) Incompleteness Theorem would arise. The fact, then—if it is a fact—that the revenge problem for the theory of truth has turned out to be the same as that for *ZF* is not reassuring.

In summary, then, though Field may have gone further than anyone else towards the Holy Grail of a consistent semantically closed theory, in the end he fails for the usual reason. The theory, if consistent, is expressively complete.

There is always, of course, the heroic solution: throw away the ladder. We declare the things that cannot be expressed, including the offending determinately-true predicate, to be meaningless. We still, after all, have the set-theoretic construction which can be carried out within *ZF*, and this at least suffices to show the consistency of the theory of truth relative to *ZF*. Field shows some sympathy with this possibility too.

The move of declaring the metatheoretic notions meaningless is, of course, open to anyone who wishes to avoid extended paradoxes. And if this is the best Field can do, he is no longer ahead of the field. But the move is one of desperation and would, I think, be somewhat disingenuous. It is clear from the informal way that Field uses the notions of determinacy/indeterminacy in his paper, that these are no mere technical device. Their intuitive sense drives the whole construction. Even Field cannot shake himself free from the meaningfulness of these notions, as the following quotation shows:[18]

> I do not wish to suggest that the notion of having semantic value 1 in the sense defined [i.e., relative to a model] has nothing to do with truth or determinate truth. On the contrary, it serves as a good model of these notions (in an informal sense of model) ...

The situation, then, is this. There are notions which, for all the world, appear to us to be intelligible; these cannot, on pain of contradiction, be expressed in the object language. If we declare them meaningless, this is for no reason, in the last resort, other than that they lead to contradiction. As far as solutions to the paradoxes go, the result is, to put it mildly, disappointing. Moreover, and importantly, ad hoc manoeuvring of this kind is not required dialethically. A dialetheic (set) theory can contain its own model-theory.[19] We are now coming to the business of a comparison of Field's approach with a dialetheic approach; before we pursue this matter explicitly, there is another matter to be discussed first.

[18] Field (2003), p. 169.
[19] See Priest (2000b).

5. BERRY'S PARADOX

Setting revenge issues aside, there is another, and clear, reason why Field's construction does not provide what is required. Field claims (sect. 5) that his construction can be applied to all the semantic paradoxes, since it generalises in a natural way to the notion of satisfaction, and hence to all semantic notions—including denotation. Now, it is true that the construction can be extended to give a consistent theory of the naive Denotation Schema. However, the denotation paradoxes, such as Berry's, use descriptions essentially. These are not part of the language that Field considers, and their addition blocks Field's construction—at least in any straightforward way. Moreover, the argument for Berry's paradox uses very little logical machinery: no principles concerning the conditional that are not validated in Field's construction, and no LEM. A proof of this fact is given in Priest (1987), 1.8.[20] Hence, even if Field's construction does solve the Liar paradox, there are equally important semantic paradoxes of self-reference that it does not solve.

In fn.14 Field replies to this point. He notes that the argument in question uses the least-number principle (LNP):

$$\exists x A(x) \rightarrow A(\mu x(A(x)))$$

and argues that this entails the LEM—or at least a restricted version thereof for statements of determinacy, $Det[A] \vee \neg Det[A]$ (I follow his notation here). He therefore rejects this principle. Several points are relevant here.

First, there is something curious about the form of Field's reply. The LNP gives contradiction in the shape of Berry's paradox. If Field were right that it entails $Det[A] \vee \neg Det[A]$, and so gives rise to revenge paradoxes, this would seem to make matters *worse* for him. Field is, in fact, simply rejecting the LNP on the ground that it gives rise to contradiction. The unprincipled nature of this rejection is clear. It is no better than the rejection of the *T*-schema for no reason other than it gives rise to paradox.

Second, and in any case, the LNP does not entail the LEM. To see this, let '$\mu x A(x)$' denote the least x (in whatever ordering is in question) such that $A(x)$ takes the value 1. For smaller y, $A(y)$ may take the value 0 or some intermediate value. (If there is no such x, we do something else. What, for the case at hand, is irrelevant.) This gives us a model of the LNP which does not validate the LEM. Field's argument from the LNP to the LEM uses the principle that:

$$1 = \mu x A(x) \rightarrow \neg A(0)$$

This fails in these semantics (since $A(0)$ may have a value other than 0). Neither is this principle employed in the argument for Berry's paradox.

Third: to see whether the LNP entails the LEM for statements of determinacy, we need to ask how determinacy is to be understood. Perhaps the most natural understanding is to take determinacy to mean having value 1 in Field's own semantics. But if

[20] The matter is further discussed in Priest (2001a).

one does this, then $Det[B] \vee \neg Det[B]$ holds anyway, even without the LNP, since set-theoretic statements are two-valued. Rejecting the LNP is therefore beside the point. Alternatively, we may understand it in such a way that it does not automatically satisfy the LEM. Thus, we may understand it as Field's own D operator (D^0). But if we do this, then Field's argument to the effect that the LNP gives $DB \vee \neg DB$ fails. This argument uses the principle that:

$$1 = \mu x A(x) \rightarrow \neg DA(0)$$

But this is not valid. To see this, take $A(1)$ to be any formula such that $D\,A(1)$, and so $A(1)$, takes the value 1. Take $A(0)$ to be such that both $A(0)$ and $D\,A(0)$ take the value 1/2 (e.g., the L_1 of Field (2003), p. 159). Then $1 = \mu x A(x)$ holds, but $\neg DA(0)$ fails.

Fourth, one could define the behaviour of the μ-operator differently. We could let '$\mu x A(x)$' denote the least x such that $A(x)$ takes the value 1, and for all $y < x$, $A(y)$ takes the value 0 (or such that $D\,A(x)$ and, for all $y < x$, $\neg DA(y)$ take the value 1). If one does this, then, of course, the offending principles fall out. But, as I have just shown, there is still an intelligible notion of the least least number operator—intelligible on Field's own semantics—which does not deliver the LEM or a restricted version thereof. And this notion—I emphasise again—is sufficient for the derivation of Berry's paradox.

Fifth, and related, the properties of the least number operator are a bit of a red-herring anyway. The argument for Berry does not require a least number operator. An indefinite description operator will do just as well. (See Priest (1983).) This demonstrably does not give the LEM, even in the context of intuitionist logic. (See Bell (1993.))

Sixth, and finally, the point remains: descriptions are involved essentially in paradoxes of denotation, and Field has not shown that his construction can handle them in such a way as to give his desired result.

6. COMPARISONS

Let us now return to the fact that there are many ways of achieving Field's goal: obtaining a conditional that allows acceptance of the T-schema. We need to evaluate which it is more rational to accept. This is to be done (as indicated in section 2) on the ground of which approach is over-all preferable. It is clear that Field's approach is consistent, whilst dialetheism is not. This will be taken by many to be clearly in his favour. In fact, I think that it is not so clear. Both Field and I take classical truth values to be the norm in truth-discourse. We both diagnose the naughty sentences as having some other status. For him, this is a consistent one; for me it is not. But given that we are dealing with an abnormality, consistency does not seem to have a great deal of advantage over inconsistency (especially given that much of the orthodox attitude to inconsistency is a prejudice with no rational ground[21]). However, let us not go into

[21] This is discussed further in Priest (2001a), sect. 4.

the matter here. Concentrate, instead, on the fact that consistency is not the only relevant consideration.

Another criterion of great importance to the evaluation of rival views is simplicity. A comparison of Field's semantics and those of dialetheism makes it clear where the virtue of simplicity lies. Both approaches deploy what can be thought of as a many-valued logic. But Field's semantics for the conditional involve the complexity of ordinal arithmetic. The construction of Field (2003), employing a three-valued logic with truth conditions that require double transfinite recursion, is perhaps best thought of as a consistency proof for certain principles concerning the conditional and truth. But the construction of Field (2004b) is even more complex in some ways, involving as it does a many-valued logic whose values are functions from a set of transfinite ordinals to the three values. Compare this with a dialetheic approach, which deploys nothing more than a certain use of impossible worlds, which there are independent grounds for supposing to be necessary anyway.[22] And if I am right about the revenge problem and Berry's paradox, further epicycles must be added to Field's theory to take account of these problems, if this can be done at all.

It also needs to be noted that the conditional that Field comes up with has quite counter-intuitive properties, since it is not a relevant conditional. Thus, for example, it validates the schema $A \vdash (B \rightarrow A)$. Now let A be 'you will not be harmed tomorrow'. This, let us pray, is true. Let B be 'you jump off the top of the Empire State Building tomorrow'. Then from the principle in question we can infer: If you jump off the top of the Empire State Building tomorrow you will not be harmed (then)—which, it would seem, is patently false.

This is one of the milder 'paradoxes of material implication', of course, and there are well known moves that one might make in connection with it (such as an appeal to conversational implicature). But there are many more virulent 'paradoxes', against which such replies are useless.[23] One of my favourites is this. Suppose that we have a light bulb, in series with two switches (currently open), *a* and *b*, so that the light will go on if (and only if) both switches are closed. Let L, A, and B be the sentences 'The light goes on', 'Switch *a* is closed' and 'Switch *b* is closed', respectively. Then we have: $(A \wedge B) \rightarrow C$. Now, for the material conditional:

$$(A \wedge B) \rightarrow C \vdash ((A \wedge \neg B) \rightarrow C) \vee (\neg A \wedge B) \rightarrow C)$$

If we could apply this, it would follow that there is one of the switches such that if it is closed whilst the other remains open, the light will go on. This is crazy.

Now, the above inference is not valid for Field's conditional, so he might be thought to avoid this problem; but in contexts where we have the LEM for the sentences involved, it does hold. And violations of the LEM arise, for Field, only when the truth predicate, or maybe vague predicates, are involved; but neither of these is the case in the switching example.

[22] For details of the semantics, see Priest (2001b), ch. 9.

[23] See, e.g., Routley et al. (1982), p. 6 ff.

Field might say that his account of the conditional was never meant to apply to cases such as this. But this highlights a new consideration. When we select a logical theory as the most preferable, we do not select in isolation: we must bear in mind all the other things that are affected by the choice. Thus, classical logic is simpler than either dialetheic logic or Field's. But, as Field and I agree, we have to take into account not just the logic, but truth as well. And classical logic plus, say, the Tarski hierarchy of truth (with all the epicycles necessary to avoid its unfortunate consequences) is perhaps more complex than Field's combined deal; it is certainly more complex than a dialetheic approach. We need to take into account a lot more than truth, however. We need to take into account, also, the adequacy of the conditional in other contexts. As we have seen, Field's conditional fares badly in this regard.

Another way in which a dialetheic account is preferable to Field's is in the matter of uniformity. All the standard paradoxes of self-reference are of a kind (inclosure paradoxes). One should therefore expect essentially the same solution for all of them. Same kind of paradox, same kind of solution (the Principle of Uniform Solution).[24] A dialetheic account respects this constraint. Field's account does not. As we have seen, it does not, on its own, resolve the paradoxes of denotation. Some essentially independent factor will have, therefore, to be invoked, violating uniformity.

It is not just the other semantic paradoxes that are inclosure paradoxes. The self-referential paradoxes of set-theory are too.[25] To the extent that Field has a solution to the set-theoretic paradoxes, it is essentially that offered by *ZF*, which is built into his account. Not only is this solution problematic in a number of ways,[26] it proceeds by denying the existence of various sets, a stratagem quite different from that deployed by Field for the semantic paradoxes. Again, we have a violation of the Principle of Uniform Solution.

Let me end this comparison of Field's approach and dialetheism with one further comment. Arguably, a strength of Field's account is that classical logic can be preserved 'where we want it'. In those situations in which the LEM holds, classical logic is forthcoming. Actually, as I have already pointed out, it is not clear that this really is a strength. We have seen that there are good reasons to doubt the adequacy of the classical account of the conditional. But I just point out here that all classical reasoning can be recaptured just as much in dialetheic logic. From a dialetheic

[24] This is defended at much greater length in Priest (1995), 11.5, and the second edition, 17.6.

[25] See Priest (1995), ch. 11.

[26] See Priest (1987), ch. 2 and Priest (1995), ch. 11. Field suggests (sect. 5) that some of the problems of *ZF* can be overcome by constructing a theory of properties, on the same lines as his theory of truth. These properties can perform, in a more satisfactory way, the function that proper classes are often invoked to perform. Of course, properties are not extensional, so we lose this much of the theory of proper classes. Field suggest that this is not a problem: 'I doubt that extensionality among proper classes plays much role anyway' (Field (2004a), p. 22). In my turn, I doubt that this is true. Here is one reason. *One* of the factors that drives us towards recognising collections other than those that exist within *ZF* is category theory, where it is natural to consider the category of all sets, or all categories—which are not *ZF* sets. (See Priest (1987), 2.3.) Now, when reasoning about categories, and in particular when reasoning about their identity, it is standard to deploy extensionality. It is not at all clear that this can be avoided.

perspective, the extensional logic of consistent situations—and classically there are no others—is classical.[27] Another supposed advantage of Field's approach therefore evaporates.

7. CONCLUSION

We have seen that Field's general worries about dialetheism are groundless, that his approach to the Liar is still subject to revenge problems, that it does not even handle all the semantic paradoxes of self-reference, and that, in any case, all the theoretical virtues with the exception of consistency pull towards a dialetheic account of the paradoxes. The 'main case for dialetheism has' not, therefore, 'disappeared' (p. 40). Field's attempt to dispose of dialetheism is markedly less successful than that of Henry II's knights to dispose of Thomas.

> When you come to the point, it does go against the grain to kill an Archbishop, especially when you have been brought up in good Christian traditions.
>
> Third Knight.[28]

REFERENCES

[1] JC Beall (2004a), 'True and False—As If', ch.12 of G. Priest, JC Beall and B. Armour-Garb (eds.), *The Law of Non-Contradiction*, Oxford: Oxford University Press.
[2] —— (2003), 'Should Deflationists be Dialetheists?', *Noûs* 37, 303–24.
[3] J. L. Bell (1993), 'Hilbert's ε-Operator and Classical Logic', *Journal of Philosophical Logic* 22, 1–18.
[4] R. Brady (1983), 'The Simple Consistency of Set Theory Based on the Logic CSQ', *Notre Dame Journal of Formal Logic* 24, 431–9.
[5] —— (1989), 'The Non-Triviality of Dialectical Set-Theory', pp. 437–70 of G. Priest, R. Routley and J. Norman (eds.), *Paraconsistent Logic: Essays on the Inconsistent*, Munich: Philosophia Verlag.
[6] H. Field (2003), 'A Revenge-Immune Solution to the Semantic Paradoxes', *Journal of Philosophical Logic* 32, 139–77.
[7] —— (2004a), 'The Consistency of the Naive(?) Theory of Properties', *Philosophical Quarterly*, 54, 78–104; reprinted as pp. 285–310 of G. Link (ed.), *One Hundred of Russell's Paradox*, Berlin: de Gruyker.
[8] —— (2004b), 'The Semantic Paradoxes and the Paradoxes of Vagueness', pp. 262–311 of JC Beall (ed.), *Liars and Heaps*, Oxford: Oxford University Press.
[9] —— (2005), 'Is the Liar Both True and False?, this volume at Ch. 2.
[10] P. Horwich (1990), *Truth*, Oxford: Basil Blackwell.
[11] G. Priest (1983), 'The Logical Paradoxes and the Law of Excluded Middle', *Philosophical Quarterly* 33, 160–5.

[27] See Priest (1987), 8.5 and Priest (2002), 7.8. One may still disagree, of course, as to whether conditionals are extensional—especially outside mathematics.

[28] T. S. Elliot, *Murder in the Cathedral*, II: 452–5.

[12] ——(1987), *In Contradiction*, Dordrecht: Kluwer Academic Publishers; 2nd (extended) edn., Oxford: Oxford University Press, 2006.

[13] ——(1995), *Beyond the Limits of Thought*, Cambridge: Cambridge University Press; 2nd (extended) edn., Oxford: Oxford University Press, 2002.

[14] ——(1999), 'What Not? A Dialetheic Account of Negation', pp. 101–20 of D. Gabbay and H. Wansing (eds.), *What is Negation?*, Dordrecht: Kluwer Academic Publishers refs. with amendments as ch. 4 of Priest (2006).

[15] ——(2000), 'Truth and Contradiction', *Philosophical Quarterly* 50, 305–19 repr. with amendments as ch. 2 of Priest (2006).

[16] ——(2001a), 'Why it's Irrational to Believe in Consistency', pp. 284–97 of B. Brogaard and B. Smith (eds.), *Rationality and Irrationality; Proc. 23rd International Wittgenstein Conference*, Vienna: öbvahpt refs. with amendments as ch. 7 of Priest (2006).

[17] ——(2001b), *Introduction to Non-Classical Logic*, Cambridge: Cambridge University Press.

[18] ——(2002), 'Paraconsistent Logic', pp. 287–303, vol. 6, of D. Gabbay and F. Guenthner (eds.), *Handbook of Philosophical Logic*, 2nd edn., Dordrecht: Kluwer Academic Publishers.

[19] ——(2000a), 'The Paradoxes of Denotation', forthcoming in V. F. Hendricks, S. A. Pedersen and T. Bolander (eds.), *Self-Reference*, Dordrecht: Kluwer Academic Publishers.

[20] ——(2001b), 'Paraconsistent Set-Theory', forthcoming in A. Irvine (ed.), *Essays on Set Theory*, Oxford: Basil Blackwell refs. as ch. 18 of the 2nd edn. of Priest (1987).

[21] ——(2006), *Doubt Truth to be a Liar*, Oxford: Oxford University Press, 2006.

[22] R. Routley, et al. (1982), *Relevant Logics and Their Rivals, vol. I*, Atascadero, CA: Ridgeview.

4

Variations on a Theme by Yablo

Hartry Field

Natural assumptions about truth lead, in classical logic, to well-known paradoxes (such as the Liar paradox and the Curry paradox). One response to these paradoxes is (i) to weaken classical logic by restricting the law of excluded middle; and (ii) to adopt an account of the conditional according to which it is not defined from negation and disjunction in the usual way, so that the biconditionals $True(\langle A \rangle) \leftrightarrow A$ can be retained in the absence of excluded middle. In "New Grounds for Naive Truth Theory" ([12]), Steve Yablo develops a new version of this response, and cites three respects in which he deems it superior to a version that I have advocated in several papers. I think he is right that my version was non-optimal in some of these respects (one and a half of them, to be precise); however, Yablo's own account seems to me to have some undesirable features as well. In this paper I will explore some variations on his account, and end up tentatively advocating a synthesis of his account and mine (one that is somewhat closer to mine than to his).

1. BACKGROUND

First some philosophical motivation for the project that Yablo and I share. A standard account of why we need a notion of truth (Quine [10], Leeds [8]) is to allow us to make and use generalizations not expressible (or not easily expressible) without the notion. For instance, even if I do not remember all the details of what you said yesterday but only the general gist of it, I may say "If everything you said yesterday is true then probably I should change my plans about such and such"; the antecedent is supposed to be equivalent to the conjunction of everything you said, which I'm not in a position to fill in. It would seem that in order for the notion of truth to fill this role, the attribution of truth to a sentence has to be fully equivalent to the sentence itself: call this the Equivalence Principle. More precisely, $True(\langle A \rangle)$ must be intersubstitutable with A in all extensional contexts, including within the scope of conditionals.[1]

I am grateful to Josh Schechter for suggesting several improvements.

[1] Possibly in some non-extensional contexts too, but there will be no need to decide this here. We certainly don't need them to be intersubstitutable in quotational contexts or in propositional attitude contexts.

(It wouldn't be enough for $True(\langle A\rangle)$ and A to be co-assertable, or for them to be co-assertable and in addition $\neg True(\langle A\rangle)$ and $\neg A$ to be co-assertable; in the example given, intersubstitutability within the antecedent of a conditional is required.)

So the Equivalence Principle is not something we should give up lightly. Unfortunately, it conflicts with classical logic: in languages with very minimal resources for developing syntax we can formulate "Liar sentences" which assert their own untruth. Such a sentence L is equivalent to $\neg True(\langle L\rangle)$; but the equivalence principle requires it to also be equivalent to $True(\langle L\rangle)$; so $True(\langle L\rangle)$ must be equivalent to $\neg True(\langle L\rangle)$, which is impossible in classical logic. The problem is not reasonably blamed on the syntactic resources that allow for self-reference: among other reasons for this, there's the fact that the motivation for the Equivalence Principle extends to a similar principle involving the notion of *true of*, and applying this extended principle to the predicate 'is not true of itself' we get a contradiction in classical logic even without the use of any special syntactic assumptions. The only two serious choices are keeping classical logic while restricting the Equivalence Principle, and keeping the Equivalence Principle while restricting classical logic.

The first of these choices has been well explored, on the technical level: see for instance Friedman and Sheard [5] for an account of the main sub-options for weakening the Equivalence Principle within classical logic. I think it is fair to say that each of these classical sub-options has a high cost: the weakenings of the Equivalence Principle are highly unnatural, and it is not obvious that they would not cripple the ordinary use of the notion of truth. That is a question that requires a more serious discussion than I can give here, but in any case, there is motivation for exploring the second choice, that of restricting classical logic.

More fully, the approach that Yablo and I share involves the use of a weakened logic—in particular, one without the law of excluded middle[2]—as one's general logic. This is compatible with allowing that the principle of excluded middle is correct (as a non-logical principle) in domains where peculiar concepts like 'true' are not involved or can be shown to be eliminable: e.g. no restriction on the use of classical logic within mathematics or within physics is required. The general logic that applies even when peculiar concepts like 'true' are in play cannot be intuitionist: intuitionism is inconsistent with the Equivalence Principle, just as classical logic is. And certain principles that are not valid in intuitionism, such as the equivalence between $\neg\neg A$ and A and between $\neg(A \wedge B)$ and $\neg A \vee \neg B$, can (and presumably should) be retained.

The idea of using logics of this sort to evade the paradoxes is not a new one, though early attempts turned out not to be consistent with the Equivalence Principle. The first work that can be viewed as demonstrating the consistency of the Equivalence Principle in a weakening of classical logic is Kripke [7]: in particular, the part of the paper that discusses the Kleene truth tables.[3] Kripke's discussion is entirely at the level of semantics, and there is more than one way to read a theory of truth off the

[2] There is an alternative non-classical route that keeps excluded middle, but gives up instead the prohibition against accepting contradictions and the principle that contradictions imply everything. I will not be discussing that here. See Beall (ch 1) and Priest (ch 3) for discussion.

[3] Kripke discusses both the weak and the strong Kleene truth tables; the strong are of more interest, and I will confine my discussion to them.

semantics; but on what is I think the most natural way of reading a theory off the semantics (viz., one that takes the theory to be the set of sentences in a particular fixed point) we get a theory that obeys the Equivalence Principle, in a logic without excluded middle.

Unfortunately, the logic that Kripke reconciles with the Equivalence Principle is so weak as to be very difficult to reason with: in particular, it does not contain a reasonable conditional. (We could define $A \rightarrow B$ as $\neg A \vee B$; but then the absence of excluded middle would preclude such things as $A \rightarrow A$ and $A \wedge B \rightarrow A$ from being valid. The lack of the former means that we also do not validate either half of the Tarski schema, i.e. either $True(\langle A \rangle) \rightarrow A$ or its converse.) The logic is expressively weak in other ways too; for instance, it has no way of registering the fact that Liar sentences are in some sense "pathological".

What Yablo and I are both interested in is showing the consistency of the Equivalence Principle in expressively richer logics, which contain at least a reasonable conditional (and in the case of my own account at least, contain ways of asserting pathology). Unfortunately the simplest ways of adding a new conditional to the logic lead to paradoxes of their own: it is easy to see that the conditional cannot be a 3-valued truth function, and even the continuum-valued truth function of "fuzzy logic" can be shown to give rise to paradox ([11], [6]). Something more elaborate is required.

2. A SIMPLIFIED VERSION OF YABLO'S ACCOUNT

Yablo develops his account[4] using a 4-valued semantics, rather than the 3-valued semantics I used in [1]. I am going to simplify things by using a 3-valued analog. All the virtues of his account that he cites survive this simplification; and the complaints I will have about his account would arise for the 4-valued version as well. Besides simplification, the use of the 3-valued semantics leads to a more powerful logic for the connectives other than the conditional: with a 4-valued semantics one must apparently sacrifice either the disjunctive syllogism ($A \vee B, \neg A \vdash B$) or the rule of disjunction elimination, whereas these can be jointly maintained on a 3-valued semantics.

2.1 Kripkean background

Let L be a standard first order language, adequate to arithmetic and the theory of finite sequences (and hence adequate to the syntax of first order languages, even ones with uncountably many symbols), and let M be a classical model for L which is standard with respect to arithmetic and the theory of finite sequences. For notational convenience (i.e., to remove the need to talk of assignments of objects to free variables), I will assume that L has a name for every object in the domain of M (which if M is uncountable will mean that L contains uncountably many expressions). We can

[4] By "Yablo's account" I shall mean what he calls *Kripke-style possible world semantics*. Prior to giving this account he sketches a different account, which he calls *Field-style possible world semantics*, but this is not one that he has any great interest in, nor do I.

think of M as consisting of a domain, an assignment of an object in the domain to each name of L and of an operation on M to each function symbol of L, and an assignment of a 2-valued extension to each n-place predicate of L, where a 2-valued extension is a function assigning exactly one of the values 1 and 0 to each n-tuple of objects in the domain of M. We want to extend L to a language L^+ by adding a new 1-place predicate 'True' and a new 2-place conditional '$\rightarrow$'; when the syntax of L^+ is developed within L^+, 'True' will mean 'is a true sentence of L^+'. We also want to extend M to a 3-valued model M^+; M^+ will have the same domain as M, and treat the names and function symbols just as M does, and assign the same 2-valued extension to the predicates of L that M assigns them; but it will also assign a 3-valued extension to 'True', that is, a function that assigns exactly one of the three values 1, $\frac{1}{2}$ and 0 to each member of the domain of M. (2-valued extensions are a special case of 3-valued extensions, so that in general all predicates are assigned 3-valued extensions; it is just that predicates other than 'True' are assigned ones in which the value $\frac{1}{2}$ never appears.) If we denote this assignment to 'True' by T, then M^+ is given by the pair $\langle M, T\rangle$.

Once T is specified (in addition to M), that will be enough to determine a semantic value for every sentence of L^+ *not containing the* $\rightarrow$, by the following "strong Kleene" rules:

$$|\neg A|_{M,T} = 1 - |A|_{M,T}$$
$$|A \vee B|_{M,T} = \max\{|A|_{M,T}, |B|_{M,T}\}$$
$$|A \wedge B|_{M,T} = \min\{|A|_{M,T}, |B|_{M,T}\}$$
$$|\exists x A|_{M,T} = \max\{|A(x/t)|_{M,T}\}$$
$$|\forall x A|_{M,T} = \min\{|A(x/t)|_{M,T}\}$$

But the value of conditionals will require a separate rule, and the main question is going to be what this rule should be. For the moment we can bypass this crucial question in an uninformative manner, by introducing the idea of a *valuation for conditionals*. This is simply a function that assigns one of the three semantic values to each conditional in L^+ (including conditionals that have other conditionals as subformulas). Then if v is a valuation for conditionals, clearly the semantic value of every sentence of L^+ is determined by M^+ *together with* v. (The rules for connectives like $\neg$ and $\vee$ and $\exists$ merely need to be extended to include sentences with conditionals; e.g., the rule for $\neg$ is now that $|\neg A|_{M,v,T} = 1 - |A|_{M,v,T}$.)

Let us turn to the question of what the 3-valued extension for 'True' should be. As mentioned, we want to maintain the Equivalence Principle; given that the language does not contain quotation marks, propositional attitude constructions and the like, we can state this in the following unrestricted form:

> **The Equivalence Principle (EP):** For any sentence C of L^+ in which a sentence A of L^+ occurs, the result of substituting $True(\langle A\rangle)$ for one or more occurrences of A has the same semantic value as does C.

If L^+ *had not contained the new conditional*, a necessary and sufficient condition for attaining (EP) would be that the assignment of a 3-valued extension to 'True' be a *Kripkean fixed point*; that is,

Kripke Fixed Point Requirement (KFP): For any sentence A of L^+, $|True(\langle A \rangle)|_{M,\,v,\,T}$ must be the same as $|A|_{M,\,v,\,T}$. (And if T does not denote a sentence of L^+, $|True(t)|_{M,\,v,\,T}$ must be 0.)

(Of course the subscript v is not really needed when the language does not contain the conditional.) But with the conditional in the language, this is no longer sufficient for (EP): we need in addition a requirement on the valuation of conditionals, viz.

Transparency Requirement (TR): For any *conditional* C of L^+ in which a sentence A of L^+ occurs, the result of substituting $True(\langle A \rangle)$ for one or more occurrences of A has the same semantic value as does C.

(Again, the conditionals in question include ones with other conditionals as subformulas.) But the requirement (KFP) on the assignment to 'True' and the transparency requirement (TR) on the valuation of conditionals together suffice for the Equivalence Principle, as a simple inductive argument shows.

Moreover, Kripke showed that satisfying (KFP) is easy: although he didn't discuss languages with additional conditionals, his argument can be extended to show that for any valuation for conditionals v, there are a wide variety of *fixed points over* v, that is, 3-valued extensions of 'True' that satisfy (KFP). In particular there is a *minimal fixed point over* v, i.e. one which assigns the value 1 or 0 to a sentence only if every fixed point over v assigns the same value to that sentence.

Let us simplify the notation. I will throughout be concerned with a single ground model M, so there will be no need to keep including it in the subscripts. Moreover, from now on I will be concerned only with pairs $\langle v, T \rangle$ for which T is a Kripke fixed point over v. And given this, there is really no need to keep v in the notation, for it is determined by T: v is that function that assigns to any conditional $A \rightarrow B$ whatever value $True(\langle A \rightarrow B \rangle)$ gets in T. I will call this v_T; so we will be concerned with assignments T to 'True' each of which is a Kripke fixed point over a unique valuation v_T. Given all this, the notation $|A|_{M,\,v,\,T}$ simplifies to $|A|_T$.

So to repeat, if v is any transparent valuation of conditionals, there are Kripke fixed points over v, and by evaluating sentences in accord with any such fixed point, the Equivalence Principle is guaranteed. And the evaluation agrees with the originally given valuation M for sentences without 'True' or '$\rightarrow$'.

2.2 The Yablo conditional

The material in section 2.1 (which is common ground between Yablo's approach and my approach in [1]) does not by itself provide much of a theory, since so far there is no serious account of how the conditional works: the valuation of conditionals v has been left completely arbitrary, except for the requirement that it be transparent. There is no guarantee that sentences that ought to come out logical truths (e.g. instances of $A \rightarrow A$ or $A \wedge B \rightarrow A$) will get value 1; indeed, every conditional could get value $\frac{1}{2}$, or every one could get value 0. Nor is there a guarantee that Modus Ponens will be validated. What we need is a reasonable way to assign values to conditionals.

Yablo's proposal—again, modified to fit a 3-valued framework—is elegantly simple. For any transparent valuation v (of conditionals), let $S[v]$ be the set of transparent valuations that extend v (i.e. which assign 1 to every conditional to which v assigns 1 and 0 to every conditional to which v assigns 0); since v is transparent, $v \in S[v]$, so $S[v]$ is not empty. For any nonempty set S of valuations (of conditionals), let $w[S]$ be the valuation given as follows: for any A and B,

$w[S](A \rightarrow B)$ is
1 if $(\forall v)(\forall T)$(if $v \in S$ and T is a Kripke fixed point over v then $|A|_T \leq |B|_T$),
0 if $(\forall v)(\forall T)$(if $v \in S$ and T is a Kripke fixed point over v then $|A|_T > |B|_T$),
$\frac{1}{2}$ otherwise.

Clearly $w[S]$ is transparent if all members of S are. Moreover if v_1 extends v_2 then $S[v_1] \subseteq S[v_2]$; and if $S_1 \subseteq S_2$ then $w[S_1]$ extends $w[S_2]$; consequently, if v_1 extends v_2 then $w[S[v_1]]$ extends $w[S[v_2]]$.

Let a *Yablo fixed point* be a valuation v for which v is identical to $w[S[v]]$; that is, a valuation v such that for any A and B,

(YFP) $v(A \rightarrow B)$ is
1 if $(\forall u)(\forall T)$ (if u is a transparent extension of v and T is a Kripke fixed point over u then $|A|_T \leq |B|_T$)
0 if $(\forall u)(\forall T)$ (if u is a transparent extension of v and T is a Kripke fixed point over u then $|A|_T > |B|_T$),
$\frac{1}{2}$ otherwise.

Yablo thinks that a reasonable valuation of conditionals should be a Yablo fixed point. He says that this gives the conditional an appealing modal-like semantics: if v is a Yablo fixed point and T is a Kripke fixed point over it, then the "possible worlds" accessible from $\langle M, v, T\rangle$ are the $\langle M, u, U\rangle$ for which u is a transparent extension of v and U is a fixed point over u. (Presumably the idea is that the "worlds" in the semantics do not really represent *possibilities* in any normal sense—each possibility is represented just by a ground world M. Rather, a "world" represents a *minimally adequate way of valuating sentences given the facts of the ground world.* A conditional sentence $A \rightarrow B$ is "modal" in something like the way that a sentence DA asserting what is determinately the case is modal in many treatments of vagueness: the value of $A \rightarrow B$ or DA is determined by looking at *a range* of valuations of the sentences A and B to which it applies, rather than just at a single valuation.)

It is easy to show that there are Yablo fixed points; indeed, there is a natural Kripke-like construction of the smallest one. We define a transfinite sequence of transparent valuations, as follows:

v_0 assigns each conditional the value $\frac{1}{2}$
$v_{\alpha+1}$ is $w[S[v]]$;
v_λ is the minimal extension of each v_β for $\beta < \lambda$, when λ is a limit ordinal.

[Or to write the successor clause without the abbreviations: $v_{\alpha+1}(A \rightarrow B)$ is

1 if $(\forall u)(\forall T)$ (if u is a transparent extension of v_α and T is a Kripke fixed point over u then $|A|_T \leq |B|_T$)
0 if $(\forall u)(\forall T)$ (if u is a transparent extension of v_α and T is a Kripke fixed point over u then $|A|_T > |B|_T$),
$\frac{1}{2}$ otherwise.]

A trivial inductive argument shows that if $\alpha < \beta$ then v_β extends v_α; so by a standard fixed point argument analogous to Kripke's, there must be an ordinal ξ such that $(\forall\alpha \geq \xi)(v_\alpha = v_\xi)$. v_ξ is *the minimal Yablo fixed point.*

Yablo's proposal (modified to fit 3-valued semantics) is to use this minimal Yablo fixed point v_ξ as the valuation for conditionals, and the minimal Kripke fixed point over v_ξ (call it Z_ξ) as the assignment to the truth predicate.

2.3 Discussion

Aside from its elegant simplicity, Yablo's proposal has many attractive features. First, it clearly validates many desirable laws (i.e., gives all instances of them value 1, in the case of sentences; preserves value 1, in case of interfences). For a *very* simple illustration, consider $A \wedge B \rightarrow A$; for any fixed point T over any valuation at all, $|A \wedge B|_T \leq |A|_T$, so the construction gives this conditional the value 1 at v_1 and hence at every valuation thereafter. Somewhat more interesting is the inference from $(A \rightarrow B) \wedge (A \rightarrow C)$ to $A \rightarrow (B \wedge C)$. If the premise gets value 1 at v_ξ then by the Yablo fixed point property (YFP), $|A|_T \leq |B|_T$ whenever v_T is a transparent extension of v_ξ, and also $|A|_T \leq |C|_T$ in the same circumstances; from which it follows that $|A|_T \leq |B \wedge C|_T$ in those circumstances, and hence that $A \rightarrow (B \wedge C)$ has value 1 at v_ξ. Modus ponens is validated as well: if $A \rightarrow B$ has value 1 at v_ξ, then for any fixed point T over a transparent extension of v_ξ, $|A|_T \leq |B|_T$; so in particular when Z_ξ is the minimal Kripke fixed point over v_ξ, $|A|_{Z_\xi} \leq |B|_{Z_\xi}$; so if A has value 1 at Z_ξ, so does B. A list of some other laws that are validated in the theory is given in [12]. (The list is of things validated in the 4-valued semantics; but anything validated in the 4-valued is validated in the 3-valued as well.)

Second, the quantification over non-minimal Kripke fixed points (in the definition of the w operator and hence in (YFP)) produces very intuitive results for conditionals in which the antecedent and consequent could consistently be assigned values in more than one way. (These cases form the basis of one of Yablo's objections to my account in [1], the objection from "insufficient strictness".)[5]

Consider for instance the conditionals $L \rightarrow I$ and $I \rightarrow L$, where L is a Liar sentence (one which asserts its own untruth) and I is a Truth-Teller (one which asserts its own truth). On Yablo's account, L and I get value $\frac{1}{2}$ in the designated fixed point Z_ξ (the minimal fixed point over v_ξ); but whereas L gets value $\frac{1}{2}$ in all other fixed points as well, I gets value 0 in some fixed points over v_ξ and value 1 in others. Because of this,

[5] In my opening remarks I mentioned that Yablo gives three objections to my account in [1]. The other two will not be considered until section 4.

the conditionals $L \to I$ and $I \to L$ get value $\frac{1}{2}$ on Yablo's account. I agree with Yablo that this seems intuitively right; my semantics in [1] (which also gave value $\frac{1}{2}$ to L and I) was unintuitive in giving these conditionals value 1. That's one illustration of why Yablo says, correctly I think, that my conditional in [1] *was not sufficiently strict.*

For a second example in which quantifying over non-minimal as well as minimal fixed points produces a desirable strictness, consider the conditional $I \to \neg I$ and its converse, where again I is a Truth-teller. An oddity of my own account in [1] was that these got value 1. ($I \to I$ got value 1 as well, as it should.) In the case of a Liar sentence L, it is inevitable that $L \to \neg L$ as well as $L \leftrightarrow L$ should get value 1: that $L \leftrightarrow \neg L$ gets value 1 follows from the Equivalence Principle (and with excluded middle gone, it does not lead to contradiction). But it does seem that we ought to minimize the number of sentences A for which $A \leftrightarrow \neg A$ (as well as $A \leftrightarrow A$) holds, and it seems undesirable that it holds for Truth-tellers. The quantification over non-minimal as well as minimal fixed points in Yablo's account is enough to guarantee that $I \leftrightarrow \neg I$ and its converse each get value $\frac{1}{2}$.

Yablo gives a third example along the same lines. Suppose Jones and Smith each say that what the other says is not true. Any account that respects the naive theory of truth (the Equivalence Principle plus the Tarski biconditionals) will yield $J \leftrightarrow \neg S$ (and so by the symmetry of the situation, any reasonable 3-valued account will give each of J and S the value $\frac{1}{2}$). But my account in [1] also yielded $J \leftrightarrow S$, which seems undesirable; and by quantifying over non-minimal fixed points as well as minimal ones, Yablo's account avoids this.[6]

It is worth noting that while these examples clearly illustrate the virtues of quantifying over non-minimal fixed points in the clause for a conditional *having value* 1, they do not turn at all on the fact that Yablo also quantifies over non-minimal fixed points in the clause for a conditional *having value* 0. Here is a minor variant of Yablo's account: instead of using the operator w of section 2.2, we use the following operator w^*, where Z_v stands for the minimal Kripke fixed point over v:

> $w^*[S](A \to B)$ is
> 1 if $(\forall v)(\forall T)$(if $v \in S$ and T is a Kripke fixed point over v then $|A|_T \leq |B|_T$),
> 0 if $(\forall v)$(if $v \in S$ then $|A|_{Z_v} > |B|_{Z_v}$),
> $\frac{1}{2}$ otherwise.

This leads to a *Yablo* fixed point*, by the same argument; that is, a v such that

> (YFP*) $v(A \to B)$ is
> 1 if $(\forall u)(\forall T)$ (if u is a transparent extension of v and T is a Kripke fixed point over u then $|A|_T \leq |B|_T$)
> 0 if $(\forall u)$ (if u is a transparent extension of v then $|A|_{Z_u} > |B|_{Z_u}$),
> $\frac{1}{2}$ otherwise.

[6] For another illustration of the (3-valued) Yablo account, let L_1 and L_2 be two Liar sentences (each asserting its own untruth), and I_1 and I_2 two Truth-tellers. The Yablo semantics yields that $L_1 \leftrightarrow L_2$ gets value 1, seemingly making the Liar sentence essentially unique, but yields that $I_1 \leftrightarrow I_2$ gets value $\frac{1}{2}$. (The reason for the 'seemingly' will appear in note 9.)

This account strikes me as slightly more natural than the actual Yablo account, but the differences will not matter to anything that follows.[7] Both accounts have the virtues cited above.

Despite its virtues, I have serious reservations about Yablo's account (and the Yablo* variant of it). Many of these reservations center on what it says (or doesn't say) about conditionals that have other conditionals embedded within them.

In the first place, let me note a point that Yablo himself cites as a weakness in his account: that on the account there seem to be no significant validities involving nested conditionals. Among the laws one might expect to hold of a conditional are the following:

$(A \rightarrow \neg B) \rightarrow (B \rightarrow \neg A)$;
$(A \rightarrow \neg A) \rightarrow \neg(\top \rightarrow A)$, where $\top$ is a tautology such as $B \rightarrow B$;

and the inferences

$$A \rightarrow B \vdash (C \rightarrow A) \rightarrow (C \rightarrow B);$$

and

$$A \rightarrow B \vdash (B \rightarrow C) \rightarrow (A \rightarrow C).$$

These all fail on Yablo's account and the Yablo* variant (though associated rules without embedded conditionals, like $A \rightarrow \neg B \vdash B \rightarrow \neg A$, hold).

The loss of the last pair of inferences is quite important: it blocks the proof of the substitutivity of equivalents (the inference from $A \leftrightarrow B$ to $X_A \leftrightarrow X_B$, where X_B is the result of substituting B for one or more occurrences of A in X_A). And indeed, that substitutivity principle fails dramatically in the Yablo (and Yablo*) semantics. For instance, though $A \leftrightarrow (A \vee A)$ is valid, $[A \rightarrow C] \leftrightarrow [(A \vee A) \rightarrow C]$ is not. For consider any A and C for which $A \rightarrow C$ gets value $\frac{1}{2}$ in v_ξ; then $A \vee A \rightarrow C$ also gets value $\frac{1}{2}$ in v_ξ. So in some extensions of v_ξ, one of $A \rightarrow C$ and $A \vee A \rightarrow C$ will get value 0 while the other one gets a value different from 0, and this means that $[A \rightarrow C] \rightarrow [(A \vee A) \rightarrow C]$ and its converse will each get value $\frac{1}{2}$. Clearly this situation arises because the extensions of v_ξ that one quantifies over in the truth conditions at v_ξ can be extraordinarily badly behaved; one might try to fix this by modifying the theory so that badly behaved valuations are excluded from the start, but it is not at all evident how this might be done without destroying the proof that the valuation of conditionals reaches a fixed point.[8]

[7] An example of the difference: if I is a Truth-teller, $I \rightarrow (0 = 1)$ gets value 0 on Yablo*, $\frac{1}{2}$ on Yablo. (Whereas if L is a Liar, $L \rightarrow (0 = 1)$ gets value 0 on both.)

[8] The fixed point proof above relied on the fact that when S is a set of transparent valuations, $w[S]$ is transparent; but if S is, say, a set of (transparent) valuations that validate the rules $A \rightarrow B \vdash (C \rightarrow A) \rightarrow (C \rightarrow B)$ and $A \rightarrow B \vdash (B \rightarrow C) \rightarrow (A \rightarrow C)$, $w[S]$ need not validate those rules. (If $A \rightarrow B$ doesn't get value 1 throughout S then we can have $|C \rightarrow A| > |C \rightarrow B|$ for some members of S. This can happen even if $|A| \leq |B|$ throughout S; in that case, $A \rightarrow B$ gets value 1 in $w[S]$ but $(C \rightarrow A) \rightarrow (C \rightarrow B)$ does not.)

The failure of substitutivity means that though both the Tarski biconditionals and the Equivalence Principle hold in the Yablo semantics, one cannot infer the latter from the former in the way one might have expected.[9]

A related point is that Yablo's claims to have given the $\rightarrow$ a modal semantics seem considerably overstated, for when a conditional is embedded inside another conditional, the "modal semantics" applies only to the outer conditional, not to the occurrence of the conditional embedded inside it. The analogs of "possible worlds" on the Yablo semantics are the Kripke fixed points over extensions of the Yablo fixed point v_ξ; in an embedded conditional, the inner conditionals are thus evaluated at extensions of v_ξ. But these extensions of v_ξ are, for the most part, not themselves Yablo fixed points, and the evaluation of conditionals at them does not proceed by considering the values of their antecedents and consequents at other worlds. Rather, the evaluation of conditionals at them is just built in by brute force, it is built into the specification of which extension of v_ξ is in question.

It might be thought that some of the issues I have raised could be resolved by iterating Yablo's construction. To explain: another way of looking at the Yablo construction is as starting from the set S_0 of all transparent valuations, and for each α letting $S_{\alpha+1}$ be $S[w[S_\alpha]]$, taking intersections at limits; this has a nonempty intersection S_∞, and v_ξ is $w[S_\infty]$. On this way of looking at things, what we have done in constructing the fixed point is to successively throw out valuations that are not candidates for our final valuation, and construct the next valuation in the sequence by quantifying only over what remains. But from this viewpoint, it would seem we could go further: the only real candidates for our final valuation are Yablo fixed points; now that we know there are some, why not introduce a new sequence of sets starting with the set S_0^1 of all Yablo fixed points, with its corresponding valuation $v_0^1 = w[S_0^1]$, and successively decrease the former and build up the latter until a new "second level Yablo fixed point" is reached? (And we might then want to iterate still further.) The motivation for the Yablo account would seem to extend to this iterated version, and the iterated version would seem as if it might give rise to a more fully modal semantics.

Unfortunately, the iterated version breaks down right at the start. To see this, consider the Curry sentence K, which says $True(\langle K \rangle) \rightarrow 0 = 1$. This has value $\frac{1}{2}$ not only in v_ξ but in every ("first level") Yablo fixed point.[10] So defining S_0^1 and v_0^1 as above, every member of S_0^1 gives K the value $\frac{1}{2}$; so by the valuation rules for the conditional, v_0^1 gives K the value 0, and hence is not even a first level Yablo fixed point, i.e. not a member of S_0^1. As a result, the iterated procedure does not

[9] It also means that one cannot infer from the fact that the biconditional connecting two Liar sentences gets value 1 that one Liar sentence is substitutable for another in all contexts; and in fact it is not, as reflection on the example in the previous paragraph should make clear.

[10] Proof: If K has value 1 at a valuation v, then it has value 1 in every extension of v and so in every Kripke fixed point over such an extension; but then the evaluation rules for $True(\langle K \rangle) \rightarrow 0 = 1$ yield that it has value 0 at $w[S[v]]$, so v cannot be a Yablo fixed point. Similarly, if K has value 0 at a valuation v, then it has value 0 in every extension of v and so in every Kripke fixed point over such an extension; but then the evaluation rules for $True(\langle K \rangle) \rightarrow 0 = 1$ yield that it has value 1 at $w[S[v]]$, so v cannot be a Yablo fixed point. (This works for the Yablo* rules as well.)

evolve toward a fixed point, and thus a fundamental feature of Yablo's account would be destroyed.[11]

Even if iteration is a bad idea, one might still hope that the (uniterated) Yablo account could be given a genuine modal semantics, by finding some accessibility relation on the set $S[v_\xi]$ (the set of Kripke fixed points over transparent extensions of v_ξ) such that for each T in $S[v_\xi]$,

> $v_T(A \rightarrow B)$ is
> 1 if $(\forall U \in S[v_\xi])$ (if U is accessible from T then $|A|_U \leq |B|_U$)
> 0 if $(\forall U \in S[v_\xi])$ (if U is accessible from T then $|A|_U > |B|_U$), and there are U accessible from T
> $\frac{1}{2}$ otherwise.

(Or this with the additional restriction in the 0 clause that U be minimal over v_U, if you prefer the Yablo* approach.) I don't think this is at all promising. First, note that for every T, there must be U accessible from it: otherwise every conditional would have value 1 at T, which cannot happen since $0 = 0 \rightarrow 0 = 1$ clearly gets value 0 in every member of $S[v_\xi]$. (So the second conjunct of the clause for value 0 can be dropped.) Now consider the Curry sentence K (which is equivalent to $K \rightarrow 0 = 1$); using that equivalence, the above yields

> $v_T(K)$ is
> 1 if $(\forall U \in S[v_\xi])$ (if U is accessible from T then $|K|_U = 0$)
> 0 if $(\forall U \in S[v_\xi])$ (if U is accessible from T then $|K|_U > 0$)
> $\frac{1}{2}$ otherwise.

And since K is equivalent to a conditional, $|K|_U$ is just $v_U(K)$. We know that there are in $S[v_\xi]$ plenty of valuations where K has value 1; so in all nodes accessible from such a node (and there are some accessible from it), K has value 0. Clearly then the accessibility relation cannot be reflexive, and cannot be connected in any nice way with the extendability relation. It also cannot be transitive. For consider a node s_2 where K has value 0 that is accessible from a node s_1 where K has value 1. Since K has value 0 at s_2, it must be that in all nodes s_3 accessible from s_2 (and there are some), K has value > 0; so such nodes s_3 cannot be accessible from s_1 given that K has value 1 at s_1. I suspect that one could prove that there is no accessibility relation whatever that would work, but the above makes pretty clear that at the very least any one that did work would have to be extraordinarily unnatural.

The lack of a specifically modal semantics is not particularly troubling, but what does seem to me *a bit* troubling is that the Yablo account comes with no model-theoretic semantics of *any* sort that is compositional: no model-theoretic semantics in which we can assign fine-grained semantic values to sentences in each model, in such a way that semantic values of sentences built from them can be determined.[12]

[11] As we will see later, there are ways to give up the demand for fixed points, and perhaps the suggestion of iterating the Yablo construction could be pursued in that context. But I think that the synthesis to be suggested in section 3 is simpler.

[12] Qualification: Obviously there are trivial ways of getting "fine-grained values" that meet this condition; e.g., we could take the "fine-grained value" of A to be simply the function that assigns one

(The reason for the 'fine-grained' is that we *obviously* cannot expect a semantics which is compositional with respect to the assignment of the *coarse-grained* values 0, $\frac{1}{2}$ and 1 to the sentence: we already know that the conditional is not a 3-valued truth function.) In a 3-valued modal semantics, you could take the fine-grained value of a sentence to consist of the set of worlds at which it has value 1 together with the set of worlds at which it has value 0; using the accessibility relation, fine-grained values for complex sentences would then be determined from fine-grained values for simple ones. There are other, non-modal, ways in which one might specify fine-grained semantic values that behave compositionally.[13] But the blindness toward the properties of embedded conditionals on Yablo's account appears to rule out any significant compositional semantics.

I will conclude this section with a worry of a different sort about Yablo's account: that at least as it stands, its expressive power is too limited. One thing we should want in a treatment of the paradoxes is to be able to consistently express in the language the idea that certain sentences of the language (Liar sentences, Curry sentences, and Truth-teller sentences) are in some sense "pathological". But just as the addition of a conditional to the language must be done with extreme care, to prevent new arguments for inconsistency from arising, so too the addition of predicates like 'pathological' must be done with extreme care: we have to make sure that apparently paradoxical sentences like 'I am either untrue or pathological' do not actually lead to inconsistency with the Equivalence Principle. One way of trying to do this is by defining "pathology predicates" from the conditional; if one can do this, then the consistency of one's treatment of the conditional guarantees the consistency of one's pathology predicates. That is the course I took in [1]. If one's treatment of the conditional does not allow for this, then one needs to expand the language to include the appropriate pathology predicates before one has an adequate overall theory. My worry about Yablo's account is that his conditional does not appear to allow for the definition of adequate pathology predicates, so that until we know how they might be added non-definitionally, his account is incomplete.

I will not attempt to prove that there is no way to define adequate pathology predicates on his account, but the prospects do not look good. The usual way to define them is to first define an operator D meaning 'determinately', with the property that if A has value 1 or 0, DA has the same value, and if A has value $\frac{1}{2}$, DA must have value no greater than $\frac{1}{2}$. Also, we would like it to be the case that if A has value $\frac{1}{2}$ then either DA, or DDA, or $DDDA$, or some further (possibly transfinite) iteration D^{α} of D applied to A must have value 0; there are some technical issues that block a complete implementation of this (having to do with the impossibility of a single fully general method

of the values 0, $\frac{1}{2}$ and 1 to each sentence containing A! What we want, I assume, is a *non-trivial* compositional semantics, but I admit I do not know how to make the non-triviality requirement precise.

[13] Indeed, the approach of mine that Yablo is criticizing does have a fine-grained compositional semantics—two of them really—though they did not appear in the paper that Yablo was primarily addressing. An algebraic semantics for it is spelled out in [3] and [4], and a broadly modal semantics, though one employing a richer structure than simply an accessibility relation, is spelled out in [2].

of defining the set of transfinite iterations of D),[14] but we would certainly hope that for all but the most *recherché* sentences this holds unproblematically. If such a determinately operator can be defined, then the pathology predicates will have the form $\neg D^{\alpha}True(x) \wedge \neg D^{\alpha}True(neg(x))$, where '*neg*' stands for negation.

But how on Yablo's theory are we to define D? As remarked above, the fact that the conditional has a modal element, where the modality is not a quantification over alternative possible worlds but rather over alternative ways of evaluating sentences in the actual world, does make for an intuitive connection between the conditional and the notion of determinateness. However, the ways of defining D that tend to work for other versions of the conditional are $\top \rightarrow A$ and $\neg(A \rightarrow \neg A)$ and minor variations of these, but these do not work on Yablo's: for instance, applying any iteration of them to a Truth-teller sentence or its negation leaves the value $\frac{1}{2}$, so $\neg D^{\alpha}True(\langle I \rangle) \wedge \neg D^{\alpha}True(\langle \neg I \rangle)$ is never 1, so we could not assert that Truth-tellers have any degree of pathology.[15] Again, this is not a criticism of Yablo's account if that is viewed merely as a treatment of the conditional; I am simply saying (i) that it is not obvious that the theory can be attractively supplemented to contain pathology predicates, (ii) that unless it can, we do not have an adequate treatment of the paradoxes, and (iii) that it is worth looking at alternative conditionals from which the pathology predicates can be defined, since they do not raise this worry.[16]

Nothing I have said is intended to be a knock-down objection to Yablo's approach. My points are intended only as reasons why we might hope to do better, while preserving the good points of his approach. It is to this that I now turn.

3. THE BASIC SYNTHESIS

I think that the worrisome features of Yablo's account stem from the fact that even at the final stage (the minimal Yablo fixed point), the evaluation of conditionals is done by quantifying over a large array of Kripke fixed points *over quite bad valuations for conditionals*: valuations which, though they extend the minimal Yablo fixed point, can do so in quite arbitrary and unprincipled ways.

[14] One needs the truth predicate to define D^{λ} for limit λ, and the required definitions get more complicated as λ gets more complicated. Because of this last fact, any precise definition of a set of predicates D^{α} extends only through a proper initial segment of the recursive ordinals, and a different method of defining the allowed iterations would have allowed for iterations through a larger initial segment. On a given method of defining the class of iterations, there are bound to be sentences A that get value $\frac{1}{2}$ for which no iteration D^{α} *that is definable by that method* is such that $D^{\alpha}A$ has value 0. What we seem to want is that whenever a sentence A gets value $\frac{1}{2}$, "there should be some method of defining iterations such that on some iteration definable by that method, $D^{\alpha}A$ gets value 0", but it is doubtful that precise sense can be made of this.

[15] This does not seem to depend at all on the inability to extend the iteration far enough that was discussed in note 14.

[16] I should point out that at the end of [12] Yablo expresses some skepticism about whether my definitions of pathology predicates in [1] are really adequate. If he is right, that tends to undermine this criticism of his own account. I do not think he is right, but the issue is too big to discuss here.

I propose that we modify Yablo's—or rather, Yablo*'s—inductive sequence of v_αs, so as to avoid this. The central change is in the rule for successors: instead of the Yablo* rule that $v_{\alpha+1}(A \rightarrow B)$ is

> 1 if $(\forall u)(\forall T)$ (if u is a transparent extension of v_α and T is a Kripke fixed point over u then $|A|_T \leq |B|_T$),
> 0 if $(\forall u)$ (if u is a transparent extension of v_α then $|A|_{Z_u} > |B|_{Z_u}$),
> $\frac{1}{2}$ otherwise,

I propose that we omit the quantification over extensions of v_α, and take $v_{\alpha+1}(A \rightarrow B)$ to be

> 1 if $(\forall T)$ (if T is a Kripke fixed point over v_α then $|A|_T \leq |B|_T$),
> 0 if $|A|_{Z_{v_\alpha}} > |B|_{Z_{v_\alpha}}$,
> $\frac{1}{2}$ otherwise.

This looks like a simple revision, but in fact it has a drastic consequence for the mathematical character of the theory: the rule is no longer monotonic, that is, $v_{\alpha+1}$ will no longer be an extension of v_α. Because of this, a change at the limit stage is called for: the appropriate rule is now that $v_\lambda(A \rightarrow B)$ is

> 1 if $(\exists\beta < \lambda)(\forall\gamma)(\forall T)$ (if $\beta \leq \gamma < \lambda$ and T is a Kripke fixed point over v_γ then $|A|_T \leq |B|_T$),
> 0 if $(\exists\beta < \lambda)(\forall\gamma)$ (if $\beta \leq \gamma < \lambda$ then $|A|_{Z_{v_\gamma}} > |B|_{Z_{v_\gamma}}$),
> $\frac{1}{2}$ otherwise.

For the moment I will keep v_0 as in the Yablo and Yablo* accounts—assigning $\frac{1}{2}$ to every conditional—though I'll reconsider this in section 5.

The fact that this rule is not monotonic means that the construction no longer reaches a fixed point for conditionals (i.e. an analog of the Yablo fixed points). But two things can be said to ameliorate this. The more minimal is that there is none the less a natural sense in which the theory produces *ultimate values*: we can take the ultimate value of a sentence A to be

> 1 if $(\exists\beta)(\forall\gamma)(\forall T)$(if $\gamma \geq \beta$ and T is a Kripke fixed point over v_γ then $|A|_T = 1$),
> 0 if $(\exists\beta)(\forall\gamma)(\forall T)$(if $\gamma \geq \beta$ and T is a Kripke fixed point over v_γ then $|A|_T = 0$)
> $\frac{1}{2}$ otherwise.

(Or we could stick to minimal Kripke fixed points in the clauses for 1 and/or 0: it would make no difference in this context.) It is easily shown (using an analog of the Continuity Lemma of [1]) that for conditional sentences this is equivalent to

> 1 if $(\exists\beta)(\forall\gamma)(\forall T)$(if $\gamma \geq \beta$ and T is a Kripke fixed point over v_γ then $|A|_T \leq |B|_T$),
> 0 if $(\exists\beta)(\forall\gamma)$(if $\gamma \geq \beta$ then $|A|_{Z_{v_\gamma}} > |B|_{Z_{v_\gamma}}$),
> $\frac{1}{2}$ otherwise;

this makes the ultimate value of a conditional analogous to its value at limits. The more substantial point, which plays an important role in ensuring that the logic works neatly, is that it can be shown that the construction eventually cycles and that there are certain special ordinals (*acceptable ordinals*) in the cycles at which every conditional gets its ultimate value (so that at minimal Kripke fixed points over acceptable ordinals, every sentence gets its ultimate value). These claims were established at length in [1] for a somewhat simpler theory which was like this one except that the construction involved only the minimal Kripke fixed points; an inspection of the proof offered there shows that it carries over to the modified theory without any hitch.

This account gives rise to a richer set of laws than does Yablo's (or Yablo*'s), especially with regard to embedded conditionals. And because of the quantification over non-minimal fixed points in the clause for conditionals having value 1, this account agrees with Yablo's on the cases cited early in 2.3 that my original account got intuitively wrong.

There are, however, some other examples of Yablo's where this account runs afoul of Yablo's intuitions. These examples were part of the basis for two of Yablo's criticisms of my earlier theory that I have not yet discussed.

One of the examples is the Conditional Truth-teller. Yablo gives two slightly different versions of this, and the more complex version raises issues I will defer till section 5; but in its simplest version, this is a sentence I^* that asserts that it is true if $0 = 0$; that is, I^* is equivalent to $0 = 0 \rightarrow True(\langle I^* \rangle)$. My account in [1] gave this sentence the value 0, and the account just sketched does so as well; whereas Yablo thinks it ought to get value $\frac{1}{2}$, which is what his account delivers.[17] Yablo's reason for thinking, independent of his theory, that $\frac{1}{2}$ is the appropriate answer, seems to be as follows: any of the assignments 0, 1 and $\frac{1}{2}$ to the sentence seem consistent with obvious principles; and in situations where this is so, the value $\frac{1}{2}$ (which is best thought of not as a value on par with 0 and 1, but rather as the absence of the values 0 and 1) is the only non-arbitrary assignment to make. (He calls this the "arbitrariness objection" to my semantics.)

The reason that I resist this argument is that on the account of determinateness I will give, I^* will be seen to, in effect, assert its own determinate truth. (This will be evident shortly; for now I'll just say that as in the case of Yablo's theory, the quantification over "nearby valuations" in the clauses for the conditional gives the conditional an intuitive connection with the notion of determinateness.) And given that I^* calls itself determinately true, it could not be true without being determinately true; in contrast, it can be false without being determinately false. So the situation with regard to I^* is not really symmetric: it is much easier for it to be false than to be true. Because of this, it is not particularly surprising if it ends up having value 0

[17] In the account I have sketched, it is easy to prove inductively that I^* gets value 0 in all v_α for $\alpha \geq 1$. (This relies on the fact that the starting valuation v_0 gave this conditional a value less than 1.) Why does I^* get value $\frac{1}{2}$ on Yablo's account? If it had another value, there would have to be a first ordinal at which it had that value, which is easily seen to be a successor $\beta + 1$; the value at β is $\frac{1}{2}$. But then there are transparent extensions of v_β in which I^* gets value 1, which is incompatible with $v_{\beta+1}$ (I^*) being 0; and the fact that I^* gets value less than 1 at v_β is itself incompatible with $v_{\beta+1}(I^*)$ being 1.

(whereas it would seem surprising if it ended up having value 1). I do not say that this makes it pre-theoretically obvious that the sentence should come out having value 0 rather than value $\frac{1}{2}$, but I do think it removes the appearance that the assignment of value 0 is arbitrary.

Yablo's other example (which he uses in his "groundedness objection") involves an infinite chain of sentences $B_1, B_2, \ldots$ Each B_i asserts that if it is true, so is the next one: $True(\langle B_i \rangle) \rightarrow True(\langle B_{i+1} \rangle)$. My account in [1], and the account above, declares that each of these B_is is true; i.e. it gives value 1 to each claim $True(\langle B_i \rangle)$ and hence to each B_i. (This is independent of the decision to assign value $\frac{1}{2}$ to conditionals at the initial stage of the revision procedure.)[18] Yablo says that while this assignment of values to the B_is is not *arbitrary* (there are reasons why we shouldn't view the B_is as false), it is objectionable because the assignment is *ungrounded*: "To suppose that B_i is true is to suppose it has a true antecedent. But then its truth is owing to the truth of its consequent $True(\langle B_{i+1} \rangle)$, with the buck being passed forever down the line" (p. 320). Yablo's own account gives each B_i the value $\frac{1}{2}$.[19]

I grant that this ungroundedness consideration has a certain pre-theoretic pull, but I think that there is at least equal weight to the following: because the sequence $B_1, B_2, \ldots$ is isomorphic to the sequence with B_1 dropped, each B_i is "essentially equivalent" to the next. So in the conditionals $B_i \rightarrow B_{i+1}$ the antecedent is "essentially equivalent" to the consequent, and that motivates assigning the conditional the value 1. (From which it follows that each conditional $True(\langle B_i \rangle) \rightarrow True(\langle B_{i+1} \rangle)$ should get value 1, i.e. that each B_i should get value 1.)

Again, my claim is not that this pre-theoretic argument is decisive; the point is only that while groundedness considerations give some intuitive support to assigning the value $\frac{1}{2}$ to the B_is, the alternative assignment of value 1 has some intuitive support as well. The intuitive considerations do not seem to me nearly strong enough to decide between two theories that yield different verdicts about the case.

[18] It is completely obvious that the three somewhat natural assignments at the initial stage—those that assign the same value to each B_i—yield the value 1 for each B_i at acceptable points: they reach this value at the very next stage, and it can never change after that. But in fact *any assignment of values whatever* yields the value 1 for each i at acceptable points (indeed, for all points from stage $\omega + 1$ on). For in the first place, no B_i can be assigned 0 at two successive stages. It follows from this (using the Continuity Lemma of [1], which carries over to the present theory and is independent of the valuation used at stage 0) that no B_i can be assigned 0 at stage ω (or any other limit stage). Also, if a B_i is assigned 1 at stage ω, the Continuity Lemma says that it is assigned 1 at all finite stages after stage n for some natural number n, and from this it follows that for all $j \geq i$, B_j has value 1 at stage n; which in turn implies that at all stages after $n + i$ (not just the finite stages), every B_j has value 1. The only alternative left to consider is that every B_i is assigned $\frac{1}{2}$ at stage ω; but in that case, every B_i gets value 1 at all later stages.

[19] Suppose not, and let α be the first stage in the Yablo construction at which at least one B_i gets value 0 or 1. α clearly is not 0 or a limit, so it is of form $\beta + 1$. So v_β assigns each conditional B_i (or equivalently, each $B_i \rightarrow B_{i+1}$) the value $\frac{1}{2}$, and so for each i, v_β has a transparent extension that assigns B_i the value 1 and B_{i+1} the value 0. Since the value of B_i is greater than that of B_{i+1} in this extension, and no greater than it in v_β itself, the value of each $B_i \rightarrow B_{i+1}$ must be $\frac{1}{2}$ in $v_{\beta+1}$, contrary to supposition.

4. FURTHER DISCUSSION

The considerations that incline me to favor the account in section 3 over Yablo's are:

(I) its richer set of laws, including especially laws involving embedded conditionals;
(II) its being more amenable to assigning "fine-grained semantic values" that behave compositionally; and
(III) its giving rise to a natural determinately operator and hence to a sequence of pathology predicates.

I have already explained why I find Yablo's theory unsatisfying in these respects. I will be brief in indicating how the account in section 3 fares in these respects, because I have discussed these points elsewhere in connection with the account offered in [1], and the differences between that account and the account offered in section 3 make little difference to the three points in question.

Let us begin with (III). The definition of the determinately operator offered in [1] was:

DA is $(\top \rightarrow A) \wedge A$, where $\top$ is some trivial truth.

Employing this definition in connection with the revision theory of the previous section, we get that in any fixed point U over $v_{\alpha+1}$, $|DA|_U$ is

1 if $(\forall T)$(if T is a Kripke fixed point over v_α then $|A|_T = 1$) and $|A|_U = 1$,
0 if $|A|_{Z_{v\alpha}} < 1$ or $|A|_U = 0$,
$\frac{1}{2}$ otherwise.

And by the monotonicity property of Kripke fixed points, the quantification over non-minimal fixed points in the clause for value 1 is redundant: that clause is equivalent to

1 if $|A|_{Z_{v\alpha}} = 1$ and $|A|_U = 1$.

As a result, the behavior of the determinately operator at successors is precisely the same as in [1]. And the same holds for limits, as is easily seen.[20]

Basically, then, the entire theory of the determinately operator, developed at some length in [1], carries over to the current theory. Let me just mention a few salient points. First, as mentioned in the discussion of Yablo, the operator gives rise to a series

[20] It is important that the theory in section 3 took off from the Yablo* account rather than the Yablo account, i.e. that there was no quantification over non-minimal fixed points in the clause for a conditional having value 0; for a quantification over them in *that* clause would *not* be redundant for conditionals of form $\top \rightarrow A$. The resulting determinately operator would not only differ from that in [1], it would be inadequate: when I is a Truth-teller, $|D^\alpha I|$ would never be 0, no matter how high the α.

That is the same criticism I made of the attempt to define a determinately operator in Yablo's own account, raising the question of whether the shift to the Yablo* variant would have evaded the criticism of his account. The answer is no: the problem for the Yablo account arises prior to the consideration of non-minimal fixed points, it arises already from the consideration of extensions of the base valuation.

of "pathology predicates" $P_\alpha(x)$, each defined as $\neg D^\alpha\, True(x) \wedge \neg D^\alpha\, True(neg(x))$ where D^α is the αth iteration of D (transfinite iterations being definable using the truth predicate, through a proper initial segment of the recursive ordinals, according to some fixed method). These pathology predicates have the following properties. (Here Δ is any acceptable ordinal, i.e. ordinal at which the values of conditionals coincide with their ultimate values.)

(i) They all have the same anti-extensions; that is, for any sentence A, and any α and β, $|P_\alpha(\langle A\rangle)|_{Z_\Delta} = 0$ if and only if $|P_\beta(\langle A\rangle)|_{Z_\Delta} = 0$.
(ii) They have strictly increasing extensions; that is, if $\alpha < \beta$ (but β is not so large that D^β and hence P^β are undefined) then
(a) for all A, if $|P_\alpha(\langle A\rangle)|_{Z_\Delta} = 1$ then $|P_\beta(\langle A\rangle)|_{Z_\Delta} = 1$, but (b) there are A for which $|P_\alpha(\langle A\rangle)|_{Z_\Delta} = \frac{1}{2}$ and $|P_\beta(\langle A\rangle)|_{Z_\Delta} = 1$.

The simplest pathological sentences, such as Liar sentences, Curry sentences and Truth-tellers, are all easily seen to be pathological at the first or second level—that is, the claim that they are P_2 has value 1. But use of the determinately operator or the pathology predicates can produce sentences for which one cannot say whether they are P_α for small α, but can say that they are for high α. For instance, consider the "α^{th} level Hyper-Liar" L_α, which says $\neg D^\alpha\, True(\langle L_\alpha\rangle)$; then $|P_\beta(\langle L_\alpha\rangle)|_{Z_\Delta}$ is $\frac{1}{2}$ if $\beta \leq \alpha$, but 1 if $\beta > \alpha$. In [1] I have discussed a wide range of such transfinite sequences of paradoxical sentences, the members of each of which can all be declared pathological at some level.[21]

Moving on to issue (II) about compositional semantics, I mentioned (in a footnote) that the account in [1] admits compositional semantics in either of two formats: algebraic and broadly modal. Both versions of the semantics can be extended to cover the account in section 3, but I will discuss only the broadly modal version, since it is closer to the semantics that Yablo proposes for his own account. (In fact the broadly modal version offered in [2] barely needs extension at all: it was offered in a very general form, so as to apply to vagueness as well as to the paradoxes; what I will do here is mostly just formulate the special case appropriate to the semantics of section 3. But

[21] As remarked in note 14, there is an inevitable arbitrariness in the system of transfinite iterations used in defining the D^αs and P^αs which affects how far the iterations extend; no given method of defining a system of P_αs can be maximal. Because of this, on any given definition of the class of P_αs, one cannot reasonably demand that for every sentence A of the language, either $|P_\alpha(\langle A\rangle)|_{Z_\Delta} = 0$ for all P_α or there is a P_α such that $|P_\alpha(\langle A\rangle)|_{Z_\Delta} = 1$; there are bound to be some sentences A for which $|P_\alpha(\langle A\rangle)|_{Z_\Delta} = \frac{1}{2}$ for all α for which P_α has been defined. But (1) it does seem intuitively (though I do not know how to make this precise enough to prove it) that for any A for which this holds, a natural extension of the iteration procedure to larger ordinals is possible which would make the sentence "pathological with respect to a larger ordinal". (2) Even putting extensions of the iteration procedure aside, sentences A for which $|P_\alpha(\langle A\rangle)|_{Z_\Delta} = \frac{1}{2}$ for all α for which P_α has been defined must be extremely *recherché*: in particular, they must be such that the final cycle of values gives the sentence a sequence of 1s *that is at least as long as the first ordinal that outruns the iteration procedure*, followed by something other than a 1 (or analogously for 0 instead of 1). I doubt that one can produce such sentences except by building into them an explicit reference to the somewhat arbitrary system of ordinal notations used in the iteration procedure.

there will need to be a very small modification, due to the fact that I decided not to quantify over non-minimal fixed points in the 0 clause for conditionals.)

In the broadly modal semantics for the account in section 3, the "possible worlds" are the (non-minimal and minimal) fixed points over the *persistent valuations*, i.e. those valuations that appear over and over in the revision process. The "actual world" is the minimal fixed point over the valuation v_Δ that occurs at acceptable ordinals, i.e. the valuation that gives the ultimate values of all conditionals. It is a feature of this space of worlds that every valuation in it extends the valuation at the actual world, just as in Yablo's theory; but only very special extensions of v_Δ are in the space, which is part of what is responsible for the differences from Yablo's account.

The other difference from Yablo is that rather than giving a simple modal semantics based on an accessibility relation, I give a more complicated one based on the idea that $\rightarrow$ is in Lewis's phrase [9] a "variably strict conditional" (though not one of quite Lewis's sort).

Picture the space of worlds as on a cylinder. For each persistent valuation v, the fixed points over v occur on a line L_v parallel to the axis of the cylinder. Moreover, the circular order of these lines L_v (say in the "clockwise" direction) corresponds to the order of the valuations in the cycle: starting with L_{v_Δ} (where Δ is acceptable), the next line is $L_{v_{\Delta+1}}$, then $L_{v_{\Delta+2}}$, and so on until you reach a sufficiently high ρ for $v_{\Delta+\rho}$ to be identical to v_Δ, at which point you are back around the cylinder at L_{v_Δ}.

Now given this picture, we can describe what Lewis calls a system of "spheres of similarity" around each "world" T in the space—though here they are not spheres, but sections of the cylinder parallel to the axis. More precisely, a sphere of similarity for any fixed point on a line L_{v_β} will consist, for some line L_{v_α} distinct from L_{v_β} of the set $S_{v_\alpha v_\beta}$ of fixed points that are *on a line that is strictly between* L_{v_α} *and* L_{v_β} *in the clockwise order, or on* L_{v_α} *itself.* (The latter disjunct is to ensure that none of the spheres of similarity is empty.) We can now describe **what it is for a conditional $A \rightarrow B$ to have value 1 at a "world" T: it is for there to be a sphere of similarity around that world such that at all worlds in that sphere, the value of A is less than or equal to that of B.**

If I had kept the quantification over all worlds in the 0 clause, the account of what it is for $A \rightarrow B$ to have value 0 at a world would be the same, except with 'greater than' instead of 'less than or equal to'. But since I did not, I need an additional piece of structure: one point on each of the lines, corresponding to the minimal fixed point over that valuation, must be distinguished. (If you like, you can think of there being a distinguished cross-section of the cylinder, on which these distinguished worlds lie.) Then **$A \rightarrow B$ has value 0 at a world T iff there is a sphere of similarity around that world such that at all *distinguished* worlds in that sphere, the value of A is greater than that of B.**

A slight oddity here is that points in L_{v_β} are not in any of their own spheres of similarity. However, the minimal fixed point on L_{v_Δ} has a distinguishing feature: any sentence A gets value 1 at Z_{v_Δ} when and only when there is a sphere of similarity around it throughout which A gets that value, and similarly for 0. This means that *it would make no difference if we allowed* Z_{v_Δ} *to appear in its own spheres of similarity.*

It is this special feature of Z_{v_Δ} that makes it natural to single it out as "the actual world".

We can now take the fine-grained semantic value of any sentence to be its "positive extension"—the set of worlds at which it has value 1—together with its "negative extension"—the set of worlds at which it has value 0. Fine-grained values of negations, disjunctions, quantifications etc. are determined in the usual way, and fine-grained values of conditionals are determined as in the boldfaced claims above. This is perhaps a more complicated modal semantics than one might have hoped for (and I grant that it could use a philosophical justification), but it is a genuinely compositional semantics in a way that Yablo's was not.

Turning finally to the issue (I) about laws, it is not hard to verify that almost all of the laws for the conditional that were established in [1] for the account there carry over to the modified account of section 3: this can be established either by direct appeal to the account there, or (more perspicuously) by the semantics just sketched. The only one that fails here is the relatively unimportant

B4* $\neg[(C \rightarrow A) \rightarrow (C \rightarrow B)] \vdash \neg[A \rightarrow B]$;

but its much more important contrapositive

B4 $A \rightarrow B \vdash (C \rightarrow A) \rightarrow (C \rightarrow B)$

does hold, as does $A \rightarrow B \vdash (B \rightarrow C) \rightarrow (A \rightarrow C)$, with the consequence that the general substitutivity principle holds on this theory. (In addition, several other laws valid in the account of [1] but not noted there are valid here as well, e.g. $\neg(A \rightarrow B) \rightarrow (B \rightarrow A)$ and the rule $\neg(A \rightarrow B) \vdash A \vee \neg B$.[22])

5. THE STARTING VALUATION

In the course of his "arbitrariness objection" to my earlier account, Yablo points out an anomaly in that account which remains in the synthesis of section 3. The problem arises because of the choice of initial valuation v_0. I should note that the only requirement that must be imposed on v_0 for the basic theory of [1] to be derivable was that v_0 be transparent. Because of this, I employed a simple choice of transparent valuation as my starting point, the one that assigns each conditional the value $\frac{1}{2}$. But though this choice had no effect on the theory developed, and affects the ultimate values of only a few very special sentences, Yablo's point is that it does produce results that seem anomalous in some examples.

The example that Yablo gives to illustrate this point is a modified version of the Conditional Truth-teller discussed in section 4. Instead of an I^* that asserts of itself that if $0 = 0$ then $True(\langle I^* \rangle)$, Yablo considers an I^{**} that asserts of itself that if $B \rightarrow B$

[22] In [2] I mistakenly asserted the stronger conditional form of this rule. In fact the conditional form is invalid even in the account of [1]: take A to be the Curry sentence and B to be its negation.

then $True(\langle I^{**} \rangle)$, where B is any conditional that one chooses. $(B \rightarrow B) \rightarrow True(x)$ is of course equivalent to $0 = 0 \rightarrow True(x)$ in the theory, so one might think that there could be no real difference between I^* and I^{**}, but that thought involves a fallacy. Compare the predicates

D_1 The number of syllables in x is divisible by two

and

D_2 The number of syllables in x is divisible by the smallest prime;

these predicates are equivalent, but on any standard method for producing self-referential sentences, the sentences E_1 and E_2 that assert $D_1(\langle E_1 \rangle)$ and $D_2(\langle E_2 \rangle)$ respectively will have opposite truth values since D_2 has an odd number of additional syllables over D_1.

Even so, it does seem odd that I^{**} should get a different value from I^*. Another oddity is that the value it gets is 1, which in light of the fact that I^{**} in effect says of itself that it is determinately true seems especially hard to motivate. The reason it gets this value is that $B \rightarrow B$, though it has value 1 at each fixed point over any valuation *from* v_1 *on* in the construction, none the less has value $\frac{1}{2}$ at all fixed points over the chosen starting valuation v_0. I^{**}, as a conditional, also gets value $\frac{1}{2}$ at this stage; so since its antecedent and consequent have the same value at this stage it gets value 1 at the next stage, and this guarantees that it will get value 1 at each stage after this.

We can avoid this particular anomaly by beginning the construction from a more "regular" starting valuation. I am currently undecided as to which starting valuation would be best to use: the choices I have thought of all seem a bit ad hoc. (But as I have said, the choice of the starting valuation plays little role in the overall theory, as long as it is transparent, and the ultimate value of "most" sentences is independent of the choice of transparent starting valuation.) One possibility I have contemplated is to use as a starting valuation the minimal Yablo (or minimal Yablo*) fixed point; this would increase the extent to which the current account was a synthesis of the account in [1] with Yablo's. But even this would not altogether avoid the sort of anomaly that Yablo has raised, because of certain conditionals B_0 that should get value 1 but do not in Yablo's minimal fixed point, e.g. the conditionals of form $(A \vee A \rightarrow C) \rightarrow (A \rightarrow C)$ considered earlier. There is no problem with such a B_0 itself: unlike on the Yablo and Yablo* accounts, it gets the desired value 1 as its *ultimate* value on the synthesized account, whatever the starting valuation. But now consider an alternative conditional Truth-teller I^{***} that says that if B_0 then I^{***} is true; this will end up with value 1 on the proposed starting valuation, which seems rather analogous to the anomaly above, though for a more marginal sentence. It may be that there is no way to avoid all such anomalies involving conditional Truth-tellers, without a more substantial alteration in the account; how serious a defect this would be, and whether there is a better approach that avoids such anomalies while preserving the advantages of the account, are questions that I leave for the reader.

REFERENCES

[1] Hartry Field. A revenge-immune solution to the semantic paradoxes. *Journal of Philosophical Logic*, 32: 139–77, 2003.

[2] ——. The semantic paradoxes and the paradoxes of vagueness. In JC Beall, ed., *Liars and Heaps*. Oxford University Press, 2003.

[3] ——. The consistency of the naive theory of properties. *Philosophical Quarterly*, 54, 2004.

[4] ——. Is the liar sentence both true and false? In JC Beall and Bradley Armour-Garb, eds, *Deflationism and Paradox*. Oxford University Press, 2004.

[5] Harvey Friedman and Michael Sheard. An axiomatic approach to self-referential truth. *Annals of Pure and Applied Logic*, 33: 1–21, 1987.

[6] Petr Hajek, Jeff Paris, and John Shepherdson. The liar paradox and fuzzy logic. *The Journal of Symbolic Logic*, 65: 339–46, 2000.

[7] Saul Kripke. Outline of a theory of truth. *Journal of Philosophy*, 72: 690–716, 1975.

[8] Stephen Leeds. Theories of reference and truth. *Erkenntnis*, 13: 111–29, 1978.

[9] David Lewis. *Counterfactuals*. Harvard University Press, Cambridge, MA, 1973.

[10] W. V. O. Quine. *Philosophy of Logic*. Prentice-Hall, Englewood Cliffs, 1970.

[11] Greg Restall. Arithmetic and truth in Lukasiewicz's infinitely valued logic. *Logique et Analyse*, 139–40: 303–12, 1992.

[12] Stephen Yablo. New grounds for naive truth theory. In JC Beall, ed., *Liars and Heaps*. Oxford University Press, 2003.

5

A Minimalist Critique of Tarski on Truth

Paul Horwich

The recent 'minimalist' view of truth is in fundamental respects very close to the account offered by Alfred Tarski in 1933.[1] It agrees with him that—putting the matter informally—just about the whole story of what it is for the statement or belief, <snow is white>, to be true is given by the equivalence:

<snow is white> is true ↔ snow is white

It agrees with Tarski that a full theory of truth should do nothing more than in some way *generalize* that trivial biconditional. It agrees that such an account will implicitly capture the idea that 'truth is correspondence with reality', but with the advantage of not having to resort to the obscure notions of 'correspondence' or 'reality': thus it will qualify, in Jan Wolenski's terms, as a "weak correspondence theory".[2] And it agrees that an even worse mistake would be to attempt to define truth in terms of 'coherence' or 'verification' or 'utility'.

So where does minimalism part company with Tarski? The difference concerns *how* one should generalize the above-mentioned, statement-specific account of truth in order to obtain a complete theory. And the root cause of the divergent strategies is that Tarski insisted on a *finite* specification of the conditions for a statement to be true—indeed, a specification to be given in the style of an explicit definition. In contrast, the minimalist view is that such a thing is neither possible nor necessary. For "true" is a primitive term; so the only interesting account that can be given of its meaning is one that identifies which underlying property of the word (i.e. which aspect of our use of it) is responsible for its possessing that meaning. In particular, our truth predicate

This is a revised version of the paper published, under the same title, in *Philosophy and Logic: In Search of the Polish Tradition*, edited by J. Hintikka, T. Czarnecki, K. Kijania-Placek and A. Rojszczak, Kluwer Academic Publishers, 2003. I am indebted to Hartry Field for his insightful constructive criticism of a draft of that paper.

[1] See Alfred Tarski's "The Concept of Truth in Formalized Languages" in his *Logic, Semantics, Metamathematics: Papers from 1923 to 1938*, Oxford University Press, 1958; and his "The Semantic Conception of Truth and the Foundations of Semantics", *Philosophy and Phenomenological Research* 4, 1944, 241–75. For a presentation and defense of minimalism see my *Truth* (2nd edition, Oxford University Press, 1998).

[2] See J. Wolenski, "Semantic Conception of Truth as a Philosophical Theory", in J. Peregrin (ed.) *Truth and its Nature (If Any)*, 51–65, Kluwer, 1999.

means what it does, according to minimalism, in virtue of our underived commitment to the equivalence schema

<p> is true ↔ p

Moreover—turning from the meaning of the word to the property it stands for—the minimalist thesis is that the *basic* facts (i.e. the axioms of the theory that explains *every* other fact about truth) will all be instances of the above schema.

Apart from its disdaining to provide an explicit (or even finite) definition, the minimalist proposal would have been quite congenial to Tarski. Indeed that rough idea may be regarded as his starting point. However, it is no simple matter to convert it into the form he requires. One might begin by trying

x is true ≡ [x = <snow is white> and snow is white; or
x = <snow is red> and snow is red; or
x = <dogs bark or snow is red>, and dogs bark or snow is red; or
. . . and so on]

But, suggestive as this may be, it involves infinitely many disjuncts and therefore will not do for Tarski.

In order to overcome this difficulty—the need to cover all of the infinitely many things that might be true—he makes the assumption that the truth of each statement derives from what its constituents stand for and from how those constituents are put together. But he does not articulate this assumption in terms of *propositions*. For both the notion of proposition, and the idea that they have constituents, are murky and controversial. Moreover, if the theory is to be finite, it will be able to specify the referents of only finitely many elements—and there are infinitely many potential propositional constituents. So, for these two reasons, Tarski focuses, not on propositions, but rather on the *sentences* of a given language and on the way in which their truth is determined by their structure and by the referents of their limited stock of component words. Thus his plan becomes that of specifying, by means of the following kinds of principle, what it is for a sentence of a given language L to be true:

A finite set of axioms specifying what each name in L refers to, and what each predicate of L is true of

For each connective (i.e. each way of combining expressions of L), an axiom specifying how the truth-value or referent of the combination depends on the truth-values or referents of its constituents

For a variety of simple formalized languages he was able to supply principles of this sort and to show how to deduce, from the finitely many axioms governing any one of these languages, correct conditions for the truth of the sentences in it. Moreover he was also able to show how each such *recursive* definition of "true in L" could be transformed into an *explicit* definition of that notion.

Tarski's approach is based on important philosophical insights and its execution is technically brilliant. None the less, as has often been observed, it is questionable in various respects:[3]

(1) Our ordinary concept of truth is deployed in expressing agreement with other peoples' beliefs and statements, in enunciating the primary aim of science, in specifying the criterion of sound reasoning, in giving the oath of a witness in court, and so on. Truth, in this normal sense, is attributed to *what* people believe, suppose, and assert, and not to the marks or noises that are sometimes used to articulate or express those propositions. Thus Tarski's account, with its focus on *sentential* truth, seems somewhat off-target.

(2) As we have seen, the source of this anomaly is his desire for a finite (indeed, explicit) definition. It is for this reason that he has to explain the truth of wholes in terms of the referents of their finitely-many parts; and is therefore driven to suppose that the relevant parts are all the words in a specified language (which are limited in number), rather than all the basic propositional constituents (which are infinite). But there appears to be no good reason to expect, or to offer, an explicit definition of "true". After all, very few terms can be so defined. Moreover the absence of an explicit or finite definition of the truth predicate need not leave it in any way obscure. The minimalist proposal—that its meaning is fixed by our acceptance of the schema '<p> is true ↔ p'—is completely demystifying, even though it does not take the form of an explicit definition or finite set of postulates.[4]

(3) Only for certain simple formal languages did Tarski explain (and do we know) how to supply principles that specify how the truth conditions of sentences depend on the referents of their parts. Attempts to treat *natural* languages in this way encounter many well-known difficulties. For example, nobody has been able to show, for sentences involving "that"-clauses, probabilistic locutions, attributive adjectives, or mass terms, how their truth could be explained as a consequence of the referents of their parts. Moreover, even in the case of more tractable constructions (e.g. universal generalizations), there is the problem of specifying the rules that transform ordinary language sentences (such as "All emeralds are green") into the equivalent formal sentences (such as "(x) [emerald(x) → green(x)]") to which Tarski's compositional principles would directly apply. Thus there are good reasons to suspect that Tarski's approach will prove not to be generally workable.

[3] See, for example, Max Black, "The Semantic Definition of Truth", *Analysis* 8, 49–63; Hartry Field, "Tarski's Theory of Truth", *Journal of Philosophy*, 60, 113–35; and Hilary Putnam, *Representation and Reality*, MIT Press, Cambridge, Mass. 1988.

[4] Note that the minimalist account of which property of the truth-predicate constitutes its meaning is finite. What is not finite is the minimalist theory of truth itself—i.e. the theory specifying those fundamental facts about truth that suffice (in conjunction with theories of other matters) to account for *all* the facts about truth. But bear in mind that a Tarskian answer to that question would not be finite either—since a full account of sentential-truth would have to concern truth relative to every possible language. Moreover, it is far from obvious that the insistence on a finite theory of truth is appropriate. We do not have (or feel we need for) such a theory of *disjunction* or of *negation*. And it is not at all unnatural to assimilate *truth* to such logical phenomena.

(4) Even if we restrict our attention to those simple languages for which the approach *is* workable, one might well wonder what the *value* of Tarskian definitions of truth would be. For it is hard to think of any important question to which they provide the answer.

Let *Ling* be such a simple language. One question we may have concerns what it *means* to describe a sentence as "true in Ling"; and we might think—given that his account is advertised as a "definition"—that Tarski is addressing just that question. But if so, it may be objected that the meaning of "true in Ling" could surely be grasped by someone even if he didn't understand every single word of that language—which would be impossible if Tarski's 'definition' were really the definition. Surely the correct approach to specifying the meaning of a complex expression, such as "true in Ling", would be via accounts of the meanings of its parts. We would need to be told (a) what it means to say, of an arbitrary language, that a given sentence is "true" in that language; and (b) what it means to designate a specific language, "Ling"; and only then, by putting these two accounts together, could we fully understand what we are saying in describing a sentence as "true in Ling".

A second possibility is that a Tarskian so-called 'definition' of "true in Ling" may be offered (despite some of his remarks to the contrary), not as a *description* of the familiar meaning of "true in Ling", but rather as a *recommendation* about what *should* be meant by it. But if so, his definitions would have to be proposed in conjunction with some motivated goal, together with some demonstration that the new meanings are needed to achieve it. Yet Tarski himself gives no such rationale for his account.

Thirdly, it may be that Tarski has in mind a sort of 'theoretical reduction' of *being true in Ling*—a specification of which underlying characteristic of a sentence is the explanatory basis for its having that truth-theoretic property. On this construal he would not be offering an account of what it means (or should mean) to apply the predicate "x is true in Ling", but rather an account of how the property it expresses is constituted or engendered at a more fundamental level (—an account analogous to the claim that 'being a sample of water' is constituted by 'being made of H_2O molecules'). But, taken in that way, it seems clear that Tarski's theory cannot be right. For compare

(M*) x is true ≡
[x = <snow is white> and snow is white; or
x = <snow is red> and snow is red; or
x = <dogs bark or snow is red>, and dogs bark or snow is red; or
...]

and

(T*) x is true in Ling ≡
[x = "A" and snow is white; or
x = "B" and snow is red; or
x = "C%B", and dogs bark or snow is red; or
...]
(where "A" in Ling translates into "snow is white" in English, "B" translates into "snow is red", etc.)

which, as we have seen, offer improperly formulated initial indications of the competing accounts that the minimalist and the Tarskian are aiming to give. Now there is some plausibility in supposing, as suggested by (M*), that the whole explanatory basis for the truth of the proposition, <snow is white>, is simply snow being white. But it is, by contrast, highly implausible that this state of affairs should also, as suggested by (T*), be a sufficient basis for the truth of the Ling sentence, "A". For, surely, a crucial part of what makes "A" true in Ling is the *meaning* of that sentence—how it is used by the speakers of Ling. Therefore, although (T*) may accurately happen to specify the extension of "true in Ling"—for it satisfies Tarski's requirement that it must entail all biconditionals of the form, "s is true in Ling ↔ p" (where "p" translates s)—it does not give us a full account of which underlying facts constitute the facts about truth.

Thus my objection (4) to Tarski's approach, and to the 'definitions' to which it gives rise, is not that they are mistaken, but that they do not respond to any puzzlement we might have about truth. They don't tell us what truth-in-L *is*, or what "true in L" *means*, or even what we *should* mean by it.[5]

Summarizing these four reservations about Tarski's account: there is reason to suppose that his definitions of "true in L" are misdirected (in so far as they do not elucidate our actual concept of truth), ill-motivated (in so far as they reflect an insistence on explicit definitions), not generally workable (in so far as they cannot be devised for natural languages), and pointless (in so far as they address no question worth answering).[6] In contrast, the above-mentioned minimalist account—which was Tarski's intuitive starting point—exhibits none of these undesirable characteristics. One should refrain, it would seem, from attempting to go beyond it.[7]

However, we cannot rest content with this conclusion until we have addressed arguments on the other side—considerations that might be thought to weigh in favor of Tarski's approach and against minimalism. Therefore, I shall now examine what I think are the most promising of such arguments: one of them concerns the liar paradox, and the other concerns the derivation of generalizations about truth.

[5] Objections resembling this fourth one have been made by Donald Davidson ("The Structure and Content of Truth", *Journal of Philosophy*, 87, 1990, 279–328), and Hilary Putnam ("On Truth", in his *Words and Life*, Harvard University Press, 1994, 315–29).

[6] Various further objections to Tarski's approach are considered by Jan Wolenski in his "Semantic Conception of Truth as a Philosophical Theory" (op. cit.). In particular, he addresses the following complaints: (1) Black's point that Tarski's theory is counterintuitive in relativizing truth to languages; (2) Kripke's point that infinitely many truth predicates are needed to deal with the liar paradox; and (3) Etchemendy's complaint that Tarski's definitions have implications that do not concern the concept of truth. But the problems I emphasize here are distinct from these objections.

[7] Alongside Tarski's theory and the minimalist approach, another form of deflationism about truth is given by the 'disquotational' account. (See, e.g., Hartry Field, "Deflationist Views of Meaning and Content", *Mind*, 94, 1994, 249–85). This point of view resembles minimalism in rejecting the need for, or possibility of, an explicit or finite theory; but it diverges from minimalism in focusing, like Tarski, on *sentential* truth and in giving central place to the schema, "p" is true ↔ p.

What is wrong with this strategy, from a minimalist perspective, is that once the goal of a finite account has been rejected, there is no longer any good reason to focus on sentential truth and thereby to miss our ordinary concept. Granted, one may feel that the notion of proposition is problematic, and so one may want to avoid it for reasons unrelated to the desire for a finite account. But given the modifications of the disquotational schema that will be needed to accommodate the truth of foreign sentences and of context-sensitive sentences, it is going to be impossible for the disquotationalist to

A respect in which Tarski's approach may seem to have an advantage over minimalism is in its capacity to deal with the liar paradox; for solving that problem was one of his main desiderata. This paradox arises (in its simplest form) with respect to the claim that whatever statement satisfies a certain definite description, "D", is not true—where it turns out that that very claim is the unique satisfier of the description: that is

<D is not true> = D[8]

For in that case, given Leibniz's Law, we have

<D is not true> is true ↔ D is true

But, given the equivalence schema for truth

<D is not true> is true ↔ D is not true

And so we arrive, by transitivity, at the contradiction

D is true ↔ D is not true

Tarski's solution to this paradox is to legislate that no decent language can contain a truth predicate that applies to the statements of that very language. Rather, there are object languages, such as L_0, involving sentences like "snow is white" which don't contain any truth-theoretic terms. In addition there is a meta-language L_1, including L_0 and containing a truth predicate "true_1" which may be applied to the statements of L_0, subject to the equivalence, "p_0" is $\text{true}_1 \leftrightarrow p_0$. Then there is a meta-meta-language L_2, including L_1 and containing a further truth predicate "true_2" which may be applied to the sentences of L_1, subject to the equivalence, "p_1" is $\text{true}_2 \leftrightarrow p_1$. And so on. As a consequence of these strictures, the only languages that can contain "D is not true_k" are L_k and L_{k+1} and L_{k+2}, etc. However, if "D is not true_k" is to be identical to D—as the paradox requires—then D must be a sentence of L_{k-1}. Therefore, D cannot exist; so no liar paradox can arise.

avoid relying on the notion of proposition—or at least on notions (e.g. translation, or interpretation) from which that notion could easily be built. For the modified schema will have to take the form:

The interpretation of u in my present language and context is "p" → (u is true ↔ p)

And, with the conceptual resources acknowledged here, the concept of proposition could then be introduced via the principles

v is the interpretation of u ↔ v and u express the same proposition

and

"p" (in my present language and context) expresses the proposition that p

Thus disquotationalism is rhetorically unstable.

[8] For example, let "D1 is not true" abbreviate "The proposition expressed by the second quoted sentence in footnote 8 of Paul Horwich's 'A Minimalist Critique of Tarski on Truth' is not true". Of course, for Tarski the paradox is articulated in terms of *sentences*. To obtain such a formulation, simply change my angle brackets to quotation marks.

Now our question is whether the availability of this proposed solution to the liar paradox favors Tarski's *general* approach to truth. And the answer is pretty clearly no. For Tarski's solution is quite independent of his compositional strategy for defining truth and could perfectly well be adopted by a minimalist. In other words, we can reject Tarskian compositional explanations of the truth of sentences in terms of the referents of their parts, yet still choose to avoid the paradox by embracing Tarski's hierarchy and imposing his ban on a language containing its own 'well-behaved' truth predicate. Thus Tarski's solution, whatever its merits or defects, gives his compositional truth definitions no advantage over minimalism.

But now a couple of further questions arise. We might well wonder whether it is not possible to improve on Tarski's solution to the liar paradox; and we might wonder, if a better solution can be devised, whether it would turn out to favor a Tarskian system of compositional truth definitions. The answers to these two questions, it seems to me, are yes and no: Tarski's solution to the paradox is indeed unsatisfactory; but the natural way of improving it will cohere with minimalism just as smoothly as it will with Tarskian truth definitions. Let me very briefly indicate why.

Some marks against Tarski's solution are (1) that it is implausible to suppose that we cannot—using a *single* sense of "true"—say of an attribution of truth that it is not true; (2) that it is objectionable for there to be no sense of "true" in which we can assert, for example, "All instances of '$p \rightarrow p$' are true"—where "p" can be any sentence, containing any truth predicate; (3) that it is counterintuitive to claim that we could not reflect on the hierarchy of truth predicates and then say of a sentence that it is not true in any of these senses; and (4) that the collection of new concepts and principles needed to implement Tarski's solution is undesirably complex.[9]

An approach to the paradox that promises to avoid these defects would be to *identify* "true_0", "true_1", etc—to suppose that they jointly cover the extension of a single truth predicate—but to restrict, in something like the way that Tarski does, instantiation of the equivalence schema. Thus we might say that our language L is the limit of the expanding sub-languages L_0, L_1, L_2, . . . where L_0 lacks the truth predicate; L_1 (which contains L_0) applies it, via the equivalence schema, to the propositions of L_0; similarly, L_2 (which contains L_1) applies it to the 'grounded' propositions of L_1 (i.e. the propositions, together with their negations, that are entailed by L_1's non-truth-theoretic facts in conjunction with the immediate results of applying the equivalence schema to them); L_3 applies it to the grounded propositions of L_2; and so on.

The intuitive idea is that an instance of the equivalence schema will be acceptable, even if it governs a proposition concerning truth (e.g. <What John said is true>), as long as that proposition (or its negation) is *grounded*—i.e. is entailed either by the non-truth-theoretic facts, or by those facts together with whichever truth-theoretic facts are 'immediately' entailed by them (via the already legitimized instances of the equivalence schema), or. . . and so on. Thus the potentially paradoxical <D is not true> will not be a grounded proposition of L_1 because there are no facts of L_0 which (given the equivalence schema) will entail either it or its negation; and similarly, it will

[9] Thanks to Hartry Field for helpful discussion of these problems.

not be a grounded proposition of any of the other sub-languages; so there will be no axiom governing it; so the contradiction will not be derivable.[10]

In other words, one might suppose that each axiom of the theory of truth takes the form '<p> is true ↔ p', and that a good solution to the liar paradox should articulate grounding constraints, as just indicated, on which particular instances of that schema are axioms. To put these constraints a little more precisely: the acceptable instances are those that concern grounded propositions—where every proposition of L_0 is grounded, and (for $k > 0$) a proposition <p_k> of L_k is grounded if and only if either it or its negation is entailed by the grounded facts of L_{k-1} and L_{k-2} and..., in conjunction with the instances of the equivalence schema that are legitimized by these facts.

Evidently, this strategy does not call for compositional principles. So, if it will do, it shows that the liar paradox does not provide any reason to reject minimalism in favor of Tarskian definitions of truth.[11]

The second argument I want to consider—one that may be given in support of Tarski and against minimalism—concerns the derivability of *general* facts about truth: for example, that every instance of <p→p> is true, and that all instances of the inference schema, 'p, p→q ∴ q', preserve truth. A Tarskian, who has a so-called definition of "true in LogicalEnglish", is able to arrive at such results because the explicit definitions (or recursive principles) he can deploy as premises are *already* generalizations about truth. But a minimalist has no such resources. He might, for example, begin with "dogs bark→dogs bark" and deduce (given the equivalence schema) "<dogs bark→dogs bark> is true"; and he might in this way deduce *every instance* of "<p→p> is true"; but the generalization, "All instances of <p→p> are true", appears to be out of reach—and similarly for other generalizations about truth.[12]

[10] Note that there is no contradiction in supposing that D is true (or in supposing that it is false): the problems arise only if the equivalence schema were to be applied. Therefore, we can and should preserve the full generality of the Law of Excluded Middle and the Principle of Bivalence, by maintaining that D is either true or false. Of course we cannot come to know which of these truth values it has. For confidence one way or the other is precluded by the meaning of the word "true"—more specifically, by the fact that its use is governed by the equivalence schema. Thus, just as it is 'indeterminate' whether a certain vague predicate applies, or does not apply, to a certain borderline case (although certainly it does or does not), so (and for the same sort of reason) it is indeterminate whether D is true or whether it is false. For further discussion of this view of indeterminacy see chapter 4 ("The Sharpness of Vague Terms") of my *Reflections on Meaning*, Oxford University Press, 2005. For further discussion of its bearing on the liar paradoxes, see B. Armour-Garb's and JC Beall's "Minimalism, Epistemicism and Paradox".

[11] Needless to say, this proposal is the merest of sketches and requires considerable development. A well-known worked-out approach based on the notion of grounding is given in Saul Kripke's "Outline of a Theory of Truth" (*Journal of Philosophy*, 72, 690–716), but in a way that invokes Tarski-style compositional principles. The present suggestion is that such principles can be avoided, offering a solution that squares with minimalism.

[12] A version of this problem was raised by Tarski himself (in section 5 of "The Concept of Truth in Formalized languages") and has been recently emphasized by Anil Gupta (in "A Critique of Deflationism", *Philosophical Topics* 21 (1993) 57–81) and by Scott Soames (in "The Truth About Deflationism", E. Villanueva (ed.) *Philosophical Issues* 8, Atascadero, Cal., Ridgeview Publishing Company, 1997).

In order to assess this argument we must first clarify why it is important to be able to arrive at these generalizations. One good answer concerns the requirement that an adequate theory of *any* phenomenon (e.g. truth) must explain *all* the facts concerning that phenomenon (e.g. general facts about truth). I will address this version of the problem in footnote 14. But to begin with let me focus on another reason for demanding these derivations—one that has to do with how we can tell whether a proposed account of the *meaning* of a term is adequate. Our overall deployment of a term—including the collection of all the sentences containing it that we accept—is dependent on (amongst other things) what we *mean* by it. Therefore, an account of what engenders the term's meaning must be capable of explaining (in conjunction with other factors) why we accept those sentences. In particular, any account of the meaning of the truth predicate—whether it be Tarskian, minimalistic, or something else—can be adequate only if it helps explain why we accept those sentences containing it that we do—and these include generalizations such as "All instances of $<p \rightarrow p>$ are true".

However, contrary to earlier indications, the minimalist is not in such a bad position to do this. Granted, it will not be enough to cite our allegiance to the equivalence schema: some further explanatory premise is needed if every use of "true" is to be accounted for. But this concession provides an objection to minimalism only if the needed additional premise *specifies properties of the word "true"*. For only then will it emerge that our commitment to the equivalence schema, together with facts that have nothing specifically to do with the truth predicate, are insufficient to explain its overall use. But actually it is far from obvious that the premise we should add will explicitly concern the truth predicate.

Suppose, for example, it were a fact that whenever someone is disposed to hold, for each F, that it is G, then he comes, on that basis, to believe that every F is G. Combined with such a fact (which does not explicitly concern the truth predicate) our disposition to accept, for each proposition of a certain form, that it is true would suffice to explain our acceptance of the generalization, "Every proposition of that form is true".

Of course this response to the objection will not do as it stands, because the proposed extra explanatory premise is clearly incorrect. It is certainly *not* always the case that having shown, for each F, that it is G, one will inevitably come to the belief that all Fs are G. For such demonstrations may well coincide with the mistaken conviction that not all the Fs have been considered. For example, suppose someone mistakenly suspects that there are planets within the orbit of Mercury. He might nevertheless be able to show, of every planet, that its distance from the sun is not less than Mercury's; but he does not believe the generalization that all the planets have this property.

It would seem, then, that we need to restrict the proposed extra premise to kinds of entity, F, and properties, G, that satisfy the following condition: that we cannot conceive of there being additional Fs—beyond those Fs we are disposed to believe are G—which we would not have the same sort of reason to believe are Gs. And it would seem that this restriction is satisfied when (a) it is essential to our conception of the Fs to maintain that all Fs result from the application of certain operations to certain basic Fs (thus F's might be propositions, numbers, or sets); and (b) given any such F, there is a uniform way of proving it to be G.

This suggests that a more plausible version of our extra premise would run along the following lines:

> Whenever someone is disposed to accept, for any *proposition* of type K, that it is G (and to do so for uniform reasons) then he will be disposed to accept that every K-proposition is G

It seems to me that this is more or less what we need to explain our acceptance of the generalization about truth. We are disposed to accept, for any proposition of the form, <p→p>, that it is true. Moreover, the rules that account for this acceptance are the same, no matter which proposion of that form is under consideration.[13]

Thus we have a plausible explanatory premise which, in conjunction with our endorsement of the equivalence schema, will enable us to explain the acceptance of generalizations about truth. And since that premise does not explicitly concern the truth predicate, the need for it does nothing to suggest that the basic regularity governing the truth predicate has to go beyond our underived commitment to the equivalence schema.[14]

I have been suggesting in this paper that the admirable deflationary sentiments that lie behind Tarski's theory of truth are better accommodated by means of the minimalistic approach. In contrast with Tarski's so-called 'definitions', minimalism responds to a genuine problem by offering an account of our actual concept of truth; it is not needlessly tied to the form of an explicit definition or finite theory; it is not burdened with the probably insuperable problems of compositionality; it squares with both Tarskian and better-than-Tarskian responses to the liar paradox; and there appear to be no facts about truth that lie beyond its scope.

[13] Although this strategy works for "All propositions of the form <p→p> are true", one might well wonder whether *all* general beliefs about truth can be explained in that way. But I think that we have some reason to think that they can be. For it would seem that any such beliefs could be put into the form: All propositions of type K have property G. For example: (1) Given any conjunction, if it is true then so are its conjuncts; (2) Given any proposition of the form <p→q>, if it and its antecedent are both true, then so is its consequent; (3) Given any atomic proposition, it is true if and only if its predicate is true of the referent of its subject; etc. Now, for any such generalization, if we can show, with the help of the equivalence schema, that it holds of an arbitrary proposition, we can then invoke the proposed additional premise to explain our acceptance of that generalization.

[14] I have been stressing that any decent account of how the meaning of "true" is engendered must show us how generalizations about truth may be derivable. But I mentioned another reason for demanding such derivations: namely, that a good theory of *truth* (as opposed to a theory of the meaning of "true") is a body of basic axioms that can explain all the facts about truth—and such facts include generalizations. With respect to this variant of the problem, as before, the Tarskian can easily solve it. As for the minimalist, he needs to show how general facts about truth could be explained in terms of what he alleges to be the *basic* facts about truth—i.e. facts of the form, '<p> is true ↔ p'. But he is of course licensed to cite further explanatory factors (as long as they do not concern truth). And this license yields a solution. For it is plausible to suppose that there is a truth-preserving rule of inference that will take us from a set of premises attributing to each proposition of a certain form some property, G, to the conclusion that *all* propositions have property G. And this rule—not *logically* valid, but none the less necessarily truth-preserving given the nature of propositions—enables the general facts about truth to be explained by their instances.

The idea comes from Tarski himself that generalizations about truth may be deduced from their instances by means of some such rule ("infinite induction"). His own reluctance to rely on it derives, not from any skepticism about its validity, but from not seeing how its consistency could be *proved*. See "The Concept of Truth in Formalized Languages", section 5.

6

Minimalism, Epistemicism, and Paradox

Bradley Armour-Garb and JC Beall

1. INTRODUCTION

Paul Horwich's Minimalism (1999) is familiar to many contemporary philosophers but one aspect of the theory has received little attention, namely, its stance on paradox—both soritical (vagueness) and semantic (Liar family). Horwich's approach to soritical paradox is along so-called *epistemic* lines, an increasingly familiar approach due to recent work by Sorensen (1988) and Williamson (1994). The question is: What is Horwich's approach to semantic paradox, and in particular to the Liar?

While Horwich (1999, p. 109) has made some remarks about Minimalism's stance on the Liar, the position has never been explicitly laid out. One aim of this chapter is to lay out the position in further detail; the other aim is to evaluate it.

When made explicit the Minimalist's stance on the Liar represents a genuinely novel approach to semantic paradox, an approach enjoying numerous virtues. For lack of a better term we shall dub the approach Semantic Epistemicism (in contrast with the more familiar Vagueness Epistemicism).[1] Despite its virtues, novelty and other interesting features, Semantic Epistemicism, as we shall argue, does not sit well with the overall Minimalist position out of which it arises.

The structure of this paper runs as follows. §2 gives a very brief review of Minimalist Semantics. §3 presents Minimalism's approach to the Liar, namely, Semantic Epistemicism, and explains why the Minimalist is committed to it.[2]

[1] As we understand things, Vagueness Epistemicism, as endorsed by Horwich (1997, 1998a, 1999), Sorensen (1988) and Williamson (1994), is so called because it is an epistemic approach to vague predicates (and, in turn, to vague sentences). Horwich's novel approach to semantic paradox, as we shall explain, is similarly epistemic. The view could be called 'Truth-theoretic Epistemicism', as it applies to the truth predicate; however, it could also be called 'Falsity-theoretic Epistemicism', as it similarly applies to the falsity predicate; but it could equally well be called 'Reference-theoretic Epistemicism', as it applies to (semantic paradoxes of) reference. In fact, as we shall note, it applies to the whole family of semantic paradoxes, including the so-called epistemic paradoxes. Rather than invoke (or create) some convoluted tag, we shall simply refer to the target position as Semantic Epistemicism. Perhaps a better name will emerge in the future.

[2] We should note that in conversation Paul Horwich has accepted that Minimalism's stance on the Liar is (what we are calling) Semantic Epistemicism. Indeed, Horwich (in conversation) maintains that Semantic Epistemicism, while not explicitly laid out in his work (cf. 1998a, 1998b, 1999), is certainly implicit in that work.

§4 turns to apparent virtues of Semantic Epistemicism, and explains how Semantic Epistemicism sits well with Minimalism's approach to vagueness. In §5 we raise various difficulties confronting the overall Minimalist position; the upshot of such difficulties is that, despite its other interesting features, Semantic Epistemicism does not afford Minimalism a stable approach to the Liar (or semantic paradox, generally). Finally, §6 offers a brief summary and closing remarks.

2. MINIMALIST SEMANTICS

Horwich's Minimalism is a two-fold theory of truth (and truth-theoretic notions, generally). One fold covers the concept of truth, the other fold (the property of) truth. Minimalism is combined with a use-theoretic approach to meaning (1998a) to yield Minimalist Semantics. The entire theory is underwritten by classical logic (or some conservative extension thereof). In this section we briefly review these background features of Minimalism, before turning, in §3, to the target feature of Minimalism, namely, its stance on semantic paradox.

2.1 Minimalist Truth

As noted above, the Minimalist account of truth comprises an account of the concept of truth and an account of the property of truth. We will discuss each of these in turn.

2.1.1 Concept of Truth

On the Minimalist view, the meaning of 'true' is not given by providing another expression with the same meaning, or by providing a rule transforming every sentence containing the truth predicate into a content-equivalent sentence without it. Rather, it is given by specifying a fundamental regularity of use—a basic acceptance property—in terms of which our overall use of 'true' is best explained. According to Horwich (1998a, p. 104), the sum of everything we do with the word 'true' is best explained by taking the fundamental fact about its use to be our disposition to accept the instances of the truth schema[3]

(ES) <*A*> is true iff *A*,

where

(a) each *A* is replaced with a token of an English sentence;
(b) these tokens are given the same interpretation as one another;

[3] Following Horwich (1998b), we employ the convention that surrounding any expression, *e*, with angled brackets produces an expression referring to *the propositional constituent expressed by e*. Accordingly, <*A*> is the proposition *that A*.

(c) under that interpretation they express a proposition; and
(d) the terms 'that' and 'proposition' are given their (standard) English meanings.[4]

2.1.2 *(Property of) Truth*

A theory of the concept, κ, aims to provide an account that best explains our overall use of '$C_κ$', where '$C_κ$' expresses the concept, κ. By contrast, a theory of the property, κ, aims to provide an account that best explains all of the facts about κ itself.[5] In general, there will be a significant difference between these two sorts of accounts; after all, the former aims to account for facts about words while, in general, the latter aims to account for facts about what those words stand for. That said, Minimalists hold that in the case of truth the two accounts more or less converge on the equivalence schema (ES):[6] The axioms of the Minimalist's theory of truth, MT, are instances of (ES) meeting conditions (a)–(d), above, and, as noted, our tendency to accept such instances constitutes our meaning what we do by 'true'. To be sure, in light of the Liar, the axioms of MT cannot (consistently) comprise all of the instances of MT that we can formulate, but more on that later.[7]

2.2 Minimalist Meaning

Although the Minimalist account is sometimes described as a *use* theory of meaning, this characterisation might be a bit misleading. The thesis is not that meanings are uses, or that meaning properties are identical to use properties; rather, the thesis is that meaning properties are *constituted* by use properties, where κ constitutes *κ* just in case 'their co-extensiveness is the basic explanation of facts involving *κ*' (Horwich, 1998a, p. 25).

2.2.1 *Basic Regularities and Their Role*

The Minimalist account of meaning comprises three theses:

> Thesis I: Meanings are concepts; they are abstract entities from which beliefs, desires and other mental states are composed. Thus, linguistic expressions *mean* concepts.

[4] Note that a similar account would be given for the concept of falsity. Of course, in the case of falsity, the relevant disposition is to accept those instances of

(FS) <*A*> is false iff ∼*A*

that meet certain specified conditions.

[5] Note that this division holds even if, with Horwich, one identifies properties with predicative concepts.

[6] The same holds for falsity: both the account of the concept and of the property of falsity converge on (FS).

[7] For more, see Armour-Garb and Beall (2003b).

Thesis II: The overall use of a word stems from its possession of a basic acceptance property, a basic regularity of use on the basis of which all other facts about its use are to be explained. That a given word possesses the basic acceptance property that it does constitutes its meaning what it does.

Thesis III: Two words express the same concept in virtue of having the same basic acceptance property. Thus, 'vrai' means *true*, that is, expresses the concept of truth, because a certain acceptance property is responsible for its overall use, and that acceptance property is also the basic acceptance property, for 'true'.

2.2.2 *Indeterminacy*

According to Horwich (1997, 1998b), if Barry is a borderline case of baldness then it is *indeterminate* whether or not Barry is bald. To say that it is indeterminate is not to say that there is no fact of the matter as to whether Borderline Barry is bald; rather, it is to say that we could come to know neither that Borderline Barry is bald nor that he is not bald, even though he is either bald or not (and we can know *that*). For ease, we will refer to Horwich's notion of indeterminacy as *indeterminacy*$_H$.

This *epistemicist* line is familiar from the work of Williamson and Sorensen. What distinguishes Horwich's position from theirs is his view of the source of *indeterminacy*$_H$, which derives from the meaning-constituting basic acceptance properties for vague predicates, and, per Horwich, comprise gaps—i.e., circumstances in which we would be unwilling both to apply the predicate and to withhold it, and in which we are confident that no further investigation could yield a decision on the matter.

Although the source of vagueness-related *indeterminacy*$_H$ lies in the gappy character of vague predicates, *indeterminacy*$_H$ can, and should, be understood independently of considerations of vagueness. Characterised more generally, a proposition is *indeterminate*$_H$ if, and only if, though either true or false, there is a semantically induced impossibility of knowing which. Conversely, a proposition is *determinate*$_H$ (i.e., *determinately*$_H$ true) when it is true and it is conceptually possible to know that it is. Spelling this out a bit more:[8] A proposition of the form <*b* is F> is *determinately*$_H$ true if, and only if, it is not the case that the facts about *b*, in virtue of which it is F, and the facts about 'F', in virtue of which it means what it does, together entail that 'F' is not known to apply to *b*.

We shall return to semantically induced *indeterminacy*$_H$ in §3. We end this section with a brief discussion of classical logic.

2.3 Minimalism and Classical Logic

Horwich's Minimalism is wedded to classical logic, as Horwich (1999) makes clear.[9] Among the most important (or, at any rate, relevant) of the 'laws' of classical logic, at least from Horwich's perspective, is excluded middle:

[8] See (1997) and (1998a), for more on this notion of determinacy. Note that a proposition is *determinately*$_H$ false if, and only if, its negation is *determinately*$_H$ true.

[9] By 'classical logic' we mean classical consequence, including consequences of the null set (zero-premise 'arguments'), over a language containing truth and falsity predicates.

(LEM) A v ∼A

Another important 'law' is bivalence:

(BIV) T<A> v F<A>

These principles play a pivotal role in the Minimalist's approach to semantic (and soritical) paradox; we shall return to them in subsequent sections. For now, we turn to the target topic: the Minimalist's stance on semantic paradox.

3. MINIMALISM'S SEMANTIC EPISTEMICISM

Semantic Epistemicism is Minimalism's stance on semantic paradoxes and, in particular, on the Liar. The Liar paradox arises from a sentence used to say of the proposition it expresses (only) that it is false (or untrue). For example:

> The proposition expressed by the first displayed sentence in §3 of 'Minimalism, Epistemicism and Paradox' is not true.

Let 'κ' name the proposition expressed by the first displayed sentence in §3 of 'Minimalism, Epistemicism and Paradox'. Then, for short, κ = <κ is not true>. As is well-known, the κ-instance of (ES), coupled with classical logic, yields a contradiction.

What to do? Horwich (1999, 41–2) considers the following four options:

1. Reject Classical Logic.
2. Reject that 'true' coherently applies to propositions involving truth.
3. Reject that 'paradoxical sentences' express propositions.
4. Restrict (ES) so that only certain instances are correct.

Horwich rejects (1) as being too radical; he rejects (2) and (3) as being too costly (and otherwise too implausible); his preferred option, then, is (4). Some might worry that (4) is merely ad hoc; interestingly, the Minimalist has a reasonable reply to the charge; however, we shall put off discussion of the issue until a later section (see §4.1).

Beyond noting that his choice among (1)–(4) is (4), Horwich says very little about Minimalism's stance on the Liar (or other semantic paradoxes); however, the Minimalist's stance on the Liar is none the less implicit in his overall framework. His stance is Semantic Epistemicism, to which we now turn.

In the following subsections we present the basic picture of semantic epistemicism and how it relates to the Minimalist's overall theory. Subsequent discussion, especially in §4 and §5, will serve to further clarify the view.

3.1 Semantic Epistemicism

In giving the basic import of Semantic Epistemicism we shall concentrate only on the Liar, discussing, in particular, κ; however, the position is intended to apply across the board to all semantic paradoxes.[10]

[10] We should note that, while Horwich (in conversation) agrees that Minimalism's position on the Liar is (what we call) Semantic Epistemicism, he has not written or otherwise said anything about the

The basic import of Semantic Epistemicism is captured in the following two theses, where L is any paradoxical proposition:

(SE_1) L is either true or false.[11]
(SE_2) It is conceptually impossible to know that L is true and it is conceptually impossible to know that L is false.[12]

With respect to κ, then, the Semantic Epistemicist asserts that, while κ is either true or false, we can never know which it is. As with vague propositions, Liar propositions are *indeterminate*$_H$.

To make sense of the view one needs to consider why each of (SE_1) and (SE_2) is maintained. The explanation, in each case, stems from the Minimalist's prior commitments. We consider each of (SE_1) and (SE_2) in turn.

3.1.1 Rationale for (SE_1)

The Minimalist, as in §2.3, is committed to both (BIV) and (LEM), where these 'laws' range over *all* propositions, including paradoxical propositions, such as κ. (BIV) yields its κ-instance, namely

T<κ is not true> v F<κ is not true>.

Whence comes (SE_1).

While we think that there are serious questions to be asked at this stage we shall postpone them for subsequent discussion (viz., §5). We turn now to (SE_2).

3.1.2 Rationale for (SE_2)

The rationale for (SE_2) is similarly straightforward, though slightly more involved than that for (SE_1).

Two items play a role in the rationale behind (SE_2), a principle about knowledge and truth ascriptions, and the Minimalist's basic strategy for avoiding paradox-generated inconsistency (discussed in §3). First, the principle about knowledge and truth ascriptions:

other semantic paradoxes. We assume, however, that Minimalism's Semantic Epistemicism applies across the board or, at least, that it is intended to do so, on pain of ad hocery and other familiar charges.

[11] Note that, from a dialetheic framework, (SE_1) does not exclude the case in which L is both true and false. But Semantic Epistemicism, as developed, is intended to be incompatible with a dialetheic approach to the Liar (on which κ is both true *and* false). For more on dialetheism and, in particular, on issues regarding its compatibility with Minimalism (and deflationary semantics, generally), see Armour-Garb and Beall (2001, 2003b).

[12] In various places (1997, 1998a, 1998b), Horwich makes use of the notion of conceptual impossibility. Though we do not aim to explicate this hoary notion, we should note that the semantically induced impossibilities of which Horwich speaks are conceptual impossibilities.

(KP) If it is conceptually impossible to deduce <<A> is true> via (ES), then it is conceptually impossible to know <<A> is true>, for any proposition, <A>.[13]

(KP) might appear objectionable, but notice that it merely registers the logical role that the Minimalist ascribes to truth.[14] What is at issue at the moment is not the plausibility of (KP) but, rather, the rationale behind (SE_2).

As noted in §3, the (Horwichian) Minimalist rejects options (1)–(3) as candidates for avoiding paradox-generated inconsistency. The Minimalist strategy for avoiding such (would-be) inconsistency is option (4): namely, restrict (ES) and (FS) in such a way that there is no 'correct' *L*-instance of (ES) or (FS) for any paradoxical proposition, *L*. In particular, the following instance of (ES) is not among its 'correct' instances; that is, it is not part of MT:

(ES_κ) <κ is not true> is true iff κ is not true.

Without (ES_κ) one cannot prove that κ is true and one cannot prove that κ is not true, though given (LEM) one can prove the disjunction.

Whence comes (SE_2): from (KP) and the Minimalist's restriction of (ES),[15] (SE_2) follows.

So go the rationales for two main theses of Minimalism's Semantic Epistemicism. We turn, now, to some of the apparent virtues of the position.

4. VIRTUES

There are two notable virtues of the Minimalist's Semantic Epistemicism. We cover each in turn.

4.1 Absence of Ad Hocery

One problem with attempts to restrict (ES) or (FS) in response to paradox is the air of ad hocery. In many cases the charge of ad hocery is spot on; however, it does not apply in the (Horwichian) Minimalist's case. That this is so falls out of the Minimalist's story about indeterminacy.

The semantically induced *indeterminacy*$_H$ discussed in §2.2.2 comes in two forms. We shall call these two forms *vagueness-related-indeterminacy*$_H$ (VRI_H, for short) and Liar-related-*indeterminacy*$_H$ (LRI_H, for short). (VRI_H) occurs when the regularities of the use of a predicate imply nothing about its application in a given case and, thus, yield no inclination to apply it or to withhold it. By contrast (LRI_H) arises when

[13] Note that to deduce <<A> is true> via (ES) is to conclude <<A> is true> on the basis of one or more instances of (ES) together with other premises.

[14] We will remain agnostic on (KP). Indeed, though (KP) plays a crucial role in Semantic Epistemicism, we shall not concentrate on it beyond noting the role it plays.

[15] Similarly for (FS).

use-regularities give rise to conflicting inclinations—both to apply and to withhold the predicate.

According to Horwich (1998a, p. 64), (LRI_H) arises with respect to the κ-instance of (ES). The reason for this is that the regularity underlying our use of 'not' is incompatible with that underlying our use of 'true'.[16] In such a circumstance, Horwich (1998b, p. 136) claims, our inclination to accept the κ-instance of (ES) is overridden: The meaning-constituting regularities of use for our predicates preclude the acceptance of that instance. More simply put: Given the meaning of 'not', the meaning of 'true' debars the κ-instance of (ES) from MT, thereby disallowing the derivation of a contradiction.

4.2. Unified Approach to Paradox

Many philosophers are pessimistic about finding a unified solution to both semantic and soritical (vagueness-inducing) paradox. Most philosophers agree, however, that a unified approach is highly desirable, as it would afford a simpler, more unified semantic theory.[17] One virtue of Horwich's Semantic Epistemicism is that, if successful, it affords just such a unified approach to both soritical and semantic paradox.

Indeed, in so far as semantically induced *indeterminacy*$_H$ is (allegedly) at the heart of both soritical and semantic paradox, Epistemicism is the recommended approach to each (at least given (BIV)): though both vague and liar-type propositions are either true or false, in each case it is conceptually impossible to know which.

5. DIFFICULTIES

We have presented Minimalism's Semantic Epistemicism (§3) and have identified some of its apparent virtues (§4). At this stage we consider difficulties with the view. Our discussion focuses only on Semantic Epistemicism as understood above, and, in particular, as it coheres with Minimalism. We shall raise three problems for the Minimalist's Semantic Epistemicism, each corresponding to a subsection below.

5.1 Justification and (BIV)

There is something curious about the Minimalist's stance on semantic paradox. Consider, for example, the case of κ. The Minimalist maintains that κ is either true or false but that, since there is no 'correct' κ-instance of (ES), we cannot know that κ is true (false). What is curious about this position is that the absence of a 'correct' κ-instance of (ES) would seem to suggest similar treatment with respect to (BIV); that

[16] Although Horwich does not indicate the aspect of the basic regularity of use for 'not' that is incompatible with that for 'true', it is clear, from a consideration of his view of negation (1998b, p. 72), that it is our (alleged) disposition to accept principle (K): 'not-*p*' is acceptable to the degree that '*p*' is unacceptable.

[17] Jamie Tappenden (1993) discusses further motivation for a unified approach.

is, it would seem to suggest that there should be no 'correct' κ-instance of (BIV), either.[18] Admittedly, most philosophers agree that (LEM) is true *a priori*; however, when problematic propositions enter the scene (BIV) becomes questionable.[19] The question is: Why, exactly, does the Minimalist accept (BIV), and, in particular, its κ-instance?

Horwich makes his reasoning clear on this point. The Minimalist is committed to (ES) and (FS). Moreover, it is (arguably) true *a priori* that every proposition satisifies (LEM); the Minimalist, at any rate, accepts (LEM) on a priori grounds. According to Horwich (1999, pp. 76–83), these three principles—(ES), (FS) and (LEM)—*entail* (BIV), and in particular entail its κ-instance. Hence, the Minimalist's commitment to the κ-instance of (BIV) arises from its being entailed by prior commitments.

The trouble with this explanation is that it relies on faulty premises. The problem is that (ES), (FS) and (LEM) entail (BIV)—and, hence, its κ-instance—*only if* (ES) and (FS) are *un*restricted. That this is so is clear: If there is no κ-instance of (ES) or (FS) then there is no way of *deducing* the κ-instance of (BIV) from (ES), (FS) and (LEM).[20] Accordingly, the (Horwichian) Minimalist's rationale for accepting the κ-instance of (BIV)—or (BIV) itself, for that matter—fails. The Minimalist's Semantic Epistemicism stands without a firm rationale for its first thesis, (SE$_1$).[21]

We think that this is a serious problem for the Minimalist's Semantic Epistemicism. The problem is especially serious given (self-imposed, as it were) constraints on acceptable explanation: Given Minimalism, the explanation for why κ is true or false must fall out of either the *explanatorily basic* (ES)/(FS) or 'Logic'. Given restrictions on (ES) and (FS), <T<κ is not true> v <F<κ is not true>> does not fall out of logic; so, it must fall out of either (ES) or (FS). But, as above, it does not, given that (ES) and (FS) exclude the κ-instance from being 'correct'. Accordingly, the Minimalist's motivation for (SE$_1$) remains unclear, if not also questionable.

5.2 (BIV) and Instability

In §5.1 we discussed the question of how the Minimalist justifies (SE$_1$). We now set that question aside. Well-founded or not, (SE$_1$) is a key thesis in the Minimalist's Semantic Epistemicism. The trouble, as we shall now explain, is that (SE$_1$), combined with the Minimalist's general approach to truth, generates a dilemma.

[18] We shall make this apparent curiosity sharper in §5.2. For now, we rely on the surface appearance, as it were.

[19] Bas van Fraassen (1968, 1969) made the distinction clear with his creation of supervaluations, which affords an embrace of (LEM) without requiring a commitment to (BIV). This view is particularly popular with respect to soritical paradox, as a result of Kit Fine's development (1975) of van Fraassen's basic idea.

[20] When the given principles are unrestricted, the normal proof goes through easily, though it uses Modus Ponens or Modus Tollens on ('arbitrary') instances of (ES) and (FS). Given restrictions on these principles, such standard proofs do not work.

[21] Interestingly, given classical consequence (BIV) follows from (ES) and only very weak principles concerning falsity, as Beall and Bueno (2001) point out (in a different dialectical context). Still, the Beall–Bueno result applies only if (ES) and the very weak falsity principles are *unrestricted*, and so not even such weakening will help ground the Minimalist's Semantic Epistemicism.

The dilemma arises as follows. The Minimalist asserts the κ-instance of (BIV): Either κ is true or κ is false. Consider the left disjunct (or the sentence expressing the left disjunct):

(✦) <κ is not true> is true

There are two occurrences of 'true' in (✦); call the left and right occurrences 'internal' and 'external', respectively.

The dilemma comes to this: Either each occurrence of 'true' in (✦) ascribes Minimalist truth or not. Suppose the latter. Then the Minimalist admits more to truth than what her Minimalist theory entails; but this is the end of Minimalism. Suppose the former. Then, in particular, the external 'true' disquotes and the internal 'true' enquotes; otherwise, this is not Minimalist truth after all, contrary to supposition. But, now, the usual Liar reasoning shows the position to be inconsistent (and, indeed, trivial, given classical logic).

We think that the Minimalist is stuck; neither horn of the dilemma above is acceptable (at least to the Minimalist). On one hand, if the Minimalist refuses to acknowledge that the external and internal occurrences of 'true' in (✦) satisfy disquotation and enquotation—in short, satisfy (ES)—then we have lost any grip on what 'true' amounts to in (✦); and without a grip on 'true' in (✦), we can hardly be confident that we have a grip on (SE_1), the κ-instance of (BIV). In this case the Minimalist's Semantic Epistemicism seems to be unclear (at best) or unintelligible (at worst). On the other hand, admitting that the given occurrences of 'true' satisfy (ES) results in an inconsistent (and, indeed, trivial) theory. Either way, Semantic Epistemicism, resting on (SE_1), is unstable, at least when combined, as it currently is, with Minimalism.

5.3 Revenge Problems

In the previous two sections (§§5.1–5.2) we focused on problems involving the Minimalist's (SE_1). We now set (SE_1) aside and turn to one last problem, a problem that arises on many approaches to semantic paradox, which is not avoided by adopting Semantic Epistemicism. The problem is a *revenge problem*, as they are standardly called; it appears to highlight a tension in the position. Whether the given tension is as serious as the previous problems (§§5.1–5.2) is a matter we leave open; that it is a problem for the (Minimalist) Semantic Epistemicist, we think, is clear.

The tension arises from the following premisses:

(e) Structurally similar paradoxes require the same solution.
(f) If nobody knows that <A> is true then nobody knows *that A*.

A consequence of (e), as we intend it, is that, for example, the simple Liar ('this sentence is false') and the strengthened Liar ('this sentence is not true') require the same solution; any 'solution' to the former (latter) that fails to solve the latter (former) is thereby inadequate. Similarly, however, for other structurally similar paradoxes, including, for example, Grelling's ('heterological'), various denotation paradoxes (e.g., Berry's, Richard's), and, in particular, the Knower.[22]

The tension for the Semantic Epistemicist arises from the Knower. Consider, for example, the following sentence:

> Nobody knows the proposition expressed by the first displayed sentence in §5.3 of 'Minimalism, Epistemicism and Paradox'.

Let 'κ' name the proposition expressed by the first displayed sentence in §5.3 of 'Minimalism, Epistemicism and Paradox'. Applied to κ, Semantic Epistemicism amounts to the claim that κ is true or false but nobody knows that κ is true and nobody knows that κ is false. Given (e) and the structural equivalence of κ and κ, Semantic Epistemicism must apply to κ if it applies to κ. This poses a problem.

By his own (Semantic Epistemicist) lights, Horwich knows that nobody knows that κ is true. Given that he knows that nobody knows that κ is true, then, given (f), Horwich ought to conclude that nobody knows κ—and that he knows as much. Knowing *that*, however, is tantamount to knowing κ. Contradiction.

Horwich can avoid contradiction by maintaining that (f) is false. The trouble is that if (f) is false then its antecedent is true and consequent false,[23] in which case nobody knows that <A> is true even though somebody knows *that A* (for some *A*). But how can this situation arise given Minimalist truth? To this question there is no apparent answer. Without such an answer the Minimalist's use of Semantic Epistemicism remains problematic.[24]

6. SUMMARY AND CLOSING REMARKS

The general import of Horwich's Minimalist Semantics is fairly well known in contemporary philosophy; however, its stance on paradox, especially semantic paradox, has never been worked out in the literature. We hope that this paper fills the gap, or at least makes a start.

While epistemic approaches to vagueness and soritical paradox are now familiar terrain in contemporary philosophy, an epistemic approach to semantic paradox is unfamiliar and, indeed, novel. Semantic Epistemicism, which is implicit in Horwich's overall Minimalist framework, is just such an approach. Beyond its novelty, Semantic Epistemicism is an interesting approach to Liar-related paradox, an approach which enjoys a number of desirable virtues (including a unified approach to paradox and a

[22] That these 'different' paradoxes have a common structure has been shown by Priest (1995, 2001), who also shows that the familiar set-theoretic paradoxes, in addition to various paradoxes of infinity, share the same structure as the mentioned 'semantic' paradoxes. Priest (1998, 2000) provides further discussion and defense of the structural similarities and (e). For now, we leave (e) without further defense or discussion.

[23] Horwich, we believe, accepts this (standard) semantics for conditionals.

[24] The remaining options are to reject (e) or that κ and κ share the requisite structural similarity. While neither of these options directly conflicts with Minimalism or Semantic Epistemicism neither option, we think, is likely to succeed. That said, we shall not discuss this option further.

principled restriction on (ES) and (FS)). Despite all this, however, the approach does not ultimately succeed, at least as a Minimalistically acceptable position. The position is not only unstable; it falls prey to revenge problems that are not tolerable within a Minimalist framework.

The problems that we have raised in this are specific to the Minimalist's framework. Perhaps Semantic Epistemicism might succeed given a more substantial notion of truth. Given the (apparent) tenability of Vagueness Epistemicism, such a possibility might well be worth exploring. However, doing so would take us beyond the stated topic of this.

REFERENCES

[1] Alan Ross Anderson and Nuel D. Belnap. *Entailment: The Logic of Relevance and Necessity*, vol. 1. Princeton: Princeton University Press, 1975.

[2] Bradley Armour-Garb and JC Beall. Can deflationists be dialetheists? *Journal of Philosophical Logic*, 2001 30: 593–608, 2001.

[3] ———. Minimalism and the Dialetheic Challenge. *Australasian Journal of Philosophy*, 2003b, 383–401.

[4] JC Beall and Bradley Armour-Garb. Should deflationists be dialetheists? *Noûs* 37: 303–24, 2003a.

[5] —— and Otàvio Bueno. The simple liar without bivalence? *Analysis*, 2002.

[6] Kit Fine. Vagueness, truth and logic. *Synthese*, 30: 265–300, 1975.

[7] Paul Horwich. The nature of vagueness. *Philosophy and Phenomenological Research*, 57: 929–36, 1997.

[8] ——. *Meaning*. Oxford: Oxford University Press, 1998a.

[9] ——. *Truth*. Oxford: Oxford University Press, 1998b.

[10] ——. The minimalist conception of truth. In Simon Blackburn and Keither Simmons, eds, *Truth*, pp. 239–63. Oxford: Oxford University Press, 1999.

[11] Graham Priest. *Beyond the Limits of Thought*. Cambridge: Cambridge University Press, 1995.

[12] ——. The import of enclosure: Some comments on Gratten-Guiness. *Mind* 107: 835–40, 1998.

[13] ——. On the principle of uniform solution: A reply to Smith. *Mind* 109: 123–6, 2000.

[14] ——. *Beyond the Limits of Thought* (expanded, revised edn). Oxford: Oxford University Press, 2001.

[14] Roy Sorensen. *Blindspots*. Oxford: Clarendon, 1988.

[15] Jamie Tappenden. The liar and sorites paradoxes: Towards a unified treatment. *Journal of Philosophy* 90, 1993.

[16] Bas van Fraassen. Presupposition, implication and self-reference. *Journal of Philosophy* 65: 136–52 1968.

[17] ——. Facts and tautological entailments. *Journal of Philosophy* 66: 477–87, 1969. Reprinted in *Entailment*, vol. I.

[18] Timothy Williamson. *Vagueness*. Routledge, 1994.

7

Minimalists about Truth Can (and Should) Be Epistemicists, and it Helps if They Are Revision Theorists too

Greg Restall

Minimalism about truth is the appealing position that the function of the predicate "true", when applied to propositions, is revealed in the class of the *T*-biconditionals of the following form:[1]

$\langle p \rangle$ is true if and only if p. (1)

It is well known that some of these biconditionals lead to paradox. For example

(2) is not true (2)

yields an instance of (1), namely

(2) is true if and only if (2) is not true (3)

since the proposition (2) simply *is* $\langle$(2) is not true$\rangle$.[2] Now, endorsing (3) is too much for many to bear. So, minimalists endorse *many* *T*-biconditionals, but not all. Horwich for example says that he accepts the *non-paradoxical* instances of the *T*-scheme [10]. Instances of the *T*-scheme arising from liar propositions are canonical examples of paradoxical instances, and Horwich and many others do not endorse *those* instances.

But exactly which are the non-paradoxical instances of (1)? Which instances can we endorse? Some are unproblematic: the *grounded* propositions pose no problem in

Thanks to Otávio Bueno, Mark Colyvan, Daniel Nolan, Graham Priest, Roy Sorensen and Achille Varzi and to the audience at the University of Otago for enjoyable discussions on this topic. Thanks to JC Beall and Brad Armour-Garb for their paper "Minimalism and the epistemic approach to paradox" [5], which raised many of the issues discussed here.

[1] Following Horwich, I use "$\langle p \rangle$" as a name of the proposition and "p" to indicate the use of a sentence expressing the proposition. Nothing, as far as I can tell, hangs on the use of the propositional formulation of minimalism, granting that we take paradoxical sentences to express propositions. The arguments of this paper could be transferred to forms of minimalism which take the important *T*-biconditionals to feature sentences and not propositions.

[2] Of course, a minimalist could say that (2) does not express a proposition, but I have set that position aside for this chapter.

T-biconditionals. (For the definition of *groundedness* see Kripke's "Outline of a Theory of Truth" [11, p. 694].) But not all ungrounded propositions are paradoxical. Take the seemingly more benign cousin of the liar, the truth-teller:

(4) is true. (4)

This is ungrounded, but the *T*-biconditional for (4) is not inconsistent—it is the innocuous *tautology* "(4) is true if and only if (4) is true". Furthermore, some liar-like propositions travel in packs. Take this pair of sentences.

(5) is not true. (5)

(6) is not true. (6)

Some reflection will show that although *T*-biconditionals are not grounded when applied to (5) and (6), they can consistently apply. Unfortunately, they can consistently apply in two different ways. Either (5) is true and (6) is not, or (6) is true and (5) is not. Nothing from among the *T*-biconditionals tells us which option to take.

As a more difficult instance, consider *this* pair of sentences.

(8) is true. (7)

(7) is not true. (8)

If we endorse both of the corresponding *T*-biconditionals we get

(7) is true if and only if (8) is true. (9)

(8) is true if and only if (7) is not true. (10)

These aren't *both* true; however, if (9) is false, then there is no harm in asserting (10). On the other hand, if (10) is false, we do not contradict ourselves by asserting (9). If (9) is a paradoxical *T*-biconditional, then (10) is de-fanged, and it can be harmlessly endorsed. On the other hand, if we reject (10) as paradoxical then (9) loses its bite, and can be accepted.

This is not an isolated example. The 'contingent' liar loops discussed by Kripke [11], Yablo's paradox [4, 9, 13, 15, 17], and the many tangles discussed by Barwise and Etchemendy [3] show us that this kind of phenomenon is pervasive. For many of these structures there will be different ways to break the cycle and maintain consistency.

It follows that paradoxicality, for *T*-biconditionals, is not an all-or-nothing business. We cannot easily discern the *culprits* responsible for inconsistency. Sometimes the work is a team effort, and any way of breaking up the team will do to restore law and order. So we do not need to reject every ungrounded instance of the *T*-scheme to restore consistency, and there is no straightforward rule—and apparently, no rule at all [12]—to tell us which ones to pick in cases like (9) and (10).[3]

* * *

[3] McGee takes the minimalist to be committed to endorsing a *maximal* consistent set of instances of the *T*-schema. I see no compelling reason for the minimalist to be committed to this. To be sure, maximality is *desirable* for a larger set decides more truths. However, whether or not the set of

Minimalism about truth is the doctrine that *all* there is to say about truth is given in the appropriate instances of the *T*-biconditional. In the version of minimalism under consideration here, only the *non-paradoxical* instances are true. If this is the case, we have seen many instances in which the class of true *T*-biconditionals just do not determine an answer as to whether or not a proposition is *true*. There appears to be a tension here. This tension can be worked into an *objection* against minimalism about truth.[4]

OBJECTION: If the class of non-paradoxical *T*-biconditionals do not determine an answer in the case of the truth-teller sentences, the looped liar sentences and other paradoxes, then something else must determine an answer. Endorsing any particular answer at all will tell us something else interesting about truth, something not revealed in *T*-biconditionals. Any answer in these cases involves a move away from minimalism to some richer notion of truth appealing to other considerations [6, 7, 14].

RESPONSE: The appropriate response for a minimalist is *epistemicism* [16]. Here is why: only the *nonparadoxical T*-biconditionals govern the extension of "true". Which *are* the genuine non-paradoxical instances? We have no idea. As far as we can tell, non-paradoxicality determines that "true" has *some* extension, constrained by certain *T*-biconditionals. That means truth has some extension or other. Exactly which extension we can never know, for the only rules governing "true" don't tell us enough to decide the matter. Some instances are genuinely paradoxical—such as (3)—so we know that the biconditional cannot apply to *them*. If that is all there is we can say about the extension of truth, then there is nothing else we can say about whether or not (3) is true.

There is at least an analogy with vague terms. Our use of the language determines that certain predications of "tall" are true, and that others are not. There are borderline cases where we can ascertain no principle to demand inclusion in the extension of tallness, or exclusion from that extension. At the very least, this is a failure of our knowledge—we can determine no reason to take Charlie as tall, and we can take no reason to take him as not tall. The meaning of "tall" determines that it has an extension taking in the canonical tall cases and avoiding the canonical non-tall cases. But, so the epistemicist says, it must have *some* extension. Borderline cases arise from our failure to ascertain what that extension might be. The same, minimalism says, can and must go for truth.

* * *

OBJECTION: Certain *T*-biconditionals fail. For example, we agree that (3) must fail. But biconditionals can fail in one of two ways.[5] In the cases of failures of

instances is maximal, the theory leaves some *T*-sentences undecided. The truth-teller as an example. Perhaps a little more unsettledness than is strictly necessary is not an insuperable problem.

[4] Many of the objections discussed here are raised by Armour-Garb and Beall [5].

[5] If it is not the case that *p* if and only if *q*, then either *p* and it is not the case that *q*, or *q* and it is not the case that *p*. This holds at least if "if and only if" is a material biconditional. At the very least, in this context of the debate, if the biconditional is really a stronger notion, such as some form of entailment, we can still resort to the weaker notion of material biconditionality to make this point.

T-biconditionals, *which* way do they fail? Do we say that *p* but that ⟨*p*⟩ is not true, or do we say that ⟨*p*⟩ is true but it is not the case that *p*?

RESPONSE: If *all* there is to say about truth is revealed in the non-paradoxical *T*-biconditionals, then epistemicism is both appropriate and required here too. In the case of (3) that either (2) is true or that (2) is not true. If all there is to truth is given by the non-paradoxical instances of (1), then there is no *reason* to endorse one option over the other. But that is no further problem. One or the other is true, but we can never know which.

* * *

OBJECTION: So, we reject the biconditional in the case of the liar sentence. Suppose we accept the left part of the biconditional and not the right. We are then committed to the *truth* of (2). But if (2) is true, it is not any *T*-biconditional which gives rise to this fact. But does this not mean that we are predicating some property of (2) other than genuine minimalist truth?

REPLY: The extension of truth is constrained by all of the non-paradoxical instances of the *T*-scheme. This means that, for propositions, the carving into the true and the untrue must respect these non-paradoxical *T*-biconditionals. Since "true" must have *some* extension, (2) will be in that extension of truth or it will not. In doing so we are not using some other predicate or ascribing some other property of (2). We are still ascribing *truth* to (2), even if this is one of the rejected instances of the *T*-scheme.

Consider the analogy with the epistemicist approach to tallness. If Charlie is a non-canonical case of tallness—that is, he actually is tall but he is not one of the canonical instances of tallness—then we do not ascribe a different property of Charlie when we (truly) call him tall. No, he *is* tall, just as someone 220 cm in height is tall. Any *oddness* in this case arises from the fact that he is a non-canonical case of tallness. We can truly assert that he is tall, but, if the epistemicist is correct, we do not *know* that he is tall. The same can apply in the case of truth. Paradoxical sentences might well be true (and this is the same property "truth" ascribed as for non-paradoxical sentences) despite not falling under the appropriate instances of the *T*-scheme.

* * *

OBJECTION: There is no *recipe* for separating paradoxical *T*-biconditionals from the non-paradoxical ones [7], because any recipe would suffice for sorting out all truths from falsehoods! The instance applied to

If (11) is true then *p* (11)

is paradoxical if and only if *p* is not true. So any algorithm for sorting out paradoxicality would give us an algorithm for sorting out truth.

RESPONSE: That's right! Perhaps, as we have conceded, there is no need to take the canonical *T*-biconditionals to be all of the non-paradoxical instances, so perhaps the more restrictive class of *canonical* instances may well be decidable by some recipe. Regardless, there is no reason to suppose that we *have* any algorithm at all for determining which *T*-biconditionals are the canonical ones. If we do not have such an algorithm, do we have a theory of truth at all? It seems like a great deal is unsettled, and it is surprising that there is such agreement about the concept of truth. The analogy with vague terms continues here. There is no agreement about the extension of vague concepts, but there is a great deal of agreement about the canonical instances of those concepts. The same holds for truth: We can agree that the concept of truth is constrained by at the very least the grounded *T*-biconditionals, where no circularity or self-reference is allowed at all. These biconditionals will give us members of the extension of *T* and members of the anti-extension of *T*. This is enough to give us quite a bit of agreement about the behaviour of truth. Perhaps we know as little about the precise boundary between truth and untruth no more than we know the precise boundary between the tall and the non-tall.

* * *

OBJECTION: What about falsehood? If only some of our *T*-biconditionals are non-paradoxical, then so too are some of the instances of the corresponding *F*-biconditionals, which govern falsity:

$$\langle p \rangle \text{ is false if and only if it is not the case that } p. \tag{12}$$

But if we endorse the non-paradoxical instances of this scheme, then we leave open the option that some paradoxical sentences are neither true nor false. We also leave open the option that some sentences are both true and false. This does not involve us in any contradictions (any cases where we accept $\langle p \rangle$ and $\langle \text{not } p \rangle$) or in rejecting any instance of the law of the excluded middle (any cases where we reject $\langle p \rangle$ and reject $\langle \text{not } p \rangle$). Nonetheless, it seems more than a little surprising that minimalism requires us to be committed to failures of bivalence in this sense.

RESPONSE: It is an *option* for the minimalist to reject bivalence in just this sense. However, it is certainly not mandatory. The appeal of the scheme (12) might well arise from the more primary connection between truth and falsity. If we accept (13)

$$\langle p \rangle \text{ is false if and only } p \text{ is not true,} \tag{13}$$

then there are no gaps between truth or falsity, or any gluts where we have both. (Underwritten, of course, by our prior acceptance of each $\langle p \text{ or not } p \rangle$ and our rejection of each $\langle p \text{ and not } p \rangle$.) Is this an extra fact about truth which makes this theory less minimalist? There is no reason to suspect that this is the case. As Horwich would say [10], these are not further facts telling us something about the intrinsic nature of truth. The biconditional (13) can be read as constraining the behaviour of *falsehood*. And falsehood is no *thicker* notion, given simply its definition in terms of truth. We have simply traded one thin notion for another by connecting truth with falsehood.

* * *

OBJECTION: Minimalists think that the truth predicate is introduced into the language to do *work*. How can such a strange predicate—defined by its defining conditions in *some* places, and given free rein to vary as it pleases in others—ever do the work required of it? Why would we ever introduce a predicate like *that* into the language?

RESPONSE: Here the parallel with other kinds of epistemicism begins to pay its way. It is clear that predicates such as 'red' and 'tall' have been introduced into our vocabulary to do work, and that they are very useful indeed. We use these predicates to draw distinctions, and in very many cases, their use is unproblematic. I ask you to pass me the red book. You point out to me the tall woman. And so on. The predicates succeed even if the "rules" we can articulate that govern the use of 'red' do not manage to uniquely carve the domain into the collection of red things and its complement, the collection of non-red things. No matter, we manage to get by even though the rules we can manage to articulate and specify don't pick out a single extension, and (to be honest) we would be happy with any number of the possible extensions compatible with what we *know* of the extension of 'red'.

The case with T is similar, though in this case we have not *under*-determined the extension with our rules. We have managed to *over*-determine it. Our rules—every instance of (1)—do not allow for *many* different extensions of 'true'. They allow for none. In this case, we do not get rid of the predicate, even though our requirements are inconsistent. Instead, we get by with as much as we can safely get away with. The case has a parallel with games with inconsistent rules (at least in those cases where the inconsistency shows up only in very odd and restricted circumstances), where we manage to avoid the area of unclarity, or make up conventions where the rules do not give us a settled answer, or simply 'make do' in any of a number of ways. Our use of the truth predicate, while introduced in order to do the *impossible*—satisfy (1)—manages to pay its way even if it cannot live up to those impossibly stringent requirements.

* * *

OBJECTION: But that is to ignore one of the most important uses of a concept of truth. Truth is introduced into a discourse in order (in part) to facilitate generalisations. If you are an epistemicist minimalist, then you have no reason to assert seemingly trivial generalisations such as

An inclusive disjunction is true iff one of its disjuncts is true. (14)

For there is always the case that the disjunction (or the disjunct) is a paradoxical statement, in which case (1) does not apply and we have no reason to endorse generalisations like (14). However, generalisations like this are *central* to semantics and logic, and discarding them, even in the case of the paradoxes (especially where it seems that they won't be replaced by any other believable generalisations) is too great a price to bear. So, you might wish to *keep* generalisations like (14), but explicitly retaining them is to move away from minimalism, which takes it that T-biconditionals (and only those biconditionals) suffice for providing the meaning of the truth predicate [1].

RESPONSE: This is a serious objection, and it will not suffice to simply bite the bullet and reject generalisations such as (14). Instead, a minimalist must find a way to accept them without placing her minimalist credentials in peril. Can she do this?

I think that she can. As before, the answer is to be found in the parallel with other kinds of epistemicism. Consider Charlie. He is not a canonically tall person. He is not a canonically short person. He is a borderline case for the predicate 'tall'. Consider what we might say about the following biconditional:

Someone the same height as Charlie is tall if and only if Charlie is tall. (15)

If we say that all that we *know* about the extension of 'tall' is that the canonically tall cases are tall and the canonically not tall cases are not tall, then we have *no* assurance that a generalisation such as (15) is true. But to acquiesce in this conclusion is silly. Not all extensions of 'tall' are alike, even among those that get their canonical extensions and anti-extensions correct. We might call a proffered precisification for 'tall' *regular* if it satisfies the following constraint:

If x is no taller than y then if x is tall, so is y, (16)

and an epistemicist may happily agree that the extension of 'tall' is regular. Perhaps the same trick can be turned in the case of minimalism about truth. After all, it seems congenial to minimalism to say that the extension of T is some *appropriate* set governed by the non-paradoxical T-biconditionals, where a proffered extension for T is appropriate when and only when it satisfies the collection of generalisations such as that specified at (14). We have not specified anything *substantial* about truth in this move: we have merely expressed a preference for how possible extensions for T may be selected out of the herd of competing candidates. It seems that the condition of appropriateness is a friendly amendment for the minimalist because the appropriateness of T (over some domain of propositions, such as the grounded ones) is *entailed* by the class of T-biconditionals (for that domain), and the constraint to keep the extension of T to be as appropriate as possible over the entire domain is another way to keep as much of (1) as we can.

We must be careful at this point. I have not specified *which* generalisations are satisfied by T, and more work must be done to examine *which* generalisations are safe for the minimalist to maintain. Suffice to say, the minimalist can respond, within the spirit of minimalism, and endorse as many generalisations as possible, consistent with the constraint of consistency: no matter what we try, T does not quite live up to the full collection of T-biconditionals.

This is where things seem to end if the minimalist takes her theory of truth to consist solely of the collection of non-paradoxical T-biconditionals. But the minimalist need not be so restrictive, and one way ahead provides a novel response to the generalisation problem.

The minimalist could take her theory of truth to consist of the collection of *all* of the T-biconditionals, without thereby taking this collection to be, as a whole, *true*. That is, the minimalist can take the collection of T-biconditionals, as a whole, to govern the meaning of the truth predicate. This keeps the minimalist safe qua minimalism. Nothing *else* is required to elucidate the concept of truth other than T-biconditionals. However, if we go beyond simple epistemicist minimalism—according to which the theory of truth is merely the class of non-paradoxical T-biconditionals—then we can avail ourselves of a principled answer to the generalisation problem. The minimalist can turn this trick by endorsing a variety of the *revision theory of truth* [8]. We say that the concept of truth is governed by the entire class of *T*-biconditionals, provided that these biconditionals are read as *revision* rules. We read the *T*-biconditionals as follows:

$$\langle p \rangle \text{ is true (at stage } i+1) \text{ if and only if } p \text{ (at stage } i). \quad (17)$$

What are stages? Stages are what one uses to evaluate expressions such as '$\langle p \rangle$ is true' and other definitions—especially *circular* definitions such as that of the concept of truth. We do not need to go into the detail here (for that, read Gupta and Belnap's account of the revision theory [8]). Here, it is sufficient to note that if we wish to evaluate the liar, we may reason as follows. If we have (2) at some stage, then at the next (2) is true, but this is the negation of (2), so at the one after, (2) is not true (which is (2) again) and so at the next after that, (2) is true, and so on. The paradoxical statement oscillates in value from true to false and vice versa.

One nice feature of the revision theory is that the grounded propositions do not oscillate in values from stage to stage: in fact, this is one way to carve out the grounded propositions. And the evaluation of a grounded proposition becomes *stable* after sufficiently many stages. In fact, we can construct single stages such that non-paradoxical statements have a stable evaluation, in the sense that for each non-paradoxical p, if p holds at this stage, it does at all successor stages as well. Call such a stage *regular*. One way to construct regular stages is to start with an initial stage, and proceed up the hierarchy of stages sufficiently high up the ordinals. Once we have passed through more ordinals than $2^{|\mathcal{L}|}$ (where $|\mathcal{L}|$ is the cardinality of the class of propositions in question) then we know we have gone through as many distinct evaluations as we can and anything that can stabilise *has*. We will think of stable stages in this way: as ones that have gone through such a process of revision that all stabilisation that will occur has occurred.

Now the epistemicist can reason as follows. Here is how truth works. It is governed by a revision rule. The revision theory tells us the *dynamics* of truth. We evaluate truth at a stage using the revision rule. Now, what can we say about what is actually true? What is actually true is what is true at some particular regular stage. We do not know which. The liar sentence is either true or it is false, but we have no idea what its truth value might be. Half of the regular stages evaluate it as true, and half of them evaluate it as false.

The epistemicist revision theorist, then, pictures the concept of truth as governed by *T*-biconditionals which are read as rules of revision (17). These rules establish a series of stages. Which stage is *actually* the case is something that we do not, and cannot know. This might not seem like much of an advance on what we might call 'static' epistemicist minimalism, but it differs in one crucial respect: the answer to the generalisation problem. Now, we may give a principled answer to the generalisation problem, for we can explain why generalisations such as (14) hold, given this account of truth. For now, given an inclusive disjunction $\langle p \vee q \rangle$, we may note that it is true at stage $i+1$ if and only if we have either p or q at stage i (applying (17)) and this holds if and only if we have either p at stage i or q at stage i (taking stages to respect inclusive disjunction) and thus (applying (17) again, this time in reverse) either $\langle p \rangle$ is true at stage $i+1$ or $\langle q \rangle$ is true at stage $i+1$. So the disjunction generalisation (14) holds at successor stages. The same will hold for *any* similar generalisation. If we have at every stage ϕ obtains if and only if some boolean condition in terms of the obtaining of $\psi_1, \psi_2, \ldots, \psi_n$ obtains, then at each successor stage, $\langle \phi \rangle$ is true if and only if that same boolean condition of the truth of $\langle \psi_1 \rangle, \langle \psi_2 \rangle, \ldots, \langle \psi_n \rangle$ obtains.[6] The structure inherent in *stages* suffices to ground a large class of generalisations with respect to the behaviour of the truth predicate. Truth, even in paradoxical cases, need not be unstructured, even if the *T*-biconditionals (read as material conditionals) fail to be true.

* * *

Objection: But what about dialetheism? Is it not just *simpler* to be robustly minimalist, accept each and every *T*-biconditional, and accept the contradictions that flow from them? Is it not more sensible to accept a dialetheic response to the paradoxes instead of fiddling about at the edges and accepting only the so-called 'non-paradoxical' *T*-biconditionals [2]?

Response: In some sense dialetheism is 'simpler' than fiddling about with the class of *T*-biconditionals, but in another sense it is much more complicated. To allow for truth-value gluts is to prise apart the denial of p and the assertion of its negation. The dialetheist argues that, at least for paradoxical sentences like (2), it is appropriate to assert that sentence and its negation. But it does not follow that it is appropriate to *deny* the liar. So just what is the connection between denial and the assertion of a negation? Surely there is some connection, for in general we manage to deny quite successfully by asserting a negation. The dialetheist thinks that we do not in the case of paradoxical sentences. So, exactly *where* does denial and the assertion of a negation split apart? Perhaps it is at just paradoxical propositions. Again, a seemingly neat and simple generalisation must be restricted in some way. It is not only the classical minimalist that restricts a natural generalisation in the face of paradox.

* * *

Minimalists who wish to avoid paradox arising from an unrestricted derivation of paradoxes can respond to the challenge of justifying which instances of the *T*-scheme actually hold by taking a leaf out of the epistemicist's book. In fact, it appears that they *have* to follow in epistemicists' footsteps. If all there is to say about truth is given in *T*-biconditionals, and if the extension of truth is not totally determined by those instances, then we cannot determine the extension of the predicate "true". In as much as "true" is a predicate, it has some extension or other. Exactly which, we will never know. Exactly which, we *can* never know. If the minimalist reads these *T*-biconditionals as *rules for revision* then not only can the epistemicist position be understood as our essential ignorance of which stage is 'this' stage, we also discover an answer to the generalisation problem.

[6] And provided that you are willing also to talk of *satisfaction* at stages (or truth relative to bindings of variables with objects) then the same general technique works with quantified statements as well.

REFERENCES

[1] Bradley Armour-Garb. Minimalism, the generalisation problem and the liar. *Synthese*, 139: 491–512, 2004.
[2] ——and JC Beall. Minimalism and the dialethic challenge. *Australasian Journal of Philosophy*, 81: 383–401, 2003.
[3] Jon Barwise and John Etchemendy. *The Liar*. Oxford University Press, Oxford, 1987.
[4] JC Beall. Is Yablo's paradox non-circular? *Analysis*, 61: 176–87, 2001.
[5] ——and Bradley Armour-Garb. Minimalism and the epistemic approach to paradox. Presented at the 2001 Australasian Association for Philosophy Conference, Hobart, Tasmania. (See Chapter 5, this volume.)
[6] Christopher Gauker. Deflationism and logic. *Facta Philosophica*, 1: 167–98, 1999.
[7] —— *T*-schema deflationism versus Gödel's first incompleteness theorem. *Analysis*, 61: 129–36, 2001.
[8] Anil Gupta and Nuel Belnap. *The Revision Theory of Truth*. MIT Press, Cambridge, MA, 1993.
[9] J. Hardy. Is Yablo's paradox liar-like? *Analysis*, 55: 197–98, 1995.
[10] Paul Horwich. *Truth*. Basil Blackwell, Oxford, 1990.
[11] Saul Kripke. Outline of a theory of truth. *Journal of Philosophy*, 72: 690–716, 1975.
[12] Vann McGee. Maximal consistent sets of instances of Tarski's schema (*T*). *Journal of Philosophical Logic*, 21: 235–31, 1992.
[13] Graham Priest. Yablo's paradox. *Analysis*, 57: 236–42, 1997.
[14] Keith Simmons. Deflationary truth and the liar. *Journal of Philosophical Logic*, 28: 455–88, 1999.
[15] Roy Sorenson. Yablo's paradox and kindred infinite liars. *Mind*, 107(425): 137–55, 1998.
[16] Timothy Williamson. *Vagueness*. Routledge, 1994.
[17] Stephen Yablo. Paradox without self-reference. *Analysis*, 53: 251–2, 1993.

8

Minimalism, Deflationism, and Paradoxes

Michael Glanzberg

This paper argues against a broad category of deflationist theories of truth. It does so by asking two seemingly unrelated questions. The first is about the well-known logical and semantic paradoxes: Why is there no strengthened version of Russell's paradox, as there is a strengthened version of the Liar paradox? Oddly, this question is rarely asked. It does have a fairly standard answer, which I shall not dispute for purposes of this paper. But I shall argue that asking it ultimately leads to a fundamental challenge to some popular versions of deflationism.

The challenge comes about by pairing this question with a second question: What is the theory of truth about? For many theorists, there is an obvious answer to this question: The theory of truth is about truth bearers and what makes them true. But this answer appears to bring with it a commitment to a substantial notion of truth, which deflationists cannot bear. Deflationists might prefer a very different answer: The theory of truth is not really about anything. There is no substantial property of truth, so there is no domain which the theory of truth properly describes. Not all positions under the name 'deflationism' subscribe to this view, but I shall argue that the important class of so-called *minimalist* views do.

I shall argue that this sort of deflationist answer is untenable, and thus argue in broad strokes against minimalism. I shall argue by way of a comparison of the theory of truth with the theory of sets, and consideration of where paradoxes, especially strengthened versions of the paradoxes, may arise in each. This will bring the two seemingly unrelated questions together to form an anti-deflationist argument. I shall show that deflationist positions that accept the idea that truth is not a real or substantial property are too much like naive set theory. Like naive set theory, they are unable to make any progress in resolving the paradoxes, and must be replaced by a drastically different sort of theory. Such a theory, I shall show, must be fundamentally non-minimalist. I shall then turn to the question of how close to minimalism one can come and avoid the problem I shall raise. I shall suggest, though more tentatively, that

This is a revised and expanded version of my "Minimalism and Paradoxes", *Synthese* 135 (2003): 13–36. Thanks to Bradley Armour-Garb and JC Beall, and to Otávio Bueno, Alex Byrne, Ned Hall, Richard Heck, Jim Pryor, Susanna Siegel, Judith Thomson, Ralph Wedgwood, and Steve Yablo. Some of this material was presented at the University of Southern California. Thanks to my audience there for valuable comments and discussion.

a much wider class of deflationist views of truth is undermined by the argument I shall present.

My argument proceeds in six sections. In the first, section (1), I make the comparison between naive set theory and the minimalist version of deflationism, and explain the sense in which both theories can be said not to be about anything. In section (2), I point out how both theories suffer from nearly identical problems, as Russell's paradox and the Liar paradox may be seen to be extremely similar in important respects. In Section (3), I show where these parallels break down. The sort of response to the Liar which might be offered by minimalism proves to be unstable, in that it is vulnerable to the Strengthened Liar paradox. The standard response to Russell's paradox in set theory is not so unstable. In Section (4), I investigate the source of this difference. I argue there that any theory of truth able to evade the Strengthened Liar must at least be about some domain in the way that standard set theory is about the domain of sets. Then in Section (5), I show that the usual ways of avoiding the Strengthened Liar meet this condition by abandoning minimalism for a more correspondence-like notion of truth. Finally, I show in Section (6) that no minimalist position can meet the condition, and so none is tenable. I conclude this section by considering whether any other version of deflationism might fare better. I shall tentatively suggest none can.

1. MINIMALISM AND NAIVE SET THEORY

The term 'deflationism' covers a wide range of philosophical views. My primary concern here is with the species of deflationism known as 'minimalism'. This is again really a class of views. As a class, it is distinguished by three distinctive marks. The first is the idea that in some appropriate sense there is no substantial or genuine property of truth. For instance, Paul Horwich writes:

> Unlike most other predicates, 'is true' is not used to attribute to certain entities (i.e. statements, beliefs, etc.) an ordinary sort of property—a characteristic whose underlying nature will account for its relation to other ingredients of reality. Therefore, unlike most other predicates, 'is true' should not be expected to participate in some deep theory of that to which it refers... (Horwich, 1990, p. 2.)

Horwich does not quite claim that there is no such property as truth, but the sense in which there is a property seems to amount to little more than there being a predicate of truth in our language. There is no genuine phenomenon of being true which this predicate describes.

The remaining two marks of the class of views I shall consider center around the *T-schema*:

> '*s*' is true iff *s*.

Those who maintain that there is no substantial property of truth cannot maintain that instances of this schema hold because of the nature of the property; it cannot hold in virtue of the nature of truth. Instead, they must say that the schema holds analytically, or perhaps by definition, or perhaps by stipulation. This is the second mark of the class of minimalist views. There are, of course, important differences between the specific ideas of analyticity, definition, and stipulation; but they will not matter for our purposes here. What is important here is that any of these options provides the T-schema with a status that ensures its truth without looking to the nature of the property of truth ('underlying nature' as Horwich puts it). In what follows, I shall compare this status to that of logical truth.

The final mark of the class of minimalist views is the idea that rather than describing a feature of truth, the T-schema provides us with a device of disquotation. This device is useful, for instance, as it allows us to make infinitary generalizations. Putting these marks together, a minimalist holds that the stipulative or analytic T-schema provides us with a useful linguistic device, rather than describing a genuine property.

The class of views on which I shall focus are thus marked by the claims that there is no substantial property of truth, the T-schema is analytic, and that truth is a device of disquotation. It is more or less standard to call any view within this class *minimalism*, though as I mentioned, a number of distinct positions within the class can be discerned. It will thus be useful to identify a particularly straightforward version of minimalism, which I shall call *pure minimalism*. Pure minimalism is distinguished by taking the instances of the T-schema to hold for any well-formed declarative sentence. Beyond that, it insists that the marks of minimalism comprise all there is to say about truth.[1]

Pure minimalism factors into two components. One is a theory in the logician's sense. The core of the theory is the T-schema, taken now as an axiom schema:

$$(T) \qquad Tr(\ulcorner \phi \urcorner) \leftrightarrow \phi.$$

We need to construe this as added to a theory strong enough to do some elementary syntax. It must have a name $\ulcorner \ulcorner \phi \urcorner \urcorner$ for each sentence $\ulcorner \phi \urcorner$, and I shall assume the theory is strong enough to allow the Diagonal Lemma to apply. Let us call this theory M.

The other component consists of the philosophical commitments of pure minimalism. In many cases, we think of the philosophical commitments going with a formal theory as helping to describe the intended interpretation of the theory. For a minim-

[1] Many current minimalist positions depart from pure minimalism in some ways. I shall return to other versions of minimalism in section (6). It is not entirely clear whether anyone has actually held pure minimalism, but regardless, I believe it encapsulates an important idea, which is reflected in the positions of a number of authors. Pure minimalism is often attributed to Ayer (1946). Ayer defines truth for propositions rather than sentences, which technically make him something other than a pure minimalist. However, as I shall discuss more in section (6), his definition of proposition is sufficiently closely tied to sentences that this difference may be insignificant. Horwich (1990) likewise holds most of the theses of pure minimalism, but construes truth as applying to propositions. Some of his remarks, especially in Horwich (1994), suggest his departure from pure minimalism may be as minimal as Ayer's. The third mark of minimalism—truth as a device of disquotation—is closely associated with Quine, and Quine (1986) comes quite close to pure minimalism. Of course, Quine would never stand for an inconsistent theory like M.

alist, this is an odd way to put the idea (as I shall discuss more in a moment), but at the very least, the philosophical commitments do help explain how M is to be understood.

Pure minimalism includes the feature of minimalism about *truth bearers*. Truth bearers are appropriate candidates for truth, and have a truth status. They are true or false.[2] Truth bearers need not be true, but they must be *truth apt*. According to pure minimalism, to be a truth bearer is nothing but to figure into predications of $\ulcorner Tr \urcorner$ or $\ulcorner \neg Tr \urcorner$. In the presence of the T-schema or the axiom schema (T), this occurs for every well-formed declarative sentence. Pure minimalism is thus minimalist about truth bearers in that it says no more about what makes something a truth bearer than it does about truth. Of course, the class of well-formed declarative sentences must be delineated by the syntax component of the theory, but this tells us nothing about their status as truth bearers. When it comes to this status, all that the theory tells us derives from the analytic (or whatever other appropriate status) schema (T). There is thus no underlying property that makes it the case that declarative sentences are all truth bearers, as there is no underlying property that makes the instances of (T) hold.[3]

I shall compare pure minimalism to *naive set theory*. This will help frame the question of what, according to the minimalist, the theory of truth is about. Like pure minimalism, naive set theory factors into two components. One is again a formal theory. Again it is captured primarily by a single axiom schema, the *naive comprehension schema*:

(COMP) $\quad y \in \{x|\phi(x)\} \leftrightarrow \phi(y).$

As with (T), we must think of this as added to an appropriate base theory, which is able to construct a name $\ulcorner \{x|\phi(x)\} \urcorner$ for the set determined by $\ulcorner \phi \urcorner$. We might also assume a principle of extensionality, but it will not matter for the discussion to follow. Let us call this theory N.

Like pure minimalism, naive set theory comes with a philosophical component as well. I have in mind naive set theory as it would have been understood by someone who really held it: Frege, or in some form perhaps a traditional logician.[4] Such a theorist would hold that (COMP) is in some way a *logical* principle. Now, there have been a great many ideas about what makes something a logical principle. But common to them is one of two thoughts. Either logical principles are schematic, and so not about anything in particular, or logical principles are about absolutely everything. Both of these lines of thought reach the same conclusion: logical principles do not hold because of the nature of a *specific* range of objects or properties or phenomena.

In this regard, naive set theory turns out to be remarkably similar to pure minimalism. Both assign remarkably similar status to their fundamental principles (COMP)

[2] Views which rely on many-valued logics will rather say that truth bearers are true, false, or any of the other truth values.

[3] A well-known argument of Jackson et al. (1994) attempts to show that minimalism about truth does not lead to minimalism about truth bearers. I do think that the points I am making here reveal a genuine commitment of pure minimalism, as I shall discuss more in section (6), when discussing departures from pure minimalism.

[4] Both Frege (at some moments) and, say, the *Port-Royal* logicians, would have preferred 'extension' to 'set'.

and (T). They agree that there is no underlying nature of anything in particular which makes these principles true. Both agree that there are no specific objects or properties that the fundamental principles of their respective theories describe. Rather, these principles are in the general class of the logical, or the analytic, or the definitional. I do not want to go so far as to assimilate logical truth to analytic or definitional truth. I only need to note that the principles in these categories share the important feature of there being no underlying natures of anything in particular to which they owe their truth.

In this way, both pure minimalism and naive set theory may be described as not being about anything in particular. Now, it may be noted that the truth predicate occurs in (T) and set abstracts in (COMP), so it could be said that one is about truth and the other sets. But at best, this is so in an entirely minimal way. As we observed, for neither schema is there any special domain of objects, properties, events, or any other phenomena that makes its instances true. As they are logical or analytic, these schemas are not about anything in particular. In the case of naive set theory, this is reflected both by the philosophical gloss on the theory, and by the unrestricted nature of set abstraction. As a matter of logic, any objects of any kind may be collected into a set. There is thus no special domain of the theory. In the case of pure minimalism, we can likewise observe that the theory cannot reveal a basic feature of the property of truth, nor can it provide any more substantial an account of what makes something a truth bearer. There is no more a special domain of this theory than there is of the naive theory of sets. As I mentioned above, the truth bearers are the syntactically well-formed declarative sentences. It is thus tempting to say that the theory is about these sentences. But it is so only in a trivial way. The theory appropriates some syntax, but this tells us nothing about truth. The principles that are supposed to tell us something about truth fall into a different category, and these hold of well-formed sentences only because this is the way the stipulations themselves are syntactically well-formed. Truth is thus predicated as widely as makes syntactic sense, not on the basis of the nature of any particular domain. Though when we write the theory down we rely on some syntax to do so, as far as the basic commitments of minimalism go, there is in no substantial sense a special domain of the theory of truth.

Pure minimalism and naive set theory do differ in some ways. Pure minimalism does not quite claim to be a matter of logic, and naive set theory offers nothing like semantic ascent. But we have now seen an important similarity between them. Both theories rely on principles which hold in some other way than by accurately describing a domain, and as a result both theories are in similar ways not genuinely about anything.

2. PARADOXES

So far, we have identified pure minimalism as a representative of the class of minimalist views. We then saw that pure minimalism is in one important respect like naive set theory, as both theories can be described as not being about anything in particular.

Pure minimalism has a formal component M, and naive set theory has a formal component N. Both M and N are inconsistent, as is well-known. Russell's paradox shows N to be inconsistent, and the Liar paradox does the same for M. But the response to its paradox has been quite different for each. Naive set theory is usually taken to be a disaster, while minimalism is often taken to be in need of modification but still viable. Given the similarities between the two theories we have seen, this may appear odd. This section will show how odd it is, by showing just how similar the paradoxes are in some important respects. In the following sections, this will lead us to consider a crucial difference between responses to the paradoxes, which will in turn show us something about the viability of minimalism.

Let us first consider the familiar Liar paradox, which shows M to be inconsistent. Using the Diagonal Lemma, we can find a sentence $\ulcorner\lambda\urcorner$ such that:

$$M \vdash \lambda \leftrightarrow \neg Tr(\ulcorner\lambda\urcorner).$$

Combining this with (T) gives the contradiction:

$$M \vdash Tr(\ulcorner\lambda\urcorner) \leftrightarrow \lambda \leftrightarrow \neg Tr(\ulcorner\lambda\urcorner).$$

The Diagonal Lemma hides the procedure for producing $\ulcorner\lambda\urcorner$, but it is clear that $\ulcorner\lambda\urcorner$ 'says of itself' that it is not true. We then ask about the truth of this sentence, and see that it is true just in case it is not true.[5]

We do virtually the same thing to produce Russell's paradox, which shows N to be inconsistent. With the Liar, we found a sentence that says of itself that it is not true. Here we need a predicate that says something is not in itself, i.e. $\ulcorner\neg x \in x\urcorner$. With the Liar, we asked about the truth of that very sentence. Here we ask about this predicate applying to its own extension. Let its extension be $R = \{x \mid \neg x \in x\}$. From (COMP) we have:

$$N \vdash R \in R \leftrightarrow \neg R \in R.$$

As with the Liar, we have a contradiction.

The two paradoxes differ in that Russell's paradox involves class abstracts and membership, while the Liar paradox involves truth, but otherwise, we do basically the same thing in both. The similarity between the two may be brought out even more explicitly by replacing (T) and (COMP) with a single principle. Consider a family of predicates $\ulcorner Sat_n(x, y_1, \ldots, y_n)\urcorner$, and corresponding axioms:

$$\text{(SAT)} \qquad Sat_n(\ulcorner\phi\urcorner, y_1, \ldots, y_n) \leftrightarrow \phi(y_1, \ldots, y_n).$$

If we replace $\ulcorner Sat_0(\ulcorner\phi\urcorner)\urcorner$ by $\ulcorner Tr(\ulcorner\phi\urcorner)\urcorner$, we have (T). If we replace $\ulcorner Sat_1(\ulcorner\phi\urcorner, y)\urcorner$ by $\ulcorner y \in \{x|\phi(x)\}\urcorner$ we have (COMP).

A more general diagonal construction yields the inconsistency of (SAT). We need only be able to prove for any predicate $\ulcorner F(x, y_1, \ldots, y_n)\urcorner$ there is a $\ulcorner Q(y_1, \ldots, y_n)\urcorner$ such that:

$$Q(y_1, \ldots, y_n) \leftrightarrow F(\ulcorner Q\urcorner, y_1, \ldots, y_n).$$

[5] Many minimalists add a clause saying something like 'only non-problematic instances of (T)'. The success of this has been discussed by McGee (1992) and Simmons (1999).

This is a straightforward modification of the more familiar Diagonal Lemma (see Boolos, 1993). Let S be a theory that contains (SAT) and can prove this generalized Diagonal Lemma.

The proof that S is inconsistent is a generalization of both the Liar and Russell arguments. Consider the predicate $\ulcorner \neg Sat_n \urcorner$ for any n. Using the generalized Diagonal Lemma, we may find a predicate $\ulcorner \sigma_n(y_1, \ldots, y_n) \urcorner$ such that:

$$S \vdash \sigma_n(y_1, \ldots, y_n) \leftrightarrow \neg Sat_n\ (\ulcorner \sigma_n \urcorner, y_1, \ldots, y_n).$$

Combining this with (SAT), we have:

$$S \vdash Sat_n(\ulcorner \sigma_n \urcorner, y_1, \ldots, y_n) \leftrightarrow \sigma_n(y_1, \ldots, y_n) \leftrightarrow \neg Sat_n(\ulcorner \sigma_n \urcorner, y_1, \ldots, y_n).$$

For each n, the schema (SAT) produces inconsistency.

The argument here is the same as that used in both the Liar and Russell's paradoxes. For the case of $n = 0$, we have the Liar. The $\ulcorner Sat_0 \urcorner$ instances of (SAT) are just (T), and the generalized Diagonal Lemma yields $\ulcorner \lambda \urcorner$. For the case of $n = 1$, we have a version of Russell's paradox. The $\ulcorner Sat_1 \urcorner$ instances of (SAT) provide a version of (COMP). The generalized Diagonal Lemma give us a formula $\ulcorner \rho(y) \urcorner$ such that:

$$\rho(y) \leftrightarrow \neg Sat_1(\ulcorner \rho \urcorner, y).$$

This is essentially the Russell predicate. As with the original Russell predicate, applying it to itself we see:

$$\rho(\ulcorner \rho \urcorner) \leftrightarrow \neg Sat_1(\ulcorner \rho \urcorner, \ulcorner \rho \urcorner) \leftrightarrow \neg \rho(\ulcorner \rho \urcorner).$$

The use of (SAT) makes all the more clear that the formal differences between the Liar and Russell's paradox are incidental, amounting to no more than the presence of a parameter. This has virtually no effect on the way the paradoxes are generated.[6]

We now have seen two theories, pure minimalism and naive set theory, that are strikingly similar in an important respect. Both can be described as not being about anything in particular. We have also seen two paradoxes, or rather two versions of basically the same paradox, which show the two theories to have inconsistent formal components. From here on, however, the situations with truth and sets diverge rather drastically, as we shall see in the next section.

3. STRENGTHENED PARADOXES

Responses to these paradoxes are well known. In this section, I shall consider representative responses to each. I shall show that even taking a response to the Liar into account leaves pure minimalism vulnerable to an additional 'strengthened' paradox, while a standard way of responding to Russell's paradox is not so vulnerable.

[6] My presentation of M and N, and of the paradoxes, draws heavily on Feferman (1984). For further discussion of $\ulcorner Sat_n \urcorner$, and its relation to set theory, see Parsons (1974b).

I should mention that in pointing out the similarities between the Liar paradox and Russell's paradox, I am not particularly taking issue with the original distinction between semantic and logical paradoxes of Ramsey (1926). The issues he raised are somewhat different than those that bear here.

In the following sections, I shall use this difference to argue that not being about anything is a fatal flaw in minimalism.

Let us first consider how the pure minimalist might respond to the Liar. The pure minimalist may well want to maintain that the paradox is simply a technical 'glitch', and does not present a deep problem for the philosophical position. According to this stance, the right response is to hold on to the philosophical account of truth, as much as is possible, but find a way to modify the formal theory M to avoid what is seen as a merely technical failure. The usual approach is to say that though the basic idea behind (T) is right, it is technically misstated, and needs to be revised.

One leading idea for revising (T) is to make the truth predicate somehow *partial*, so that problematic sentences like $\ulcorner \lambda \urcorner$ come out neither true nor false. There are many different ways to implement this idea. For discussion purposes, I shall sketch one that is relatively simple, and remains in some ways close in spirit to M. The idea is to replace the axiom schema (T) with the following collection of inference rules:

$$\text{(INF)} \qquad \frac{P \vdash Tr(\ulcorner \phi \urcorner)}{P \vdash \phi} \quad \frac{P \vdash \neg Tr(\ulcorner \phi \urcorner)}{P \vdash \neg \phi}$$
$$\frac{P \vdash \phi}{P \vdash Tr(\ulcorner \phi \urcorner)} \quad \frac{P \vdash \neg \phi}{P \vdash \neg Tr(\ulcorner \phi \urcorner)}.$$

Call the resulting theory P. A theory like P can be modified or extended in many ways, but it will suffice to illustrate the point as it stands.[7] P makes truth partial in the following sense. For some sentences $\ulcorner \phi \urcorner$, we have $P \vdash Tr(\ulcorner \phi \urcorner)$, so according to P, $\ulcorner \phi \urcorner$ is true. For some sentences $\ulcorner \phi \urcorner$ we have $P \vdash \neg Tr(\ulcorner \phi \urcorner)$, so according to P, $\ulcorner \phi \urcorner$ is false. (Observe if $P \vdash \neg Tr(\ulcorner \phi \urcorner)$, then $P \vdash Tr(\ulcorner \neg \phi \urcorner)$.) But for some sentences, like $\ulcorner \lambda \urcorner$, we have neither, so P assigns such sentences neither the value true nor the value false. (In many cases, we expect to get results like $\ulcorner Tr(\ulcorner \phi \urcorner) \urcorner$ from P together with some other theory, which tells us the facts of some special science. It is the theory of truth together with the theories of physics, chemistry, etc. which tells us what is true. But the role of theories of special sciences does not matter for a sentence like $\ulcorner \lambda \urcorner$, which contains no terms from any special science not already incorporated into P. All that appear in $\ulcorner \lambda \urcorner$ are a sentence name, $\ulcorner Tr \urcorner$, and the negation operator. Hence, I shall ignore this role in what follows, and just speak of what P tells us is or is not true.)

Philosophically, it appears that the move from M to P does not change the commitments of pure minimalism. The rules in (INF) might be glossed as having the same analytic or definitional status as (T), and they do substantially the same job of introducing a device of disquotation. There are some complications, of course.

[7] Many theories implement partiality in a more model-theoretic way, along the lines of Kripke (1975). I have taken as my example for discussion a proof-theoretic approach, which modifies (T) explicitly. I have chosen this route mostly because it is simple to present, and eases the comparison with naive set theory. Most of what I say applies equally to other approaches to partiality.

The rules of (INF) appear in McGee (1991), though McGee has much more to say about the issue. For proof-theoretic investigation of similar systems, see Friedman and Sheard (1987). Much stronger systems invoking partiality are developed in Feferman (1991). I have discussed some further issues surrounding partiality in my (2004b).

Inference rules are not schemas whose instances can be analytically or definitionally true. But we can say that the transition from premise to conclusion is in some way analytically correct—perhaps correct in virtue of the meaning of 'true'—or is correct as a matter of stipulation, etc. Hence, the pure minimalist can give much the same gloss to these rules as was given to (T). Though there are a number of issues raised by the step from M to P, I think we can fairly grant P to the pure minimalist for argument's sake.

P is consistent; yet the Liar paradox makes trouble for it none the less. This is because of what is known as the *Strengthened Liar paradox*. We reason as follows. The partiality of P ensures that $\ulcorner\lambda\urcorner$ does not come out true, in that $P \nvdash Tr(\ulcorner\lambda\urcorner)$. So it seems, using P as a guide, we have come to conclude $\ulcorner\lambda\urcorner$ is not true, i.e. $\ulcorner\neg Tr(\ulcorner\lambda\urcorner)\urcorner$. But $\ulcorner\lambda\urcorner$ just 'says' $\ulcorner\neg Tr(\ulcorner\lambda\urcorner)\urcorner$. P itself tells us this, as $P \vdash \lambda \leftrightarrow \neg Tr(\ulcorner\lambda\urcorner)$. Thus, it appears that just relying on P, we have come to conclude $\ulcorner\lambda\urcorner$. We are now back in paradox.

Now, this inference cannot be carried out in P, so P remains consistent. But it still poses a problem. The conclusion we draw seems to be entirely correct, whether it can be carried out in P or not. P is designed precisely to make sure $\ulcorner\lambda\urcorner$ does not come out true. That is how consistency is achieved. So, we simply rely on P to come to the conclusion that $\ulcorner\lambda\urcorner$ is not true. In so far as P is supposed to capture the notion of truth, it appears this is just the conclusion $\ulcorner\neg Tr(\ulcorner\lambda\urcorner)\urcorner$. Opinions differ on just how serious a problem this is, and how it may be solved.[8] For our purposes here, all I need to insist upon is that the inference is intuitively compelling, and poses a problem that requires a solution one way or another.

The partiality response to the Liar, embodied in P, is vulnerable to the Strengthened Liar paradox. So, our modified pure minimalism based on P is likewise vulnerable. Continuing our comparison between the theory of truth and the theory of sets, we should consider a solution to Russell's paradox, and see if there is a strengthened version of this paradox to which the solution remains vulnerable.

There is, I believe, a standard response to Russell's paradox. It has two components, corresponding to the two components of naive set theory. First, the inconsistent formal theory N is replaced. There are a number of plausible candidates to replace it, but for illustration, let us take the Bernays-Gödel theory of sets and classes BGC. Second, the philosophical gloss on the naive theory is replaced by an account of the domains of sets and classes. Again there are a few competitors, but for argument's sake, let us assume some version of the iterative conception of set, together with the idea that (proper) classes are the extensions of predicates of sets.[9] Let us call the combination of these the *standard theory*.

[8] I have discussed this further in my (2001).

[9] BGC is a two-sorted theory, with variables $\ulcorner x\urcorner$ for sets and $\ulcorner X\urcorner$ for classes. The crucial axioms are restricted class comprehension $\ulcorner\forall X_1, \ldots, \forall X_n \exists Y(Y = \{x|\phi(x, X_1, \ldots, X_n)\})\urcorner$ where only set variables are quantified in $\ulcorner\phi\urcorner$, and axioms that say every set is a class and if $X \in Y$, then X is set. BGC also has the usual pairing, infinity, union, powerset, replacement, foundation, and choice axioms, as well as a class form of extensionality (see Jech, 1978).

For those unfamiliar with the iterative conception of set, it is roughly the idea that the sets are built up in stages. The process starts with the empty set $\emptyset$, then forms all the sets that can be formed out of those, i.e. $\emptyset$ and $\{\emptyset\}$, then all sets that can be formed out of those, i.e. $\emptyset$, $\{\emptyset\}$, and $\{\emptyset, \{\emptyset\}\}$, and so on. (For more thorough discussion, see Boolos (1971, 1989).)

In calling this theory standard, I by no means want to suggest that either of its components is beyond controversy. The iterative conception of set is still a matter of philosophical investigation and debate. Whether or not it justifies all the axioms of *BGC* is a matter of dispute. The continuum problem looms large as a difficulty of both components, and it is a commonplace idea that the formal theory *BGC* itself may not be strong enough for some purposes. None the less, both components are standard in that they are to be found in introductory set theory texts, and they enjoy reasonably wide, if often qualified, endorsement. Let us take the standard theory for granted, for purposes of this discussion.

The standard theory provides the *standard solution* to Russell's paradox. (COMP) has been dropped, and the revised theory *BGC* is presumably consistent. In the Liar paradox case, we were able to re-run the paradox to create a problem for our proposed solution via partiality. The question that needs to be asked, given remarkable similarity between the Liar paradox and Russell's paradox, is if we can do the same for the standard solution to Russell's paradox. Can we re-run Russell's paradox to get a strengthened version of it that poses a problem for this revised theory of sets?

The answer is that we cannot. As we have already observed, the formal theory *BGC* is presumably consistent (though for the usual Gödelian reasons, a proof of this is bound to be less than satisfying). But unlike the case of *P*, which is also consistent, the formal theory *BGC*, together with the philosophical component of the standard theory, give us a way to avoid the strengthened paradox.

To see why, let us first recall how the standard solution resolves Russell's paradox. According to the standard theory, the Russell class *R* is simply not a set. There is, according to the Bernays-Gödel theory, a proper class *R*, which we may think of as the extension of the predicate $\ulcorner \neg x \in x \urcorner$ where $\ulcorner x \urcorner$ ranges over sets. From the axiom of foundation, in fact, we know that *R* is coextensive with the class *V* of all sets. But *R* is a proper class; it is not a set. (Both the formal and informal sides of the theory confirm this.) Only sets are members of classes. Indeed, only set terms can occur on the left of the membership sign $\ulcorner \in \urcorner$, so we cannot even ask if $R \in R$ or $\neg R \in R$.

Pursuing the parallel between the paradoxes, we might attempt to reinstate a strengthened version of Russell's paradox by an analogous argument to the Strengthened Liar. We get the Strengthened Liar by noting that we still have the Liar sentence $\ulcorner \lambda \urcorner$, and asking what the theory in question tells us about its truth status. Of course, we still have the Russell *predicate* $\ulcorner \neg x \in x \urcorner$. In parallel with asking about the truth status of $\ulcorner \lambda \urcorner$, we might ask what falls in the extension of this predicate. In particular, we might ask if the object *R* falls in its extension. In the Liar case, we got the answer that $\ulcorner \lambda \urcorner$ is not true. Likewise, here we get the answer that *R* does not fall within the extension of the predicate $\ulcorner \neg x \in x \urcorner$. With the Liar, this led back to paradox, as we seemed to have reached exactly the conclusion $\ulcorner \neg Tr(\ulcorner \lambda \urcorner) \urcorner$.

But here the parallel ends. There is no such problem with *R*. There would have been, if the predicate $\ulcorner \neg x \in x \urcorner$ said that *x* does not fall in the extension of *x*. If so, we

BGC is convenient for this discussion because it talks about classes explicitly, which will be useful when we return to Russell's paradox. However, everything I say could be expressed perfectly well if we chose a formal theory like *ZFC* that describes only the domain of sets. We can always, on the informal side, introduce (predicative) classes as the extensions of predicates of sets.

would be forced to conclude $R \in R$, leading to paradox. But that is not what the predicate says at all. Rather, it says that the set *x* is not a member of the set *x*. We know that *R* is not a set, whereas the extension of $\ulcorner \neg x \in x \urcorner$ is a collection of sets, so *R* is not among them. This does not produce any paradox. The invitation to conclude that as *R* does not fall within the extension, then it does after all, is simply a confusion of sets with classes, and of set membership with falling within a class. The extension of the Russell predicate is determined only by the facts about set membership.

There is thus no strengthened Russell's paradox for the standard theory. It would be an over-statement to say that there are no problems for the standard theory presented by this sort of reasoning. For instance, if we ask why the set/class boundary falls were it does, and so why the universal class is not a set, we run into some well-known questions. Opinions differ on how pressing these questions are.[10] But regardless, it is striking that they do not present us with a paradox at all, and certainly do not reinstate a version of Russell's paradox. We see that both components of the standard theory—formal and philosophical—work together to ensure that the standard solution to Russell's paradox is invulnerable to a strengthened version.

We have now seen a crucial difference between the responses to the Liar and Russell's paradox. The response to the Liar via partiality is vulnerable to the Strengthened Liar, while the standard solution to Russell's paradox is not vulnerable to a strengthened version. This difference emerges in spite of the two paradoxes themselves being formally very similar, as we saw in section (2). As the difference is not in the paradoxes, it must lie in the theories of sets and of truth we build in response to the paradoxes. This shows us something important about the theory of truth. The theory given by pure minimalism, even modified to use the partial theory *P*, is unstable in the face of the paradox; while the standard set theory is not. This shows us both that this theory of truth is not adequate, and that it is lacking something which the standard set theory has. Our task now is to find out what standard set theory has and pure minimalism lacks, and see if a minimalist approach to truth can provide it.

4. STABILITY AND DIVISIVENESS

What is it about pure minimalism that makes it unstable in the face of the paradox, and what must a better theory of truth look like? We have seen that in spite of the paradoxes for sets and truth being remarkably similar in formal respects, the standard set theory is not so unstable. So, to see what form a viable theory of truth must take, we should begin by looking at what makes the standard set theory stable.

Recall the point from section (1) that both naive set theory and the pure minimalist theory of truth are in an important sense not about anything. The standard set theory is entirely different. It is genuinely about something: sets and classes. This is so in two ways. First of all, the formal theory *BGC* itself makes claims about the extent and nature of the domain of sets: claims that are true specifically of that domain, and do

[10] This sort of problem was originally pressed by Parsons (1974b). For a response, see Boolos (1998b).

not hold of other domains. It provides principles of nature, like extensionality and foundation, set existence principles like infinity and restricted comprehension, and some generation principles like powerset that show how sets are generated from other sets. The existence and generation principles work together to describe the extent of the domain of sets.

The iterative conception of set works with the formal theory, to help make clear what the intended interpretation of the theory is. This helps us to further understand the extent and nature of the sets. Together, the formal and informal components of the standard theory go some way towards describing the domains of sets and classes. Of course, they have some well-known failings. They do not by any means complete the task as they stand. But anyone who understands the two components of the standard theory can reasonably claim to understand something of what sets there are, and something of how they behave; understand well enough, at least, to understand something about the difference between sets and classes.

This is crucial to the stability of the standard solution to Russell's paradox. The formal and philosophical components of the theory come together to allow us to conclude that the Russell class R is not a set. Even if some aspects of the extent of the domain of sets remain unclear, both components clearly support this conclusion. Once the distinction between sets and classes is in place, and it is established that R is not a set, we can rely on this to decline the invitation to draw paradoxical conclusions. Once we see the difference between set membership and falling within a class, and understand the Russell predicate as a predicate of sets, the invitation may be seen clearly to be a gross mistake. We would like to make the same sort of reply to the Strengthened Liar. We would like to say that in coming to conclude the Liar sentence is not true after all, we make a similarly gross mistake. The question is what we need from the theory of truth to be able to do so.

In describing the domains of sets and classes, the standard theory of sets behaves as we expect of most theories. Most theories some way or another divide off their subject-matter from the rest of the world. It is the correctness of the description of the subject-matter provided by the theory that makes the theory true. The specification of the subject-matter can be done in part by the formal components of the theory, and in part by the informal or philosophical account of its intended interpretation. The correctness of both components are then determined by the subject-matter so specified. Let us call this feature feature *divisiveness*.[11]

Theories may be divisive in different ways and to different degrees. Perhaps the most striking case is the second-order theory of arithmetic. In this case, the formal theory itself fully determines its domain of application, by being categorical. Few theories live up to this rather demanding standard. Our standard set theory certainly does not. But together, the formal component of the standard theory—*BGC*—and the philosophical explanation of its intended interpretation—the iterative conception—do provide a substantial account of the domains of sets and classes, as we have

[11] A number of people have pointed out to me that 'divisive' may carry connotations which make it an unfortunate choice of term. An anonymous referee suggested 'discriminate' instead. However, to keep my terminology the same as that of "Minimalism and Paradoxes," I am leaving it unchanged.

observed. This is enough to at least partially specify the domain the theory is about, and to which it is responsible for its correctness. Perhaps most importantly for our purposes, the standard theory is divisive enough to draw some basic conclusions about what does *not* fall within the domain of *sets*. In particular, it makes a clear distinction between sets and classes, which enables us to conclude that the Russell class is not a set. This makes the theory divisive enough to be stable in the face of the paradox.

We expect empirical theories to be divisive to roughly this degree as well. An example much like the case of set theory is to be had from quantum mechanics. My friends in physics assure me that the domain of application of this theory is phenomena of very small scale. Just what is small scale is explained in part by the more informal gloss given to the theory, but also in part by the value of Planck's constant. More generally, it is no surprise that any decent theory should describe whatever it is about well enough to give some indication of what that domain is. Such an indication had better enable us to conclude, at least in some of the most basic cases, that something is not in the domain. For the most part, any good theory should be divisive.[12]

Both naive set theory and pure minimalism are notable for being as non-divisive as can be. Both are so by design: it is a reflection of philosophical commitments of both. This is a consequence of the point of section (1) that neither theory is properly about anything. As we saw there, neither theory describes any particular domain, to which it would be responsible for its truth. As I noted in section (1), the range of instances of (T) or (INF) is limited by syntax; but not because that is the limit of the domain these principles describe, but rather only because that is the limit of what can be written down. Pure minimalism still provides no real divisive content. It has no principles that reveal the nature of truth or the things to which truth applies. It thus has no principles that explain the nature of truth bearers and demarcate their domain. It cannot, for pure minimalism holds there is no such thing as a nature of truth or truth bearers!

Revising the formal theory by replacing M with P still leaves pure minimalism entirely non-divisive. Consider what P tells us about the domain of truths or truth bearers. It does prove some facts about truth, for instance, $P \vdash Tr(\ulcorner 1 + 1 = 2 \urcorner)$ (assuming that the theory is based on arithmetic). It even makes some existence claims, as we know $P \vdash \exists x Tr(x)$. But the theory is still as minimally divisive as can be. When the theory does prove something about the extent or nature of truth, it is

[12] In describing a theory as divisive if it divides off its subject-matter from the rest of the world, I do not mean to require that a divisive theory must only apply to a proper subdomain of *objects*, or in the case of a physical theory, a proper subdomain of physical objects. We should construe the theory's subject-matter broadly, to include not only the objects to which the theory applies, but also the properties of them it describes. (In Quinean jargon, we should consider both ontology and ideology.) Some of the important examples for this paper, including standard set theory, arithmetic, and the divisive theories of truth I shall consider below, are divisive in part by applying to particular proper subdomains of objects. I do not know if this is so for quantum mechanics, but it need not be for the theory to be divisive. It would be enough for the theory to apply to all physical objects, but to describe only their small-scale properties. To take a less difficult example, suppose that Newtonian mechanics had applied to all physical objects. My friends in philosophy of science tell me that even if it had, it would still be a theory that describes the *motions* of physical objects (when speeds are not too great). It would thus still be reasonably divisive.

only because something else having nothing to do with truth—nothing to do with its subject-matter—does most of the work. Once something else about the theory proves, for instance, $\ulcorner 1+1=2 \urcorner$, then the theory is able to deduce $\ulcorner Tr(\ulcorner 1+1=2 \urcorner) \urcorner$. From there, it can perform an existential generalization to get $\ulcorner \exists x Tr(x) \urcorner$. But the principles governing truth that are the heart of the theory only play a role in deducing these facts in the step from $\ulcorner 1+1=2 \urcorner$ to $\ulcorner Tr(\ulcorner 1+1=2 \urcorner) \urcorner$. The rest is a completely independent matter of arithmetic or logic. The theory can determine that something is the case, and then add that it is a truth, and then extract some logical consequences from this fact. But it cannot say anything about truths, the purported objects the theory is describing, more directly. None of the principles of truth in P by themselves make any substantial claims about truths in general, but only relate truth to specific sentences whose correctness has been independently decided. P states no general principles which can help us to understand the extent of the domain of objects to which truth applies. The theory P is thus only divisive where something unrelated to truth makes it so. This is just as the philosophical principles of pure minimalism would have it. Both the formal and informal components of pure minimalism make it as non-divisive as can be, and modifying the formal theory to incorporate partiality does nothing to change this.

To further our comparison with set theory, imagine a theory of sets more like our partial theory of truth P. It would have some principles which, once you concluded something else, could be used to conclude that some set exists, or has certain members. As a result, we could use the theory to generate a list of specific statements that say that something is a member of something else ($\ulcorner a \in b \urcorner$), or not a member of something else ($\ulcorner a \notin b \urcorner$). But the theory could make only trivial generalizations about membership or set existence, such as those that followed from elements of the list by logic (by analogy with $P \vdash \exists x Tr(x)$). Unlike *BGC*, it could tell us nothing more substantial about the extent and nature of the list. And unlike what the standard theory says about the Russell class, it could not tell us anything about *why* certain sentences could not be on the list.

In contrast to the standard theory, this makes the theory we are now imagining not divisive enough to enable us to reply to the attempt at a strengthened Russell's paradox. If we found a pair of objects a and b such that we determined somehow that the theory could not have on the list $\ulcorner a \in b \urcorner$, we would be able to conclude only that, as far as the theory tell us, $a \notin b$. We would not be able to draw any more subtle conclusions. Crucially, we would not be able to draw the conclusion that $\ulcorner a \in b \urcorner$ is not on the list because b is outside of the range of objects the theory is attempting to describe, or because a is the kind of object that cannot be a member of anything. Hence, if we were to observe that $\ulcorner R \in R \urcorner$ cannot be on the list, we would indeed fall into a strengthened Russell's paradox. We would have to conclude that as far as the theory tells us, $R \notin R$, from which the paradox follows.

The theory we are now imagining lacks the resources to make the reply of the standard solution to Russell's paradox. It cannot say that we do not have $\ulcorner R \in R \urcorner$ (it is not 'on the list') because R is a proper class, and so cannot enter into membership relations with any set or class. It cannot make this reply because it fails to draw a stable distinction between sets and classes. This failure in turn derives from its failure to be sufficiently divisive. A stable distinction between sets and classes could only follow from a sufficiently divisive specification of the theory's subject-matter, as we have with the standard theory. Without this much divisiveness, as we have seen, we are simply left with the paradoxical conclusion.

A theory of sets that fails to be divisive in this way cannot avoid the strengthened paradox. Pure minimalism likewise fails to be divisive, and so cannot avoid the Strengthened Liar. When we encounter $\ulcorner\lambda\urcorner$, pure minimalism, even modified by *P*, allows us nothing to say except that according to *P*, $\ulcorner\lambda\urcorner$ is not true. As pure minimalism fails to be divisive, we cannot go on to make any substantial claim about why this is so. We can cannot observe that it is so because $\ulcorner\lambda\urcorner$ falls outside the domain of the theory, or falls under a special category within the theory, as we say about the Russell class on the standard set theory. Thus, the non-divisiveness of pure minimalism leaves it with a paradoxical conclusion as well.

In section (1), I pointed out that pure minimalism, like naive set theory, is in a sense not about anything. We have seen in this section that this makes pure minimalism highly non-divisive. Following up on the discussion of paradoxes in sections (2) and (3), we have seen that failing to be reasonably divisive renders pure minimalism unable to respond to the Strengthened Liar, even when modified to use a partial theory like *P*. We have also seen that a sufficiently divisive theory, like the standard set theory, easily dismisses the attempt at a strengthened Russell's paradox, even though the two paradoxes are themselves virtually alike. The moral is that to have any prayer of avoiding the Strengthened Liar, we must look for a more divisive theory of truth. In the next section, we will consider what such a theory of truth might look like.

5. DIVISIVE THEORIES OF TRUTH

A viable theory of truth must be more divisive than pure minimalism. It must be more like the standard theory of sets in describing some specific domain. It must be about something! What would such a more divisive theory of truth look like? In this section, I shall offer some reasons to think that any more divisive theory of truth should be expected to be highly non-minimalist, or more generally non-deflationist. It will look much more like a correspondence-based theory.

As is often pointed out, it is too much to ask of a theory to characterize the domain of all truths. This would be impossibly demanding, as it would make the theory the complete theory of absolutely everything; containing all sorts of facts about all sorts of subjects.[13] But it is reasonable to ask the theory to be divisive about *truth bearers*. This could make the theory divisive about truth in the right way, as delineating a domain of truth bearers appropriately delineates the range of application of the truth predicate. If we can delineate its range of application properly, we might be able to offer a stable

[13] There is a significant question of whether there is really a coherent notion of absolutely all truths. Some reasons to be skeptical may be found in Grim (1991). Related issues are discussed in Parsons (1974a) and my (2004a). However, my worry here is much more pedestrian. It is already too much to ask of the theory of truth to contain all our current knowledge, whether or not a single complete theory of absolutely everything makes sense.

reason for declining to apply the truth predicate to the Liar sentence, which might lead to a stable solution to the Liar.

To describe what such a divisive theory might look like, we should return once more to the debate over deflationism. Deflationism is often contrasted with the idea of a correspondence theory of truth. Outside of its classical form, such as in works of Russell, it is notoriously difficult to state clearly what the correspondence theory of truth is. None the less, there is a core idea behind talk of correspondence which points towards more divisive theories.

The core idea is that truth bearers are *representational.* They describe the world as being some way, and are true if the world is that way. There is some leeway in just how we characterize truth bearers along these lines. We might say that truth bearers are propositions, where propositions are objects that encapsulate collections of truth conditions (to borrow a phrase from Hartry Field). Truth then obtains when the actual circumstance is among a proposition's truth conditions.

Propositions themselves are not really crucial to this idea. We could just as well say that truth bearers are *interpreted* sentences, where the interpretations provide truth values for sentences (in contexts, where appropriate). An extensional approach might stop there, while a more intensional approach might provide richer semantic contents for sentences. A similar theory could be given based on utterances rather than sentences.

Whether we opt for propositions or not, some idea of correspondence is usually built into these sorts of representational approaches. It comes up naturally in explaining how a sentence expresses a proposition, is given an interpretation, or is otherwise representational. In many cases, such explanations proceed by identifying the extensions—the referents—of components of a sentence (or intensions, built up from the referents). This accounts for representation in terms of 'word-to-world' relations, and how the worldly referents themselves interact. This is in essence a correspondence idea (though one that can avoid explicit commitments to facts).

More importantly, it is a highly non-minimalist idea. So long as being representational is itself construed as a substantial property, as it is on the correspondence-based approach, it implicates substantial properties of being a truth bearer and of truth. On this sort of approach, being a truth bearer is determined by whether a sentence expresses a proposition or is otherwise a representation, which is determined by substantial facts about reference. Likewise, whether or not a truth bearer is true is fixed by these facts. Such a representational account of truth and truth bearers embodies enough of the correspondence idea to stand in opposition not only to minimalism, but to most any form of deflationism.[14]

A theory along these lines could wind up being sufficiently divisive. An account of how truth bearers are representational could provide a suitably divisive picture of the domain of truth bearers, so long as it is able to make a principled distinction between

[14] I should note that in asking for a theory which is divisive about truth bearers, I am not raising the classic question of what the *primary* bearers of truth are. Rather, the issue here is one of distinguishing truth bearers, be they primary or otherwise, from non-truth bearers in a sufficiently divisive way.

sentences that genuinely provide truth bearers—express propositions or are otherwise representational—and sentences that may look like they provide truth bearers but do not. From this, we could distinguish two ways of failing to be true. One is to be a truth bearer that is not true, and the other is to fail to be a truth bearer at all. The partial theory *P* attempted to implement a distinction like this, by making the truth predicate partial. But in lacking a divisive theory of truth bearers, it failed to do so in a way that is sufficiently robust to resist the Strengthened Liar.

If we had a sufficiently robust, sufficiently divisive theory of truth bearers, we could genuinely begin to resist the Strengthened Liar. We could begin to do what pure minimalism could not. This claim needs to be made with some care. It is well known that appealing to propositions or truth-value gaps does *not* by itself suffice to solve the Strengthened Liar. My point is rather that a divisive theory of truth bearers is required to even begin to make progress towards addressing it. If we had such a theory, we could go this far in responding to the Strengthened Liar: when we conclude that $\ulcorner\lambda\urcorner$ is not true, we could come to two different conclusions. Either $\ulcorner\lambda\urcorner$ is (or expresses) a truth bearer, but is not true, or $\ulcorner\lambda\urcorner$ is not (or does not express) a truth bearer. The latter is very much analogous to concluding that the Russell class R is not a set. If we could reach this conclusion, we could resist the invitation to infer that we have concluded λ, just as when we say that R is not in the extension of the Russell predicate, we have not concluded $R \in R$. It was in not providing a principled way to draw this sort of distinction that P and pure minimalism left us nowhere to turn to avoid the Strengthened Liar.

Drawing a stable distinction between different ways of failing to be true is the first step in solving the Strengthened Liar. It is not the last. Crucially, we still need to explain what sense is to be made of the conclusion that $\ulcorner\lambda\urcorner$ is not true, even if this is because it is not a truth bearer. Many have taken this to require that we invoke a hierarchy of truth predicates. My own preference is for an approach relying more heavily on ideas about context dependence. I shall not advocate for any particular approach here.[15] I only claim that we need our theory of truth to draw the distinction between different ways of not being true to proceed at all. Drawing it requires being divisive about the domain of truth bearers, in just the way the standard theory is about sets, and in just the way that pure minimalism is not. Just as having *some* set/class distinction is not by itself enough to solve Russell's paradox, having some characterization of the domain of truth bearers is not by itself enough to solve the Strengthened Liar; but it is a necessary precondition.

I have argued that the required divisiveness might be found in the idea of truth bearers being representational, which forms the core of a correspondence-based theory of truth. Unlike the minimalist approach, this view maintains that there is some underlying nature to the property of truth, to be found in the ideas of representation and the world fitting a representation. If this yields substantial principles about what makes a well-formed sentence or utterance a genuine truth bearer, it could provide just the divisiveness we need to begin building a stable response to the

[15] I have discussed my own preferred approach to the Strengthened Liar in my (2001; 2004b; 2004c).

Liar. Of course, much more needs to be said to articulate the ideas of representation or correspondence. There have been a great many attempts to do so over the years. Rather than rehearse them here, I shall restrict myself to a much more modest goal. I shall conclude this section by pointing out that many of the leading ways of dealing with the Strengthened Liar rely on these ideas.

Most approaches to the Strengthened Liar ultimately rely on some sort of hierarchy. To see how this relates to correspondence and representation, we should start with the idea of *grounding* developed by Kripke (1975).[16] Sentences are divided into two classes: grounded and ungrounded. Grounded sentences are naturally assigned the values true or false, while ungrounded ones are not. An account of grounding can thus be used to provide a divisive account of truth bearers. The account Kripke gives of grounding is, informally speaking, one of starting by describing the world in non-semantic terms, and then building up successively more complex descriptions involving semantic expressions. This process reaches a fixed point, which circumscribes the domain of grounded sentences. This notion of grounding is naturally taken to provide just the sort of account of representation to which I alluded a moment ago. We start with the idea of reference for non-semantic terms, and on the basis of it assign truth values to sentences involving only these terms. We then progressively build up truth assignments for sentences containing semantic terms (namely the truth predicate). As is well known, the presence of self-reference and other semantic complexity makes this process transfinite, and it assigns truth values to some but not all sentences. Those that are assigned a truth value—either true or false—at the end of the process are the grounded ones. The picture that emerges is one of truth bearers being those sentences that ultimately describe the world through this iterative process. We may well say that these are the sentences that express propositions, or are representational. They are the truth bearers.

It is well known that in the face of the Strengthened Liar, Kripke ultimately appeals to "the ghost of the Tarski hierarchy" (1975, p. 80). This is a hierarchy based on grounding rather than on syntax. At the first level is the truth predicate produced by the process of generating grounded sentences just described. From the first level, we can ascend to the next level in the hierarchy by reflecting on the entire process, and noting that on the basis of it certain sentences are not true. On this view, the basis for the hierarchy is the idea of grounding. Grounding generates the first-level truths and falsehoods, and then provides the material for the construction of the next level through some sort of reflection on the process, and so on.[17]

With this in mind, we should consider the more traditional hierarchical approach stemming from Tarski (1935), which imposes a hierarchy of indexed truth predicates

[16] The term first appears in Herzberger (1970), which also makes some comparisons with paradoxes in set theory. Kripke's work provides an extensive development of the idea. Technically, in Kripke's framework, grounded sentences are those that are true or false in the least fixed point, and the informal sketch I give below echoes this idea. However, it would not change the basic points I make about grounding if one were to offer some reason for starting with a more extensive assignment of truth values and generating a larger fixed point.

[17] The idea of such reflection is fundamental to the approach of Parsons (1974a). Both Parsons and Burge (1979) pursue these sorts of ideas with much more explicit attention to the role of context. I have discussed the nature of this sort of reflection in my (2004b).

and syntactic restrictions on how they may appear in a sentence. We can see the syntactic requirements Tarski imposes as requiring an explicit syntactic representation of much the same kind of grounding process as Kripke describes (though in Tarski's work, lacking the transfinite and level-merging aspects). Hence, we can see Tarski's approach as based on the same kinds of ideas about representation or correspondence as Kripke's. It is hotly debated just how much of a deflationist Tarski is, and I do not want to take a stand on Tarski interpretation here so much as to point out how a natural understanding of his theory draws on correspondence ideas. Moreover, it is important to note that irrespective of this, his theory is divisive in one vital sense. Surface well-formedness is not sufficient to make a sentence a truth bearer. A sentence must also be, we might say, *well-indexed*: its truth predicates must be indexed so as to make it a genuine sentence of the Tarski hierarchy of languages. In so far as a characterization of this property must be part of the full theory of truth, we have a divisive principle. I have merely suggested that one source of such a principle is in correspondence-based ideas.

One other important example is the theory of Barwise and Etchemendy (1987). Their work is based on a situation theory which is explicitly modeled on ideas about the correspondence theory of truth as seen by Austin (1950).

I am not here advocating a particular solution to the Strengthened Liar; rather, I am claiming that a theory which can provide one must be divisive about truth bearers. Moreover, I claim, the general outlook of a representational approach to truth—embodying some aspects of the idea of correspondence—provides a basis for the development of such a divisive theory. We have seen how some of the leading theories that have been developed to solve the Strengthened Liar rely on this outlook.

We have now seen that pure minimalism is untenable, as it is unstable in the face of the Strengthened Liar. We have also seen why. In attempting to not be about any subject-matter, it is not sufficiently divisive to provide an adequate response to the paradox. We have also seen that theories which avoid strengthened paradoxes are divisive, both in the case of sets and of truth. Finally, we have seen that theories of truth based on ideas of representation can be sufficiently divisive to avoid the Strengthened Liar. These, we have seen, are fundamentally correspondence-based theories, and so are diametrically opposed to minimalism.

6. MINIMALISM AND DEFLATIONISM

I have stressed the parallel between pure minimalism and naive set theory on the one hand, and the divisiveness of standard set theory and a theory of truth able to address the Strengthened Liar on the other. In the face of the paradoxes, a viable theory of truth, like a viable theory of sets, must be sufficiently divisive. I have noted that the general idea of the correspondence approach to truth provides a basis for such divisiveness. This gives us good reason to expect a viable theory of truth to be non-minimalist, and more generally non-deflationist. But I have yet to consider explicitly whether any significant departures from pure minimalism could be sufficiently divisive, without giving up on their deflationist ideals.

In this section, I shall argue they cannot, in two steps. First, I shall argue that minimalist approaches cannot be sufficiently divisive, even if they depart from pure minimalism in some respects. The second step will be more tentative. In it, I shall turn my attention to whether any other sort of deflationism could be divisive enough. I shall there express some skepticism about how any philosophically rich deflationism could achieve the needed divisiveness.

Let us quickly review the problem for pure minimalism. It is clear from the arguments above that pure minimalism cannot yield a theory which is divisive on truth bearers. Philosophically, the position is intended to be as non-divisive as can be. Pure minimalism is, by its nature, not a theory about any domain, so it cannot be divisive. Formally, we have seen that moving from *M* to *P* does not help matters. This is striking, as *P* was designed to avoid the Liar. Its failure shows that just changing the formal theory does not make the view divisive. We can safely conclude that no change to the formal component compatible with the philosophical side of pure minimalism will make it divisive.

In section (1) I introduced pure minimalism as a simplified version of minimalism, useful for discussion purposes. We thus must consider whether any other minimalist positions might achieve the needed divisiveness, while staying faithful to the core ideals of minimalism. I shall address this question in two parts, and after them turn to the remaining task of discussing deflationism more generally.

First, there are a number of positions that depart from pure minimalism in ways that do not affect the issue of divisiveness about truth bearers. Some views that hold to the basic principles of minimalism take the truth predicate to apply to propositions. However, these views remain minimalist by saying that for each well-formed declarative sentence, there is a proposition expressed by it. There is no more an underlying fact about what makes a sentence express a proposition than there is an underlying nature of truth. Hence, these theories are no more divisive than pure minimalism on truth bearers.[18]

Second, we need to consider views that depart from pure minimalism in more significant ways, yet remain in some sense minimalist. An important example is a view derived from Wright (1992). Wright proposes a criterion for the truth aptness of sentences based on "surface constraints of syntax and discipline" (Wright, 1992, p. 35). Truth bearers are then the truth-apt sentences. The basic idea of "discipline" is that of norms of *use* which are typical of assertion, including the appropriateness of embedding in antecedents of conditionals, for instance. This is a significant departure from pure minimalism. As it is a departure precisely on the issue of truth aptness, it might allow for a minimalist theory to be a little more divisive than pure minimalism.[19]

[18] This is quite close to the view held by Ayer (1946). It may be the view held by Horwich (1990). There, Horwich provides a use-based account of proposition-individuation, but says little about the conditions for a sentence to express a proposition. As I mentioned, remarks in Horwich (1994) suggest a minimalist approach to this issue, which would make his view fall within the scope of the objection pressed here. (See Field (1992) for some further discussion.)

[19] Wright's use of the term 'minimalism' is slightly different from mine, making the question of whether to attribute a form of minimalism in my sense to him somewhat delicate. However, the idea

However, I do not see how anything along the lines of surface constraints of syntax and norms of use can provide a criterion that will help in the face of the Liar. The problem there is precisely that we do seem to have a sentence that meets the constraints of syntax and of discipline as well, but one that cannot be a truth bearer. Compare this once again with the set theory case. Proper classes bear all the surface marks of sets. They have members, are extensional, and so on. By these lights, the Russell class is as good a set as any other, and hence the paradox. What avoids the paradox is a much more substantial ontological distinction, between set-like objects that are sets, and those that are not. In the truth case, a criterion like Wright's still seeks to make anything that looks like a truth bearer be a truth bearer. This is the force of the constraints of syntax and discipline being *surface constraints*. The addition of discipline refines the notion of looking like a truth bearer, but the problem with the Liar is that we have something that *does* look like a truth bearer by any of these standards, and we need a theory that provides a stable answer that none the less it is not one. We need a more divisive theory than the combination of syntax and discipline can give.

Thus, a departure from pure minimalism along Wright's lines fails to be sufficiently divisive. But more importantly, the reason it fails shows us a much more general reason why anything that counts as minimalism will fail to be sufficiently divisive. A minimalist approach, however refined, is committed to there being no 'underlying nature' or 'substantial property' of truth. As a result, any minimalist approach is committed to there being nothing but overt surface properties that determine whether something is a truth bearer or not. Anything else would *eo ipso* provide an 'underlying nature' of truth, as it would provide some underlying facts about what counted as a truth bearer and what did not. This would make truth 'substantial' in just the way the minimalist says it is not. The Liar is such a problem in part because the Liar sentence really does appear on its face to be a perfectly good truth bearer. It meets all the overt or surface criteria for being one. Because of this, minimalist solutions to the Liar tend to be unstable in the face of the Strengthened Liar. When we try to make the Liar sentence not a truth bearer, we then find reasons to reinstate it as a truth bearer after all. Overt or surface criteria give us no reason to which we might appeal to reject this conclusion. Hence, the kind of divisiveness we need to begin to address the Strengthened Liar is precisely one that is not based on overt surface features. This is not something any brand of minimalism can provide.

Before leaving minimalism, we should pause to discuss briefly the argument of Jackson et al. (1994) that minimalism about truth does not by itself lead to minimalism about truth aptness. First of all, we are already in a position to see that simply avoiding commitments about truth bearers or truth aptness cannot save minimalism. As we saw in section (3), a theory like P is already formally silent on truth bearers, in that it has sentences for which it proves neither $\ulcorner Tr(\ulcorner \phi \urcorner) \urcorner$ nor $\ulcorner \neg Tr(\ulcorner \phi \urcorner) \urcorner$, yet it is vulnerable to the Strengthened Liar. It is vulnerable because it shows how to predicate truth of some sentences, and then shows that the Liar sentence is not among them. It lacks an explanation of why this is not simply the conclusion $\ulcorner \neg Tr(\ulcorner \lambda \urcorner) \urcorner$, and this in

of discipline is a natural one for a minimalist in my sense to appropriate, whether the result is Wright's own position or not.

turn leads to paradox. When it comes to the puzzle of the Liar, having a theory that is simply silent on truth bearers does not give a sufficiently divisive theory. To the contrary, what we need is a theory that gives us a principled distinction between truth bearers and things that look on the surface like truth bearers but are not, to which we can appeal in responding to the Strengthened Liar. If we somehow excise commitments on truth aptness from minimalism, we get no such thing. Instead, we get a theory which makes no substantial claims about truth bearers, but still allows the drawing of conclusions about applications of the truth predicate. This allows for the Strengthened Liar, and does not give us anything like the resources needed to resolve it.

Thus, the arguments of Jackson et al. (1994) cannot provide a safe haven for minimalism. They note that an instance of the T-schema, such as ' 'torture is wrong' is true iff torture is wrong', only confers truth conditions if the right-hand side of the biconditional is itself truth apt. This claim appears to be entirely correct, but it does not help with the issue at hand. At best, it provides a way for a minimalist to be silent about issues of truth aptness. As we have seen, this will not suffice.[20]

I conclude that no minimalism can be divisive enough to respond to the Strengthened Liar, and so no minimalism is tenable. This now brings us to the second issue of this section: the question of whether some other sort of deflationism about truth, somehow different from minimalism in any of its forms, could evade the problem I have raised. The vague nature of the category of deflationism makes this question rather hard to answer, but I shall offer some reasons why the problem is very difficult for deflationist positions to overcome.

As far as I can tell, the only deflationist positions which might find the needed divisiveness are those that, unlike minimalism, do include a substantial and divisive theory of propositions or of content, but still remain committed to a strong form of (T) and hold it to be analytic or necessary. The commitment to the necessity of (T) is a mark of deflationism, but none the less it is not easy to formulate such a position in a way that remains deflationist. Ramsey (1927) is sometimes offered as an example, but I am inclined to side with Field (1986) in saying that Ramsey is not a genuine deflationist. Ramsey interpretation aside, the point is that any view that has a substantial account of propositions as encapsulating *truth* conditions can certainly have a strong version of (T), but is no more or less deflationary than its account of truth conditions. Non-deflationism about truth conditions is non-deflationism.[21]

[20] Jackson et al. (1994) go on to offer a more substantial account of truth aptness. As I shall discuss below in footnote 22, I do not see how this winds up leaving room for minimalism at all.

It should be stressed that the notion of truth aptness at issue here is the fairly weak one of application of the truth predicate making sense. So long as application of the truth predicate is governed by enough discipline to make overt contradictions repugnant, we have to deal with paradoxes that may arise for it. This is the case whether or not the assertions in question wind up being truth apt in the sense relevant to, say, non-cognitivism. Thus, I believe that the issues primarily under consideration by Jackson et al., as well as those debated by Boghossian (1990), Wright (1992), and Soames (1999), are somewhat different than those being investigated here. (Surely no one ever really thought non-cognitivism could solve the Liar!)

[21] As was pointed out in Parsons (1974a), *any* view that contains a theory of propositions as truth conditions leads to a strong version (T). On such a view, the truth predicate is just the operation of evaluating an intension on the actual world. In the notation of intensional logic, we have

The only way to pursue this line as a deflationist seems to be to offer a *non-truth-conditional* account of propositions or content, and yet hold that propositions (or contentful sentences) are truth bearers.[22]

This is close to the view held by Field (1986; 1994). Field certainly would not opt for propositions, but he employs a robust notion of content based on conceptual role. This is coupled with a deflationary account of truth, in which the truth predicate applies to sentences that the speaker understands, and thus which have content. The relation between the two sides of (T) is one of 'cognitive equivalence', which is, presumably, at least as strong as the necessity or analyticity minimalism proposes.[23] As the notion of content to which Field appeals is itself not at all minimal, there is room for a view like this to be divisive about truth bearers. It will be, so long as it yields a substantial criterion for whether a sentence is contentful, and so can stand as a truth bearer.

Though a theory like Field's can be divisive about truth bearers, it is not at all clear to me how it can be sufficiently divisive to respond to the Strengthened Liar. It remains unclear how the theory can really explain why the Liar sentence is not one we understand, and so is not a truth bearer. The same kinds of points as I raised above about syntax and discipline apply here. The Liar looks like a well-behaved sentence. We understand each of the terms in it, and we can use it in apparently well-structured arguments. Hence, it may well appear that we should count the Liar sentence as one we understand. (As it might be put, which part of $\ulcorner \neg Tr(\ulcorner \lambda \urcorner) \urcorner$ don't you understand?) Moreover, when we consider the Strengthened Liar, we are confronted with perfectly good cases in which we do seem to understand it. Yet if we have good reason to count the Liar sentence as one we do understand, it counts as a contentful sentence—as a truth bearer. If so, then the theory is not divisive enough after all.

This is not the end of the matter. Clearly Field or others may have more to say.[24] So let me simply express skepticism about how a theory along these lines can be adequately divisive. Finally, let me note that the challenge I have raised to this sort of

something like $\ulcorner Tr(p) \leftrightarrow {}^{\vee}p \urcorner$. Coupled with the principle of intensional logic $\ulcorner {}^{\vee\wedge}\phi \leftrightarrow \phi \urcorner$, we get the T-schema in the form $\ulcorner Tr({}^{\vee\wedge}\phi) \leftrightarrow \phi \urcorner$. This has the status of a truth of mathematics, if not logic. The truth predicate is basically the operation of function evaluation. Even so, it is not clear that we should conclude that it is entirely trivial. Having self-applicative truth puts us in an untyped world, and experience with, say, the untyped λ-calculus shows that function application in such a setting is far from trivial.

22 I suspect that Jackson et al. (1994) miss this point. They consider a view of truth aptness based in part on whether a sentence expresses the content of a belief, while belief states are said to be "designed to fit the way things are" (p. 297). This appears already to bring with it a correspondence-like notion of truth for what sentences express, and so is not anything a deflationist can accept.

23 Field also considers some departures from the requirement that the truth predicate only apply to sentences the speaker understands, especially in the postscript to Field (1994) provided in Field (2001).

24 Field has in fact said more. At some points, he has asked if the cognitive equivalence of $\ulcorner Tr(\ulcorner \phi \urcorner) \urcorner$ and $\ulcorner \phi \urcorner$ really leads to (T) (cf. Field, 2001). More recently (2002), he has considered the possibility of changing the logic of $\ulcorner \rightarrow \urcorner$ to allow for the truth of all instances (T), including the paradoxical ones, while retaining consistency. This might keep the link between cognitive equivalence and (T). I remain skeptical, for several reasons. First of all, I remain somewhat skeptical of this sort of (fairly radical) revision of logic, especially if what we are offered is supposed to be metaphysically deflationary. Moreover, I remain uncertain if the kind of strengthened paradoxes that have been

theory is a general one to deflationism. The most likely way to provide a divisive yet deflationist theory, I have suggested, is to provide a theory which invokes a non-truth-conditional notion of proposition or of content. As the response to Field shows, being sufficiently divisive on truth bearers is not simply a matter of having *something* to say about content or propositions. It must be enough to explain what is problematic about sentences like the Liar. It is hard to see how this could be done without returning to the correspondence-based ideas I canvassed in section (5). At the very least, it is hard to see how this could be done without establishing a link between propositions, divisively and non-truth-conditionally described, and representational or otherwise non-deflationist aspects of truth bearers. Can this be done without converting the apparently non-truth-conditional account of propositions into a substantial account of truth and truth conditions? More generally, can it be done while retaining deflationism? I am inclined to doubt it can.[25]

Deflationism is a wide and vaguely defined area, so such sweeping conclusions should be drawn with care. At least, I think it is a fair challenge to deflationists, especially minimalists or those of Field's variety, to ask how sufficient divisiveness can be achieved.

REFERENCES

Austin, J. L., 1950. Truth. *Aristotelian Society Supplementary Volume* 24: 111–29. Reprinted in Austin (1961).

——, 1961. *Philosophical Papers*. Oxford: Oxford University Press. Edited by J. O. Urmson and G. J. Warnock.

Ayer, A. J., 1946. *Language, Truth and Logic*. 2nd edn. London: Victor Gollancz.

Barwise, J. and J. Etchemendy, 1987. *The Liar*. Oxford: Oxford University Press.

Boghossian, P. A., 1990. The status of content. *Philosophical Review* 99: 157–84.

Boolos, G., 1971. The iterative conception of set. *Journal of Philosophy* 68: 215–32. Reprinted in Boolos (1998a).

——, 1989. Iteration again. *Philosophical Topics* 42: 5–21. Reprinted in Boolos (1998a).

——, 1993. *The Logic of Provability*. Cambridge: Cambridge University Press.

——, 1998a. *Logic, Logic, and Logic*. Cambridge: Harvard University Press.

my focus here may be reintroduced into Field's theory, especially if they make use of meta-level reasoning that bypasses the special logic Field imposes on $\ulcorner\rightarrow\urcorner$. This raises a great many issues, too many to be discussed here. So let me just cautiously register my skepticism.

[25] One view that is probably not open to the objection I have raised per se is that sketched in Soames (1984). The idea there is to construe truth as a property of *abstract* interpreted languages. Though he does not pursue the matter, much of what I have said about how a theory could be made sufficiently divisive could easily be carried over to this setting. As I understand it, the view is offered as deflationist in that truth is construed as not a metaphysically important notion, but more a piece of mathematics. (Soames (1999) takes a similar stance towards deflationism, and discusses the Liar explicitly. In response to the Strengthened Liar, he there appeals to a "Tarski-like hierarchy" (p. 181).) As Soames is well aware, this is very far indeed from minimalism, and even from most other positions that offer themselves as deflationist. I see no reason to argue over who gets the term 'deflationist', but I believe Soames' position is significantly different from the kinds under discussion here.

——, 1998b. Reply to Charles Parsons' "Sets and Classes". In *Logic, Logic, and Logic*, pp. 30–6. Cambridge: Harvard University Press.

Burge, T., 1979. Semantical paradox. *Journal of Philosophy* 76: 169–98. Reprinted in Martin (1984).

Feferman, S., 1984. Toward useful type-free theories, I. *Journal of Symbolic Logic* 49: 75–111. Reprinted in Martin (1984).

——, 1991. Reflecting on incompleteness. *Journal of Symbolic Logic* 56: 1–49.

Field, H., 1986. The deflationary conception of truth. In G. MacDonald and C. Wright, eds., *Fact, Science and Morality*, pp. 55–117. Oxford: Blackwell.

——, 1992. Critical notice: Paul Horwich's *Truth. Philosophy of Science* 59: 321–30.

——, 1994. Deflationist views of meaning and content. *Mind* 103: 249–84. Reprinted in Field (2001).

——, 2001. *Truth and the Absence of Fact*. Oxford: Oxford University Press.

——, 2002. Saving the truth schema from paradox. *Journal of Philosophical Logic* 31: 1–27.

Friedman, H. and M. Sheard, 1987. An axiomatic approach to self-referential truth. *Annals of Pure and Applied Logic* 33: 1–21.

Glanzberg, M., 2001. The Liar in context. *Philosophical Studies* 103: 217–51.

——, 2004a. Quantification and realism. *Philosophy and Phenomenological Research* 69: 541–572.

——, 2004b. Truth, reflection, and hierarchies. *Synthese* 142: 289–315.

——, 2004c. A contextual-hierarchical approach to truth and the Liar paradox *JPL* 33: 27–88.

Grim, P., 1991. *The Incomplete Universe*. Cambridge: MIT Press.

Herzberger, H. G., 1970. Paradoxes of grounding in semantics. *Journal of Philosophy* 67: 145–67.

Horwich, P., 1990. *Truth*. Oxford: Basil Blackwell.

——, 1994. The essence of expressivism. *Analysis* 54: 19–20.

Jackson, F., G. Oppy, and M. Smith, 1994. Minimalism and truth aptness. *Mind* 103: 287–302.

Jech, T., 1978. *Set Theory*. New York: Academic Press.

Kripke, S., 1975. Outline of a theory of truth. *Journal of Philosophy* 72: 690–716. Reprinted in Martin (1984).

Martin, R. L., ed., 1984. *Recent Essays on Truth and the Liar Paradox*. Oxford: Oxford University Press.

McGee, V., 1991. *Truth, Vagueness, and Paradox*. Indianapolis: Hackett.

——, 1992. Maximal consistent sets of instances of Tarski's schema (T). *Journal of Philosophical Logic* 21: 235–41.

Parsons, C., 1974a. The Liar paradox. *Journal of Philosophical Logic* 3: 381–412. Reprinted in Parsons (1983).

——, 1974b. Sets and classes. *Noûs* 8: 1–12. Reprinted in Parsons (1983).

——, 1983. *Mathematics in Philosophy*. Ithaca: Cornell University Press.

Quine, W. V., 1986. *Philosophy of Logic*. 2nd edn. Cambridge: Harvard University Press.

Ramsey, F. P., 1926. The foundations of mathematics. *Proceedings of the London Mathematical Society, Second Series* 25: 338–84. Reprinted in Ramsey (1931).

——, 1927. Facts and propositions. *Aristotelian Society Supplementary Volume* 7: 153–70. Reprinted in Ramsey (1931).

——, 1931. *The Foundations of Mathematics and Other Logical Essays*. London: Routledge and Kegan Paul.

Simmons, K., 1999. Deflationary truth and the Liar. *Journal of Philosophical Logic* 28: 455–88.
Soames, S., 1984. What is a theory of truth? *Journal of Philosophy* 81: 411–29.
——, 1999. *Understanding Truth*. Oxford: Oxford University Press.
Tarski, A., 1935. Der Wahrheitsbegriff in den formalizierten Sprachen. *Studia Philosophica* 1: 261–405. Translation by J. H. Woodger as "The Concept of Truth in Formalized Languages" in Tarski (1983).
——, 1983. *Logic, Semantics, Metamathematics*. 2nd edn. Indianapolis: Hackett. Edited by J. Corcoran with translations by J. H. Woodger.
Wright, C., 1992. *Truth and Objectivity*. Cambridge: Harvard University Press.

9

Do the Paradoxes Pose a Special Problem for Deflationism?

Anil Gupta

The Liar and other semantic paradoxes pose a difficult problem for all theories of truth. Any theory that aims to improve our understanding of the concept of truth must, when fully stated, include an account of the paradoxes. Not only deflationism but also its competitors—for instance, correspondence and coherence theories—must ultimately address the paradoxes. The question that concerns me in this chapter is whether it is especially urgent for deflationism to do so. Are the paradoxes a special threat, a special problem, for deflationism? I will argue that they are not.[1] Deflationists can leave the paradoxes to the specialists to puzzle over. It is the specialists who will be well served if they keep some insights of deflationism firmly in view.

1.

Deflationism rests on some claims about our ordinary concept of truth. The central one of these claims—and the one that is threatened by the paradoxes—is that sentences of the following form

(T) '- - - -' is true iff - - - -,

the *T-biconditionals*, capture the meaning of 'true'.[2] Thus W. V. O. Quine calls truth a device of "disquotation". The effect of adding 'is true' to the quotation name ' 'Snow is white' ', Quine says, is to cancel the quotation marks and to yield the equivalent sentence 'Snow is white'.[3] According to Paul Horwich, the T-biconditionals implicitly

I am grateful to Professor Bradley Armour-Garb for helpful discussions and for nudging me to write this paper.

[1] Keith Simmons (1999) and Elke Brendel (2000) have argued that the paradoxes undermine deflationism. Bradley Armour-Garb and JC Beall (2001) have responded in detail to Simmons's argument.

[2] This is a rough formulation of the claim. It will be sharpened a little in the following discussion.

[3] Quine writes in *Pursuit of Truth* (1992), "To ascribe truth to the sentence ['Snow is white'] is to ascribe whiteness to snow.... Ascription of truth just cancels the quotation marks. Truth is disquotation (p. 80)." A little later, Quine adds that the disquotation account is "a full account: it explicates

define 'true'.[4] Similar ideas are expressed by other deflationists, including Hartry Field, Christopher Hill, and Michael Williams.[5]

Now, as is typical in philosophy, there is something very right in this central claim of the deflationists, and there is also something quite wrong. Let us try to isolate the element that is right. Let us begin by accepting that truth can, in one of its senses, be applied to sentences, and let us agree to focus on its application to the sentences of English. Further, let us agree to neglect the complications that indexicals, context sensitivity, and ambiguity create in any account of truth. The above rough formulation of the deflationists' claim does not get off the ground unless we make these concessions. Moreover, as far as our present interests are concerned, the concessions are inconsequential.

The deflationists' claim contains one principle that is undoubtedly true. This is the Closure principle:

> *The Closure principle.* The following two rules of inference, TI and TE, hold for categorical affirmations:
> (TI) A; therefore, 'A' is true
> (TE) 'A' is true; therefore, A.[6]

Note that this principle is very weak: it licenses the interchange of A and ' 'A' is true' only in categorical contexts, not in contexts of hypothetical reasoning. For example, it does not entitle one to infer 'Snow is black' from the *supposition* that ' 'Snow is black' is true'. On the other hand, if one flat out asserts ' 'Snow is black' is true' then the Closure principle commits one to 'Snow is black'. Because of its weakness, the Closure principle does not yield inconsistencies even in the presence of paradoxical sentences. Set 'the Liar' to be a name of the sentence

> The Liar is not true.

If TI and TE had unconditional validity then a contradiction would be immediate: the supposition 'The Liar is not true' would yield 'The Liar is true', and the supposition 'The Liar is true' would yield 'The Liar is not true'. But such applications of TI and TE are not licensed by the Closure principle, for they occur within hypothetical contexts. The Closure principle, it is easy to show, remains consistent even when a language is enriched with all kinds of resources for expressing self- and cross-reference.[7]

clearly the truth or falsity of every clear sentence (p. 93)." Quine's writings have exercised a great influence on contemporary deflationism, but we should be cautious about attributing any full and unambiguous deflationism to him.

[4] *Meaning* (1998), p. 107. Horwich's remark is actually directed to propositional truth. But he treats the other notions of truth in a parallel way; see Horwich (1990).

[5] See Field (2001), Hill (1987) and (2002), and Williams (1986). There are significant differences in the positions of the various deflationists, but these can be neglected for the argument of this chapter. I will work with disquotationalism as a representative deflationary theory. Let me stress, though, that I am not attributing disquotationalism to all deflationists.

[6] Here and at many places below, quotes should be understood in the manner of Quine's corner quotes.

[7] Friedman and Sheard (1987) is a rich study of the principles that can, and those that cannot, consistently be held in the context of self-referential truth. See McGee (1991) and Halbach (1994) for further illumination.

The Closure principle is plainly correct even for paradoxical sentences. For example, a person who categorically affirms 'The Liar is not true' is thereby committed to ' 'The Liar is not true' is true'. If the person refuses to recognize the commitment, he is either confused or fails to fully grasp the meaning of 'true'. The Closure principle ought, therefore, to be respected by all theories of truth, deflationist and non-deflationist alike. And, indeed, all the main approaches to the paradoxes validate the principle.[8]

2.

Let us now turn to something stronger and more troublesome, namely, the claim that the T-biconditionals are correct. Is this claim right? Plainly, on some ways of understanding 'true', the claim is doubtful. It is sometimes said, following P.F. Strawson, that sentences whose presuppositions fail—e.g., 'The king of France is bald'—are neither true nor false. And it is also said that truth attributions to these sentences—e.g., ' 'The king of France is bald' is true'—are simply false. If this is right, then the two sides of the T-biconditionals are not always equivalent, and we cannot unqualifiedly endorse the biconditionals. Nevertheless, there is a notion of truth on which the semantic value of a sentence is the same as that of its truth-attribution. On this notion, if A is neither true nor false, then ' 'A' is true' is also neither true nor false. If A has a semantic value v then ' 'A' is true' also has the semantic value v, and conversely. It is this notion—sometimes called the *weak* notion of truth (Yablo 1985)—that is of primary interest to the deflationists. Deflationists do need to give some account of the other notions of truth. But let us not pause to reflect on what they might say about them. Let us work with the weak notion and return to the question whether the T-biconditionals can now be deemed to be correct. The restriction to the weak notion ensures that the T-biconditionals of ordinary, unproblematic sentences are correct. The question is whether those of paradoxical sentences such as the Liar are also correct.

I suggest that we do not rush to give a definitive answer to this question. Let us recognize instead that a strong case can be made for both answers, that the

[8] See my paper "Truth" for a survey of the main approaches. The axiomatic theory KF articulated by Solomon Feferman (1984) does violate the Closure principle. In this theory, the inference rule "P, therefore 'P' is true" is not admissible: P can be a theorem, yet ' 'P' is true' can fail to be one. (Actually, in KF, one can prove of some theorems that they are not true.) KF is elegant, but it is not a good account of the actual logic of truth, and Feferman has not proposed it as such. McGee (1991) contains a valuable discussion of KF.

The Closure principle is not respected by the approach Horwich takes to the paradoxes (Horwich 1990, p. 42). Horwich reacts to the paradoxes by excluding some of the T-biconditionals from the theory of truth. And he does not supplement the theory in any way to prevent the loss of Closure. The failure of Closure is, I think, a grave flaw in Horwich's approach. One consequence of it is that Horwich's theory fails to sustain his own claims about the concept of truth—for example, his claims about the explanatory power of his theory and about the generalization function of truth. Horwich recognizes the problem in the second edition of his book (p. 42, fn. 21), but I think he underestimates it.

T-biconditionals are not correct and that they are correct. The T-biconditional for the Liar,

'The Liar is not true' is true iff the Liar is not true,

is equivalent, by the substitutivity of identicals, to the biconditional,

The Liar is true iff the Liar is not true,

which is only a few short steps removed from an explicit contradiction. Further, it appears, 'not' can express a concept of negation on which the semantic values of P and not-P are always distinct. If so, there are readings on which the two sides of the above biconditional have different values; hence, on such readings, the biconditional is incorrect.

On the other hand, there are equally strong reasons to think that the biconditional is correct. The Liar exhibits a specific type of semantic instability: the idea that the Liar is true forces recognition of the idea that the Liar must then not be true, and the latter idea, in turn, forces recognition of the earlier one. This semantic behavior is quite special: it is quite different, for example, from that of the Truth-teller ("the Truth-teller is true"). The T-biconditional for the Liar seems to capture something right and important about the Liar.

Let us buttress this point in another way. The Liar remains puzzling even after we recognize that its T-biconditional is not true. Our attitude towards the Liar paradox is quite different from that towards other popular puzzles and paradoxes. With the latter, our perplexity disappears completely once we concede that some crucial idea or presupposition that we brought to the puzzle is false. But with the Liar this is not so. Our perplexity remains even after we have been brought to concede that its T-biconditional is untrue. Furthermore—and this is a more important point—we continue to use 'true' in ways that presuppose some sort of general equivalence between sentences and their truth attributions. These uses are not marginal, but central and important. Here is an example. Deflationists have observed that the truth predicate enables us to generalize over sentence positions. Consider the sentence 'Self-conjunctions of truths are true', or more formally,

(1) For all sentences x, if x is true then 'x & x' is true.

Deflationists point out that this sentence serves as a universal generalization of

(2) If A then A & A.[9]

Observe that in (2) the variable 'A' occupies sentence positions. In contrast, in (1) the variable 'x' occupies name positions. The truth predicate in (1) enables us to gain the effect of generalizing over sentence positions while using variables that occupy name positions. Deflationists see in this fact the distinctive contribution of the truth predicate, and they view 'true' as having a purely logical function. This last idea should certainly be subjected to a skeptical inquiry before it is accepted. But the earlier

[9] I am not suggesting that all generalizations involving truth can be understood in this way. I am claiming only that in this example it is correct to take (1) as having the force of generalizing (2).

idea, that (1) expresses a generalization of (2), captures our ordinary understanding of (1). Observe, though, that (1) cannot serve as a generalization of (2) if we unequivocally reject the T-biconditionals for paradoxical sentences. For (1) yields only

(3) If 'the Liar is not true' is true then 'the Liar is not true & the Liar is not true' is true.

To serve as a generalization of (2), it should yield

(4) If the Liar is not true then the Liar is not true & the Liar is not true.

Without the T-biconditionals for the Liar and its self-conjunction, we lack the resources to move from (3) to (4), and back from (4) to (3).[10] The T-biconditionals, in some readings of them, are somehow in play in our understanding of (1).

Even if we are inclined to reject the T-biconditionals for the paradoxical sentences, we must recognize that the concept of truth imposes some constraints on the treatment of these sentences. The concept does not leave the status of paradoxical sentences completely open.[11] Both the Liar and its self-conjunction are paradoxical. So, if the status of these sentences were completely open, then the supposition that the Liar is true and its self-conjunction untrue should be coherent. But plainly it is not: there is a conceptual constraint that requires that the Liar and its self-conjunction be treated in the same way. The source of this constraint lies in the truth conditions—however peculiar—that the T-biconditionals attribute to these sentences. Hence, an explanation of the constraint—as well as of numerous others like it—must appeal to the T-biconditionals.

In summary, the argument I am making is this. (i) The T-biconditionals explain the distinctive character of the Liar and other paradoxical sentences. These biconditionals explain how and why the behavior of paradoxical sentences differs from that of unproblematic sentences and also from other types of pathological sentences. (ii) The concept of truth imposes constraints even on the treatment of paradoxical sentences. An explanation of these constraints will need to appeal to the T-biconditionals. And, finally, (iii) *the T-biconditionals for paradoxical sentences play an indispensable role in ordinary uses of some unproblematic sentences.* In view of these three facts, it is unlikely that we can obtain a good account of the concept of truth if we unequivocally abandon the T-biconditionals for paradoxical sentences. Our account of truth must somehow work with these biconditionals.

The intuition that the T-biconditionals are correct is so strong that some theorists of truth and paradox have been moved to espouse the *Inconsistency View*, the view that the principles governing truth are inconsistent. Alfred Tarski wrote that the paradoxes "prove emphatically that the concept of truth . . . when applied to colloquial language in conjunction with the normal laws of logic leads inevitably to confusions and contradictions" (Tarski (1935); p. 267 in Tarski (1956)). Charles Chihara has

[10] Note that the Closure principle is insufficient to yield the desired equivalence.

[11] Scott Soames (1999) has proposed that 'true' is a "partially defined" predicate: the rules governing 'true' leave it open whether paradoxical sentences fall, or do not fall, under the concept of truth. See my "Partially defined predicates and semantic pathology" (2002) for some criticisms of Soames's proposal.

defended Tarski's suggestion at some length (1979). Graham Priest has gone a step further and has argued not only that the principles are inconsistent but that they prove some contradictions to be true (1979 and 1987). I myself think that the Inconsistency View faces serious problems in explaining ordinary uses of 'true'. If the Inconsistency theorist accepts classical logic, as Tarski and Chihara do, he has difficulty explaining how even simple truth attributions (e.g., ' 'Snow is white' is true') manage to have coherent content.[12] If, on the other hand, the theorist abandons classical logic, as Priest does, then he has difficulty explaining our ordinary inferential practices. In any case, the point I want to stress is that the Inconsistency View, even if it misjudges the price of inconsistency, is based on an insight: none of the T-biconditionals can summarily be dismissed.[13]

I have been arguing that there is something correct about the T-biconditionals. I do not want to suggest, however, that this idea is a comfortable one, much less that the above considerations show us how to make sense of it. I hope the argument so far establishes this much: that we need a better understanding of the T-biconditionals and, in particular, of the connective 'iff' that occurs in them. It is not hard to supply a meaning for 'iff' under which the T-biconditional for the Liar sentence is false. The problem is to specify a meaning under which it is true. A sense of 'iff' under which the biconditional is false is as follows. 'A iff B' is true if and only if A and B have the same semantic value (i.e., they are both true, or both false, or both neither-true-nor-false, or both have the degree of truth *i* or...); otherwise, it is false. Let us call 'iff' so understood the *material biconditional* and use the sign '≡' for it. Then, the very meaning of 'not' dictates that the material T-biconditional

> 'The Liar is not true' is true ≡ the Liar is not true

is not true. It is not so easy, however, to give a reading of 'iff' under which the biconditional is true.[14] This should not be surprising: the task of specifying such a sense for 'iff' is a crucial part of a theory of truth and paradox. Let us simply mark the problem for now by symbolizing the troublesome 'iff' as '$\overset{?}{\leftrightarrow}$'. And let us accept it is a desideratum on a theory of truth that it supply an account of '$\overset{?}{\leftrightarrow}$' that sustains the following principle.

> *The Tarski principle.* The biconditionals
> (T?) '- - - -' is true $\overset{?}{\leftrightarrow}$ - - - -
> are correct for the weak notion of truth.

From now on, I shall understand by 'T-biconditionals' sentences of the form (T?). Claims about T-biconditionals will remain schematic until a sense is given to 'iff' ('$\overset{?}{\leftrightarrow}$').

[12] See Gupta and Belnap (1993), Chapter 1, for more on this point.

[13] It is this fact, I think, that has led some deflationists, and philosophers with deflationist sympathies, to opt for the Inconsistency View. See Armour-Garb and Beall (2001), Armour-Garb (200+), and Hill (2002).

[14] And only true. Priest's dialetheism yields a reading of 'iff' on which the T-biconditional for the Liar is true. On this reading, however, the biconditional is also false.

Two minimal constraints may be imposed on an adequate treatment of '$\overset{?}{\leftrightarrow}$'. First, the T-biconditionals, on the new reading, should sustain the Closure principle. Second, they should imply the material biconditionals for ordinary, non-pathological sentences. I myself would impose a third, somewhat more controversial, constraint: the biconditionals should not imply contradictions. In particular, the T-biconditional for the Liar should not imply the corresponding material biconditional.

In summary: Deflationists accept the T-biconditionals and they are correct to do so. It is a burden on the specialist on paradox to tell a story that makes the deflationists' acceptance coherent and correct.

3.

Let us now turn to the full claim of the deflationists: that the T-biconditionals fix the meaning of 'true'. One minor doubt arises here immediately, namely, that the T-biconditionals do not guarantee that only sentences are true. They allow the possibility of, for example, the Moon being true. The doubt is easily addressed by modifying a little the deflationists' claim. Let us leave the modification tacit and move on to a more important issue: the meaning of 'meaning' in the claim.[15]

'Meaning', it is widely recognized, is ambiguous. It can be understood in a weak way as "extension", in an intermediate way as "intension", and in a strong way as "sense". (Further grades can also be distinguished but these three will suffice for our present purposes.) Meaning understood in a weak way captures extensional information about an expression. For example, in this way of understanding, the meaning of 'the number of planets' and 'the square of three' is the same and can be identified with the number nine. Meaning understood in the intermediate way, i.e. as intension, captures extensional information across possible situations. (Different grades of "intension" can be distinguished on the basis of the range of possible worlds encompassed in an intension.) Thus, the intension of 'the number of planets' is different from that of 'the square of three', for in some possible situations the two expressions denote different numbers. Sense is a more fine-grained notion than intension and, it must be confessed, more murky. Sense is supposed to capture the cognitive content of an expression. The sense of 'the square of three' differs from that of 'the number of planets'; it differs also from that of 'nine', though the two have the same intension.

There is terminological tangle about meaning as extension that we need to straighten out before we return to the deflationists' claim. In one common use of 'extension', the extension of a one-place predicate is the set of objects of which the predicate is true. Thus, the extension of 'river' is the set of all rivers, the extension of 'natural number between 1 and 5' is the set {2, 3, 4}, and so on. 'Extension' so understood captures part of the extensional information about a (one-place) predicate, but it does not capture all of it. Extension does not tell us the objects of which the

[15] The condition that the theory of truth implies 'only sentences are true' is, of course, included in Tarski's Convention T (Tarski 1935).

predicate is false. In a classical context, we can recover this information if the totality of all objects is given to us. This is not possible, however, if the predicate is gappy (say because of considerations of sortal correctness) or if it is fuzzy (because of vagueness) or if it is n-valued. . . . So, extension, in this way of understanding it, does not capture all the extensional information about a predicate. Let us use the term 'signification' for total extensional information about a term. Signification includes the information carried by extension, but it is richer. For example, the signification of a gappy predicate will yield the objects of which the predicate is true, those of which it is false, and those of which it is neither true nor false; the signification of a vague predicate will yield the degree of applicability of the predicate to an object; and so on.[16]

On the weak reading of 'meaning', the deflationists' claim yields this thesis:

> *The Signification thesis.* The T-biconditionals fix the signification of the weak notion of truth. Or, more fully, given the non-semantic facts that obtain in the actual world, the T-biconditionals fix the actual signification of truth.

I think this thesis is better dubbed 'principle'; it is true and captures an important constraint on theories of truth and paradox. Consider first the T-biconditionals for nonpathological sentences. Consider, for example, these three biconditionals:

> 'Two plus two is five' is true iff two plus two is five,
> 'Two is sad' is true iff two is sad,
> 'Fred is bald' is true iff Fred is bald.

Let us assume that, because of sortal incorrectness, 'Two is sad' is neither true nor false; and that Fred is bald to the degree r. Then, the three biconditionals dictate, correctly, that 'true' is false of 'Two plus two is five', that it is neither true nor false of 'Two is sad', and that it applies to the degree r to 'Fred is bald'. The biconditionals fix properly the signification of 'true' with respect to these sentences. The point holds for all non-pathological sentences, because the T-biconditionals for these sentences imply the corresponding material biconditionals and, furthermore, our focus is on the weak notion of truth.

Let us consider next the pathological sentences such as the Liar and the Truth-teller. Do they provide a counterexample to the Signification thesis? This question cannot be answered directly, for we do not have as yet a sufficiently rich account of the connective 'iff' in the T-biconditionals. Let us therefore reformulate the question thus. Should we require a theory of truth and paradox to preserve the Signification thesis over the pathological sentences? I think that the answer to this question is "Yes". A good descriptive account of our notion of truth will not pin a particular semantic value (e.g., "false", "neither true nor false", and "applicable to degree r") on the Liar and the Truth-teller. Instead, it will simply indicate—and explain—the sort of pathological behavior that these sentences exhibit. Further, the special behavior of these sentences is rooted in the T-biconditionals. There is nothing over and above the

[16] This use of 'signification' was introduced in Gupta and Belnap (1993), pp. 30–1.

T-biconditionals (and the contingent facts) that settles the signification of truth on the pathological sentences. There is a problem, I grant, in understanding how the T-biconditionals fix the behavior of pathological sentences. It is the task of a theory of truth and paradox to provide us with this understanding. The theory should provide us with a reading of the T-biconditionals that sustains the Signification thesis. Many current theories of truth and paradox, it seems to me, neglect this desideratum, with the result that time and effort are wasted on alternatives that are easily dismissed.[17]

Let us now turn briefly to the stronger readings of the deflationists' claim: that the T-biconditionals fix the intension of 'true' (the *Intension* thesis) and that they fix the sense of 'true' (the *Sense* thesis). These theses deserve an extended discussion, but for our purposes here it is sufficient to make just one observation about them: The paradoxes threaten these theses only to the extent that they threaten the Signification thesis. I have argued that the paradoxes do not threaten the Signification thesis. It follows that they do not threaten the Intension and the Sense theses.

It is the Sense thesis that is of critical importance to deflationism,[18] and we can reinforce the idea that the paradoxes do not threaten it as follows. Consider a fragment *L* of English that is weak in self-referential resources (so that pathological sentences cannot be expressed in it) but that is otherwise as rich as one cares to make it. Suppose we grant the deflationists that the Sense thesis holds for 'true' when it is restricted to *L*. Now, what arguments might the paradoxes provide to put the Sense thesis into doubt for languages with richer self-referential resources? Suppose we enrich *L* with the name 'the Liar' and let its denotation be 'The Liar is not true'. Do we have any grounds to doubt the Sense thesis—any grounds that are not at the same time grounds for doubting the Signification thesis? No! We can rehearse the Liar argument, we can deduce the contradictions, we can induce puzzlement. But we leave the Signification thesis intact. And we bring forth no doubts against the Sense thesis—at least none that do not arise even for the paradox-free language *L*.

In conclusion: the paradoxes do not pose any special threat to the deflationsts' claim that the T-biconditionals fix the meaning of 'true'.

[17] I mean the remark to be directed only to those theories that aim to address the *descriptive* problem posed by the paradoxes—i.e., the problem of giving a description of our ordinary concept of truth, as opposed to revising the concept to suit one or another purpose.

In the fixed-point approaches of Saul Kripke (1975) and Robert Martin and Peter Woodruff (1975), the Tarski principle is sustained if 'iff' is read as the Łukasiewicz biconditional and the signification of 'true' is taken to be the least fixed point of a particular monotone three-valued scheme (e.g., the Strong Kleene). But such a theory fails to sustain the Signification thesis. The thesis can be sustained, however, if keeping the same reading of 'iff', we take the signification to be the set of all fixed points of the scheme. Note that the Łukasiewicz biconditional cannot be expressed within Kripke's and Martin–Woodruff's fixed-point languages.

[18] The argument of my "A critique of deflationism" (1993), if sound, shows that the Intension thesis is insufficient to support deflationary conclusions about truth. The Intension thesis is a generalized version of the Signification thesis. It says that the signification of 'true' in a possible world w is fixed by the T-biconditionals and the facts in w. The Intension thesis can, therefore, be sustained (see Gupta and Belnap (1993), pp. 20–5). The Sense thesis is, however, more doubtful and it—or something like it—is needed to reach deflationary conclusions.

4.

Friends of deflationism have responded to the paradoxes in several ways. An especially popular way has been to abandon classical logic in favor of a non-classical one.[19] The popularity of this approach is understandable. It blocks the derivation of absurdities from paradoxical sentences. And, on some variants, it even allows one to affirm all the material T-biconditionals and, at the same time, to explain how the concept of truth manages to do substantive work. (In such variants, the classical principle *ex falso quodlibet* fails.) Furthermore, the work of Kripke, Martin and Woodruff, Albert Visser (1984), and others has powerfully illuminated the virtues of the non-classical approaches. Nevertheless, I want to argue that deflationists, as well as theorists of paradox, should take a neutral stance on logic. They should not let the Liar dictate to them one logic over another.

Let us begin by observing that the principal claims of deflationism are neutral on logic. The plausibility of these claims—for example, that the T-biconditionals fix the meaning of 'true' and that truth enables us to generalize on sentence positions—does not alter as we shift our attention from one part of our language to another. Whether we consider classical arithmetic, or discourse with vague terms, or biological discourse—where, because of considerations of sortal correctness, the semantics of predicates may be three-valued—the deflationists' claims remain equally plausible. The claims remain plausible even in those areas of language whose semantics has eluded us, for example, hyper-intensional constructions. Moreover, if it were to turn out that we are wrong about the logic of even the simplest parts of our language—say, if it were to turn out that this logic is seven-valued (as the Jaina logicians thought)—the deflationists' claims would remain unaffected. It appears, therefore, that these claims are not sensitive to the underlying logic and semantics of language.

A theorist of truth and paradox should also, I think, keep a neutral stance on logic. The paradoxes arise not just in classical logic but in other kinds of logics as well: three-, four-, n-valued, modal, intuitionist, relevant, etc. It is true that in some logics, for example, the Strong Kleene, the paradox appears to be less damaging. But this is so only because these logics are weak in their logical resources: some kinds of negation, for example, are inexpressible in them. Once the logics are enriched, the paradox appears with the full force it exhibits in classical logic.[20] The work on the paradoxes in the last thirty years has revealed a panoply of ways of weakening expressive power while gaining unproblematic self-referential truth. Broadly speaking, these ways fall into two groups: those that restrict syntactic resources and those that restrict logical resources. The effect of either type is the same: genuinely paradoxical sentences are

[19] See, for instance, Grover (1992), Weir (1996), Gauker (1999), Armour-Garb and Beall (2001), Armour-Garb (200+), and Field (2001).

[20] The negation that is expressible in Strong Kleene is *choice* negation (∼): ∼A is true iff A is false, and ∼A is false iff A is true. If A is neither true nor false then ∼A is also neither true nor false. Exclusion negation (¬) is not expressible, however: ¬A is false iff A is true; otherwise, ¬A is true. The Liar sentence formed using exclusion negation is no less puzzling than the standard classical Liar.

eliminated from the language.[21] The work on expressively weak languages enriches our understanding of the concept of truth. But it does not by itself provide a solution to the descriptive problem of understanding truth. The project of seeking a solution to the descriptive problem is quite distinct from that of constructing expressively weak self-referential languages. A theorist engaged in the former project should aim to explain the working of the concept of truth in any logical environment: classical, as well as n-valued; intuitionist, as well as relevant; expressively weak, as well as expressively rich. Expressively weak logics provide no shelter to the descriptive theorists. Indeed, such theorists seek no shelter; they wish to face the full force of the paradox so that they can come to understand its nature and its source.

The behavior of paradoxes (and other pathological sentences) is so similar across different logics and semantics that it is fair to demand that any account of them be general, that it apply uniformly across the whole range of logics and semantics. No account of the paradoxes is likely to be plausible that makes an essential appeal to a particular semantics, e.g., the Strong Kleene. For then it would have no resources to explain similar paradoxes that arise under other semantics. If, following the Strong Kleene fixed-point route, it is said that the Liar is neither true nor false, then the question immediately arises what we should say about the variant Liar that is formulated using exclusion negation (see fn. 20). We cannot say that this Liar is neither true nor false, for that leads to absurdity.

Furthermore, in all cases, irrespective of the underlying logic, it is the T-biconditionals that are the source of the distinctive behavior of the Liar (and other pathological sentences). Hence, it is proper to demand that a theory of truth give an account of the biconditionals that is *logic neutral*. It should assign a reading to 'iff' ('$\overset{?}{\leftrightarrow}$') that works—or at least can naturally be carried over—across the whole range of logics. That is, theorists of paradox should aim at an account of the T-biconditionals that enables them to meet the following challenge. Given any logic—classical, three-valued, n-valued, relevant, ... —they can predict and explain which sentences behave pathologically in any given set of circumstances, and which sentences do not. Further, for each of the pathological sentences, they can predict and explain the particular kind of pathology that the sentence exhibits; and for each of the non-pathological ones, they can predict and explain the semantic value of the sentence. This requirement of generality, it seems to me, is the sound residue of "the universality of natural language" that has been the bugbear of theorists of paradox.[22]

There is one further requirement that I think we should impose on an account of the paradoxes: it should not attribute a special logic to sentences containing 'true'. Logical resources (e.g., negation, conjunction, and quantification) should interact with 'true' in just the way that they do with the other predicates. In our ordinary reasoning with sentences containing 'true', we do not hold them to be above the usual logical laws. We are not worried—nor should we be—if in the course of an otherwise

[21] The Liar sentence formulated using choice negation in Strong Kleene languages is not, in my view, genuinely paradoxical. It exhibits no instability if it is deemed neither true nor false.

[22] I have still to see a formulation of the thesis of "the universality of natural language" that is both clear and true.

logically valid argument we take a detour through some sentences containing 'true'. There is, to be sure, something very peculiar about 'true'. The peculiarity, I am suggesting, is all centered on the T-biconditionals and, in particular, on the little word 'iff'.

5.

I have argued that a descriptive account of the concept of truth must provide a sense of 'iff' ('↔') under which the following desiderata are satisfied.

> *Desiderata A.* (a1) The T-biconditionals are correct and fix the signification of truth. (a2) The T-biconditionals for non-pathological sentences yield the corresponding material biconditionals. (a3) The Closure principle is sustained.
>
> *Desiderata B.* (b1) The T-biconditionals do not imply contradictions. (b2) The T-biconditionals are logic neutral: they fix the signification of truth irrespective of the logic and semantics of the language. (b3) The logical rules of the language apply uniformly to sentences containing 'true'.

There should not be any dispute about Desiderata A. Desiderata B, on the other hand, are bound to be somewhat controversial, since many existing theories of paradox fail to satisfy one or more of them. I myself think that a failure to satisfy any of the desiderata is evidence against a theory. A violation of desiderata A is, I think, a fatal flaw. Violations of desiderata B may be tolerable if it can be shown that they promote overriding virtues.

If the above desiderata are correct then the paradoxes pose no special problems for the deflationists. The deflationists can happily assert their favorite slogan, "the T-biconditionals fix the meaning of 'true'." If a pesky objector invokes the paradoxes, the deflationists need only exercise a bit of caution. They should not rush—as they have been apt to do—to construct or to endorse a particular account of the paradoxes. Far too often this kind of move has led not only to a poor theory of paradox; it has led to an undermining of the deflationists' principal claims. In response to the objector, the deflationists need say only that their claims, extensionally construed, constitute an important desideratum on any account of paradox. It is the task of the specialist to show how the desideratum can be satisfied.

It may be objected that the above desiderata are too strong, that they cannot possibly be satisfied. The response to the objection is that this just is not so. There is a natural and intuitive way of satisfying the desiderata, and it is this. Following Tarski, we view the T-biconditional for a sentence *S* as defining the conditions under which *S* falls under 'true'. We observe—and this is a plain but striking fact—that the T-biconditionals sometimes define these conditions in circular ways. Often 'true' occurs in the defining conditions; sometimes the defining conditions for *S* contain as a constituent part the very thing being defined, namely, the truth attribution to *S*. The sense in which the T-biconditionals—including those of paradoxical sentences such as the Liar—are correct is one in which they are seen as laying down possibly circular defining conditions for the applicability of 'true'. 'Iff' should therefore be viewed as representing "partial, possibly circular, definitional equivalence".[23] This reading of 'iff' is logic-neutral in the desired way. Further, it is intuitively plausible that, on this reading, the T-conditionals fix the signification of truth. They dictate (in light of the contingent facts) which sentences are non-pathological and which pathological. They dictate also the particular sort of pathology that the latter sentences display.

This reading of 'iff' rests on the idea that circular definitions are legitimate. Belnap and I have defended the legitimacy of circular definitions at length in our book (1993). We have tried to show that circular definitions are logically coherent and that they are in general contentful. I provide a quick overview of our theory in the survey paper "Truth" (2001). The key to meeting the above desiderata lies, I believe, in the recognition that truth is a circular concept.[24] It is not my aim here, however, to convince the reader of this claim. All I need do for my present purposes is to counter the suggestion that the above desiderata are too strong. Perhaps there are other ways of satisfying the desiderata than that provided by the theory of circular definitions. So long as the desiderata *can* be satisfied, they are reasonable. And if they are reasonable, then the paradoxes pose no special threat to deflationism.

The deflationists' main claim—that the T-biconditionals fix the meaning of 'true'—is correct, I have argued, if it is read *extensionally*. This reading is insufficient, however, to establish deflationary conclusions about the role of truth in philosophy (e.g., in the theory of meaning). The deflationists need for their arguments much stronger readings—readings such as that the T-biconditionals fix the sense of 'true'.[25] The debate over deflationism centers—and ought to center—on two points: (i) what precise reading of the deflationists' claim is needed to establish deflationary conclusions about the role of 'true', and (ii) whether the claim is correct under this reading. The paradoxes are only a distraction in this debate; they take attention away from the central issues.

REFERENCES

Armour-Garb, Bradley (200+). Minimalism, the generalization problem and the liar. Forthcoming.

—— and JC Beall (2001). Can deflationists be dialetheists? *Journal of Philosophical Logic* 30, 593–608.

—— —— eds. (2005). *Deflationary Truth*. Chicago: Open Court Press.

Brendel, Elke (2000). Circularity and the debate between deflationists and substantive theories of truth. In Chapuis and Gupta (2000), pp. 29–47.

[23] Caution: This should not be taken to imply that the two sides of the T-biconditionals have the same sense or the same cognitive content. The biconditionals constitute at best an *intensionally* adequate definition of 'true', not a *sense* adequate definition. See Gupta and Belnap (1993), p. 130.

[24] I know of only one serious objection to Belnap's and my claim that truth is a circular concept. This was put forward by Robert Koons in his critical study (1994) of *Revision Theory*. Belnap's and my reply (1994) accompanies Koons's study.

[25] See my "A critique of deflationism" (1993).

Chapuis, André and Anil Gupta (2000). *Circularity, Definition and Truth*. New Delhi: Indian Council of Philosophical Research. Distributed outside India by Ridgeview Publishing Company, Atascadero, CA.

Chihara, Charles S. (1979). The semantic paradoxes: a diagnostic investigation. *Philosophical Review* 88, 590–618.

Feferman, Solomon (1984). Toward useful type-free theories I. *Journal of Symbolic Logic* 49, 75–111. Reprinted in Martin (1984), pp. 237–87.

Field, Hartry (2001). *Truth and the Absence of Fact*. Oxford: Oxford University Press.

Friedman, Harvey, and Michael Sheard (1987). An axiomatic approach to self-referential truth. *Annals of Pure and Applied Logic* 33, 1–21.

Gauker, Christopher (1999). Deflationism and logic. *Facta Philosophica* 1, 167–95.

Grover, Dorothy (1992). *A Prosentential Theory of Truth*. Princeton: Princeton University Press.

Gupta, Anil (1993). A critique of deflationism. *Philosophical Topics* 21, pp. 57–81. Reprinted, with a postscript, in Armour-Garb and Beall, eds. (2005), *Deflationary Truth*, pp. 199–233. Chicago: Open Court Press.

—— (2001). Truth. In Louis Goble, ed., *A Guide to Philosophical Logic* (Oxford: Blackwell Publishers), pp. 90–114.

—— (2002). Partially defined predicates and semantic pathology. *Philosophy and Phenomenological Research* 65, 402–09.

—— and Nuel Belnap (1993). *The Revision Theory of Truth*. Cambridge, MA: The MIT Press.

—— —— (1994). Reply to Robert Koons. *Notre Dame Journal of Formal Logic* 35, 632–6.

Halbach, Volker (1994). A system of complete and consistent truth. *Notre Dame Journal of Formal Logic* 1994, 311–27.

Hill, Chirstopher S. (1987). Rudiments of a theory of reference. *Notre Dame Journal of Formal Logic* 28, 200–19.

—— (2002). *Thought and World: An Austere Portrayal of Truth, Reference, and Semantic Correspondence*. Cambridge: Cambridge University Press.

Horwich, Paul (1990). *Truth*. Oxford: Basil Blackwell. Second edn (1998). Oxford: Oxford University Press.

—— (1998). *Meaning*. Oxford: Oxford University Press.

Koons, Robert (1994). Book review: *The Revision Theory of Truth*. *Notre Dame Journal of Formal Logic* 35, 606–31.

Kripke, Saul A. (1975). Outline of a theory of truth. *Journal of Philosophy* 72, 690–716. Reprinted in Martin (1984), pp. 53–81.

Martin Robert L., ed. (1984). *Recent Essays on Truth and the Liar Paradox*. Oxford: Oxford University Press.

—— and Peter W. Woodruff (1975). On representing 'true-in-L' in L. *Philosophia* 213–17. Reprinted in Martin (1984), pp. 47–51.

McGee, Vann (1991). *Truth, Vagueness, and Paradox: An Essay on the Logic of Truth*. Indianapolis: Hackett Publishing Company.

Priest, Graham (1979). The logic of paradox. *Journal of Philosophical Logic* 8, 219–41.

—— (1987). *In Contradiction: A Study of the Transconsistent*. The Hague: Martinus Nijhoff.

Quine, W. V. O. (1992). *Pursuit of Truth*. Revised edn. Cambridge, MA: Harvard University Press.

Simmons, Keith (1999). Deflationary truth and the liar. *Journal of Philosophical Logic* 28, 455–88.

Soames, Scott (1999). *Understanding Truth*. Oxford: Oxford University Press.

Tarski, Alfred (1935). Der Wahrheitsbegriff in den formalisierten Sprachen. *Studia Philosophica* 1, 261–405. Translated by J. H. Woodger, "The concept of truth in formalized languages," in Tarski (1956), pp. 152–278.

—— (1956). *Logic, Semantics, Metamathematics: Papers from 1923 to 1938*. Oxford: Clarendon Press. Second edn, 1983, John Corcoran (ed.), Hackett Publishing Company.

Visser, Albert (1989). Four-valued semantics and the liar. *Journal of Philosophical Logic* 13, 181–212.

Weir, Alan (1996). Ultra-maximalist minimalism! *Analysis* 56, 10–22.

Williams, Michael (1986). Do we (epistemologists) need a theory of truth? *Philosophical Topics* 14, 223–42.

Yablo, Steve (1985). Truth and reflection. *Journal of Philosophical Logic* 14, 297–349.

10

Semantics for Deflationists

Christopher Gauker

1. INTRODUCTION

As I understand it, deflationism about truth is essentially two theses, one positive and one negative. The positive thesis is that sentences (or assertions or propositions) ascribing truth are in some sense equivalent to the sentences (or assertions or propositions) to which truth is ascribed. If we take "is true" as a predicate properly attaching to the names of sentences, then the positive thesis is that a sentence of the form [φ] **is true** is in some sense equivalent to the sentence φ (where [φ] is the quotation name of the sentence φ). The negative thesis is that this equivalence does not have to be explained by analyzing the truth of φ in terms of real reference relations between its subsentential components and objects and sets or properties. That is, the truth of a sentence does not have to be explained in terms of reference relations of a kind that we can explicate only in terms of spatio-temporal-causal relations between uses of an expression and the object or kind of object that the expression is said to refer to.

In what sense is [φ] **is true** equivalent to φ? (I will assume throughout that φ belongs to the same language as **is true**.) At the very least, we should be able to say that [φ] **is true** and φ always have the same truth value. If we assume that every sentence is either true or false, then, in light of the semantic paradoxes, that claim can be decisively refuted. But a deflationist cannot very well allow that sentences may be neither true nor false, because a deflationist cannot very well explain the difference between falsehood and lack of truth. The broader question posed by this question about equivalence is how the deflationist might define logical validity. What is needed is a *semantic* definition, by which I mean a definition that we can use to demonstrate of valid arguments that they are valid and of invalid arguments that they are invalid (which is not to say that it must provide an algorithm for constructing such demonstrations). That need not in itself spell defeat for deflationism, for we might obtain a semantic definition of logical validity of a kind that is acceptable to a deflationist. So the question becomes, what kind of semantic definition of logical validity would be acceptable to a deflationist?

The usual model-theoretic approach defines a logically valid argument as one that preserves truth in a model, or interpretation. But if we define logical validity in terms of truth on an interpretation in this way, then, I will argue, we will inevitably suppose that there is one special interpretation, the intended interpretation, such that truth on that interpretation is truth simpliciter. The intended interpretation will be that which assigns to each nonlogical constant what it really refers to. Thus the question arises whether conceiving of truth in this way is compatible with deflationism. In particular, we have to ask whether the deflationist can give an adequate account of the pertinent reference relation, one that does not resort to treating reference as a real relation between singular terms and objects and between predicates and properties or sets of *n*-tuples. The answer, I will argue, is negative.

So if we wish to attain the goals of deflationism, we will need some other approach to defining logical validity. Fortunately, there is indeed another way to think about logical validity, one that both explicates the equivalence between [φ] **is true** and φ and eschews the reduction of truth to reference. It begins with the concept of *a context for a conversation.* The context for a conversation, as here conceived, is something objective, determined by the goals of the conversation in light of the character of the environment in which the conversation takes place. For each grammatical type of sentence, we may define the conditions under which sentences of that type are assertible in a context, deniable in a context, or neither. Logical validity may then be defined as preservation of assertibility in a context. Semantic paradoxes are avoided in as much as the inferences that seem to take us from facts about the identity of paradoxical sentences (such as that λ = " λ is not true" or that α = " α is not assertible in any context") to contradictions prove to be invalid.

2. DEFLATIONISM IN A BIVALENT SETTING

One of the weakest kinds of equivalence that a deflationist might claim for [φ] **is true** and φ is material equivalence. So the deflationist's claim might be simply that, for certain sentences φ,[φ] **is true** and φ have the same truth value. The thesis of deflationism would be question-begging if formulated as just the thesis that for certain sentences φ, [φ] **is true** and φ have the same *truth value*. But the same conception of equivalence can be expressed without employing the concept of truth. In a bivalent context, [φ] **is true** and φ will have the same truth value if and only if the corresponding instance of the T-schema, [φ] **is true if and only if** φ is true. It would again be question-begging for the deflationist to characterize these instances of the T-schema simply as *true*. But instead they can be characterized as in some sense *given*. Thus we arrive at a formulation of deflationism that we can call *T-schema deflationism*: For certain sentences φ, the T-sentence, [φ] **is true if and only if** φ, is *given*.

There are various senses in which an instance of the T-schema might be said to be *given*. It might be given in the sense that, in doing proofs, we are permitted to take that instance as a premise whenever we choose. Or it might be given in the sense that it is *analytic*. In any case, a sentence's being given has to be sufficient for its being true. Moreover, any instance of the T-schema that is in fact true must qualify as given. Again, where our purpose is to define a deflationary theory of truth, it would be question-begging to explicate givenness in terms of truth. None the less, we may take for granted that the instances of the T-schema that are supposed to explicate the T-schema deflationist's conception of the equivalence between [φ] **is true** and φ will include all and only those instances that really are true.

Taken as the thesis that *all* sentential instances of the T-schema are given, T-schema deflationism is clearly false. Not all instances of the T-schema can be given, because some are plainly not true. That some instances of the T-schema are not true is the conclusion we must draw from the semantic paradoxes. For example, we might have:

$\lambda =$ "λ is not true".

But

"λ is not true" is true if and only if λ is not true,

is an instance of the T-schema. From the above identity and this T-sentence, we may infer,

λ is true if and only if λ is not true,

which is plainly not true. It is no help to deny the possibility of identities such as the one here claimed between λ and "λ is not true", because we can construct other nontrue instances of the T-schema without relying on such identities. For example, suppose that on side A of a certain notecard we have the sentence "Every sentence on side B is true" and on side B we have, "No sentence on side A is true". Then if all instances of the T-schema are given, we may derive the conclusion that every sentence on side A is true if and only if *not* every sentence on side A is true, which is certainly not true. In showing this we will rely on the fact that the sole sentence on side A is "Every sentence on side B is true", but such identities cannot be forbidden; they will arise by accident despite our best intentions (as Kripke noted in his (1975)).

So the T-schema deflationist cannot maintain that *every* instance of the T-schema is given. In a bivalent setting, we will have to allow that some of them are actually false. (Presumably we will want to say, of the nontrue instance concerning λ, that the left-hand side is false, and the right-hand side is true.) That is why I initially formulated the T-schema deflationist's claim as only the thesis that *certain* instances of the T-schema are given. Formulated in that way, T-schema deflationism is an explicitly vague thesis. So to get a definite thesis, we will need to answer the question: Which instances of the T-schema are the ones that are given? I will now argue that there is no good answer to that question so long as we maintain that every sentence is either true or false.

Anyone who claims to have a theory of something has to have some way of communicating to others what the theory says; otherwise we may deem the theory to be *incomprehensible*. So in particular, a T-schema deflationist who claims to have a conception of the equivalence between [φ] **is true** and φ must have some way of demonstrating to others that he or she really does have it. One way to demonstrate that one is in possession of a theory is to actually state it by means of a finite number of sentences. In just that sense one might have a theory of physics. Another way might be to define a language and a model for that language and then explain that one's theory consists of the sentences of the language that are true in that model. In just that sense we might have a theory comprising all the truths of arithmetic. But the T-schema deflationist cannot claim to possess a theory in either of these ways. The pertinent set of instances of the T-schema is certainly not finite, and it would be question-begging to identify the pertinent instances in terms of truth.

However, there is another way in which a person might make a theory comprehensible, and that is to describe some definite method for generating a list of all of the sentences that constitute the theory. So unless someone can think of some other reasonable criterion for comprehensibility that T-schema deflationism might pass, we may take for granted that the instances of the T-schema that the T-schema deflationist takes to be given must be at least effectively enumerable. If the instances of the T-schema that the T-schema deflationist takes to be given are not at least effectively enumerable, then we may conclude that T-schema deflationism is strictly *incomprehensible*.

In fact, given only a few further assumptions about our language, T-schema deflationism is demonstrably incomprehensible. The additional assumptions are these: I will assume that the sentences of our language can be written using the syntax of the standard languages of formal logic. I will also assume that our language contains a quotation name for every formula in our language, which I will form with square brackets. I also assume that our language contains its own *diagonal predicate*. If $F(\nu)$ is a formula of our language containing ν as its sole free variable and $[F(\nu)]$ is its quotation-name, then $F([F(\nu)])$ is the *diagonal* of $F(\nu)$. Let the diagonal predicate of our language be $\mathbf{D}$, so that a sentence of the form $\mathbf{D}ab$ means that the sentence of our language that a denotes is the diagonal of the formula of our language that b denotes. Finally, I assume that our language includes the language of arithmetic.

A well-known observation of Gödel's, sometimes called the diagonal lemma, tells us that, under these conditions, for any formula $F(\nu)$ of our language containing ν as its sole free variable, we can construct a *Gödel-sentence* A for $F(\nu)$, which is such that A is true if and only if $F([A])$ is true. In particular, the following sentence is such a Gödel-sentence for $F(\nu)$:

$$\exists \mathbf{y}(\mathbf{Dy}[\exists \mathbf{y}(\mathbf{Dyx} \wedge F(\mathbf{y}))] \wedge F(\mathbf{y})).$$

It is evident that this sentence will be true if and only if the following sentence is true:

$$F([\exists \mathbf{y}(\mathbf{Dy}[\exists \mathbf{y}(\mathbf{Dyx} \wedge F(\mathbf{y}))] \wedge F(\mathbf{y}))]).$$

(By virtue of the meaning of $\mathbf{D}$, the first of these two sentences is true if and only if $\exists \mathbf{y}(\mathbf{y} = [\exists \mathbf{y}(\mathbf{Dy}[\exists \mathbf{y}(\mathbf{Dyx} \wedge F(\mathbf{y}))] \wedge F(\mathbf{y}))] \wedge F(\mathbf{y}))$ is true, which is so if and only if the second sentence is true.)

I will now demonstrate (assuming bivalence) that every sentence of the language is materially equivalent to some instance of the T-schema. Let $\mathbf{S}$ abbreviate some arbitrary sentence of our language, and consider the following formula in particular:

S if and only if y is true.

Substituting this for "*F*(**y**)" in the schematic Gödel-sentence above, we have:

> **∃y(Dy[∃y(Dyx ∧ S if and only if y is true)]**
> **∧ S if and only if y is true).**

Let us abbreviate this sentence as **G**. (So in what follows, wherever I write "**G**", one should read the above sentence, even when "**G**" occurs between square brackets.) Since **G** is a Gödel-sentence for **S if and only if y is true**, it is true if and only if the following sentence is true:

> **S if and only if [G] is true.**

Thus, we may reason as follows: By the argument just given, **G** and **S if and only if [G] is true** are materially equivalent. So suppose **S** is true. In that case, **G** and **S if and only if [G] is true** will be materially equivalent (assuming bivalence) only if **G** and **[G] is true** are both true or both false. So **[G] is true if and only if G** will be true. Suppose next that **[G] is true if and only if G** is true. So **G** and **[G] is true** are both true or both false. In either case, **G** and **S if and only if [G] is true** will be materially equivalent only if **S** is true. So **S** is true if and only if **[G] is true if and only if G** is true. But **[G] is true if and only if G** is an instance of the T-schema. So every sentence **S** is materially equivalent to some instance of the T-schema. (Notice that this argument fails if we do not assume bivalence. If **G** and **[G] is true** can be neither true nor false, then **G** and **S if and only if [G] is true** might have the same truth value—the value *neither*—though **S** is true and **[G] is true if and only if G** is neither true nor false.)

Say that **[G] is true if and only if G** is **S**'s *corresponding instance of the T-schema.* What we have just concluded is that **S** is true if and only if its corresponding instance of the T-schema is true. Moreover, since **S** occurs in its corresponding instance of the T-schema (embedded in quotation marks), we find that for any instance of the T-schema that in this sense corresponds to some sentence, we can "read off" from it the sentence **S** to which it corresponds.

Suppose that the deflationist can have what he or she needs, an effective enumeration of the instances of the T-schema expressing his theory of truth for our language. Next, consider an arbitrary true sentence φ of our language. Since φ is true and its corresponding instance of the T-schema has the same truth value as φ, we may conclude that φ's corresponding instance of the T-schema must be true too, and so it ought to be included in the deflationist's theory, and so it ought to turn up somewhere in the enumeration. So for every true sentence of our language, its corresponding instance of the T-schema ought to show up somewhere in the enumeration. But for each of the sentences in this enumeration, we can easily decide whether or not it is the corresponding instance of the T-schema for some sentence. If it is, then, assuming that every instance of the T-schema in the deflationist's theory of truth is true, we will know that the sentence to which it corresponds is true too. Thus an effective enumeration of the instances of the T-schema expressing the deflationist's theory of truth yields as a dividend an effective enumeration of all truths expressible in our language whatsoever.

For any given sentence we can decide whether or not it is a sentence in the language of arithmetic (since that is just a matter of the vocabulary employed). So our enumeration of the truths of our language yields an enumeration of the truths of arithmetic. But the set of truths of arithmetic is a complete theory; that is, for every sentence in the language of arithmetic, either it or its negation belongs to the theory. So our enumeration of the truths of arithmetic yields an effective procedure for deciding whether or not a sentence in the language of arithmetic is true: For any such sentence, wait until either it or its negation shows up in the enumeration. But as is well known, the truths of arithmetic are not decidable in this way. We may conclude that the set of instances of the T-schema that the T-schema deflationist would like to put forward as an explication of the equivalence of [φ] **is true** and φ is not effectively enumerable and, therefore, that T-schema deflationism is incomprehensible.[1]

T-schema deflationism, as I have defined it, treats "is true" as a predicate attaching to the names of sentences. A different kind of deflationism, call it *propositional deflationism*, might be defined as the thesis that every proposition of the following *propositional T-schematic form* is "given":

The proposition that φ is true if and only φ.

(It is not clear to me what might be meant by saying that a proposition has a certain form, but I pass over that complaint.) Such a theory must also yield a theory of truth for sentences, because we can always say (if we believe in propositions in the first place) that a sentence is true in a context if and only if the proposition that it expresses in that context is true. Thus we should expect propositional deflationism to yield a comprehensible theory of truth for sentences as well, or at least for sentences that express the same proposition in every context, such as the sentences of arithmetic. So if the propositional deflationist's account of truth for sentences has the consequence that every sentence is either true or false, then the present argument will be an argument against propositional deflationism as well. (In this way the present argument can be taken as a criticism of Horwich's attempt to state a theory of truth, since he assumes bivalence (1990, p. 80).)

3. DEFLATIONISM WITHOUT BIVALENCE

Again, one of the weakest kinds of equivalence that we might find between [φ] **is true** and φ is material equivalence. If we abandon bivalence and allow that sentences might be neither true nor false, then to say that two sentences are materially equivalent is to say that they have the same truth value, either both true, or both false, or both neither true nor false. This idea has a natural formulation in terms of inference rules. If for all φ, [φ] **is true** and φ have the same truth value, then all instances of the following two rules of inference are logically valid:

[1] This argument is a slightly improved version of the argument that I gave in my (2001). The idea of selecting the Gödel sentence for the formula **S if and only if y is true** comes from Vann McGee (1992), who also used it in an argument against deflationism.

Semantic Ascent	*Semantic Descent*
φ	[φ] **is true**
[φ] **is true**	φ

So in the setting of a three-valued semantics, the thesis that [φ] **is true** and φ are materially equivalent can be formulated as the thesis that these two inference rules (as well as their contrapositives) are valid. Call this *inference-rule deflationism*. Inference-rule deflationism does not reduce to T-schema deflationism because in a three-valued setting these two inference rules may be valid though not every instance of the T-schema is true. Let [φ] **is true** and φ be two sentences neither of which is true. Then, on the usual three-valued accounts of the biconditional (e.g., the strong Kleene scheme), the T-sentence, [φ] **is true if and only if** φ, will not be true.[2]

Inference-rule deflationism does not immediately generate paradoxes in the way that unrestricted T-schema deflationism did. By means of Semantic Ascent and Semantic Descent, together with certain other inference rules, we can indeed derive contradictions from identities such as λ = "λ is not true". But in a three-valued setting, we can block such derivations by rejecting some of the other inference rules employed in the derivations instead of rejecting Semantic Ascent and Semantic Descent. For example, we might try to derive a contradiction from a plain fact about the identity of the liar sentence as follows:

1. λ = "λ is not true". (A plain fact.)
2. Suppose λ is true.
3. Given 2, "λ is not true" is true. (From 1 and 2, by the laws of identity.)
4. Given 2, λ is not true. (From 3, by Semantic Descent.)
5. λ is not true. (From 2–4, by a form of Indirect Proof.)
6. Suppose λ is not true.
7. Given 6, "λ is not true" is true. (From 6, by Semantic Ascent.)
8. Given 6, λ is true. (From 1 and 7, by the laws of identity.)
9. λ is true. (From 6–8, by Indirect Proof.)
10. λ is true and λ is not true. (From 5 and 9.)

The soundness of this reasoning can be denied without rejecting the pertinent instances of Semantic Descent and Semantic Ascent, by rejecting the pertinent instances of Indirect Proof. (I am taking Indirect Proof to be the principle that if a set of sentences $S \cup \{$**not**-$\varphi\}$ implies φ, then S implies φ, and that if a set of sentences $S \cup \{\varphi\}$ implies **not**-φ, then S implies **not**-φ.) Similarly, the derivation of contradictory instances of the T-schema by means of instances of Semantic Ascent and Semantic Descent can be rejected by rejecting the required instances of the rule of

[2] In my (1999) I attributed inference-rule deflationism to Hartry Field. This was based on his definition of cognitive equivalence in his (1994b), note 1. The different definition of cognitive equivalence given in note 2 of Field (1994a) entails a form of deflationism at least as strong as T-schema deflationism (as I acknowledged as well in my (1999)). Field's comments in the postscript to the reprinting of Field (1994a) in Field (2001) suggest that at that time he did not wish to be pinned down to any very definite conception of cognitive equivalence.

Conditional Proof (which says that if a set of sentences $S \cup \{\varphi\}$ implies ψ, then S implies **If** φ **then** ψ).

In order to block the derivation of contradictions in this way, it is necessary to reject the unrestricted use of Indirect Proof and Conditional Proof. It is precisely the decision to reject bivalence and allow that sentences may be neither true nor false that allows us to do this. Suppose that there are counterexamples to Indirect Proof. That is, suppose there is a set of sentences S and a sentence φ such that $S \cup \{$**not**-$\varphi\}$ implies φ but S does not imply φ. Since S does not imply φ, there is an interpretation M of the language such that every sentence in S is true on M and φ is not true on M. But then since $S \cup \{$**not**-$\varphi\}$ implies φ, **not**-φ cannot be true on M either. But if φ is false on M, then (assuming that we do not say anything unusual about negation), **not**-φ is surely true on M. So since **not**-φ is not true on M, φ is not false on M. So φ is neither true nor false on M. So we cannot have the advantages of inference-rule deflationism without admitting truth-value gaps.

But what can an inference-rule deflationist say about truth-value gaps? Presumably, a deflationist would want to explicate falsehood and lack of truth value in the same manner in which he or she proposes to explicate truth. So just as the deflationist explicates truth by positing an equivalence between [φ] **is true** and φ, a deflationist would explicate falsehood by positing an equivalence between [φ] **is false** and a sentence not containing **false**, and would explicate **not true** by positing an equivalence between [φ] **is not true** and a sentence not containing **not true**. The trouble is that there is only one plausible candidate for both jobs, namely, **not**-φ. The inference-rule deflationist will be driven to say both that [φ] **is false** is equivalent to **not**-φ and that [φ] **is not true** is equivalent to **not**-φ. But if we say that *both* [φ] **is false** and [φ] **is not true** are equivalent to **not**-φ, then [φ] **is not true and not false** will be equivalent to a contradiction, **not**-φ **and not-not**-φ, contrary to our assumption that it is sometimes true that a sentence is neither true nor false.

Perhaps I am mistaken in assuming that the deflationist must explicate lack of truth value in the same way he or she explicates truth and falsehood. Instead, the deflationist might define a class of sentences *NP* (for *nonparadoxical*) and restrict the equivalence theses to the sentences in *NP*. If a sentence φ is in *NP*, *then* [φ] **is true** is equivalent to φ. And if a sentence φ is in *NP*, *then* [φ] **is false** is equivalent to **not**-φ. Both [φ] **is not true** and [φ] **is not false** may be true, but only if φ is not in *NP*.[3] But then how are we to characterize the class of sentences in *NP*? We cannot characterize it simply as consisting of the sentences that are either true or false, since that would beg the question of the nature of truth and falsehood. Since it is the paradoxical sentences (at least) that we want to characterize as neither true nor false, perhaps we could say that *NP* consists in (or is confined to) *nonparadoxical* sentences. But then how are we to characterize the nonparadoxical sentences apart from the concepts of truth and falsehood? We might try: A sentence φ is *nonparadoxical* if and only if the assumption

[3] Such an approach is suggested by Richard Holton (2000), although ultimately he does not endorse it. Holton takes seriously another idea, without endorsing it, that I ignore altogether, viz., that we cannot truly *say*, of the sentences that are neither true nor false, that they are neither true nor false.

that [φ] **is true** is equivalent to φ does not allow us to derive contradictions from plain facts about the identities of sentences. But that will not work because by this criterion plainly nonparadoxical sentences may have to be counted as "paradoxical" too. Consider a version of the notecard paradox (described in section 2 above) in which side B contains both "No sentence on side A is true" and "The moon is the moon". In that case, even the assumption that " 'The moon is the moon' is true" is equivalent to "The moon is the moon" will play a role in the derivation of a contradiction from plain facts about the identities of sentences (and the fact that the moon is the moon).

JC Beall (2002) has suggested that a deflationist can admit truth-value gaps by distinguishing between strong and weak negation. Both kinds of negation take a truth into a falsehood and a falsehood into a truth, but a strong negation takes a sentence that is neither true nor false into a truth, while a weak negation takes a sentence that is neither true nor false into another sentence that is neither true nor false. Suppose **NOT** expresses strong negation and **not** expresses weak negation. Then the deflationist might say that [φ] **is neither true nor false** is equivalent to **NOT**-(φ **or not** φ), which is true in the case where φ is neither true nor false. But suppose that **s =** [**s is NOT true**] is true, so that **s is NOT true** is a liar, and compare these three sentences: (a) **s is NOT true**, (b) [**s is NOT true**] **is true**, (c) [**s is NOT true**] **is NOT true**. Since (a) is a liar, we should regard it as neither true nor false. Since (b) ascribes truth to a nontrue sentence, it is either false or neither true nor false. In either case, because (c) is the strong negation of a nontrue sentence, it is true. But (a) results from (c) by identity substitution; so if (c) is true, (a) should be true too, contrary to our assumption. So identity substitution seems to fail. Moreover, if **s is NOT true** is neither true nor false, then likewise **s is true** should be neither true nor false, because otherwise **s is NOT true** would be either true or false. And if **s is true** is not true, then **s is NOT NOT true** cannot be true either. So [**s is NOT true**] **is NOT true** is true and **s is NOT NOT true** is not true. So we cannot maintain that in general [φ] **is NOT true** is equivalent to **NOT**-φ. But an inference-rule deflationist should expect those two forms of sentence to be equivalent.[4]

4. DEFLATIONARY MODEL THEORY

In the previous two sections I have criticized two deflationary attempts to formulate the purported equivalence between [φ] **is true** and φ. Now I want to set aside the question of how to formulate this particular equivalence in order to ask a broader question: How can a deflationist define the class of logically valid arguments? This is a

[4] While thus arguing, by appeal to strong negation, that a deflationist might regard liar sentences as neither true nor false, Beall, writing with Armour-Garb, has also been arguing that deflationists might regard liar sentences as both true and false (Beall and Armour-Garb 2003). On this view, the present problem does not arise: [φ] **is NOT true** will be equivalent to **NOT**-φ. Strangely, though, a deflationist who maintains that a sentence is both true and false must apparently hold as well that it is not either true or false (weak negation). That would seem to be a problem.

strictly broader question if we assume that the equivalence of [φ] **is true** and φ is a special case of logical validity—if we assume, that is, that the claim is that both the argument from [φ] **is true** to φ and the argument from φ to [φ] **is true** are logically valid. Perhaps some deflationists have imagined that it would suffice just to declare that certain rules of inference are valid or (in the case of rules like Conditional Proof) validity-preserving, and that all and only arguments whose conclusions can be derived from their premises by means of those rules are valid. But for several reasons that cannot be right.

First, if an argument is valid, then that fact is not just the effect of stipulation. There must be some explanation of that fact in terms that we can relate to a larger conception of the nature of linguistic communication. Such an explanation is precisely what an explanation in terms of a semantic definition of logical validity purports to be (even if the practitioners of logic do not always hold firmly in mind a conception of the relation between their definition of logical validity and a broader conception of the nature of language). Second, it is not always intuitively obvious which forms of argument are really valid, and to resolve such issues we need the guidance of a conception of semantics. If we want to say that the venerable rule of Indirect Proof is not always validity-preserving, because sometimes $S \cup \{$**not** - $\varphi\}$ logically implies φ, though *S* does not logically imply φ, that verdict should not be just an ad hoc move designed to rescue the deflationist's equivalence thesis; it should be a verdict that we can justify in light of a broader conception of the nature of language. Finally, one of the things we want in logical theory is a method by which we can demonstrate of invalid arguments that they are invalid (as well demonstrate of valid arguments that they are valid). To demonstrate invalidity we need to be able to construct counter-examples of some kind and then use our account of the semantic properties of sentences to demonstrate that the premises are true (or whatever) in the counter-example and the conclusion is not true in it. (This may not be an algorithm, for there may be no algorithm for finding a counterexample even when a counterexample exists.) We cannot demonstrate invalidity just by *failing to derive* the conclusion from the premises using the arguments that we have declared to be valid.

On the usual model-theoretic account, an argument is said to be valid if and only if the conclusion is true in every model, or interpretation, in which the premises are all true. (I use the terms "model" and "interpretation" interchangeably.) In the simplest sort of case, a model, or interpretation, specifies a domain of interpretation and specifies an assignment of objects from this domain to individual terms (the referents of these terms) and an assignment of sets of *n*-tuples of members of this domain to *n*-ary elementary predicates (the extensions of these predicates). Further, we are provided with an account of the conditions under which each grammatical type of sentence in the language is true in a model. If we want to allow that the truth of a sentence is relative to a world or a time or a context, then we will have to take some steps beyond this simplest sort of case. For instance, if we want to allow that truth is relative to a possible world, our models may contain a domain of worlds and our assignments may assign to each predicate a function from worlds onto referents or extensions. But for simplicity, I will assume in what follows that we are dealing with the simplest sort of case.

So one option for the deflationist might be to take over the standard model-theoretic conception of logical validity wholesale, but then attempt a deflationary "interpretation" (construal) of the terminology it employs. That is the approach I will consider in this section. So the kind of deflationism I am contemplating in this section is one that grants that **is true** and **is false** have *extensions*. But the deflationist expects that somehow it is the fact that [φ] **is true** is equivalent to φ and the fact that [φ] **is false** is equivalent to **not**-[φ] that determine the extensions they have. It is not the independent fact that **is true** and **is false** have these extensions that explains the equivalences.

On the surface, the usual model-theoretic conception of logical validity seems quite contrary to the deflationist outlook. If we define logical validity as preservation of truth in a model, then it seems almost inevitable that we will suppose that there is one special model, call it the *intended interpretation*, such that truth simpliciter is truth in that particular model. The intended interpretation will be that model that assigns to each elementary nonlogical constant that to which it *really refers*. Having posited such an intended interpretation, it seems we will then be committed to identifying it in spatio-temporal-causal terms in the way that the deflationist denies we can do. In this way, the model-theoretic account of logical validity seems to contradict the negative thesis of deflationism.

Here is why the definition of logical validity in terms of truth on an interpretation commits one to the claim that truth simpliciter is truth on one of those interpretations in particular: Suppose a model-theoretic definition of logical validity (for a given language) is the right way to define validity, so that to say that an argument is valid is to say just that for every model in which the premises are true the conclusion is true. And suppose, for a reductio, that there is no model (of the language) such that truth in that model is truth (in that language). Then to say that an argument is valid is to make no claim about truth. In particular, in saying that an argument is valid we are not already saying that if the premises are true in fact, then the conclusion is true in fact. In other words, saying that an argument is valid does not imply that it does not happen that the premises are true in fact while the conclusion is false in fact. So it could happen that an argument was valid in the sense that for every model in which the premises were true the conclusion was true, even though the premises were true in fact and the conclusion was not true in fact. But I take it that a necessary condition on the correctness of any definition of logical validity is that, necessarily, if the definition renders an argument valid, then if the premises are true in fact then the conclusion is true in fact as well. Having assumed that the model-theoretic definition is correct and that there is no intended interpretation, we arrive at a contradiction: Necessarily, if an argument is valid and the premises are true, then so is the conclusion. But it could happen that an argument was valid and the premises were true but the conclusion was false. So if the model-theoretic definition of validity is correct, then, contrary to our supposition, there must be an intended interpretation, that is, a model such that truth in that model is truth.[5]

[5] Against this conclusion it might be argued that those who define logical validity in terms of truth on an interpretation cannot possibly imagine that there is one special interpretation such that truth

One finds in several sources an argument that purports to show that even if the class of models over which we quantify in defining logical validity does not include an intended model, still we can be sure that all of the arguments that are valid according to our model-theoretic definition really are valid. The argument seems to originate with Kreisel (1967, pp. 153–4); it is reiterated by Etchemendy (1990, chapter 11; he demands some modifications) and Cartwright (1994, p. 10). We suppose that we have a deductive calculus that is sound and complete with respect to our model-theoretic semantics. We are not concerned that our model-theoretic definition might invalidate *too many* arguments. So we may assume that all arguments that really are valid are also valid by our definition. Moreover, all of the arguments valid by our definition are provable, since our deductive calculus is complete with respect to our model-theoretic semantics. Finally, all of the arguments that are provable are presumably really valid. So we have come full circle and may conclude that the arguments that really are valid are exactly those that are valid according to our definition. But in drawing this conclusion we have nowhere assumed that our models include an intended interpretation. So it seems we can dispense with that assumption. The trouble with this argument lies in the assumption that all of the provable arguments really are valid. This just takes for granted what we were led to doubt. The deductive calculus is sound; so we can be sure that all of the provable arguments are valid *by our definition*. But to infer that all of the provable arguments really are valid, we need to know that all of the arguments valid by our definition really are valid. If we cannot be sure that truth and falsehood are captured in one of the models over which we quantify in the definition of logical validity, we cannot be entirely sure of that.

Having reached the conclusion that adopting the model-theoretic conception of logical validity commits us to there being an intended interpretation, that is, a model such that truth in that model is truth, we can take a further step and conclude that we are committed to somehow *identifying* the intended interpretation. It would be plainly unsatisfactory to say that *there is* an intended interpretation but we cannot in any way give an informative account of *which* model the intended interpretation *is* (which is not to say that we have to explicitly specify its interpretation of every term in the language).

Presumably the domain for the intended interpretation includes at least everything that exists. The term assignment of the intended interpretation may be stipulatively defined as that which assigns to each individual term what it really refers to and assigns

on that interpretation is truth simpliciter. Any such "intended interpretation" would have to assign the set of all ordinals to the predicate "is an ordinal" and the set of all sets to the predicate "is a set", but, as almost everyone takes for granted, there is no set of all ordinals or set of all sets. On the contrary, I would say that the model-theoretic definition does indeed commit one to supposing that there is an intended interpretation, as I have explained, and the fact that, for the reason just given, there cannot be one is a major, outstanding problem that almost everyone just sweeps under the rug. One approach to this problem attempts to construct a set theory that allows a universal set (see Forster (1992)). Another strategy, initiated recently in Rayo and Williamson (2003) defines logical validity by means of a second-order quantification over interpretive relations rather than by means of a first-order quantification over models. Although such approaches might get us around the problem of the domain's inevitably being too small, they do not allow us to deny that there is an intended interpretation.

to each predicate the extension it really has. Using the word "refers" to encompass the relation between predicates and their extensions as well as the relation between individual terms and their referents, we can say that the intended interpretation assigns to each term what it *refers to*. Thus the requirement that the intended interpretation somehow be identified may be reformulated as the requirement that the reference relation somehow be identified. In this way, the model-theoretic conception of logical validity poses the question, "What is the reference relation?" If we have no satisfactory answer to that, then that is reason to doubt the theory of logical validity—the model-theoretic conception—that puts us in the position of needing an answer to that.

None the less, a deflationist might hope to mimic the methods of model-theoretic semantics while defending a deflationist account of the terminology it employs. In particular, a deflationist might agree that if we define logical validity in terms of truth in a model, then there must be one special model, the intended interpretation, that assigns to each nonlogical constant that to which it really refers. But the deflationist might maintain that this appeal to reference relations is not a problem unless it commits us to constructing a substantive account of the reference relation that attempts to explain in a general way, without restriction to any particular language, what relation must obtain between the use of an expression and some object or set of things in the world in order for the expression to refer to that object or set of things in the world. So a deflationist might deny that we need any such general theory of reference, applicable to other languages as well as our own, and may maintain that we can identify the intended interpretation for our own language by means of a deflationary account of reference. For instance, a deflationist might propose that all we need to understand about reference is the following equivalences:

Reference Equivalence Schemata
[*b*] **refers to** *a* :: *b* **is** *a*.
o **belongs to the extension of** [*F*] : : *o* **is** *F*.
$\langle o_1, o_2 \rangle$ **belongs to the extension of** [*R*] : : o_1*R*'**s** o_2.

The deflationist might claim that such equivalences specify the intended interpretation of our language as precisely as we could wish.

One problem is still how to allow a three-valued semantics. Suppose the deflationist proposes to explain truth-value gaps in terms of extensions and antiextensions in the usual way. So the deflationist might say that a sentence of the form *Fa* is neither true nor false if the thing that *a* refers to is a member of neither the extension of *F* nor a member of the antiextension of *F*. But then the deflationist will have to supplement the deflationary account of membership in an extension with a deflationary account of membership in an antiextension and will have to do so in a way that allows that an object may belong to neither the extension nor the antiextension of a predicate. The problem will be to say something about failure to belong to the extension of a predicate that is different from what the deflationist says about membership in the antiextension of the predicate. The deflationist might propose to treat the predicate **belongs to the extension of** [*F*] as equivalent to **is** *F*, and might propose to treat the predicate **belongs to the antiextension of** [*F*] as equivalent to **is not** *F*. But then there does not seem to be anything left to which the deflationist can treat the predicate **does not belong to the extension of** [*F*] as equivalent.

Another problem is that it is doubtful whether we can really think of the intended interpretation as one model among others if we think of the intended interpretation as specified in this way. We cannot likewise give a deflationary account of models other than the intended interpretation. We have to think of the assignments provided by the nonintended interpretations as literally functions from elementary nonlogical constants to objects and sets of *n*-tuples. Accordingly, if we are to think of the nonintended interpretations as alternatives to the intended interpretation, then we will have to think of the assignment provided by the intended interpretation as genuinely a function from elementary nonlogical constants to objects and sets of *n*-tuples, which it apparently will not be on the deflationist's account. For instance we cannot define a function f by writing: For all x, for all y, $f(x) = y$ if and only if there exists an a such that $[a] = x$ and $a = y$ and $[a]$ refers to a. We cannot define a function in that way because such a definition employs a nonsensical quantification binding a variable that occurs both within and outside of square bracket quotation marks.

Further, it is doubtful whether we really can use instances of the above Reference Equivalence Schemata to identify the reference relation. Whether we can do that will depend on how many vocabulary items have to have their reference specified separately, that is, not by means of some kind of recursion. If in order to specify the intended interpretation we have to specify separately the reference of infinitely many different expressions, then no finite amount of drawing of inferences by means of the Reference Equivalence Schemata will ever do it. It is often said that if a language is to be learnable, then the number of vocabulary items that have to have their reference specified separately has to be finite. But learnability considerations notwithstanding, it is for several reasons not very plausible that the number of such vocabulary items in natural languages really is finite. (Think about numerals. Think about "that"-clauses.) In any case, the learnability argument rests on dubious assumptions about what it is that we learn when we learn a language. (For a detailed development of this objection, see my (1999).)

5. BASIC CONTEXT LOGIC

The rest of this chapter will develop an alternative conception of semantics that deserves to be called deflationist. This will yield a definition of logical validity that we can use to demonstrate that arguments are or are not valid, as the case may be. Moreover, it will establish an equivalence between [φ] **is true** and φ without falling prey to semantic paradoxes. It will not appeal to reference relations at all; a fortiori it will not appeal to reference relations of a kind for which we require a substantive theory. However, this approach to semantics will employ a semantic vocabulary that I do not expect to be explicable in the deflationary way. In that respect my theory may fall short of what some deflationists have aspired to.

The first step will be to explain what I mean by a *context*. In the tradition stemming from Kaplan (1989), a context is supposed to be a set of values of parameters such as time, speaker, hearer, etc. In the tradition stemming from Stalnaker (1974), a context is supposed to be a set of shared assumptions, or a set of assumptions that the speaker supposes are shared. In my terminology, a context is neither of these things. For me, a context can more accurately be described as structure built up from simple sentences that captures what is objectively relevant about the environment in which the conversation that the context pertains to takes place. (For criticism of Stalnaker's definition of contexts in terms of shared assumptions, see my (1998) and my (2003), chapter 5.)

An account of contexts in my sense will have two aspects, a formal aspect and a substantive aspect. The formal aspect explains the formal structure of a context. The formal structure that we have to build into a context will depend on the logical devices present in the language. Initially, we will consider only a very simple language with logical symbols for negation and disjunction only. Every time we add something of a logical nature to the language, such as quantifiers or a truth predicate, we will have to complicate the formal account of contexts as well. The substantive account of contexts will explain what it takes for a structure of the pertinent formal kind to be *the* structure of this formal kind relative to which we wish to evaluate the sentences uttered in a given conversation. At each stage in the development of my theory I will be able to give a precise formal account of the pertinent kind of context. However, I will attempt a substantive account only here at the beginning, for the simplest kind of case.

So to begin, let *PL* be a language containing denumerably many *individual terms*, and, for each n, countably many n-ary *predicates*, as well as the connectives "$\neg$" and "$\vee$". (Syntactically, *individual terms* here are what others might call *individual constants*. I do not want to call them that because there is no presumption here that they constantly *denote*.) As usual, an atomic sentence consists of an n-ary predicate followed by n individual terms. Say that a *literal* is any sentence that is either an atomic sentence or the negation of an atomic sentence. For such a language, a context can be defined simply as a formally consistent, but not necessarily maximal set of literals, thus:

> A *context* for *PL* is a set Γ of literals of *PL* (possibly empty) such that for no sentence φ do both φ and $\neg\varphi$ belong to Γ.

Given this definition of context, we can formulate the conditions under which each type of sentence is assertible or deniable in a context, thus:

- (A0) If $\varphi \in \Gamma$, then φ is assertible in Γ.
- (A$\neg$) If φ is deniable in Γ, then $\neg\varphi$ is assertible in Γ.
- (A$\vee$) If φ is assertible in Γ or ψ is assertible in Γ, then $(\varphi \vee \psi)$ is assertible in Γ.
- (ACl) Nothing else is assertible in Γ.
- (D0) If $\neg\varphi \in \Gamma$, then φ is deniable in Γ.
- (D$\neg$) If φ is assertible in Γ, then $\neg\varphi$ is deniable in Γ.
- (D$\vee$) If φ is deniable in Γ and ψ is deniable in Γ, then $(\varphi \vee \psi)$ is deniable in Γ.
- (DCl) Nothing else is deniable in Γ.

In terms of assertibility in a context for *PL*, we can define logical validity for arguments in *PL* thus:

If S is a set of sentences of *PL* and φ is a sentence of *PL*, then the argument having the sentences in S as premises and the sentence φ as conclusion is *logically valid* if and only if for every context Γ for *PL*, if every member of S is assertible in Γ, then φ is assertible in Γ too.

So, for example, the argument from $\{(\mathbf{Fa} \vee \mathbf{Gb}), \neg \mathbf{Gb}\}$ to $\mathbf{Fa}$ is valid: Suppose $(\mathbf{Fa} \vee \mathbf{Gb})$ is assertible in Γ, so that either $\mathbf{Fa}$ or $\mathbf{Gb}$ is assertible in Γ, which means that either $\mathbf{Fa}$ or $\mathbf{Gb}$ is a member of Γ. Suppose also that $\neg\mathbf{Gb}$ is assertible in Γ, so that $\mathbf{Gb}$ is deniable in Γ; which means that $\neg\mathbf{Gb}$ is a member of Γ. Since it cannot happen that $\mathbf{Gb}$ and $\neg\mathbf{Gb}$ are both members of Γ, $\mathbf{Fa}$ must be a member of Γ, which means that $\mathbf{Fa}$ is assertible in Γ. By contrast, the inference from $\{(\mathbf{Fa} \vee \mathbf{Gb})\}$ to $\mathbf{Fa}$ is invalid. Let $\Gamma = \{\mathbf{Gb}\}$. Then $(\mathbf{Fa} \vee \mathbf{Gb})$ is assertible in Γ, but $\mathbf{Fa}$ is not.

According to the formal account, a context for *PL* is just a consistent set of literals of the language *PL*. The substantive account of contexts for *PL* will explain what it is for such a context to be *the* context pertinent to a conversation, that is, the context relative to which we should judge sentences of *PL* to be assertible or deniable in the conversation. In explaining this, I will assume that conversations have goals. In paradigm cases, these goals will be practical goals such as hunting buffalo, building a house, or cooking a meal. In addition, there may be goals that are themselves linguistic, such as finding an answer to a question. Conversations do not always have real goals, but it will be hard to find a case in which a conversation is not guided at least by feigned goals. Apart from the guidance of goals, a conversation is liable to reduce to a sequence of verbal routines.

I will suppose, moreover, that we can distinguish between courses of action, in pursuit of a goal, that *accord* with a given set of literals and those that do not. I will not be able to define this accordance, but I can give an example. Suppose that our goal is to obtain clean water for cooking. Consider then the following set of sentences (which I am thinking of as close enough, for purposes of illustration, to a set of literals):

{Water is in the well. The well is next to Namu's house. Water is in the barrel. *This* pail is not clean. *That* pail is clean.}

An action that accords with this set of sentences relative to the goal will be fetching water from the well next to Namu's house using *that* pail, not *this* one. Another action that accords with this set might amount to cleaning *this* pail and then using it to fetch water from the well next to Namu's house.

Given these assumptions, the context pertinent to a conversation may be defined as follows:

The context for a conversation is the set of literals such that:
(i) all courses of action in accordance with it relative to the goal of the conversation are good ways of achieving the goal, and
(ii) no proper subset of that set has this property.

In short, the context is the smallest consistent set of literals such that every action in accordance with it is a good way of achieving the goal. Continuing the example, if we added "This pail is red", then the resulting set of literals would be too big; the addition of that sentence would do nothing to narrow down the class of good ways of achieving the goal. If we removed "This pail is not clean" and "That pail is clean", then some actions in accordance with the resulting set of sentences would not be good ways of achieving the goal, namely, using the dirty pail to get the water.

I am not in a position to give a similar substantive account of contexts for each of the languages that we will encounter in what follows. In each case, however, the objective in developing such an account would be to explain how the contents of the context comprise exactly what is in some sense most *relevant* given the goals of the conversation and the actual circumstances in which the conversation takes place. Contexts, so understood, are objective in the sense that interlocutors may be unaware of or even mistaken about their contents. That can happen because interlocutors may be unaware of the circumstances in which their conversation takes place or because they are not very good at determining what is relevant given their goals and the circumstances. Contexts change because goals are either achieved or abandoned in favor of new goals, or because external circumstances change; they do not change because someone decides to speak *as if* the context had a certain content. (For further discussion of the nature of communication and contexts, see chapter 3 of my (2003) or chapter 1 of my (forthcoming).)

Suppose now that we want to add quantifiers to the language. Let *QL* be a language like *PL* except that in addition *QL* contains denumerably many individual variables and the quantifier "$\exists$". Suppose, moreover, that one of the binary predicates of *QL* (and *PL*) is the identity sign "=". Let $\forall\nu\varphi$ abbreviate $\neg\exists\nu\neg\varphi$ in the usual way. Say that $\varphi c/\nu$ is the result of substituting c for ν wherever ν occurs free in φ. Say that two individual terms c and d are *identity-linked* in a set S if and only if either $c = d \in S$ or there is a term e such that c is identity-linked to e in S and e is identity-linked to d in S. We define contexts for *QL* as follows:

A *context* Γ for *QL* is a pair $\langle B_\Gamma, N_\Gamma\rangle$ such that:

(1) B_Γ, the *base*, is a set of literals of *PL* such that:
   (a) for all φ,φ and $\neg\varphi$ are not both in B_Γ, and
   (b) if for each i, $1 \leq i \leq n$, c_i and d_i are identity-linked, then not both $\varphi c_1/\nu_1 \ldots\ c_n/\nu_n$ and $\neg\varphi d_1/\nu_1 \ldots\ d_n/\nu_n$ are in B_Γ, and

(2) N_Γ, the *domain*, is a nonempty set of individual terms that includes every individual term that occurs in any member of B_Γ (and possibly other individual terms as well).

To the conditions on assertibility and deniability, we will now add conditions for the identity sentences and the quantified sentences, thus:

(A=) If $\varphi c/\nu$ is assertible in Γ and $c = d$ or $d = c$ is assertible in Γ, then $\varphi d/\nu$ is assertible in Γ.

(A$\exists$) If for some individual term c, $\varphi c/\nu$ is assertible in Γ, then $\exists\nu\varphi$ is assertible in Γ.

(D=) If $\varphi c/\nu$ is deniable in Γ and $c = d$ or $d = c$ is assertible in Γ, then $\varphi d/\nu$ is deniable in Γ.

(D∃) If for all individual terms $c \in N_\Gamma$, $\varphi c/\nu$ is deniable in Γ, then $\exists\nu\varphi$ is deniable in Γ.

As always, if a sentence is not assertible or deniable in a context by any of the conditions already laid down, then it is neither assertible nor deniable in the context. Logical validity may be defined as before (with "*QL*" in place of "*PL*").[6]

To illustrate the use of this apparatus, let us see how a sentence on the order of "Every *F* is *G*" might be assertible in a context although "Everything is *G*" is not assertible in that context. Suppose $B_\Gamma = \{\mathbf{Fa}, \mathbf{Ga}, \mathbf{Gb}, \neg\mathbf{Fc}\}$, and $N_\Gamma = \{\mathbf{a}, \mathbf{b}, \mathbf{c}\}$. $\forall\mathbf{xGx}$ ("Everything is *G*") is not assertible in Γ, for while **c** is in N_Γ, **Gc** is not assertible in Γ because it is atomic and does not belong to B_Γ. But $\forall\mathbf{x}(\neg\mathbf{Fx} \vee \mathbf{Gx})$ ("Every *F* is *G*") is assertible in Γ because for all *c* in N_Γ, either $\neg\mathbf{F}c$ is assertible in Γ or $\mathbf{G}c$ is assertible in Γ. As for **a** and **b**, **Ga** and **Gb** are both assertible in Γ because they both belong to B_Γ. As for **c**, $\neg\mathbf{Fc}$ is assertible in Γ since $\neg\mathbf{Fc}$ is in B_Γ.

The resulting logic is not classical, but that is not a bad thing at all. $(\varphi \vee \neg\varphi)$ is not assertible in every context, and that is a reasonable result, because it is not relevant in every conversation. If we are planning a picnic, then "Either it will rain or not" might be relevant, at least as a reminder that rain is an issue, but in most contexts it will be perfectly irrelevant. Furthermore, $\forall\nu\varphi$ does not imply $\varphi c/\nu$ for arbitrary terms *c* of the language. That too is a reasonable result. There will be contexts in which we can relevantly assert "Everyone has arrived" even if Vladimir Putin has not arrived (and is not expected to arrive). So "Everyone has arrived" may be assertible in some context even though "Vladimir Putin has arrived" is not assertible in that context. (For detailed discussions of this failure of universal instantiation, see my (1997) and my (2003), chapter 7.) Classical logic (for arguments containing at most finitely many premises) is recoverable by confining the class of contexts to contexts whose bases are maximal (in the sense that for every atomic sentence either it or its negation belongs).

Before proceeding, let me explain how and to what extent this approach to semantics circumvents the problem of reference. As I observed in section 4, one of the ways in which we are driven to posit a reference relation is by defining logical validity as preservation of truth on an interpretation; for this forces on us the supposition that there is one special interpretation such that truth (simpliciter) is truth on that interpretation, and then we expect to use the concept of reference to characterize the intended interpretation. The present approach to logical validity avoids that particular motive in as much as in judging an argument to be logically valid we do not have to entertain a variety of possible interpretations of the language at all.

There is perhaps some danger that when all is said and done, we will have to resort to real reference relations in order to explicate some of the concepts that this alternative approach relies on. In particular, there might be some temptation to appeal to correspondence relations of some kind in identifying the context pertinent to a conversation. We might be tempted to say that the set of literals pertinent to a conversation is that which *describes* the set of facts that are relevant to the conversation.

[6] This definition has undesirable consequences in the case of infinite sets of premises (e.g., the omega rule is valid). These can be avoided by means of Leblanc's method of rewrite functions (1976).

But since we are no longer appealing to any kind of mapping from expressions into objects or sets of n-tuples of objects in the semantics itself, it should not seem just obvious that we will have to do it in that way.

Further, we might still have to appeal to some kind of reference relation when we go to give the semantics for indexical and demonstrative expressions. We might say that what varies from context to context for a demonstrative is which object in the world it *refers* to. Here I will not attempt to develop a logic of demonstratives; so that too will remain an open question. However, the fact that speakers can use indexicals and demonstratives to refer to different objects on different occasions is certainly not a sufficient reason to suppose that we have to explicate the semantic properties of sentences in terms of reference relations that hold between each of the elementary nonlogical constants and appropriate referents. Pointing at an object and uttering "That!" certainly creates some kind of real relation between the utterance of "That!" and the object; but that fact alone does not show that we can explicate truth by assigning a reference to every noun, verb and adjective.

6. CONTEXT LOGIC FOR "IS TRUE" AND "IS FALSE"

Next we want to define conditions of assertibility and deniability in a context for the sentences of a language containing predicates meaning *true* and *false*. So let *WL* (the "W" standing for the German "wahr") be a language like *QL* except that, in addition: (i) For every sentence φ of *WL*, *WL* contains a name of φ, which we form by putting square brackets around φ, thus: $[\varphi]$. We will call these names of sentences *sentence terms*. (ii) *WL* contains denumerably many *sentence variables*. Predicates that may be followed by a sentence term or sentence variable at a given place (as well as by an individual term or individual variable at that place) will be said to be *sentential* at that place. (iii) The predicates of *WL* include the one-place predicates "**T**" and "**F**", to be understood as meaning *true* and *false*, respectively. These predicates will be *sentential* in their one and only place. (iv) *WL* contains a *sentential quantifier* "Σ", and if τ is a sentence variable, and $\varphi[\psi]/\tau$ (the result of substituting $[\psi]$ for τ wherever τ is free in φ) is a sentence of *WL*, then $\Sigma\tau\varphi$ is a sentence of *WL* too. Let $\Pi\tau\varphi$ abbreviate $\neg\Sigma\tau\neg\varphi$.

In addition, we will need a language which is just like *PL* (our quantifier-free language), except that in addition it contains all the sentence terms of *WL*. Call this language *PL+*. Suppose (for the sake of later illustrations) that *PL*, and thus *PL+*, contains the predicate "**U**", which we understand as meaning *utters*, and which is sentential in its second place. *PL+* does not contain **T** or **F** or Σ, except as parts of sentence terms.

We may now define a context for *WL* as follows:

A *context* Γ for *WL* is a triple $\langle B_\Gamma, N_\Gamma, S_\Gamma \rangle$ such that:

(1) B_Γ, the *base*, is a set of literals of *PL+* such that:
   (a) for all φ, φ and $\neg\varphi$ are not both in B_Γ, and
   (b) if for each i, $1 \leq i \leq n$, c_i and d_i are identity-linked, then not both $\varphi c_1/\nu_1 \ldots c_n/\nu_n$ and $\neg\varphi d_1/\nu_1 \ldots d_n/\nu_n$ are in B_Γ, and

(c) if $\varphi \neq \psi$, then $[\varphi]$ and $[\psi]$ are not identity-linked in B_Γ, and

(2) N_Γ, the *domain*, is a nonempty set of individual terms that includes every individual term that occurs in any member of B_Γ, and

(3) S_Γ, the *sentential domain*, is a nonempty set of sentence terms that includes every sentence term that occurs in any member of B_Γ (and possibly other sentence terms as well).

Supposing that contexts are now defined in this way, we may add assertibility and deniability conditions for sentences containing the new vocabulary as follows:

(A**T**) If φ is assertible in Γ, then $\mathbf{T}[\varphi]$ is assertible in Γ.
(A**F**) If φ is deniable in Γ, then $\mathbf{F}[\varphi]$ is assertible in Γ.
(AΣ) If for some sentence ψ, $\varphi[\psi]/\tau$ is assertible in Γ, then $\Sigma\tau\varphi$ is assertible in Γ.
(D**T**) If φ is deniable in Γ, then $\mathbf{T}[\varphi]$ is deniable in Γ.
(D**F**) If φ is assertible in Γ, then $\mathbf{F}[\varphi]$ is deniable in Γ.
(D Σ) If for all sentences ψ such that either ψ is assertible or deniable in Γ or $[\psi] \in S_\Gamma$, $\varphi[\psi]/\tau$ is deniable in Γ, then $\Sigma\tau\varphi$ is deniable in Γ.

(The usual closure clause still applies, allowing these new conditions on assertibility and deniability.)

For example, let us see how a sentence meaning, "Every sentence John uttered is true" can be assertible even when "Every sentence is true" is not assertible but "John uttered some sentence" is assertible. To construct such a context we need to ensure that for each sentence that is either assertible or deniable or named in the sentential domain, if that sentence is deniable, then it is deniable that John uttered it. Thus, we will have to employ a recursion, such as the following:

$$N_\Gamma = \{\mathbf{a}, \mathbf{b}, \mathbf{j}, \mathbf{d}\}$$
$$S_{\Gamma_0} = \{[\mathbf{Fa}], [\mathbf{Hc}]\}$$
$$B_{\Gamma_0} = \{\mathbf{Uj}[\mathbf{Fa}], \neg\mathbf{Uj}[\mathbf{Hc}], \mathbf{Fa}, \mathbf{Gb}\}$$
$$S_{\Gamma_{i+1}} = S_{\Gamma_i} \cup \{[\varphi] | \varphi \text{ is deniable in } \langle B_{\Gamma_i}, N_\Gamma, S_{\Gamma_i}\rangle\}$$
$$B_{\Gamma_{i+1}} = B_{\Gamma_i} \cup \{\neg\mathbf{Uj}[\varphi] | \varphi \text{ is deniable in } \langle B_{\Gamma_i}, N_\Gamma, S_{\Gamma_i}\rangle\}$$
$$S_\Gamma = \bigcup S_{\Gamma_j}, j \geq 0.$$
$$B_\Gamma = \bigcup B_{\Gamma_j}, j \geq 0.$$

$\Sigma\mathbf{sUjs}$ ("John uttered some sentence") is assertible in Γ because $\mathbf{Uj}[\mathbf{Fa}]$ is assertible in Γ. $\Pi\mathbf{sTs}$ ("Every sentence is true") is not assertible in Γ, because, although $[\mathbf{Hc}]$ is in S_Γ, $\mathbf{T}[\mathbf{Hc}]$ is not assertible in Γ (because $\mathbf{Hc}$ is not assertible in Γ). Still, $\Pi\mathbf{s}(\neg\mathbf{Ujs} \vee \mathbf{Ts})$ ("Every sentence John uttered is true") is assertible in Γ, because for every sentence φ, if φ is assertible or deniable in Γ or $[\varphi]$ is in S_Γ, then either $\neg\mathbf{Uj}[\varphi]$ is assertible in Γ or $\mathbf{T}[\varphi]$ is assertible in Γ. (In the case of $\mathbf{Hc}$ and every sentence deniable in Γ, $\neg\mathbf{Uj}[\varphi]$ is assertible in Γ, and in the case of $\mathbf{Fa}$, $\mathbf{Gb}$ and every sentence assertible in Γ, $\mathbf{T}[\varphi]$ is assertible in Γ.)

Logical validity is defined in the same way as before: If S is a set of sentences of *WL* and φ is a sentence of *WL*, then the argument having the sentences in S as premises and φ as conclusion is logically valid if and only if for every context Γ for

WL, if every member of S is assertible in Γ, then φ is assertible in Γ too. It is apparent that Semantic Ascent and Semantic Descent are valid without qualification. The validity of Semantic Ascent is obvious from the assertibility conditions for sentences of the form $\mathbf{T}[\varphi]$. So consider the case of Semantic Descent: Suppose $\mathbf{T}[\varphi]$ is assertible in arbitrary context Γ. There are two ways this might happen. Case 1: φ is assertible in Γ. Case 2: For some individual term c, $c = [\varphi]$ (or $[\varphi] = c$) is assertible in Γ and $\mathbf{T}c$ is assertible in Γ. But given that $c = [\varphi]$ is assertible in Γ, and given that for any sentence ψ distinct from φ, $[\psi]$ and $[\varphi]$ are not identity-linked in Γ, $\mathbf{T}c$ can be assertible in Γ only if $\mathbf{T}[\varphi]$ is assertible on some other grounds, which takes us back to case 1. So in either case, φ is assertible in Γ.

Still, there are no paradoxical sentences in *WL*. We can readily allow that there may be contexts Γ such that a sentence like "λ = 'λ is not true' ", or $\mathbf{a} = [\neg\mathbf{Ta}]$, is a member of B_Γ and so is assertible in Γ. But this does not generate any contradiction. We simply find that $\neg\mathbf{Ta}$ cannot be either assertible or deniable in such a context. (Likewise, $\mathbf{Ta}$ cannot be either assertible or deniable in such a context.) This is not because no sentence of the form $\neg\mathbf{Ta}$ can ever be assertible. For instance, $\neg\mathbf{Ta}$ would be assertible in a context in which $\mathbf{a} = [\mathbf{Gb}]$ were assertible and $\mathbf{Gb}$ were deniable. We cannot duplicate the paradoxical reasoning of section 3, because we cannot rely on Indirect Proof. We find that $\{\mathbf{a} = [\neg\mathbf{Ta}], \mathbf{Ta}\}$ implies $\neg\mathbf{Ta}$, since $\mathbf{a} = [\neg\mathbf{Ta}]$, and $\mathbf{Ta}$ are never assertible together in a single context (so that $\{\mathbf{a} = [\neg\mathbf{Ta}], \mathbf{Ta}\}$ implies every sentence of the language). However, $\{\mathbf{a} = [\neg\mathbf{Ta}]\}$ does not imply $\neg\mathbf{Ta}$, because $\neg\mathbf{Ta}$ may fail to be assertible (indeed, cannot be assertible) in a context in which $\mathbf{a} = [\neg\mathbf{Ta}]$ is assertible.[7]

Notice that the present semantics finds no semantic difference between falsehood and nontruth. That is, $\mathbf{F}[\varphi]$ and $\neg\mathbf{T}[\varphi]$ are assertible in exactly the same contexts (those in which φ is deniable) and are deniable in exactly the same contexts (those in which φ is assertible). So the sentence $\neg(\mathbf{T}[\varphi] \vee \mathbf{F}[\varphi])$ is a contradiction, assertible in no context. The semantics is none the less three-valued, because it is a semantics of assertibility in a context, not of truth, and sentences may be neither assertible nor deniable in some contexts.

7. CONTEXT LOGIC FOR "ASSERTIBLE" AND "DENIABLE"

If I left it at that, I could be accused of cheating. The challenge posed by the semantic paradoxes is not just to construct a consistent artificial language. It is not even to construct a consistent artificial language containing a predicate having a logic

[7] Some theorists of truth who have put forward diagnoses of the semantic paradoxes have wished to claim that in some context-relative sense we may be able to assign truth or falsehood to liar sentences (e.g., Simmons (1993)). But as JC Beall has pointed out (2001), this should not be the position of a deflationist. A deflationist should happily concede that in the case of a simple predication, such as $\mathbf{Ta}$ (as opposed to, say, an occurrence of $\mathbf{T}$ under the scope of a quantifier), there should be some equivalent sentence not containing the truth predicate, and if there is not, then the sentence is meaningless, or at least truth-value-less.

that looks like the logic we expect from the predicate "is true". Rather, at the very least, the challenge is to show that we can formulate our semantical theories of languages in terms of a metalanguage that does not in turn lend itself to semantic paradoxes. (As Simmons (1993) has shown, other authors are not always very scrupulous in facing up to this aspect of the challenge.) Here we are formulating our semantics as concerned with the property of assertibility in a context. So to meet the challenge we must show that a semantics of the same kind can be constructed for a language of the kind that we use in formulating our semantic theories, and we must be able to assure ourselves by means of that semantics that our language does not lend itself to semantic paradoxes.

Let *AL* be a language like *WL* except that, in addition: (i) If φ is a sentence of *AL*, then $[\varphi]$ is sentence term of *AL*. (ii) *AL* contains denumerably many terms called *context terms* and, correspondingly, denumerably many *context variables*. (iii) *AL* contains the two-place predicates **Asst**$(\ldots, \ldots)$ and **Den**$(\ldots, \ldots)$, and if γ is a context term and α is either a sentence term or an individual term of *AL*, then both **Asst**(α, γ) and **Den**(α, γ) are sentences of *AL* as well. **Asst**$([\varphi], \gamma)$ is understood as meaning "φ" *is assertible in* γ, and **Den**$([\varphi], \gamma)$ is understood as meaning "φ" *is deniable in* γ. (These predicates carry parenthesis for clarity.) (iv) *AL* contains the quantifier "§" (call it the *double ess*), and if ω is a context variable and γ is a context term and $\varphi\gamma/\omega$ is a sentence of *AL*, then $\S\omega\varphi$ is a sentence of *AL*. Let $\P\omega\varphi$ abbreviate $\neg\S\omega\neg\varphi$.

In addition, we will need a language which is just like *PL* (our quantifier-free language), except that in addition it contains all the sentence terms of *AL*. Call this language *PL‡*.

In terms of *PL‡* we will now define contexts for *AL* inductively. Initially, we define the set of *basic* contexts for *AL*, and then in terms of those we define the rest of the contexts for *AL*.

A *basic context* Γ for *AL* is a quintuple $\langle B_\Gamma, N_\Gamma, S_\Gamma, C_\Gamma, f_\Gamma\rangle$ such that:

(1) B_Γ, the *base*, is a set of literals of *PL‡* such that:
   (a) for all φ, φ and $\neg\varphi$ are not both in B_Γ, and
   (b) if for each i, $1 \leq i \leq n$, c_i and d_i are identity-linked, then not both $\varphi c_1/v_1 \ldots c_n/v_n$ and $\neg\varphi d_1/v_1 \ldots d_n/v_n$ are in B_Γ, and
   (c) if $\varphi \neq \psi$, then $[\varphi]$ and $[\psi]$ are not identity-linked in B_Γ, and
(2) N_Γ, the *domain*, is a nonempty set of individual terms that includes every individual term that occurs in any member of B_Γ, and
(3) S_Γ, the *sentential domain*, is a nonempty set of sentence terms that includes every sentence term that occurs in any member of B_Γ, and
(4) C_Γ, the *context domain*, is a set of context terms, and
(5) f_Γ, the *context assignment function*, is a function whose domain is C_Γ such that for all $\gamma \in C_\Gamma$, $f_\Gamma(\gamma) = \emptyset$.

(The empty set, $\emptyset$, is *not* a context for *AL*.) Now we can define the set of contexts for *AL* stagewise, as follows:

Let M_0 = the set of basic contexts for *AL*, as defined above.
For each $i \geq 0$, let M_{i+1} = the set of quintuples $\langle B_\Gamma, N_\Gamma, S_\Gamma, C_\Gamma, f_\Gamma\rangle$ such that

(1) B_Γ,N_Γ,S_Γ,and C_Γ are as in the definition of basic contexts for *AL* above, and
(2) f_Γ is a function whose domain is C_Γ such that for all $\gamma \in C_\Gamma$, either
    (a) $f_\Gamma(\gamma) = \emptyset$, or
    (b) $f_\Gamma(\gamma) \in M_i$.

Let the set of contexts for *AL* be $M = \bigcup M_i, i \geq 0$.

Supposing that contexts are defined in this way, we may add assertibility and deniability conditions for sentences containing the new vocabulary as follows:

(A**Asst**) If $\gamma \in C_\Gamma$ and $f_\Gamma(\gamma) \neq \emptyset$ and φ is assertible in $f_\Gamma(\gamma)$, then **Asst**($[\varphi]$, γ) is assertible in Γ.

(A**Den**) If $\gamma \in C_\Gamma$ and $f_\Gamma(\gamma) \neq \emptyset$ and φ is deniable in $f_\Gamma(\gamma)$, then **Den** ($[\varphi]$,γ) is assertible in Γ.

(A§) If for some context variable ω and some context constant γ, $\varphi\gamma/\omega$ is assertible in Γ, then $\S\omega\varphi$ is assertible in Γ.

(D**Asst**) If $\gamma \in C_\Gamma$ and $f_\Gamma(\gamma) \neq \emptyset$ and φ is not assertible in $f_\Gamma(\gamma)$, then **Asst**($[\varphi]$,γ) is deniable in Γ.

(D**Den**) If $\gamma \in C_\Gamma$ and $f_\Gamma(\gamma) \neq \emptyset$ and φ is not deniable in $f_\Gamma(\gamma)$, then **Den**($[\varphi]$, γ) is deniable in Γ.

(D§) If for some context variable ω and every context constant $\gamma \in C_\Gamma$, $\varphi\gamma/\omega$ is deniable in Γ, then $\S\omega\varphi$ is deniable in Γ.

In light of the new use for sentence terms, we need to revise the deniability conditions for sentences formed with the quantifier Σ, thus:

(DΣ) If for all sentences ψ such that either $[\psi]$ is a member of S_Γ or ψ is assertible or deniable in Γ *or* (this is the new part) for some γ in C_Γ, ψ is assertible or deniable in $f_\Gamma(\gamma)$, $\varphi[\psi]/\tau$ is deniable in Γ, then $\Sigma\tau\varphi$ is deniable in Γ.

Logical validity for *AL* may be defined according to the usual pattern: Where *S* is a finite set of sentences of *AL* and φ is a sentence of *AL*, the argument having the sentences in *S* as premises and φ as conclusion is *logically valid* if and only if for every context Γ for *AL*, if every sentence in *S* is assertible in Γ, then φ is assertible in Γ too.

One thing to notice about these new assertibility conditions is that we do not define the deniability conditions for **Asst**($[\varphi]$, γ) in terms of the deniability of φ, which would be the usual pattern; likewise, we do not define the deniability conditions for **Den**($[\varphi]$, γ) in terms of the assertibility of φ. Rather, we define the deniability conditions for **Asst**($[\varphi]$, γ) in terms of the *non*assertibility of φ, and we define the deniability conditions for **Den**($[\varphi]$, γ) in terms of the *non*deniability of φ. The rationale for these departures from the usual pattern is that we want to be able to say in this language that a sentence is neither assertible nor deniable. Given the assertibility conditions laid down in the previous paragraph, a sentence of the form $\neg$(**Asst**($[\varphi]$, γ) $\vee$ **Den**($[\varphi]$, γ)) will be assertible in Γ provided φ is neither assertible nor deniable in $f_\Gamma(\gamma) \neq \emptyset$ (But (**Asst**($[\varphi]$, γ) $\vee$ **Den**($[\varphi]$, γ)) is not assertible in every other context, because it may happen that, for some Γ, γ is not in C_Γ, or γ is in C_Γ but $f_\Gamma(\gamma) = \emptyset$.)

For an example, let us construct a context in which the sentence Σ**s**¶**gAsst**(**s**, **g**) ("Some sentence is assertible in every context") is assertible. Suppose:

$B_\Gamma = \varnothing$, $N_\Gamma = \{$**b**$\}$, $C_\Gamma = \{\Delta, \Lambda\}$, $f_\Gamma(\Delta) = \Psi$, $f_\Gamma(\Lambda) = \Theta$.
$B_\Psi = \{$**Fa**$\}$, $N_\Psi = \{$**a**$\}$, $C_\Psi = \{\Delta\}$, $f_\Psi(\Delta) = \varnothing$.
$B_\Theta = \{$**Fa**, ¬**Hc**$\}$, $N_\Theta = \{$**a**$\}$, $C_\Theta = \{\Lambda\}$, $f_\Theta(\Lambda) = \varnothing$.

(The membership of the sentential contexts is irrelevant for purposes of this example.) **Fa** belongs to B_Ψ. So **Fa** is assertible in $\Psi = f_\Gamma(\Delta)$. So **Asst**([**Fa**], Δ) is assertible in Γ. Also, **Fa** belongs to B_Θ. So **Fa** is assertible in $\Theta = f_\Gamma(\Lambda)$. So **Asst**([**Fa**], Λ) is assertible in Γ. But Δ and Λ are the only context terms in C_Γ. So ¶**gAsst**([**Fa**],**g**) is assertible in Γ. So Σ**s**¶**gAsst**(**s**, **g**) is assertible in Γ.

An important feature of the construction of the set of contexts for *AL* is that it can never happen that, for some γ in C_Γ, $f_\Gamma(\gamma) = \Gamma$. That is, for all contexts Γ for *AL*, and for all $\gamma \in C_\Gamma$, $f_\Gamma(\gamma) \neq \Gamma$. Call this the *well-foundedness assumption* for contexts for *AL*. In the next section, I will defend the reasonableness of this assumption. For now let us observe that in consequence of this feature of the construction of contexts, we cannot formulate in *AL* any paradoxes of assertibility in a context. Here I can only illustrate how the paradoxes are evaded. For a general proof, we would need to prove that in general it cannot happen that for some sentence φ and some context Γ for *AL*, both φ and $\neg\varphi$ are assertible in Γ. More generally, we need to show that, if for each i, $1 \leq i \leq n$, c_i and d_i are identity-linked, then not both $\varphi c_1/v_1 \ldots c_n/v_n$ and $\neg\varphi d_1/v_1 \ldots d_n/v_n$ are assertible in Γ. These things can be done, but I will not take the space to do them here.

For example, suppose $\alpha =$ "α is not assertible in any context". From this it might seem that we could derive a contradiction as follows:

1. $\alpha =$ "α is not assertible in any context".
2. Suppose α is assertible in some arbitrary context Γ.
3. Given 2, "α is not assertible in any context" is assertible in Γ.
4. Given 2, for all $c \in C_\Gamma$, "α is not assertible in"$^\frown c$ is assertible in Γ.
5. Given 2, for all $c \in C_\Gamma$, "α is assertible in"$^\frown c$ is deniable in Γ.
6. Given 2, for all $c \in C_\Gamma$, α is not assertible in $f_\Gamma(c)$.
7. Given 2, α is not assertible in Γ.
8. α is not assertible in any context. (From 2–7.)
9. Suppose α is not assertible in any context.
10. Given 9, "α is not assertible in any context" is not assertible in any context.
11. Given 9, for every context Γ, there is a $c \in C_\Gamma$ such that "α is not assertible in"$^\frown c$ is not assertible in Γ.
12. Given 9, for every context Γ, there is a $c \in C_\Gamma$ such that "α is assertible in"$^\frown c$ is not deniable in Γ.
13. Given 9, for every context Γ, there is a $c \in C_\Gamma$ such that α is assertible in $f_\Gamma(c)$.
14. Given 9, α is assertible in some context.
15. α is assertible in some context. (From 9–14.)
16. α is both assertible in some context and not assertible in any context.

However, there is a fallacy in this argument, in the step from 6 to 7. From the fact that for all $c \in C_\Gamma$, α is not assertible in $f_\Gamma(c)$, it does not follow that α is not assertible in Γ, because we cannot assume that Γ is in the range of f_Γ. Indeed, by the well-foundedness assumption, we can be sure that it is not.

There has to be a fallacy in the second half of the argument too, since we can easily construct a context in which both of the following two sentences are assertible:

$\alpha =$ "α is not assertible in any context".
α is not assertible in any context.

We can even arrange that in that same context, the following sentence is assertible:

"$\alpha =$ 'α is not assertible in any context' " is assertible in every context.

(We took this for granted in the step from 5 to 6 and the step from 12 to 13.) That is, $\mathbf{a} = [\neg\S\mathbf{gAsst}(\mathbf{a}, \mathbf{g})]$, $\neg\S\mathbf{gAsst}(\mathbf{a}, \mathbf{g})$, and $\P\mathbf{gAsst}([\mathbf{a} = [\neg\S\mathbf{gAsst}(\mathbf{a}, \mathbf{g})], \mathbf{g})$ may all be assertible in a single context. Such a context Γ may be constructed as follows:

$B_\Gamma = \{\mathbf{a} = [\neg\S\mathbf{gAsst}(\mathbf{a}, \mathbf{g})]\}$, $N_\Gamma = \{\mathbf{a}\}$, $C_\Gamma = \{\Delta\}$, $f_\Gamma(\Delta) = \Theta$, where:
$B_\Theta = \{\mathbf{a} = [\neg\S\mathbf{gAsst}(\mathbf{a}, \mathbf{g})]\}$, $N_\Theta = \{\mathbf{a}\}$, $C_\Theta = \{\Delta\}$, $f_\Theta(\Delta) = \Lambda$, where:
$B_\Lambda = \{\mathbf{a} = [\neg\S\mathbf{gAsst}(\mathbf{a}, \mathbf{g})]\}$, $N_\Lambda = \{\mathbf{a}\}$, $C_\Lambda = \{\Delta\}$, $f_\Lambda(\Delta) = \Omega$, where:
$B_\Omega = \emptyset$, $N_\Omega = \{\mathbf{a}\}$, $C_\Omega = \{\Delta\}$, $f_\Omega(\Delta) = \emptyset$.

Clearly, $\mathbf{a} = [\neg\S\mathbf{gAsst}(\mathbf{a}, \mathbf{g})]$ is assertible in Γ. Since it is also assertible in $f_\Gamma(\Delta) = \Theta$, and Δ is the only member of C_Γ, $\P\mathbf{gAsst}([\mathbf{a} = [\neg\S\mathbf{gAsst}(\mathbf{a},\mathbf{g})]], \mathbf{g})$ is assertible in Γ. To show that $\neg\S\mathbf{gAsst}(\mathbf{a}, \mathbf{g})$ is assertible in Γ, we have to do a little more work: Observe that $\mathbf{Asst}(\mathbf{a}, \Delta)$ is not deniable in Ω; so $\S\mathbf{gAsst}(\mathbf{a}, \mathbf{g})$ is not deniable in Ω; so $\neg\S\mathbf{gAsst}(\mathbf{a}, \mathbf{g})$ is not assertible in $\Omega = f_\Lambda(\Delta)$. So $\mathbf{Asst}([\neg\S\mathbf{gAsst}(\mathbf{a}, \mathbf{g})], \Delta)$ is deniable in Λ. Since $\mathbf{a} = [\neg\S\mathbf{gAsst}(\mathbf{a}, \mathbf{g})]$ is assertible in Λ, $\mathbf{Asst}(\mathbf{a}, \Delta)$ is deniable in Λ. Since Δ is the only context term in C_Λ, for all γ in C_Λ, $\mathbf{Asst}(\mathbf{a}, \gamma)$ is deniable in Λ. So $\S\mathbf{gAsst}(\mathbf{a}, \mathbf{g})$ is deniable in Λ. So $\neg\S\mathbf{gAsst}(\mathbf{a}, \mathbf{g})$ is assertible in $\Lambda = f_\Theta(\Delta)$. So $\mathbf{Asst}([\neg\S\mathbf{gAsst}(\mathbf{a}, \mathbf{g})],\Delta)$ is not deniable in Θ (indeed, it is assertible in Θ). Since $\mathbf{a} = [\neg\S\mathbf{gAsst}(\mathbf{a}, \mathbf{g})]$ is assertible in Θ, $\mathbf{Asst}(\mathbf{a}, \Delta)$ is not deniable in Θ (it is assertible). So for some γ in C_Θ, $\mathbf{Asst}(\mathbf{a}, \gamma)$ is not deniable in Θ. So $\S\mathbf{gAsst}(\mathbf{a}, \mathbf{g})$ is not deniable in Θ (but is assertible). So $\neg\S\mathbf{gAsst}(\mathbf{a}, \mathbf{g})$ is not assertible in $\Theta = f_\Gamma(\Delta)$. So $\mathbf{Asst}([\neg\S\mathbf{gAsst}(\mathbf{a}, \mathbf{g})], \Delta)$ is deniable in Γ. Since $\mathbf{a} = [\neg\S\mathbf{gAsst}(\mathbf{a}, \mathbf{g})]$ is assertible in Γ, $\mathbf{Asst}(\mathbf{a}, \Delta)$ is deniable in Γ. So for all γ in C_Γ, $\mathbf{Asst}(\mathbf{a}, \gamma)$ is deniable in Γ. So $\S\mathbf{gAsst}(\mathbf{a}, \mathbf{g})$ is deniable in Γ. So, finally, $\neg\S\mathbf{gAsst}(\mathbf{a}, \mathbf{g})$ is assertible in Γ. The precise location of the fallacy in the second half is the step from 13 to 14. As the example shows, from the fact that for every context (consider Θ) that we can talk about in our context (which might be Γ), there is, from the point of view of that context (Θ) a context in which α is assertible (consider Λ), it does not follow that from the point of view of our own context (Γ) there is a context in which α is assertible (α not being assertible in Θ).

For a simpler example of how paradox is avoided, suppose we had a context term "Δ" such that f_Γ("Δ") $= \Gamma$ and a sentence β, which read "β is not assertible in Δ".

Then it might appear that from the fact that $\beta =$ "β is not assertible in Δ" we could derive the contradictory conclusion that β both is and is not assertible in Γ (see my (2003), p. 209). However, the derivation will not go through without the assumption that $f_\Gamma(\text{“}\Delta\text{”}) = \Gamma$, and that equation is precluded by the well-foundedness assumption for contexts for *AL*.

8. THE CONTEXT WE ARE IN

The language *AL* is consistent in the sense that there is no sentence φ of *AL* such that both φ and $\neg\varphi$ are assertible in a single context. Furthermore, if for each i, $1 \leq i \leq n$, c_i and d_i are identity-linked in Γ, then not both $\varphi c_1/v_1 \ldots c_n/v_n$ and $\neg\varphi d_1/v_1 \ldots d_n/v_n$ are assertible in Γ. (These claims require a proof, which I am not giving here.) It is essential to these results that the context assignment function for a context Γ cannot assign Γ itself to any context term in the context domain for Γ. In other words, we must deny the possibility of anyone's talking about the context that he or she is in. This is what I have called the well-foundedness assumption. Only due to this limitation are we able to block the derivation of contradictions from plain facts such as the fact that α = "α is not assertible in any context". That restriction is guaranteed by our construction of the set of contexts. But now we must ask whether the well-foundedness assumption is a reasonable restriction that we can motivate independently.

As I explained in section 5 above, we are to think of the context pertinent to a conversation as comprising everything that is relevant to the conversation in light of the goals of the conversation and the actual circumstances in which it takes place. The context for a conversation, so conceived, is objective in the sense that the participants in the conversation may be entirely mistaken about the contents of the context. What is relevant to the goals of the conversation in light of the actual external circumstances does not depend on the interlocutors' states of mind.

In light of this conception of the context as comprising what is objectively relevant to the conversation, we can perhaps understand the necessity of the well-foundedness assumption. Suppose that Γ is the context *pertinent* to a conversation *C*, that is, the context relative to which the assertibility of sentences in *C* ought to be evaluated. Then the content of Γ is a matter of what is relevant to *C*. In particular, a context Δ is in the range of the context assignment function for Γ only if Δ is relevant to *C*. Thus, to defend an account of the content of context Γ would be to establish the relevance to *C* of every context that is taken to belong to the context assignment function for Γ. So if Γ itself were in the range of the context assignment function for Γ, then we would be in the impossible position of having to establish the relevance of Γ to *C* before we had established the content of Γ. So, assuming that it will be possible to defend an account of the content of Γ, Γ cannot itself be a member of the range of the context assignment function for Γ. It is fair to assume that it must be possible to defend an account of the content of a context, because, while contexts may be objective, they must also be the sort of thing whose content can in principle be discovered.

It may seem to us on occasion as though we were referring to the very context we are in. For instance, if we are madly driving around desperately trying to find the location where we are supposed to return the rented car we are driving, you might say to me, "Last time, you didn't have any problem", and I might reply, with irritation, "That's not relevant in this context; it does not help us one bit". Here it might look as though I was saying something assertible about what was assertible in the context we are in. But it is not actually so obvious that the context in which my sentence is assertible is the same as the context I am talking about. We can carry on multiple conversations that interweave with one another in time, and it might very well be that when I utter my sentence I am, so to speak, taking a break from the conversation we had been having, whose goal was to find the rental car return office, in order to have a brief conversation about that conversation, where the goal of this second conversation is to correct your manner of contributing to the first.

This limitation on what we can talk about is at the same time a limitation on our ability to formulate the semantics for our own language. Certainly, we may formulate various generalizations about assertibility in a context. We might, for instance, declare an argument valid, meaning that for every context in which the premises are assertible, the conclusion is assertible as well. But the context pertinent to the conversation in which we assert this generalization is not in the range of the context assignment function for that context, and so, as we can observe from the perspective of another context, our generalization is not really about absolutely every context. This limitation need not matter in any practical way at all; for it may still be the case that, in any context in which the question arises, the same generalization will be assertible; in no context is that form of words deniable. Of course, even in saying this I am failing to speak of absolutely every context.

Many philosophers, from diverse traditions, have perceived an analogous quandary pertaining to reference to one's self. Consider, for instance, this passage from Kant:

> Through this I or he or it (the thing) that thinks nothing more is represented than a transcendental subject of thoughts = x, which cognizes itself only through the thoughts which are its predicates and of which, separated out, we can never have the slightest concept; consequently we perpetually revolve in a circle around it, in that we must always make use of its representation in order to form some judgment of it. (Kant (1956/1781), A346/B404)

A similar thought forces itself on Wittgenstein:

> If I wrote a book called *The World as I Found It*, I should have to include a report on my body, and should have to say which parts were subordinate to my will, and which were not, etc., this being a method of isolating the subject, or rather of showing that in an important sense there is no subject; for it alone could *not* be mentioned in that book. (Wittgenstein (1961/1921), 5.631)

Here is Jean-Paul Sartre on the same theme:

> Thus consciousness (of) belief and belief are one and the same being, the characteristic of which is absolute immanence. But as soon as we wish to grasp this being, it slips between our fingers, and we find ourselves faced with a pattern of duality, with a game of reflections. For consciousness is a reflection (*reflet*), but *qua* reflection it is exactly the one reflecting (*réfléchissant*), and if we attempt to grasp it as reflecting, it vanishes and we fall back on the reflection. (Sartre (1956/1943), pp. 75–6)

The idea is expressed most plainly, with the least implication of profound mystery, by Gilbert Ryle:

> A higher order action cannot be the action upon which it is performed. So my commentary on my performances must always be silent about one performance, namely itself, and this performance can be the target only of another commentary. Self-commentary, self-ridicule and self-admonition are logically condemned to eternal penultimacy. Yet nothing that is left out of any particular commentary or admonition is privileged thereby to escape comment or admonition for ever. On the contrary it may be the target of the very next comment or rebuke. (Ryler (1949), p. 195)

What Kant, Wittgenstein, Sartre and Ryle are all remarking upon is a difficulty in attempting to reflect on one's own self. Necessarily some aspect of oneself is omitted from the content of one's reflection, namely, that very act of reflection.

We do not have to read these passages as denying the possibility of self-reference. These philosophers do not claim that a thought cannot refer to itself, although their claims may entail that there will always be something about itself that such a thought fails to represent. Moreover, these philosophers cannot be understood as imposing a hierarchy. They are not suggesting that the self is sliced into moments or planes and that one's reflection on oneself always belongs to a different plane from the self reflected upon. Their claim is rather that, for any given representation that one may form of oneself, there is always an aspect of oneself that falls not within the purview of that representation, namely, that aspect of oneself that consists in one's representation of oneself.

As these philosophers claim that an act of reflection always fails to encompass itself, I claim that a generalization over contexts always fails to encompass the context with respect to which the generalization ought to be judged assertible or not. That is an analogous point that remains after we have abandoned referential semantics in favor of contextual semantics and have taken the primary locus of conceptual representation to be the assertions of interlocutors in conversation rather than the judgments of isolated minds. Likewise, just as these philosophers supposed that any act of reflection can become the object of a further reflection, so too we allow that any context of assertion can fall within the scope of generalizations assertible in other contexts. One's sense that one can in fact talk about the context one is in stems from the knowledge that one can always shift to a different context and from that point of view talk about the context one was in just before.

REFERENCES

Beall, JC (2001). "A Neglected Deflationist Approach to the Liar", *Analysis* 61: 126–9.
—— (2002). "Deflationism and Gaps: Untying 'Not's in the Debate", *Analysis* 62: 299–305.
—— and Bradley Armour-Garb (2003). "Should Deflationists be Dialetheists?", *Noûs* 37: 303–24.
Cartwright, Richard (1994). "Speaking of Everything", *Noûs* 98: 1–20.
Etchemendy, John, (1990). *The Concept of Logical Consequence*, Harvard University Press.

Field, Hartry (1994a). "Deflationist Views of Meaning and Content", *Mind* 103: 249–85. (Reprinted in Field (2001).)
—— (1994b). "Disquotational Truth and Factually Defective Discourse", *Philosophical Review* 103: 405–52. (Reprinted in Field (2001).)
—— (2001). *Truth and the Absence of Fact*, Oxford University Press.
Forster, T. E. (1992). *Set Theory with a Universal Set: Exploring an Untyped Universe*, Oxford University Press.
Gauker, Christopher (1997). "Universal Instantiation: A Study of the Role of Context in Logic", *Erkenntnis* 46: 185–214.
—— (1998). "What is a Context of Utterance?", *Philosophical Studies* 91: 149–72.
—— (1999). "Logic and Deflationism", *Facta Philosophica* 1: 167–96.
—— (2001). "T-Schema Deflationism versus Gödel's First Incompleteness Theorem", *Analysis* 61: 129–36.
—— (2003). *Words without Meaning*, MIT Press.
—— (forthcoming). *Conditionals in Context*, MIT Press.
Holton, Richard (2000). "Minimalism and Truth-Value Gaps", *Philosophical Studies* 97: 137–68.
Horwich, Paul (1990). *Truth*, Blackwell.
Kant, Immanuel (1956/1781). *Kritik der Reinen Vernunft*, ed. Raymund Schmidt, Felix Meiner Verlag.
Kaplan, David (1989). "Demonstratives: An Essay on the Semantics, Logic, Metaphysics, and Epistemology of Demonstratives and Other Indexicals", in Joseph Almog, John Perry, and Howard Wettstein, eds., *Themes from Kaplan*, Oxford University Press, pp. 481–564.
Kreisel, Georg (1967). "Informal Rigour and Completeness Proof", in Imre Lakatos, ed., *Problems in the Philosophy of Mathematics*, North-Holland, pp. 138–57.
Kripke, Saul (1975). "Outline of a Theory of Truth", *Journal of Philosophy* 72: 690–716.
Leblanc, Hugues (1976). *Truth-Value Semantics*, North-Holland.
McGee, Vann (1992). "Maximal Consistent Sets of Instances of Tarski's Schema (T)", *Journal of Philosophical Logic* 21: 235–41.
Rayo, Agustín and Timothy Williamson (2003). "Unrestricted First-Order Languages", in JC Beall, ed., *Liars and Heaps: New Essays on Paradox*, Oxford University Press, pp. 331–56.
Ryle, Gilbert (1949). *The Concept of Mind*, Barnes and Noble Books.
Sartre, Jean-Paul (1956/1943). *Being and Nothingness*, tr. Hazel E. Barnes, Philosophical Library.
Simmons, Keith (1993). *Universality and the Liar: An Essay on Truth and the Diagonal Argument*, Cambridge University Press.
Stalnaker, Robert (1974). "Pragmatic Presuppositions", in Milton K. Munitz and Peter K. Unger, eds., *Semantics and Philosophy*, New York University Press, pp. 197–213.
Wittgenstein, Ludwig (1961/1921). *Tractatus logico-philosophicus*, trans. D. F. Pears and B. F. McGuiness, Routledge & Kegan Paul.

11

How Significant Is the Liar?

Dorothy Grover

In their search for an understanding of *truth*, some philosophers place high priority on explaining the liar sentence ('this is false'). The belief is that unless a theory of truth provides an explanation of the liar sentence, the theory is seriously flawed as a theory of *truth*.

The challenge is presented roughly as follows. "Given what we mean by 'false' and 'true', the sentence 'this is false' is false if true and true if false. This (apparent) derivation of a contradiction raises doubts as to the coherence of our truth concept. And so it becomes crucial that we find an account of the liar that will restore confidence in the coherence of our talk of truth and our pursuit of truth." This is certainly the way I used to try and persuade non-philosophers and beginning students that the liar sentence should occupy a significant place in our deliberations.[1] But it is not easy to convince others that we need to "resolve the paradox of the liar"; or that analysis of the liar may reveal crucial insights. Non-philosophers may grant there is a curious puzzle, but it is a "don't care" puzzle. How, and where, is the liar so crucial to our understanding? I will now argue there is something right in the naive reaction of unconcern.

Many who have sought, and claimed to have found, a resolution of the liar, will in the end reject the purported inference to contradiction. Their theories, designed in part to resolve the liar, will be presented as explaining why the argument must be rejected. By contrast, I deny there is an argument of any kind—valid, invalid, or spurious. There is no threat; there is nothing to resolve. Nor do I see grounds for thinking there is an unraveling of the liar that will yield insights into truth,[2]

Special thanks to Walter Edelberg for his insightful promptings on an early draft. Appreciative thanks to colleagues at the University of Canterbury for helpful comments; and to Jerry Kapus, Nuel Belnap, and Anil Gupta, for their invaluable thought provoking exchanges on these and related topics on this occasion, and over the years.

[1] See, also, Barwise and Etchemendy (1987), p. 4: "An adequate analysis of a paradox [including the liar] must diagnose the source of the problem the paradox reveals, *and thereby help us to refine the concepts involved, making them truly coherent.*" [Emphasis added.] Vann McGee (1988) comments in his Preface, p. vii, "There are scarcely any philosophical problems of greater urgency than the liar paradox, for there are scarcely any concepts more central to our philosophical understanding than the concept of truth."

[2] Truth-related philosophical issues arise in a number of contexts. I will not review these here as I address this topic in two recent papers, Grover (2000) and Grover (2001). These discussions have a

self-reference, category mistakes, presupposition, or any of the other very interesting issues that get raised. If we do become concerned about the coherence of our truth-talk, our focus should be on our actual (and potential) uses of 'true', 'false', 'truth', and 'falsity', in contexts where we seek to *communicate*, rather than on a sentence we do not use.[3]

Part of my discussion will focus on the fact that, in natural language, the ties between syntax and semantics are relatively loose. This is, at least in part, because we need openness in word usage so that we can modify our language as we seek ways of communicating in new circumstances. However, the absence of uniform ties between syntax and semantics does mean we must be wary of unreflectively "endorsing" syntactic moves that may not have semantic moves accompanying them. I will argue there are syntactic-only moves in the purported arguments from the liar.

In section 1 I highlight some of the differences between natural and formalized languages. Those designing formalized languages have wanted the following features. First, a word should carry with it, *in all its occurrences*, a fixed meaning; that is, if in one sentence an expression means *m*, it will mean *m* in all other sentences.[4] Second, designers of formalized languages have required that a sequence of sentences that qualifies on syntactic grounds as a proof, should qualify on semantic grounds as an inference, or as a sequence of inferences. I provide reasons for denying that anything close to these assumptions is true of natural languages. While previous and concurrent uses of tokens of a word can influence the way we use another token of the word, those other uses do not *fix* (that is, fully determine) use in a new situation. Nor do past or concurrent uses determine that a token is meaningful when it is not being *used* in discourse, not even if it occurs in a syntactically well-constructed sentence. As a result, unless a word, phrase, or sentence is used in a given context in a communicatively significant way, it does not have "operative meaning", though each of the words may have one or more meanings listed in a dictionary.

In section 2 I give my reasons for holding the liar is not a sentence that is used in a communicatively significant way.[5] This means that though the liar is syntactically well-formed, and its individual words have dictionary meaning, the liar does not have "operative meaning". It is a sentence with limited philosophical interest. This discussion uncovers significant similarities between the liar and division by zero. I recommend that our reaction to the liar should be similar to our reaction to '6 ÷ 0'.

parochial slant as I saw a need to explain how the deeply interesting truth-related issues are not denied prosentential theorists.

[3] My message resonates with that of Gupta and Belnap (1993), p. 17, where they say, "we should try to understand the principles that underlie the ordinary unproblematic uses of the concept of truth" and "we need to give *less* attention to the paradoxes than we have given them." However, on p. 6, they do claim, "A central problem in the theory of truth is to resolve the paradox" and on p. 17, "we need a proper understanding of the Liar paradox." My contrasting position is that there is little to understand in the liar, unless it has to do with matters not uniquely connected with the truth concept.

[4] I am ignoring recognition that is now granted such features as vagueness, indexicals, and ambiguity.

[5] I focus on the significance of the liar in natural language. There are reasons why the status of its analogues in formalized languages can be different. I touch on these issues in passing, and then briefly elaborate in 5.2.

In section 3 I address cases where there is a "risk" of a liar-like construction being used. In sections 2 and 3 I have limited discussion to views that hold 'true' and 'false' are used to ascribe properties. I review the position of the prosentential theory in section 4, defending theses similar to those offered on behalf of a property-ascribing view.

1. LIVING LANGUAGES

"... all communication by speech assumes the interplay of inventive construction and inventive construal."

"On What Metaphors Mean", Donald Davidson (1978), p. 245.

The features of natural languages that I highlight are, by and large, features that in part distinguish natural languages from formalized languages. Accordingly, as I develop my position, I shall draw comparisons between the two.

1.1 Openness to Change

During much of last century it was often said that formalized languages epitomize the "ideal language". Analytic philosophers tended to talk of the shortcomings of natural languages in so far as they lack those characteristics deemed desirable in formalized languages.[6] But the truth of the matter is quite to the contrary. Natural languages are in many ways *necessarily different* from formalized languages as the two serve quite different purposes. A natural language serves our needs well, *only* if it allows us to improvise as our circumstances change. This calls for a kind of openness and flexibility that has not (so far) been viewed as desirable in formalized languages. By contrast, formalized languages have not been designed for general everyday use. They are task-specific. It is true that designers of formalized languages have been concerned with idealizations—in concept analysis, theory construction, and in the creation of useful linguistic resources. But idealizations are one thing, an "ideal language" another.

Formalized languages are often used in the development and presentation of theories that contribute to the development of fruitful linguistic resources for engaging in rational thought. This has included analysis of important concepts, which often come hand in hand with enriching *additions* to our pool of linguistic resources. I emphasize 'addition', as formalized languages must be embedded in natural languages, if they are to be used and not just talked about.[7]

Formalized and natural languages are both created by us, but in completely different circumstances and in quite different ways. In the case of a formalized language its designers *stipulate* its various components. The alphabet, sentences,

[6] See, for example, Fine's (1975, p. 265) characterization of vagueness as involving "deficiency" of meaning. This negative overtone is from someone who takes vagueness seriously. Given the model he uses Fine could as well have talked of "riches" of meaning.

[7] As Tom Bestor put it, "Formalized languages don't provide their own context."

axioms, rules, and semantics are recursively enumerated. A formalized language exists as soon as its features are defined, and independently of whether it has or might be used. Mastery of the language—if it is appropriate to talk this way—would be a matter of following the fully articulated rules with respect to sentence construction, the rules governing proofs, and so on. If the specified rules of a formalized language are not followed, then if anything is said it is not being said in that language.

By contrast, the creation of a natural language is ongoing.[8] There is no way of effectively specifying that a natural language shall be a certain way, without exception. There is no way, for example, that I might effectively stipulate that speakers cease labeling their female partners as "sheilas". Teachers try to get students to follow accepted patterns of usage, but with limited success. Nor can bodies of experts effectively stipulate. Consider the school child who immediately after learning what 'H_2O' is supposed to be used to refer to, will immediately use 'H_2O' to refer to a whole variety of watery liquids. We communicate—and often communicate well—when we exercise such flexibility in word usage. Nor can the alphabet of a natural language be recursively enumerated—except by hindsight. This is because, with more or less success, we can also add symbols as it suits. Consider the backwards 'R' of 'Toys "Я" Us'. Nor can the set of words or the set of sentences of a living language be recursively generated, prior to the language being used. Natural languages do not come into existence through definition, but evolve as its speakers try in all manner of ways (through imitation, improvisation, and so on) to communicate about those things we wish to communicate about. The alphabet, syntax, and word usage of a language all evolve over time.[9]

In the case of formalized languages, uniformity is prized. This is one reason why a predetermined mapping between syntax and semantics has been assumed desirable. It is assumed all well-formed terms and sentences should have a semantic value—even if some are expeditiously assigned the null set as value. These defining events at the onset determine the present and future meaning of a sentence in that language.[10] Things are

[8] To the extent the views I express here are on target, I am indebted to Wittgenstein's discussion of language in *Philosophical Investigations*, and more recently, Mark Wilson's writings. In Wilson (1982), where the focus tends to be our use, over time, of predicates that target scientific properties, Wilson points to complexities that make the task of assigning extensions to predicates difficult. This is because our "classificatory skills" often do not get the property right and so there is a process of correcting them as we learn more about the world. Wilson's analysis of this process shows that, among other things, Kripke's and Putnam's accounts of reference to "natural kinds" is much too simplistic. This detailed analysis of word usage delves deeper than what I offer here. Others have also touched on issues that relate to the ways in which language can be flexible. See, for example, Michael Lynch (1998). He describes concepts as "fluid". Fluidity appropriately encompasses Wittgenstein's notion of family resemblance as well as the "openness" I speak of.

[9] Of course authorized groups have specified some significant aspects of language, as has happened when an oral language is changed to a written language. For example, both Korean and Maori languages acquired written versions in relatively controlled ways. As with other languages, however, the written form has evolved and continues to evolve.

[10] Thus, in Tarski (1933/56), pp. 165–6, "*formalized languages* . . . can be roughly characterized as artificially constructed languages in which the sense of every expression is unambiguously determined by its form."

quite different in the case of natural languages.[11] Indeed, it would be a disaster if there were analogous pre-determined ties between syntax and semantics. For natural languages would not then have the features that make them especially useful to us, given the kinds of seekers of knowledge that we are, the attitudes and feelings we seek to express or evoke, and given the changing environment in which we live. Natural languages that are *living* languages—and the ones we use *are*—must allow for changes in the language through improvisation.

Consider, for example, the communicative demands that software designers faced when they first began talking and writing about the software they were designing for computers. Because the invention of personal computers introduced new occasions for communication, software designers had to improvise as they looked for ways of writing and talking about new entities and processes. In this creative process, pre-existing words like 'file', 'paste', 'save', and 'software' were selected for use. Software designers faced several options as they selected ways for talking about the operations computers perform. They could have attempted to introduce new words; borrow words from other languages; extend the use of pre-existing words from their own language; or form new compounds out of pre-existing words (e.g., 'software'). In each case it was not a matter of finding *the* right choice, but a matter of making *a* good choice.[12] This is illustrated by the fact that while Mac and PC designers tended to use pre-existing words, they sometimes picked different words. For example, Mac uses 'aliases' where Word uses 'shortcut'. Rarely did they make really bad choices, as a choice of 'rubbish' instead of 'save' would have been. At the very least, economic considerations sent them chasing "user-friendly" choices.

Beyond inventions like that of the personal computer, there are many other circumstances where an interest in communicating leads us to improvise as we seek ways of talking about new things. Because we are not omniscient *and* seek knowledge, there are new discoveries to talk about and new theories to articulate. We also modify our language usage as we seek to change attitudes. Consider the effort to change racist attitudes through use of the terms 'black American' and 'African American'; similarly, the effort to change sexist attitudes through the replacement of inappropriate uses of 'chick' and 'girl' by 'woman'. Poets, novelists, dramatists, and the rest of us, introduce new locutions and nuances in the interests of effectively conveying new perspectives and new ways of evoking sensitivity to the depth and variety of human experience. There are also the changes we make in the interests of novelty and humor. Consider

[11] Of natural languages, Tarski (1933/56) says on p. 164, "For [a natural] language is not something finished, closed, or bounded by clear limits. It is not laid down what words can be added to this language . . ."

[12] Wilson (1982) selects examples from the history of science of "choices" that might have been made differently. For example, on p. 580, "the idea that all Au-atoms belong to this set [the extension of 'gold'] ignores many of the complexities and vicissitudes in the history of 'element'. Given the complicated intertwining of "chemical" (combination properties) and "physical" (optical and mass spectroscopy) experiments in our actual scientific development, our final identification of 'element' with atomic number was perhaps historically inevitable. However, I fail to see this scheme is the only rational one. Certainly proof of its uniqueness would require a more careful study of alternate historical developments than "natural kind" proponents typically provide."

the dialogue Sheridan writes for Mrs Malaprop. All these activities make new demands on our language. For these many enriching reasons, there is improvisation.

Note that deliberate innovation is not the only source of successful variation. We can successfully communicate even though we make grammatical mistakes, including use of incomplete sentences. Communication can also proceed when we use the wrong word, a non-word,[13] borrow a phrase from another language, or rely on implicatures to carry the day.[14]

Natural languages are flexible in the sense that they accommodate innovation, whether deliberate or not. As long as we need to creatively exploit the flexibility, there will be openness in word usage, and natural languages will evolve.

1.2 Communicative Significance

Given the number of options facing the designers of computer software, there is no way we could have predicted in 1960 the uses pre-existing words like 'file' and 'paste' would have today.[15] Dictionaries pre-dating 1960 will record only the variety and changes in uses, *up to that time*. Questions concerning possible future uses are necessarily left open by the compilers of dictionaries.

With future uses left open, *context (broadly construed) plays an essential role in determining the communicative significance of new tokens*. In some cases or possibly most cases, a token will be used in the "same way" as past tokens of the word have been used.[16] But this does not eliminate the crucial importance of context. For one reason, most words already have a history of *several* uses. This fact is made clear in dictionaries. The 2001 edition of the Concise Oxford Dictionary distinguishes, for example, nine uses of 'burn', two of 'knuckle', three of 'pre-empt'. So even if a new token is used as tokens of the same word have been used before, we will not know which particular set of past uses is pertinent to understanding the new token—unless we know the context of use. So past use never (alone) determines, for a new token, which among the dictionary meanings of a word is operative, whether the token is being used in a new way, or whether the speaker has mis-spoken.

When participating in a discourse we undoubtedly first rely on our tutored intuitions in acquiring an understanding of what others are saying—intuitively

[13] Most novelists attempt to capture this feature of language usage. Consider, for example, Mrs Gamp in Dickens' *Martin Chuzzlewit*. The other characters understood her, even though there is hardly a speech of Mrs Gamp's that doesn't contain a mistake, e.g., '[H]e must take the consequences of sech a sitiwation,' and 'I've brought another, which engages to give every satigefaction.'

[14] See Grice (1989).

[15] Wilson (1982) frequently remarks on the limits to which word usage can be predicted. For example, pp. 579–80, "In truth, the *implicit parameters* appropriate to these predicates [e.g., 'is an electron'] will have widened enormously over the past four centuries and no linguist could have predicted how their application was to be extended in the new circumstances."

[16] I have not said anything about what it is for a token to be used as previous tokens of the same word have been used. Communication and certain kinds of knowledge depend on our ability to sometimes (mostly?) refer to the same thing, or ascribe the same property, as others have on other occasions. See Millikan (2000) for a deeply insightful discussion of the importance of re-identifying substances and the role of language in this.

putting together beliefs we have of past uses of words with information we are gathering about the context. But if this somewhat unreflective approach fails to yield understanding, other kinds of more deliberately reflective effort must be made. We may look for a pertinent analogy between past uses of words and present uses, given the knowledge we have of the communicator, the possible purpose of the communication, and other features of the context. Understanding may take a while, as we question the speaker, read forward and back, or as we learn more about the subject being talked about. In the case of learning the language of computer software instructions, I found it was necessary to not just read on, and talk to experts, I also needed to try things on the computer. We usually need to know *something* of the subject matter, or at least *be learning* something of the subject matter, for communication to proceed. Successful participation in a discourse is a multidimensional activity, involving ever so much more than a search through dictionaries.

Unless a token is *used* in communication (and not just mentioned) the question of its meaningfulness, in the sense of its communicative significance in its context, just does not arise. Consider, for example, a token of the word 'horse', written on a blackboard. If the token is displayed only for the purpose of demonstrating how letters are written, and so is not itself contributing to what is being said, there is no case for arguing it is communicatively significant. This is not to deny that we can know that in earlier or later contexts other tokens of the word might have been used in communicatively significant ways. As, for example, if 'horse' is used in talking of a child's rocking horse, a clothes' horse, a picture of a racehorse, etc.

A pre-existing word, phrase, or sentence has associated with it a history of a variety of different uses of its past tokens. It is knowledge of this history, together with what we know of the speaker and context more generally, that leads to successful communication. We need to have some knowledge of the context of use to know which of its past uses is operative, or whether a new use (possibly derivative from an earlier use) is operative. Given these facts, I will sometimes need to refer to the *history of uses that a word has at a given time*. (The index to time is needed because the record of uses is forever accumulating. This is one reason why dictionaries must be updated.) This history needs to be distinguished from *the use* (if any) *that a token of a word has in its context*. The former I refer to as the *dictionary meaning of a word*. The latter, I refer to as *the operative meaning of a token*. Note, not all tokens have operative meaning, since there are tokens that are not used in communicatively significant ways. The blackboard token of 'horse' mentioned above is a case in point.[17] There is significant interplay between the two kinds of "meaning". An accepted use of a token that gives it operative meaning will be reflected in (possibly later) dictionary meanings of the word tokened. In turn, our knowledge of the history of uses of a word will typically be exploited in our use and understanding of the operative meaning of new tokens.

[17] Operative meaning is not to be identified with *what the speaker means*. The history of uses of the word tokened, other uses of the word in the immediate context, knowledge of those using tokens of the word, and possibly many other factors, will help determine a given token's use, which in turn determines operative meaning.

There are riches in a language structure that accommodates creative modification. However, it does mean there will be no simple account of what a word or sentence means, or how it is used. There will be no pre-determined domain that a predicate can be said to bifurcate. Nor, given that syntactic structure and uses of words evolve over time, will there be a simple account of the identity conditions of a natural language. Nor do natural languages evolve linearly, but with many branchings. For different communities of speakers (e.g., scientists, teenage rock fans, groups separated by geographic distance) generate some of their own ways of communicating. I have seen, for example, that there is now a New Zealand Concise Oxford English Dictionary. If we do need to draw a line, then, as in the case of vague words, we may have to somewhat arbitrarily find a suitable place to draw it.

So, natural languages are living evolving languages so long as we continue to use them, to acquire knowledge, be evocative, imaginative, and embrace innovation. Relevant to our present concerns, a particular use of a token is not (fully) determined by other uses—a context of use is essential to a token having operative meaning.

2. THE LIAR SENTENCE

So why is the liar sentence of limited interest? It is not a sentence that is used.

Of course a token of 'this is false' can be used. There is the case where 'this' of 'this is false' is used deictically to refer to another sentence or utterance. Suppose 'this', accompanied by a pointing, is used to refer to a headline in the newspaper, "Israelis Invade West Bank." On a property-ascribing view, the sentence 'this is false' would be used to ascribe the property falsity to either the sentence "The Israelis have invaded the West Bank," or a proposition it expresses. By contrast, on the prosentential reading the modified prosentence 'this is false' is used to affirm, with anaphoric overtones, the contradictory "The Israelis have not invaded the West Bank." As there is no contradiction arising out of either of these readings, there is no more interest in this use of 'this is false' than in the use of most other sentences containing an indexical and the predicate 'is false'.

2.1 Operative Meaning and Inference

'This', 'is' and 'false' have usually been assumed to have their dictionary meaning operative in 'This is false', with 'this' referring to the very sentence in which it occurs. In this section I assume a property-ascribing reading of the truth and falsity predicates.[18] It is on such a reading that it has been claimed a contradiction derives from each of the two assumptions, *the liar is true* and *the liar is false*. But we have now seen that dictionary meaning (past use) does not determine operative meaning, given our need for flexibility in language, and the ensuing need for openness in word usage. In

[18] I am considering only those property-ascribing theories that at a minimum would, in a formalized language context, endorse the logical properties exhibited in the truth schema—whatever that might mean.

order to establish the liar sentence has operative meaning (of any kind), we need to know something of the discourses (if any) in which 'this is false' is used. We need to identify contexts where 'this is false' has operative meaning.[19]

It is clear the liar sentence is talked about—over and again in this paper and in many others. But mentioning the liar sentence is one thing, *using* the liar sentence is another. And, even if I try projecting past uses of the words involved, I fail to see how the liar sentence might be used. I hazard a guess that one reason why many non-philosophers do not seem concerned about the liar is that they too do not anticipate finding a use for it. For thinking of a context where the liar might be significantly used involves thinking of a way of integrating its use in activity-related discourse. If I am right, there are no uses of the liar that give it operative meaning. So there are no uses to be reflected in the dictionary meanings of the words involved. So the liar is irrelevant to the issue of the coherence of the truth concept, or to our understanding of truth related issues in general.

But some will quickly respond that we do use the liar. There are versions of the liar, for example Kripke's "risky" cases, which may be used inadvertently by any speaker. I leave the discussion of these cases until section 3. Others will respond that philosophers *use* the liar in inferences. Indeed, in the very inferences used in deriving the contradictions. So the words tokened in the liar not only have a history of uses, but also, when combined in a token of the liar, would have operative meaning. Let us look at one version of the inference. A critique of this one proposed inference (together with the two to follow) should suffice to show how I would attempt to disassemble similar candidates.

For convenience in philosophical discussion, the simple version of the liar is often discussed in a different form. The indexical 'this' is replaced by a name. 'L' can name 'L is false', for example. One way the derivation to contradiction can be presented is as follows.

1. L = 'L is false'	stipulation
2. *L is false*	hypothesis
3. 'L is false' is false	substitution for 'L'
4. 'p' is false iff ∼ p	falsity schema
5. 'L is false' is false iff ∼(L is false)	(4), substitution
6. ∼(L is false)	(3), (5), classical logic
7. L is true or L is false	classical logic
8. L is true	(6), (7), classical logic
9. L is true and L is false	(2), (8), classical logic
10. *L is true*	hypothesis
11. 'L is false' is true	(10), substitution
12. 'p' is true iff p	truth schema
13. 'L is false' is true iff L is false	(12), substitution
14. L is false	(11), (13), classical logic

[19] My concern is not unrelated to Dummett's (1959) claim that we need to know the point of classifying a sentence as true or false. What would be the point of using the liar sentence?

15.	L is true and L is false	classical logic
16.	L is false V L is true	classical logic
17.	L is true and L is false	disjunction elimination, (1)–(15)
18.	(L is false) & ~(L is false)	(4), (12), (17), classical logic

Each line is "justified" as either an instance of an accepted schema or as following from one or more earlier lines according to one of the accepted rules of inference. At least this is how lines (1)–(18) would be viewed if they belonged to a formalized language with an appropriate vocabulary, schemas, and rules.[20] The sequence of sentences would qualify as a proof that shows a contradiction would be derivable if "L = 'L is false' " were a sentence of such a formalized language.

However, my project does not concern formally constructed languages but the concept of truth in natural languages. In a natural language, a lone sequence of sentences does not constitute an inference, no matter what syntactic connections obtain between the various lines. Much idealizing has been done in arriving at such formalized language notions of proof.

Inference is a much more complex phenomenon in a natural language context. Speakers using a natural language might perform any of a variety of linguistic acts through the use of a sequence of sentences. The speaker might be engaged, for example, in describing a scene, in giving expression to a set of promises, in hurling abuse at another, or as in the case of a political speech or domestic quarrel, a combination of these. So the linguistic act of arguing a point will be only one among many things a speaker or writer might hope to accomplish through use of a sequence of sentences. But, as linguistic acts are involved, each sentence gives expression to a kind of propositional attitude, like, a supposition, a belief, a concluding, or a wondering. Furthermore, there will not be any kind of inferring done, unless each sentence involved has operative meaning in its context of use. So, there is much besides syntactic structure that is required, if a communication (or rumination) involving the use of a sequence of sentences is to be correctly understood as giving expression to an inference.

I have already mentioned that one goal of those constructing a formalized language has been to design the syntax so that it perspicuously mirrors targeted semantic features of the language. Where there is a match, results concerning syntactic properties can be interpreted as neatly yielding information about the mirrored semantic features of the language. The resulting focus on syntax has at times led to the unfortunate description of logicians as engaged only in "symbol-pushing maneuvers". This superficial description sadly ignores the deep insights and imaginative constructions that have been necessary for logic's successful development and useful applications.[21] However, the criticism is to a degree pertinent where our engagement with logic has led to an under-appreciation of the many riches and subtleties of natural language. Indeed, examples from introductory texts and lectures illustrate how the

[20] I am also assuming a formalized language that lacks a discriminative treatment of the truth and falsity predicates.

[21] Unfortunately, there is not space to theorize about the many positive contributions of formalized languages to our understanding of the linguistic resources of natural languages.

abstractions required for the syntactic characterization of inference may unwittingly have led us to ignore the breadth of features that constitute linguistic acts. Thus, when teaching the concept of *logical form*, we sometimes resort to talk of inferences, even when nonsense constructions are involved. I recall examples like the following.

(i) All didgets are nadgets.
No nadgets are spadgets.
Therefore, no didgets are spadgets.

We want students to understand we need pay no attention to the meaning of the non-logical terms when we are looking for the logical form of an inference. Unfortunately, because we must cover the syllabus, most of us pay little attention to the fact that strings of non-sentences like those in (i) do not even begin to qualify as inferences in a natural language context. In expeditiously referring to such nonsense constructions as *inferences*, we ignore the fact that in reaching such a point in the enterprise of logic we have already abstracted heavily from real life (i.e., from live) examples. For if, in a natural language context, all we have is a string of non-sentences, then that is all we have.[22] (i) is not an inference and so it does not have a logical form. We have also just seen that even in the case of a string of well-formed sentences, there may not be an inference. For the string might be used in describing something, in laying out a set of instructions, in telling a story, etc. Consider, also,

(ii) Blatant grasses run furiously homeward
Therefore, grasses can run

Perhaps there are poetic contexts where such a string could be used to give expression to an inference, but new or metaphorical uses of the words are not in question in the alleged derivation of contradiction from the liar.

2.2 The Liar Is Not Used

Are there grounds for saying the sequence of sentences in (1)–(18) is an inference? Or is the sequence no more than a much talked about, displayed string, satisfying certain syntactic properties?

Those who believe the liar leads to a contradiction have assumed the liar has operative meaning with 'true' and 'false' used in (1)–(18) in the way they have been used historically in other contexts. But my sketch of the features that make natural languages admirably suited for our use—given our epistemic situation, our desire to understand, and our changing situation generally—shows this is not something that can be assumed without argument. For, while pre-existing words (and phrases of certain kinds) have a history of past uses, including a history of the way individual words have—on occasion—been combined to form meaningful sentences, such histories do not determine future uses of tokens in the full range of possible syntactic combinations. "Blatant grasses run furiously homeward" illustrates this point.

[22] I allow there is no telling what someone might do with such nonsense. The sequence might be used in making a joke.

Indeed, given the need for openness in word usage, the question of new tokens of pre-existing words having operative meaning is *always* open. In the case of tokens of 'this is false' we must ask, for example, what reason there is for thinking the liar sentence is being *used* in line (2) and if it is being used, what is its operative meaning. Simply calling (i) and (ii) inferences does not provide operative meaning for either 'nadget' or 'Blatant grasses run furiously homeward'. Similarly, placing 'L is false' in the sequence (1)–(18) does not provide operative meaning for the liar.

As a result, those denying my skepticism are begging the question when they respond, "The liar *is* used in (1)–(18), because it is used in drawing an inference. So of course (2) has an operative meaning." From 'there is an inference only if each line has operative meaning', we have allegedly arrived at '(2) has operative meaning because (1)–(18) is an inference'!

Nor is line (2) the only line that poses a challenge in the natural language context. Again for comparison, the hint of an inference in (ii) derives from the suggestion of an inferential move from the first to the second line by Modus Ponens and instantiation in the schema, 'if **x** runs yly then **x** can run.' But when we think about it a second, we realize this schema generates meaningful instances only in the case of a relatively small, vaguely identifiable, group of the sentences of our language. (By contrast, in an appropriately designed formalized language, all instances *could* be deemed meaningful.) Similarly, while the truth and falsity schemas of (1)–(18) generate instances that in the right contexts have operative meaning when 'Snow is white' is substituted, substitution of many other sentences will not generate such instances. Consider substituting a question; or a sentence that contains indexicals, ambiguous names, or anaphoric pronouns without antecedents; or substituting a sentence like 'Blatant grasses . . . ', etc. We lack evidence that the result of substituting 'L is false' in the truth and falsity schemas yields sentences that have operative meaning.

While in a formalized language context (1)–(18) may qualify syntactically as a "proof", there are many factors about living languages that undermine the claim the sequence could give expression to an inference in a natural language context. So (1)–(18) has not established the liar is used. Without evidence the liar is used, there is no reason to think we need worry about "resolving" the liar before engaging in the deeper issues raised in our discussions of truth-related matters. Openness in word usage gets us off the liar hook.

2.3 The Liar Cannot Be Used

Logicians have sought to provide clear and concise ways of saying things in contexts where this is important, as in mathematics; or in providing analyses of logical relations; or in analyses of the relations between important concepts, like that of *proof* and *truth*. Crucial to a number of these enterprises has been Tarski's groundbreaking theory that makes available metalinguistic truth and falsity predicates.[23] (As most have had in mind property-ascribing truth and falsity meta-linguistic

[23] By 'metalinguistic predicate' I mean only a predicate that combines with the name of a sentence to form a sentence.

predicates,[24] I continue with that assumption.) As in the case of other theorizing, it is appropriate that comprehensiveness is highly valued. In the context of formalized languages this would seem to suggest that all well-formed sentences, including the liar, should be included in the domain of a metalinguistic predicate. Surely we should be able to say of a sentence that it, itself, is false? And so it is argued, the resulting sentence (e.g., the liar) should feature in a *theory* of inference.

I have claimed there is no reason for thinking the liar is used in our deliberations as to what is true. From a property-ascribing perspective, I now explain why I think tokens of the liar cannot *ever* be used in a communicatively significant way, if the tokens of words in a given token of the liar are assumed used in conformity with uses in other contexts. This means, despite appearances, the liar does not say anything. It does not have operative meaning; despite the intuition many have that the liar does "say something". Note that something can seem to make sense when it does not. We have all had the experience of reading a passage that "sounds" as though it should make sense, but then closer examination of its rhetoric and high-sounding words shows a lack of content. We can think we have something to say, but with failure to articulate the thought wonder if there was something to articulate. So, there are reasons, even beyond openness in word usage, for taking nothing for granted as to whether a syntactically well-formed sentence has operative meaning.

Those who have at some stage believed (1)–(18)—or something similar—shows a contradiction is derivable from the liar will have assumed the tokens appearing in it are being used in a way that conforms with the way tokens of the same words have been used historically. They have assumed the liar is used in a communicatively significant way that gives it operative meaning. This assumption should be made explicit for the argument presented in (1)–(18).

> (0) L has operative meaning in (1)–(18)—under the condition the tokens of words appearing in the liar are used in conformity with the way tokens of the same words have been used in other contexts.

My argument, that L cannot have operative meaning under the condition stated, proceeds as follows.

> (0) is assumed for reductio. Under this assumption, (1)–(18) would show both that the liar leads to a contradiction and the denial of the liar leads to a contradiction. (That is, under assumption (0), we would not just have a series of syntactic-only moves to a formula with the form of a contradiction.) So a contradiction would follow from assumption (0). By reductio, either (0) must be denied or one of the steps in (1)–(18) must be denied.
>
> But those I am trying to persuade accept (1)–(18). So that leaves only (0) to be denied.
>
> The denial of the condition on (0) could mean that at least one of the words in the liar is being used in a new way. Such a reading of L is not relevant to addressing the paradox. The only other alternative is to deny the condition by

[24] Neil Tennant (2002) is an important exception.

denying L is *used*. That would grant me my point that L does not have operative meaning in (1)–(18).

So, the assumption that L is (counterfactually) used must be denied.

It will be observed that my argument involves a counterfactual. Counterfactual claims are (at best) tricky to evaluate. However, the only moves I have resorted to, under the assumption of the counterfactual hypothesis, are syntactically characterized moves that have traditionally been made by those who have accepted assumption (0)—they have assumed the syntactic structure reflects semantic structure.

Any intuition that we might have had that the liar "says something" has been shown ill served. Sometimes our assessment of operative meaning is made intuitively. Sometimes we need to be much more reflective. Either way, so-called paradoxical sentences are not exempt from appearing to say something, but failing us. If L does not have operative meaning, and cannot have operative meaning, it cannot be used in a communicatively significant way. So the liar does not have a role in inference—despite the syntactic moves. The liar does not need to be included in theories of inference.

A slight irony is emerging here. Logicians and mathematicians have helped us by providing many useful algorithms as, for example, for multiplying and dividing large numbers, drawing conclusions from sentences containing quantifiers, providing languages suitable for use in computers, etc. The syntactic maneuvers make otherwise complex (sometimes, intuitive) operations easy. These accomplishments have in part been achieved, as Frege has pointed out, through deeply insightful selection of syntax.[25] (Imagine trying to carry out a long division using Roman numerals!) The work of logicians and mathematicians has been so successful that we typically employ algorithms without giving any thought as to how they work or what is happening as we manipulate the symbols. So it is not surprising that our "thoughtless" syntactic moves might sometimes bring surprises. The possibility of concatenating '6', '÷', and '0' is obvious. We do so for many other triples; but in this case a referring term is not the result. Syntax can outstrip semantics. Sometimes the reverse happens, also. We can try to express something, but there are not the words. Some resort to use of foreign phrases; the rest of us must start the process of introducing a new word or a new use for an old word.

2.4 A Comparison with Division by Zero

If, in a natural language context, we try to use either the term '6 ÷ 0', or the liar sentence, we risk appearing incoherent. Unknowingly, or just carelessly, we may be trying to use a sentence that lacks operative meaning. If we remain unaware of our mistake, application of standard syntactic moves can place us in the position of appearing to assert a contradiction. There are other parallels.

[25] "It only becomes possible at all after the mathematical notation has, as a result of genuine thought, been so developed that it does our thinking for us, so to speak." Frege (1884).

In the case of dividing by zero there are nondenumerably many numbers (including, say, 7) that we can consider as candidates for the value of '6 ÷ 0'. But each such candidate would lead (counterfactually) to '6 = 0'. No matter what number we were to pick as the referent of '6 ÷ 0' a contradiction results. Note that, in arriving at '6 = 0' from '6 ÷ 0 = 7', each side would (counterfactually) have been multiplied by zero. But such multiplying would be possible only if '6 ÷ 0' denoted a number, which it does not. Syntactic maneuvers would be made without a follow-through of accompanying semantics.

Continuing with the assumption that 'true' and 'false' are property-ascribing predicates, the liar is (counterfactually) a candidate for being either true or false. But we have seen on this (counterfactual) assumption, something with the form of a contradiction would be derivable from each of 'L is true' and 'L is false'. But just as the step of "multiplying by zero" was merely a rote maneuver that has no substance when applied to a non-denoting term; so, also, several of the steps in (1)–(18) are merely rote syntactic maneuvers, having no substance when applied to tokens that have no operative meaning.

Despite these parallels, our reaction to the two has been quite different. There has been no suggestion that the concept of division is rendered incoherent by the failure of division by zero. By contrast, many of us have thought the liar seems to threaten the coherence of our truth-talk. This is clearly a mistake. The liar does not render our truth-talk incoherent any more than division by zero renders division incoherent—though in each case carelessness can lead to an *appearance* of incoherence. To think otherwise is to subscribe to a wrong picture of concepts and/or meaning. Openness in word usage means neither that there are predetermined domains that predicates bifurcate, nor that all operations are completely defined. In mathematics, we isolate division by zero, saying that it is not defined. We accept division as a partial function and guard against incoherence by attaching clauses like "providing x $\neq$ y", when 'x = y' appears as a divisor. Sometimes it can be appropriate to prove existence and consistency theorems when introducing a new term or operation. It would be appropriate to adopt similar attitudes and procedures in the case of the liar.

2.5 Strengthened Version

I have had no intention of offering a "solution" to the liar in this paper. My project has been to explain why we should simply ignore the liar—unless we are in the business of developing formalized languages where the ties between syntax and semantics are tight, and so we must find ways to circumvent liar-like constructions. However, Walter Edelberg has pointed out that because it might look as though I am proposing a solution, a quick response from those versed in the liar literature will be: "What of the strengthened liar?" Walter's candidate paradoxical sentence is,

1. S = 'S is false or S lacks operative meaning' stipulation

It is claimed a contradiction follows from each of the hypotheses 'S is true', 'S is false', 'S lacks operative meaning'.

2. S is true iff S is false or S lacks operative meaning.	*1*, truth schema
3. S is false iff ~(S is false or S lacks operative meaning).	*1*, falsity schema
4. (S is true V S is false) V S lacks operative meaning ('V' is exclusive disjunction)	hypothesis
5. S is true	hypothesis
6. S is either false or S lacks operative meaning.	*2, 5*, classical logic
7. S is false	hypothesis
8. S is not true.	*4, 7*, classical logic
9. S is true and S is not true	*5, 8*, classical logic
10. S lacks operative meaning.	hypothesis
11. S is not true	*4, 10*, classical logic
12. S is true and S is not true	*5, 10*, classical logic
13. S is true and S is not true	*6–12*, classical logic
14. S is false	hypothesis
15. ~(S is false or lacks operative meaning)	*3, 14*, classical logic
16. ~S is false and ~ S lacks operative meaning	*15*, classical logic
17. S is true.	*4, 16*, classical logic
18. S is not true.	*4, 14*, classical logic
19. S is true and S is not true	*17, 18*, classical logic
20. S lacks operative meaning	hypothesis
21. S is true.	*2, 20*, classical logic
22. S is not true.	*4, 20*, classical logic
23. S is true and S is not true	*21, 22*, classical logic
24. S is true and S is not true.	*4, 5–13, 14–19, 20–23*, three-way disjunction elimination

If *(1)–(24)* were an inference, and not just a series of syntactic maneuvers, each line would have operative meaning. Also, it would be assumed S has operative meaning. As with the liar derivation, (1)–(18), we need to make this hypothesis explicit. So,

0. S has operative meaning. hypothesis

Note that the truth and falsity schemas are used throughout. But *(2)* and *(3)* follow from *(1)* and the truth schema, *only if* S has operative meaning, since S is substituted in the schemas. Following a similar reductio argument to that used in section 2.4, based this time on the counterfactual assumption *(0)*, we can conclude that *(0)* is false. So S lacks operative meaning.

But those critiquing my presentation might try again, claiming that the conclusion 'S lacks operative meaning' is not acceptable. This is because the sub-argument from *(20)* shows a contradiction is derivable from the hypothesis 'S lacks operative meaning'. We seem to have another contradiction on our hands. But, no. Given S lacks operative meaning we cannot arrive at *(2)*. The limits on substitution in the truth schema deny that step. So *(21)* does not follow from *(20)*. Syntactic maneuvers are one thing, operative meaning and inference are another. I do not see the strengthened liar introducing anything more than the *appearance* of an inference to a contradiction.

But note that under assumption *(0)*, the right hand side of the strengthened liar sentence in *(1)* has a false disjunct. So, given the counterfactual assumption of operative meaning, the strengthened liar in effect "reduces" to the liar sentence. So to speak, we might have stipulated that S = 'S is false'. Just as in a complex formula a "hidden" division by zero may lead to an appearance of inconsistency, so might "hidden" liar sentence constructions.

Classical logic, as well as the truth and falsity schemas, can be used without restriction in proofs *only if* all sentences involved in the substitutions have operative meaning. In guarding against unintended use of liar-like sentences we may need to employ cautionary techniques, as we do in guarding against division by zero. So, just as we say, "providing $x \neq y$", and "providing the divisor does not equal zero", we might say, "providing 'p' has operative meaning".[26]

3. OTHER CASES

3.1 Neither True Nor False

Given a property-ascribing role for 'true' and 'false', we should be able to say of 'Blatant grasses run furiously homeward' that it is neither true nor false. Similarly, it can be said of commands, requests, and the big boulder in my garden, that each is neither true nor false. Judgments involving a claim that a property neither applies nor does not apply to an object (or pseudo object) are not uncommon. In a class on reproduction, for example, there can be occasion to point out, "Amoebas are neither male nor female. Most reproduce through fission." Also, "Amoebas are neither true nor false, as they are not linguistic entities of any sort, but one-celled organisms. You seem confused about something." And then there is,

(N) The liar sentence is not true and not false.

[26] Nuel Belnap's (1973) conditional assertion 'p/q' might prove useful in handling, in a formal language, well-formed terms and sentences that lack operative meaning. The semantics of conditional assertion p/q is as follows: q is "asserted" only if the condition p (the antecedent) is true; otherwise, there is no assertion. The closest to a conditional assertion in English might be, "There are biscuits on the table, if you want some," said in a situation where the speaker intends that her guests ignore the comment, if they do not want a biscuit. (Perhaps the speaker does not want to interrupt a meeting.) Using conditional assertion, the truth schema could then be expressed 'p' has operative meaning/'p' is true iff p. The assertion that would result after substitution of 'snow is white' for 'p' would be " 'snow is white' is true iff snow is white." Whereas, if 'Blatant grasses run furiously homeward' were substituted, no assertion results. Also, a property-ascribing person could use "S has operative meaning/S is true or S is false" instead of *(4.)*. For then, whether or not S has operative meaning, there is no risk (in a formal context) of a mismatch between syntax and semantics arising after application of the truth schema. This device could similarly be considered in the case of, "providing $x \neq y$," and "providing the divisor does not equal zero".

However, by contrast with the amoeba-sentences, concern will be expressed that (N) would threaten incoherence of the truth concept, as (N) seems to lead to a contradiction. The purported derivation could involve the following sequence.

(N)	L is not true and L is not false	hypothesis
	∼(L is true) and ∼(L is false)	classical logic
	∼(L is false) and ∼ ∼(L is false)	truth and falsity schemas, classical logic
	∼(L is false) and (L is false)	classical logic

This sequence of sentences would qualify as a formal proof, if substitution of the liar in the truth and falsity schemas were allowed. But substitution of L does not yield instances of the truth and falsity schemas that will have operative meaning. So, despite the syntactic moves, there is no inference from the second to the third line. There is no inference to a contradiction from (N) based on this sequence of sentences.

We cannot infer from the fact that something is not false that it is true; just as we cannot infer from the fact that something (e.g., an amoeba) is not male that it is female. (Though the converse is true.) When denying that the big boulder in my garden is false, a speaker is unlikely to affirm the boulder is true. In such cases we may need to ask for more information before we can know the specific reason for denying application of either of such a pair of predicates. So, in general, there are no grounds for simply assuming the logic of the truth and falsity schemas applies. In the case of claiming something is neither true nor false, the reason a speaker has for withholding both will depend on what objects they think are potential candidates for being true or false. Perhaps the sentence does not have operative meaning, or it is a question, or the subject is a non-linguistic object like the boulder in my garden. It might prove helpful to think of 'not' as sometimes used as a connective that negates one or more presuppositions. In the case of 'x is neither true nor false', the presuppositions in question are those that must be true if either one of the pair <'true,' 'false'> were to apply to x. In the case of 'x is neither male nor female', the presuppositions in question are those that must be true if either one of the pair <'male', 'female'> were to apply to x.

3.2 Risky Cases

Though tokens of a sentence may have operative meaning when used in a variety of contexts, there can be inauspicious contexts where a token of the same sentence, if "used" by a speaker, would seem to be paradoxical. Kripke (1975) describes a couple of cases as follows.

> The versions of the liar paradox which use empirical predicates already point to one major aspect of the problem: ***many, probably most, of our ordinary assertions about truth and falsity are liable, if the empirical facts are extremely favorable, to exhibit paradoxical features.*** Consider the ordinary statement, made by Jones:
>
> (1) Most (i.e., a majority) of Nixon's statements about Watergate are false.
>
> Clearly, nothing is intrinsically wrong with (1), nor is it ill-formed. Ordinarily the truth value of (1) will be ascertainable through an enumeration of Nixon's Watergate assertions, and

assessment of each for truth or falsity. Suppose, however, that Nixon's assertions about Watergate are evenly balanced between the true and the false, except for one problematic case,

(2) Everything Jones says about Watergate is true.

Suppose, in addition, that (1) is Jones's sole assertion about Watergate, or alternatively, that all his Watergate-related assertions except perhaps (1) are true. Then it requires little expertise to show that (1) and (2) are both paradoxical. . . .

. . . It is said that Russell once asked Moore whether he always told the truth, and that he regarded Moore's negative reply as the sole falsehood Moore had ever produced. Surely no one had a keener nose for paradox than Russell. Yet he apparently failed to realize that if, as he thought, all Moore's *other* utterances were true, Moore's negative reply was not simply false but paradoxical. (pp. 691–2)

Cases like those Kripke describes would typically happen by mistake, but that does not rule out someone deliberately uttering the inauspicious token, in full appreciation of the effect the context has in depriving the relevant token of operative meaning. The speaker might be playing a trick on philosophers, for example. However, my focus will be with the case where a speaker unwittingly utters a seemingly paradoxical token, the situation Kripke describes as the one Russell was in. Since Russell is participating in a discourse, one assumes there is something he hoped to communicate in using the sentence token in question. So there is a sense in which the problematic sentence *is* used in communication. But how is this possible if liar-like utterances have no operative meaning?

It is a commonplace that we often successfully communicate, despite mistakes. Aside from Mrs Malaprop and Mrs Gamp, we have all used the wrong word, as well as the wrong non-word. Our writing contains typos and omissions. We sometimes do not hear all that was said. Yet in many such instances we do communicate. For, as linguistically competent people, we have the skills necessary for "second-guessing" what a speaker is hoping to convey. Given our background knowledge, linguistic and otherwise, and knowledge of the context, then—as Davidson (1986) put it—through "wit, luck, and wisdom", we can understand speakers like Mrs Malaprop, and others can understand us. Faced with Russell's utterance, and the given context, we could try guessing how Russell might correct his utterance, if prompted. One possibility is that he would clarify his assumption that Moore is talking about only his previous statements. Under those circumstances, Moore's answer is his only falsehood, according to Russell. When there are mistakes, we may not be in a position to tell *exactly* what was intended, but then close enough is often good enough. On this reconstruction, Russell's utterance was a mistake.

Note that the fact that we can usually or sometimes figure out what a speaker hoped to communicate does not confer operative meaning on a speaker's non-words. Nor does our second-guessing confer operative meaning on Russell's utterance. Similar (linguistic) mistakes can arise when speakers forget we cannot divide by zero. Suppose an instruction is given, as follows.

Count the number of refugees. Count the number of tents. Divide the second number into the first. Use the resulting number as a guide in assigning family groups to tents.

But suppose there are no tents. Then the purported instruction in the third sentence cannot be followed. Those receiving the instruction must either ask for further instructions, or do some second-guessing. A better set of instructions might have begun with the following.

> If there are no tents, notify the International Red Cross office immediately. If there are tents, then . . .

4. THE PROSENTENTIAL ACCOUNT

In this section, I briefly touch on a couple of issues connected with the prosentential account of the liar, taking cognizance of the theses about language that I have defended here.[27]

On the prosentential account 'true' and 'false' are not property-ascribing predicates. They are predicates with a prosentential role. 'That is true' and 'it is true' are prosentences; modifications such as 'that was true' and 'that is false' are modified prosentences. Like pronouns, prosentences are parasitic in that they do not have operative meaning[28] unless tied to an appropriate antecedent expression with operative meaning, from which their own operative meaning derives. In the simple cases, whereas an anaphoric pronoun inherits a referent from its antecedent, a (modified) prosentence inherits (modified) sentence operative meaning from its antecedent. In 'Mary is wise but she is busy' the pronoun 'she' inherits its referent from its antecedent 'Mary'. In a case where 'that is true' has 'grass is white' as its antecedent, it would be used to affirm that grass is white; 'that is false' would be used to deny grass is white. But if there is not an appropriate antecedent, the anaphor (pronoun or prosentence) is "ungrounded". The anaphor then fails to have operative meaning. (Pronouns and prosentences can be "bound". Just as bound individual variables do much the same work that bound pronouns do in natural languages, so also bound propositional variables are the formal analogues of bound prosentences.)

The liar sentence is a modified prosentence that would (if used!) purport to affirm the contradictory of its antecedent. However, as it is itself its own antecedent, it is "ungrounded". For there is no antecedent with grounded operative meaning to inherit. The liar cannot be used to say anything.

So in this one respect the prosentential and property-ascribing theories are similar. On neither account does the liar have operative meaning. I had earlier claimed as an advantage for the prosentential theory the fact that lack of operative meaning of the

[27] Readers are referred to Grover (1992) for accounts of the prosentential role of the truth and falsity predicates. The liar is discussed in "Inheritors and Paradox", pp. 121–36; 'Neither true nor false' in "Truth: Do We Need It?" pp. 193–204.

[28] I have to be a little sloppy as I try to tie property-ascribing and prosentential accounts together. It makes some sense on the property-ascribing view to talk of the truth "concept" and to talk of dictionary meaning and operative meaning. (And that is only for now, as I do not like some presuppositions of concept and meaning talk.) On the prosentential view, I prefer to talk simply of the "role" or the "logical role" of the truth predicate and in this paper will speak of prosentences (with appropriate antecedents) as having operative meaning.

liar fell out neatly from the theory—whereas property theories seemed to face insurmountable problems with the liar. But this is not a basis for choosing between the theories. That choice should probably be based on such issues as the different expressibility offered, explanatory role issues, and general comprehensiveness and potential for coherent articulation—possibly formal articulation—of the theories.

I have argued that neither the liar, nor the strengthened liar, provides grounds for thinking prosentential truth-talk leads to contradiction. However, Jerry Kapus (1991) is skeptical. He has raised a number of important issues. The only part I will address here is an argument borrowed from Anil Gupta and Nuel Belnap (1993). They dismiss any attempt to "resolve" the liar that denies the liar expresses a proposition.

> If in the propositional analogue of the Simple Liar we understand 'not' to have wide scope, we again land in difficulties. Consider this reformulation of the analogue:
>
> (6) It is not the case that there is a true proposition that this sentence—i.e., (6)—expresses.
>
> Sentence (6) is paradoxical if we assume it expresses a proposition. But there is a difficulty even if we assume that it does not. For now we must deny the existential claim that
>
> There is a true proposition that (6) expresses.
>
> Consequently we must assert
>
> (7) It is not the case that there is a true proposition that (6) expresses.
>
> But if we say that (6) does not express a proposition, it would appear that we should say equally that (7) does not express one either. This is strange: We are asserting (7) and yet denying that it expresses a proposition. (Gupta and Belnap (1993), pp. 9–10.)

Gupta and Belnap make an intuitive appeal to there being a point to affirming (7). They make no attempt to demonstrate there is a use for (6). Their reason for thinking (6) and (7) have the same status seems based on syntactic considerations and their placing a high priority on uniformity of treatment. But we have seen that in natural languages, one set of uses of tokens of a sentence does not determine that another token has the same, or even any, operative meaning. How can context generate a difference between (6) and (7)?

Token (6) is mentioned in (7) but not used. Only token (7) is used. Whereas, token (6) is both mentioned *and* (allegedly) used in (6). This is a difference that makes the difference. It is one thing to talk about a token that does not have operative meaning, and another to purport to use it. Things are complex, but not dubious as Gupta and Belnap suggest.

Similar issues arise for Gupta and Belnap's other cases. They are concerned that those who deny the liar expresses a proposition must provide "a separate account of the logic and semantics of sentences" like

> (5) St. Paul believed that all Cretans are liars. (p. 8.)

I am afraid that is the case. Similarly there are special challenges in the case of

St. Paul believed that $6 \div 0 = 7$.

And this probably calls for a different treatment than that which might be given of

St. Paul believed that Pegasus flew overhead.

I question whether there are conditions that would show St. Paul had the alleged belief. I assume we want to draw a distinction between uttering and believing. So St. Paul's uttering the sentence will not suffice. Similarly, the second case is puzzling. Many of us were told at school that $6 \div 0 =$ infinity. We certainly believed that the teacher told us infinity was the right answer. Is there anything else we believed? I am not sure where the value of these examples, as examples, lies.

5. SUMMARY

5.1 Natural Language

I have argued the liar does not have to be "resolved". My argument begins with the observation that the liar is not a sentence that is used (unless used inadvertently). Indeed, I have difficulty envisaging what point there would be in trying to use the liar sentence. The argument then splits in two because I have wanted to provide arguments for both, those who think 'true' is property-ascribing, and those who think 'true' has a prosentence-forming role.

1. *From a property-ascribing perspective,* I show the liar is not even used in inferences to contradiction, because the sequences of sentences that look like inferences are not, in fact, inferences. This is because the liar sentence does not substitute in truth and falsity schemas—since it has not been independently shown that it has operative meaning.

2. *From a prosentential perspective,* I remind readers that prosentences need to be grounded if they are to be used in a communicatively significant way. As the liar is an ungrounded modified prosentence, it cannot be used in a communicatively significant way.

Given openness in word-usage, a token that is not used does not have operative meaning. If no token of the liar has operative meaning, it does not contribute to dictionary meaning. So there is nothing hidden in the liar that contributes to our concept of truth.

My negative thesis is limited, for there are genuine questions in other respects that we can raise about the liar. For example, we might prefer that a good theory of the *role* of the truth predicate in natural language should have fall out of it (have as a corollary) an explanation of why we are not tempted to use tokens of the liar.[29] Graham MacDonald and Anil Gupta have raised this issue with me. We might ask, What would be the point in uttering the liar sentence? What would we be trying to say in using the liar sentence? The prosentential theory gives negative answers to these questions, as ungrounded prosentences provide us with nothing to say. From a

[29] This is roughly the converse of the position I have argued against: the position that we should seek insight *from* the liar in the interests of explaining our "other" truth-talk.

property-ascribing perspective I think the negative story will be a little more complex. While the possibility of asserting a contradiction would suffice as a reason for not trying to use the liar; I am skeptical that *that* is why people never use the liar sentence.

We should also allow that explanations (or partial explanations) of our not using the liar might be helpful with other projects. Take the concept of rationality, for example. Our understanding of rationality has probably deepened through a study of behavior that is not rational, behavior like that of people who suffer ongoing delusions, or the behavior of other animals. Similarly, our understanding of which sentences are useful might be deepened through consideration of the fact that we judge the liar (and 'Blatant grasses run furiously homeward') is not useful in our usual discourse.

Another issue we can address concerns belief. Does it make sense to ascribe to a Cretan the belief that all Cretans are liars? Mere utterance of the sentence hardly suffices.

There is also the challenging task of trying to identify those occasions where we would run the risk of mistakenly (trying to) use liar-like constructions. We do not usually want to run the risk of *appearing* to assert a contradiction.

5.2 Formalized Languages

I will discuss two formal treatments of the truth predicate, as they will give me the opportunity to illustrate some of the points I have briefly alluded to earlier in the paper.

The places where we most often find talk of resolving the liar is in the motivating sections of writings on the truth predicate in formalized languages. Undoubtedly this has been due in large part to Tarski's (for example, Tarski (1933/56)) despair of natural language as containing a truth predicate and other features *suitable for his needs*. In response, philosophers have sought to restore confidence in the intuitive truth concept. However, I do not believe Tarski himself sought to do anything like "resolve" a paradox. Nor did he seek a deeper understanding of truth *through the liar*.[30] So what did Tarski do? And how was it that he seemed to pay some attention to the liar?

A part of his project was to provide philosophers with a metalinguistic truth predicate that would be useful in formalized languages; that is, in languages where there are fixed "unambiguous" ties between syntax and semantics.[31] The stipulated ties between syntax and semantics make a metalinguistic truth predicate a good choice in formalized languages. (A more perspicuous choice than a prosentence-forming predicate, for example.)[32] Tarski's recognition of the role T-sentences could play in his

[30] This assessment is consistent with his comment, "A thorough analysis of the meaning current in everyday life of the term 'true' is not intended here," Tarski (1933/56), p. 153.

[31] Again, by a "metalinguistic" truth predicate I mean a truth predicate that attaches to names of sentences. It happens Tarski had a truth predicate for each level of language, but I am not including that in 'metalinguistic.'

[32] In "Truth: Do We Need It?" §6, and "Two Deflationary Truth Theories" (reprinted in Grover (1992) pp. 173–206, and pp. 215–33) I point out that a metalinguistic predicate (prosententially interpreted) can be used to perspicuously "draw attention to the syntax of the language". The

definition of truth was profound. By contrast, indexicals, ambiguity, openness in word usage, and so on, mean that T-sentences cannot have anything like the same role outside the formalized language context. The resulting theory, with its adequacy conditions and the formal results that followed, have provided ***the paradigm*** of how important, intuitive, natural language concepts, operators, and predicates may be provided perspicuous useful formal explications.[33] As for the liar, Tarski simply circumvented it. His contributions have little to do with the liar, and a lot to do with the provision of a truth predicate that he was able to use in establishing highly important results.

Clearly, those who work on the development of formalized languages, with its ties between syntax and semantics, are forced to make a choice as to the status they will give the liar sentence. Tarski's approach was to exclude the liar from the set of well-formed sentences. While the semantic implications of this choice match our not using (and Tarski's not using) the liar, there is no reason to think he sought to capture this aspect of linguistic usage.[34] Another alternative is to allow the liar as a well-formed sentence and then provide a semantic value deemed suitable—which will not introduce inconsistency. Some have tried the "third" value option. Gupta (with Belnap, in Gupta and Belnap (1993)) has presented another possibility. He begins by taking more seriously—one might say—the idea of using the whole set of well-formed T-sentences (including instances formed with the liar[35]) as a way of defining an extension for the truth predicate. More accurately, in Gupta's terminology, "the T-sentences *fix the signification of truth*." On this explication of the truth concept, the liar receives, appropriately, an ever-shifting semantic assignment[36] that earns the liar the classification "pathological". This status of the liar falls nicely out of his theory. As with Tarski's theorizing, I do not see that Gupta's theory needs to be *motivated* by the liar. I personally see his most important insights as arising in his groundbreaking theory of circular definitions. While Gupta arrives at this from his account of truth *via* T-sentences, his work on circularity should deepen our understanding well beyond

conditions need to be right, as they are in formalized languages. I do not see that Tarski's (or Kripke's (1975)) truth predicates need to be interpreted as property-ascribing. As a separate issue, I have often wondered whether a metalinguistic truth predicate is *necessary* in establishing the formal results of, say, Godel and Tarski. Tennant (2002) (based on results of Feferman) shows that in one case a metalinguistic predicate is not necessary.

[33] I use the word 'explication' here in recognition that a formal analogue cannot exactly (whatever that might mean) replicate an intuitive concept. Tarksi told us he hoped to target "the so-called *classical* conception of truth ('true—corresponding to reality')" (p. 153).

[34] To digress from Tarski's project for a minute: If analysis of natural language were the task, we would again not need to include semantics for the liar even for saying, of it, that it is "neither true nor false". The liar need only be mentioned for that. I am assuming the analysis of "neither true nor false" suggested in §3.1 that disallows instancing the truth and falsity schemas with the liar sentence.

[35] Note that Gupta and Belnap (1993) have claimed the focus should be "the principles that underlie the ordinary unproblematic uses of the concept of truth." As the principle encapsulated in the T-schema has a limited range of applicability, in the sense that not all well-formed sentences are included, sentences containing indexicals, sentences like "Blatant grasses run furiously homeward," etc., are excluded. Consistent with my position, the liar would not then substitute in the T-schema.

[36] There is an interesting massaging here of Tarski's (1933/1956) requirement that the sense of every expression be "unambiguously determined by its form".

this, in light of the fact that circularity of various kinds seems pervasive in the development of language.

I add just one more point. The picture of living languages that I have presented, according to which there is openness in word usage, means that we should not expect to find *the* correct formal explication of *the* intuitive concept of truth, nor *the* correct determination of the status of the liar. The fact that word usage is open means that there is not necessarily a unique concept, nor (if there were one) will there be just one way of "extending" it in a formal context.[37] In a formal explication there will be choices to be made. The goal, or goals, of the formalization may influence these. For example: Is the point an analysis of some aspect of the role of 'true' in natural language? Is the point the development of a predicate that will be useful in establishing new results? Is the point to provide a theory of belief ascription? (Nor do I mean to suggest these are distinct enterprises.)

5.3 Attitudes

I have advocated that we adopt an attitude to the liar similar to the attitude we have towards division by zero. We do not regard division incoherent on the ground that inconsistency would seem to threaten if we were to counterfactually assume we could divide by zero. So, also, we should not regard truth-talk incoherent on the ground that inconsistency would seem to threaten, if we were counterfactually to assume the liar could be used in inferences.

There are also contrasts to be made with other cases in mathematics. I assume zero was "added" to the number system so terms like '6 − 6' would have referents. Similarly, the introduction of irrational and complex numbers took us from a partial to a complete square-root function. By contrast, I understand there is not a satisfactory way of introducing a new number or set of numbers to make complete the division function. Nor do results from formalized language analyses of the role of the truth predicate make it seem likely we can extend our *use* of 'true' and 'false' to include use of liar sentences.

At the time I wrote "Inheritors and Paradox" I had assumed those who advocated a property-ascribing role for 'false' faced an insurmountable problem in the liar. I now realize this view was based on a faulty picture of concepts. Our truth-talk is not to be held hostage by paradox. For a given concept, operative meaning, or logical role, is not attached willy-nilly to each and every conceivable token of the word in question. We are the creators of our ever-evolving language, through our creative introduction of new uses of words, as we face a variety of new demands on our communicative resources. The resulting openness in word usage means there is no earthly reason why we need assume *the existence* of tokens of the liar raises issues of inconsistency. As most people do, we might as well go about the business of using the truth predicate in asking the questions we want to ask, like, Are scientific truths the only truths there are?

[37] I follow Lynch (1998) in thinking concepts—including truth, if one is a property theorist—are fluid in the respect that there is the possibility of developing their use in a variety of different ways. This would apply particularly in formalized languages.

Under what conditions are we justified in claiming our beliefs are true? Do we need to assume a truth property? But, of course, there is a question that covers all of these and more: What is true?

REFERENCES

Barwise, Jon and John Etchemendy (1987). *An Essay on Truth and Circularity*, New York, Oxford: Oxford University Press.

Belnap, Nuel D. (1973). "Restricted Quantification and Conditional Assertion", in *Truth, Syntax, and Modality*, ed. H. Leblanc, Amsterdam: North-Holland, pp. 48–75

Davidson, Donald (1978). "What Metaphors Mean". Reprinted in *Truth and Interpretation* (1985), Oxford: Clarendon Press pp. 245–64.

—— (1986). "A Nice Derangement of Epitaphs", in *Truth and Interpretation: Perspectives on the Philosophy of Donald Davidson*, ed. E. LePore, Oxford: Basil Blackwell.

Dummett, Michael (1959). "Truth", *Proceedings of the Aristotelian Society*, 59, pp. 141–62. Reprinted in *Truth and Other Enigmas* (1978) Cambridge, MA: Harvard University Press.

Fine, Kit (1975). "Vagueness, Truth and Logic", in *Synthese* 30, 265–300.

Frege, G. (1884). *The Foundations of Arithmetic*, trans. J.L. Austin, Chicago: Northwestern University Press.

Grice, Paul (1989). *Studies in the Way With Words*. Cambridge, MA: Harvard University Press.

Grover, Dorothy (1992). *A Prosentential Theory of Truth*, Princeton: Princeton University Press.

—— (2000). "On Locating Our Interest in Truth", in *What is Truth?*, ed. Richard Schantz, Berlin: Walter de Gruyter, pp. 120–32.

—— (2001). "The Prosentential Theory: Further Reflections on Locating Our Interest in Truth", in *The Nature of Truth*, ed. Michael P. Lynch, Cambridge, MA: MIT Press, pp. 505–26.

Gupta, A and N. D. Belnap Jr. (1993). *A Revision Theory of Truth*, Cambridge, MA: MIT Press.

Horwich, Paul (1990). *Truth*, Cambridge, MA and Oxford: Basil Blackwell Ltd.

Kapus, Jerry (1991). "The Liar and the Prosentential Theory of Truth", in *Logique & Analyse* vol. 135–6, pp. 283–91.

Kripke, Saul (1975). "Outline of a Theory of Truth", *The Journal of Philosophy* 72, pp. 690–716.

Lynch, Michael (1998). *Truth in Context: An Essay on Pluralism and Objectivity*, Cambridge, MA: MIT Press.

McGee, Vann (1988). *Truth, Vagueness, and Paradox*, Indianapolis, IN: Hackett Publishing.

Millikan, Ruth Garrett (2000). *On Clear and Confused Ideas: An Essay about Substance Concepts*, Cambridge, UK: Cambridge University Press.

Tarski, Alfred (1933/56). "The Concept of Truth in Formalized Languages", in *Logic, Semantics, Metamathematics* (1956), Oxford: Clarendon Press. First published in Polish in 1933.

Tennant, Neil (2002). "Deflationism and the Godel Phenomena", in *Mind*, 111, pp. 551–82.

Wilson, Mark (1982). "Predicate Meets Property", in *Philosophical Review* 91, pp. 549–90.

12

The Deflationist's Axioms for Truth

Volker Halbach and Leon Horsten

Aber es geht um die höhere Wahrheit, an die man glauben muß; und unsere Aufgabe ist es, diese Wahrheit in die Niederungen des Beweises herabzuziehen.

Hofrat Brunner to Ernst Stockinger
TV series *Stockinger* (episode *Stille Wasser*)

1. DEFLATIONISM

In this introduction we shall be very sketchy. We do not want to fatigue the reader by refuting in detail claims that have lost credibility a long time ago. For instance, we sketch only the arguments for the insufficiency of the T-sentences as axioms for truth.

We will state some claims that seem central to deflationism *as we understand it.* Naturally there will be philosophers who disagree with our conception of deflationism. We believe, however, that many will agree that the deflationist has to subscribe to these claims. They are weak in the sense that they describe more a methodology than a real philosophical doctrine. The claims are not intended to cover the deflationist position completely, and probably the deflationist will put forward much stronger claims.

In the first place, according to deflationism, a logico-mathematical notion of truth is central to the deflationist conception of truth. Thus whether a sentence or proposition is true does not depend on contingent facts such as our causal relations with the world. Consequently, for instance, a causal-historical notion of reference will not form the basis for a deflationist theory of truth. Rather truth behaves like a logical or mathematical expression: when it is combined with other logical and mathematical notions it forms sentences or propositions that obtain independently of any contingent facts in the world.[1] Presumably the deflationist will also need more 'substantial' notions of truth which are not logico-mathematical in this sense. But for the deflationist logico-mathematical truth is primary and the starting point from which other notions should be defined.

[1] See, e.g., Field [7], Halbach [13], Horsten [17].

Second, truth is axiomatized, that is, truth is conceived as a primitive and undefined notion. This approach does not exclude the possibility that truth turns out to be definable or reducible in another sense.[2] Deflationism, as we understand it, does not necessarily articulate a notion of truth that is 'thin' in the sense that it might easily be reduced away. Rather deflationists have tried to describe the purpose of truth that can only be achieved if truth is available. Or they say that truth would be dispensable if we could use infinite conjunctions or certain forms of quantification.[3] An axiomatization of truth also coheres with its status as a logico-mathematical notion.

According to the conception of deflationism outlined so far, *semantical* theories of truth like Kripke's fixed-point theory or the rule-of-revision theory[4] are not deflationist theories. These theories provide definitions of truth in set theory. Thus truth is no longer conceived as a primitive concept. Moreover, these semantical concepts of truth are dispensable, because they are definable. In this respect semantical theories are similar to 'substantial' theories of truth; most varieties of the correspondence, coherence and pragmatist theory are supposed to *define* truth in terms of states of affairs, correspondence, coherence, utility, etc.

The semantical conceptions of truth from Tarski to Kripke and the revision theory rely on the availability of a stronger metalanguage where truth is defined. Consequently these notions of truth are not universal in the sense of being notions of truth for the whole language (or at least its logico-mathematical part) that we are using.[5] Frequently they show how to add to an arithmetical language a truth predicate and how to expand the standard model of arithmetic to a model of the extended language with the truth predicate. Although this may be informative with respect to an analysis of the semantical paradoxes, it does not provide a notion of truth for the language (or, more precisely, for the theory) we are using. In general, studying toy languages and theories from a set-theoretic standpoint will not satisfy the deflationist because he is seeking a notion of truth for the language of the theory he is using. Concepts of truth for weak toy languages for which we can define truth by set-theoretic means are of little immediate use to the deflationist.

In sum, in a certain sense semantical approaches provide a more 'deflationary' picture of truth because they purport to define truth. So according to these semantical theories, truth is ultimately redundant because it is definable. However, definable

[2] The discussion has focused on a very special sense of reducibility. It is pretty obvious from Tarski's theorem on the undefinability of truth that truth will not be reducible in the sense that it is definable. Truth, however, might be reducible in another sense, and in proof theory many concepts of reduction have been discussed and applied. Several authors like Shapiro [27], Ketland [19] and Field [8] and Azzouni [1] have discussed whether the deflationist is committed to the conservativeness of his theory of truth. See Halbach [13].

[3] Field [8] and Azzouni [1] might be exceptions. They seem to believe that a truth theory ought to be conservative. See Halbach [13] for a discussion. We shall return to the discussion of conservativeness below.

[4] See Kripke [22] and Belnap and Gupta [2].

[5] Some deflationists disagree with this view. Soames [30], for instance, conceives Kripke's theory as a deflationist theory of truth.

notions of truth are not of primary interest to the deflationist because they are always just notions of truth for at best a part of our 'real' language.

Many axiomatic approaches are also formulated for toy languages and theories such that finally models for these axiomatic theories can be defined (in relatively weak theories). For instance, very often logicians add truth axioms to the language of Peano arithmetic. Although Peano arithmetic is very weak compared to our usual mathematical assumptions (set theory), these investigations are nevertheless relevant. If adding certain truth axioms to Peano arithmetic yields a consistent theory, adding axioms of the same kind to Zermelo-Fraenkel ought to produce a consistent theory as well. This is not guaranteed, however. For adding truth axioms usually increases the proof theoretic strength of a theory, and one cannot even obtain a proof of relative consistency. That is, in most cases we are not able to prove that set theory plus the truth axioms are consistent even if set theory itself is assumed to be consistent. In fact, the situation is sometimes even worse than that. Examples can be found of apparently innocent axioms concerning the notion of satisfaction which can consistently be added to Peano Arithmetic, but which result in an inconsistent system when they are added to the Zermelo-Fraenkel axioms.[6]

However, several considerations are independent from the chosen base language. If some truth axioms are inconsistent with Peano arithmetic, they will be inconsistent with set theory as well. Moreover, arithmetic is a convenient setting for the study of axiomatic truth theories because we have names of expressions at our disposal. Numerals (of codes of expressions) may serve the same purpose as quotational names in natural language. The language of set theory lacks such names (although they could easily be added). Therefore building truth theories on arithmetical theories is simply a convenient approach but arithmetic merely serves as an example here.

2. TARSKI'S THEORIES OF TRUTH

Many deflationists have advanced 'disquotational' axioms for truth. In particular, some have relied on some variety of the T- or disquotational sentences

$$\mathrm{T}\ulcorner A \urcorner \leftrightarrow A.$$

Here $\ulcorner A \urcorner$ is a name for the sentence A or its Gödel number. Horwich's theory is similar, but there $\ulcorner A \urcorner$ would be a name for the proposition that A.[7]

In order to avoid inconsistency one can restrict the instances to such sentences A that do not contain the truth predicate.[8] As Tarski has noted, the T-sentences are far too weak to prove any interesting generalization. In particular, if a base theory plus the T-sentences prove a generalization of the form $\forall x(A(x) \rightarrow \mathrm{T}x)$ then the base theory

[6] See Horsten [16].

[7] See Horwich [18].

[8] Some consistent restrictions of the T-scheme yield unwanted consequences. McGee [25] has shown that Horwich's idea of excluding only the 'bad' instances of the schema does yield neither a unique nor a satisfying theory of truth.

proves that there are at most n objects satisfying $A(x)$, that is, the base theory proves $\exists_n x A(x)$ for some fixed number n.[9]

The deductive weakness of the T-sentences is *our* motivation for embracing a compositional theory of truth. Other authors—like Davidson—had different reasons (like finite axiomatizability) for relying on Tarski's compositional axioms for truth. In the first axiom P is any n-place predicate symbol (except T) and val(x) represents the function that assigns to any closed term t its value.

$$\forall t_1 \ldots t_n\, (\mathrm{T}\ulcorner P t_1 \ldots t_n \urcorner \leftrightarrow P\mathrm{val}(t_1) \ldots \mathrm{val}(t_n)) \tag{T1}$$

$$\forall A \in \mathcal{L}\, (\mathrm{T}\ulcorner \neg A \urcorner \leftrightarrow \neg \mathrm{T}\ulcorner A \urcorner) \tag{T2}$$

$$\forall A, B \in \mathcal{L}\, (\mathrm{T}\ulcorner A \wedge B \urcorner \leftrightarrow \mathrm{T}\ulcorner A \urcorner \wedge \mathrm{T}\ulcorner B \urcorner) \tag{T3}$$

$$\forall A(v) \in \mathcal{L}\, (\mathrm{T}\ulcorner \forall v A(v) \urcorner \leftrightarrow \forall t \mathrm{T}\ulcorner A(t) \urcorner) \tag{T4}$$

The first axiom says that for any string of closed terms $t_1, \ldots, t_n$, P followed by this string of terms is true if and only if P applies to the values of these terms. In the case of arithmetic there is no difficulty in defining val( ). According to axiom T4 a universally quantified sentence $\forall v A(v)$ is true if and only if all its instances $A(t)$ for any closed term t are true. Thus T4 captures a substitutional understanding of the quantifier. In an arithmetical framework this approach is sound because there are closed terms for any object because there is a numeral for every number.

In the general case, where some objects might lack terms designating them, however, we would have to employ satisfaction instead of the unary truth predicate. What we say below would go through for satisfaction instead of truth as well. Employing truth instead of satisfaction makes our notation somewhat more perspicuous.

$\forall t_1$ expresses quantification over closed terms, while $\forall A \in \mathcal{L}$ expresses quantification over all sentences of the base language $\mathcal{L}$, i.e., the language without the truth predicate, and $\forall A(v) \in \mathcal{L}$ expresses quantification over all formulas of $\mathcal{L}$ with only-v free. Quantification in quotational contexts can be explained in different ways: we do not provide details here.

Axioms T2–T4 say that truth commutes with connectives and quantifiers. We do not provide an exact formulation because for our purposes a rough sketch ought to be sufficient.

If the axioms T1–T4 above are added to a theory like Peano arithmetic or some set theory it seems attractive not only to add these truth-theoretic axioms but to extend the axiom schemes to the new language with the truth predicate as well. In the literature there has been some discussion on these additional truth-theoretic axioms.[10] Most authors (including us) agree that the axiom schemes should be extended to the language with the truth predicate in the case of PA or ZF. The details are tricky and will not be dealt with in this paper.[11]

[9] This observation is basically Tarski's: see his [31]. The proof relies on the fact that a proof contains only finitely many instances of the T-schema. So the T-sentences prove only *finite* generalizations. This holds even if the allow the truth theory to contain all instances of the induction scheme (including those with T) assuming that, e.g., PA is our base theory.

[10] See Shapiro [27], Field [8] and Halbach [13].

[11] See Feferman [6] for more information on the role of axioms schemes in truth theories.

3. DESIDERATA FOR AXIOMATIC THEORIES OF TRUTH

Tarski's solution of the liar paradox was an undivided success in mathematical logic and opened the road to model theory. In philosophy of language it was only a partial success. Tarski himself did not think that his solution of the liar paradox applied to natural language.

The deflationist is confronted with the problem of having to come up with a less restrictive solution of the liar paradox. Of course the derivation of an inconsistency has to be blocked, but not in Tarski's coarse way. It is not in the scope of the present paper to discuss all proposals that have been made to this end. However, we shall discuss some of the main contenders.

Once the deflationist has decided in favor of an axiomatic approach to truth, he can attempt to articulate general features that any such theory S must possess in virtue of its logico-mathematical function in ordinary discourse. Here is the list of desiderata that we propose:

1. S must satisfy a requirement of naturalness and simplicity. It must contain as few ad hoc elements as possible.

2. S must explicate the compositional nature of truth. S must explain as fully as possible how the truth-value of a sentence is determined by the truth-values of its component parts.

3. S must prove as many (true) infinite conjunctions as possible. The chief reason for having a truth predicate is to express infinite conjunctions. But expressing infinite conjunctions is of little use if we are not able to prove many of them.[12]

4. The logic in which S reasons about the truth predicate must be the same as the logic under which the truth predicate is closed according to S. In quasi-technical terms: the *outer logic* of S, i.e., the set of the sentences provable in S, must equal the *inner logic* $\{A | S \vdash T\ulcorner A \urcorner\}$ of S.

5. It is desirable that classical logic is used. This applies not only to the outer logic, but—by the previous desideratum—to the inner logic as well.

These desiderata considerably overlap and were partly inspired by Michael Sheard's list of 'naive criteria' which he thinks theories of truth—both axiomatic and semantic—need to satisfy as much as possible.[13]

Our Desideratum 1 is a paraphrase of Sheard's third criterion, which he also calls the criterion of simplicity. Of course, it is not easy to put forward criteria for naturalness and simplicity. We think that the T-sentences are simple and that T1–T4 are simple and natural as well, though less simple than the T–sentences. T2–T4 express that the truth predicate commutes with connectives and quantifiers. Therefore T2–T4 describe a simple 'algebraic' property of truth.

Desideratum 2 implies that the truth predicate should commute with quantifiers and connectives. Therefore it is a generalization of Sheard's fifth principle which says

[12] See Halbach [11, 13]. [13] See Sheard [29].

that theories of truth should contain the Barcan principle $\forall A(v) \in \mathcal{L}(\mathrm{T}\ulcorner\forall v A(v)\urcorner \leftrightarrow \forall t \mathrm{T}\ulcorner A(t)\urcorner)$. Strictly speaking $A(t)$ is no subformula of $\forall v A(v)$, but the axiom would be compositional in the strict sense if a satisfaction predicate were employed. For the axiom would then say that $\forall_v A(v)$ is true if $A(v)$ is satisfied by all objects. Therefore we consider axioms as T4 above and C4 below as compositional. We shall have to discuss compositionality again below.

Desideratum 3 is not explicitly present in Sheard's list. It is to some extent entailed by Sheard's sixth principle, which he formulates tentatively, and which says that S should be arithmetically nonconservative over the arithmetical basis over which S is formulated.[14] Deflationists might object to adopting this desideratum if they believe that truth has to be a simple and innocent concept in every respect. We believe that deflationist truth is a tool for formulating and *proving* generalizations (or, if you like, infinite conjunctions).

Deflationist truth is as insubstantial as other logico-mathematical concepts like the concept of elementhood. It does not rely on any 'substantial' concepts like causality, correspondence, coherence or utility. But this does not force the deflationist in any way to maintain that a theory of truth ought to be deductively weak. This implies in particular that we do not expect a theory of truth to be conservative in any reasonable sense. Rather if the concept of truth is useful it will turn out to be proof-theoretically strong and irreducible. This is in accord with the deflationist doctrine that truth is an indispensable tool for making generalizations.

Desideratum 4 expresses that we want to capture truth for the language or theory we are using. In particular, we want to avoid asymmetries like axiomatizing in classical logic a notion of truth in partial logic. This desideratum implies Sheard's demand that provability should entail truth. For, if a sentence A is provable, then A is in the outer logic and there it ought to be contained in the inner logic as well; i.e., it should be (provably) true.

Desideratum 5 for a truth theory framed in classical logic is motivated by the deflationist conviction that truth is primarily a logico-mathematical notion. Historically, classical logic has emerged from a conscious attempt to explicate the form of mathematical reasoning. So if truth is indeed a logico-mathematical notion, then it ought to be governed by classical logic.

Desideratum 4 overrules the last desideratum. That is, if one opts for non-classical logic, e.g., partial logic, for the inner or the outer logic, then both, the inner and the outer logic, must be governed by partial logic.

4. BEYOND TARSKI

Once one drops Tarski's solution of the liar paradox and allows the truth predicate to apply to sentences containing the truth predicate, we see basically two ways to go: Either one sticks to classical logic or one adopts partial (or many-valued) logic or at least a partial conception of truth (which may be described in classical logic).

[14] Sheard remarks that under fairly general conditions, this feature of S is a consequence of S's containing the Barcan formula for T.

The main bulk of proposals consists in solutions based on non-classical logic. One can allow truth value gluts or gaps, or make even more severe incisions in classical logic. As pointed out above, the deflationist seeks an axiomatic approach, not a semantical approach. However, semantical theories can be used in order to motivate axiomatic approaches. A typical example is axiomatization of Kripke's approach in partial logic, e.g. Kremer [21]. Solutions based on nonclassical logic can be axiomatized in classical logic as well. In this case the truth theory itself is formulated in classical logic, but it describes a nonclassical concept of truth. Important examples of such systems are the variants of the *Kripke–Feferman* theory KF (see Feferman [6], Reinhardt [26] and Cantini [4]), which is motivated by Kripke's [22] fixed point theory with the strong Kleene scheme, and VF of Cantini [3], which is motivated by Kripke's [22] fixed point theory with the supervaluations scheme.

Typically these systems are inconsistent with either the "consistency" axiom

$$\forall A \in \mathcal{L}_{\mathrm{T}} \neg(\mathrm{T}\ulcorner \neg A \urcorner \wedge \mathrm{T}\ulcorner A \urcorner),$$

which excludes truth value gluts, or with the "completeness" axiom

$$\forall A \in \mathcal{L}_{\mathrm{T}} (\mathrm{T}\ulcorner \neg A \urcorner \vee \mathrm{T}\ulcorner A \urcorner),$$

which excludes truth value gaps. Proof-theoretical investigations have shown that such theories are very good at proving infinite conjunctions. In fact, Feferman [6] has provided a proof-theoretic analysis of the weak and strong reflective closures of Peano arithmetic (variants of KF) by means of infinite conjunctions. Although Feferman's paper has gone mostly unnoticed by the deflationists, his paper certainly has advanced the understanding of the relation of infinite conjunctions and truth a great deal.

KF and its relatives are notorious for their asymmetry between internal and external logic: they describe a notion of partial truth in classical logic. One can prove in KF that the liar sentence L is not true, i.e., $\mathsf{KF} \vdash \neg\mathrm{T}\ulcorner L \urcorner$. Since KF is classical and $L \leftrightarrow \neg\mathrm{T}\ulcorner L \urcorner$ is provable in the basic theory of syntax, the liar sentence itself is a theorem of KF. That is, KF proves both the liar sentence *and* that the liar sentence is not true! Therefore

$$\{A \mid \mathsf{KF} \vdash A\} \not\subseteq \{A \mid \mathsf{KF} \vdash \mathrm{T}\ulcorner A \urcorner\},$$

i.e. the inner logic of KF does not coincide with its outer logic. According to KF, the extension of the truth predicate is closed only under *partial* logic. Indeed, KF was discovered by a conscious attempt to formalize Kripke's *semantical* inductive theory based on the strong Kleene-scheme. In sum, KF scores miserably on Desideratum 4.

One could (and should) formulate KF in partial logic outright.[15] That way, at least the inner logic of the resulting system would coincide with its outer logic,[16] and it would cohere better with the partial picture behind the theory.[17] But the fact remains that we have abandoned classical logic.

[15] We have tried to formulate KF in Strong Kleene logic in [14].

[16] The obvious way of formulating KF in partial logic results in a system which *differs* from the inner logic of KF. It is, according to [14] stronger than CT but weaker than KF. Cf. also Kremer [21] for a formulation of Kripke's theory in partial logic.

[17] Kripke [22] was ambiguous on precisely this point. Reinhardt [26] is more consistent here, and so is Soames [30].

KF is still compositional, if the concept of compositionality is liberalized. For KF features axioms like $\forall A \in \mathcal{L}_{\mathrm{T}}(\mathrm{T}\ulcorner \mathrm{T}\ulcorner \dot{A} \urcorner\urcorner \leftrightarrow \mathrm{T}\ulcorner A \urcorner)$ saying that an atomic sentence T_n is true if and only if n is (the code of) a true sentence. Unlike the case of the quantifier axiom, using a satisfaction predicate will not render this axiom compositional in the strict sense. We tend to view A as a component of $\mathrm{T}\ulcorner A \urcorner$. In this sense KF is still compositional.[18]

Stronger systems like the above-mentioned system VF of Cantini [3], which formalizes the Kripkean construction based on the supervaluation scheme, have the same deficiencies as KF. The inner logic of VF also differs from its outer logic.[19] Moreover VF is not compositional and there is no known way to reformulate the VF axioms in a compositional manner. Proof-theoretic results suggest that this is not possible. In [12] it was conjectured that what compositionality for truth theories corresponds to predicativity for subsystems of analysis, i.e. with the aid of compositional truth theories we can motivate the arithmetical part of predicative analysis, but not more. If this thesis is sound, VF cannot be reformulated as a compositional system. For VF is impredicative. The irreducibly non-compositional feature of VF is the presence of a reflection axiom

$$\forall A \in \mathcal{L}_{\mathrm{T}}(\mathrm{Bew}_P(\ulcorner A \urcorner) \rightarrow \mathrm{T}\ulcorner A \urcorner)$$

where P is some (weak arithmetical) theory formulated in the language $\mathcal{L}_{\mathrm{T}}$. This axiom implies that, e.g., $B \vee \neg B$ is true, even if B is some paradoxical sentence like the liar. Thus a disjunction may be true even if both disjuncts lack a truth value, but it also might lack a truth value. $B \vee B$ will neither be true nor false. VF even proves that neither the liar sentence L nor its negation $\neg L$ are true; nevertheless it proves that $L \vee \neg L$ is true. Thus the truth of a sentence does not only depend on the truth value of its components but also on the syntactical shape of the sentence. This is a clear violation of compositionality.

As we shall see, reflection axioms can be reduced in some cases to compositional axioms. But if Halbach's thesis on compositionality and predicativity holds, then in the case of VF this is not possible.

In favor of VF it is to be said that VF is one of the strongest natural truth theories known so far. Therefore VF scores best at Desideratum 3 among all truth systems.

5. CLASSICAL REFLECTIVE TRUTH

Because of the problems with KF and VF we propose a system describing a *classical* notion of truth. The system explicitly denies the existence of truth value gluts and gaps. Here we do not argue that classical concepts of truth are superior to partial notions. We simply presuppose that classicality is a desirable feature. At least we find reasoning in partial logic awkward and not natural and thus we do not want to use

[18] See Halbach [12] for further discussion.

[19] So we do not agree with Sheard that VF scores much higher than KF on Desideratum 4.

partial logic.[20] And if we use classical logic in order to axiomatize a concept of partial truth, then the awkward asymmetry of inner and outer logic arises as in the case of KF.

We emphasize, however, that we do not believe that there is a single best set of axioms for the deflationist. Tarski's theorem on the undefinability rules out the "best" system as inconsistent. All desiderata we have listed cannot be satisfied equally well at the same time. Therefore we cannot come to a final decision and settle for a single system.

An obvious way to generalize T1–T4 is simply to let the quantifiers not only range over formulas without the truth predicate but also over formulas with the truth predicate. This yields the following axioms:

$$\forall t_1 \dots t_n \; (\mathrm{T}\ulcorner Pt_1 \dots t_n \urcorner \leftrightarrow P\mathrm{val}(t_1) \dots \mathrm{val}(t_n)) \tag{T1}$$

$$\forall A \in \mathcal{L}_\mathrm{T} \; (\mathrm{T}\ulcorner \neg A \urcorner \leftrightarrow \neg \mathrm{T}\ulcorner A \urcorner) \tag{C2}$$

$$\forall A, B \in \mathcal{L}_\mathrm{T} \; (\mathrm{T}\ulcorner A \wedge B \urcorner \leftrightarrow \mathrm{T}\ulcorner A \urcorner \wedge \mathrm{T}\ulcorner B \urcorner) \tag{C3}$$

$$\forall A(v) \in \mathcal{L}_\mathrm{T} \; (\mathrm{T}\ulcorner \forall v A(v) \urcorner \leftrightarrow \forall t \mathrm{T}\ulcorner A(t) \urcorner) \tag{C4}$$

We call the base theory plus these axioms CT_0 (for "classical truth").

We cannot allow P to be truth predicate in the first axiom, because otherwise the system would be inconsistent.[21]

The deflationist surely wants his theory to be sound, that is, he wants all theorems of his theory to be true. But of course Gödel's second incompleteness theorem shows that a truth theory can hardly prove its own soundness. The soundness for a truth theory S is expressed by:

$$\forall A \in \mathcal{L}_\mathrm{T}(\mathrm{Bew}_s(\ulcorner A \urcorner) \rightarrow \mathrm{T}\ulcorner A \urcorner) \tag{GRFN}$$

This sentence is called the *global reflection axiom* for S.[22] If the truth theory proves the unproblematic T-sentence $\mathrm{T}\ulcorner \bot \urcorner \leftrightarrow \bot$, then GRFN implies also the consistency statement $\neg\mathrm{Bew}_s(\ulcorner \bot \urcorner)$ for S.

However we are free to add the reflection axiom GRFN to the truth theory S in order to obtain a new theory S_1. The result of iteratively adding reflection axioms to a theory has been investigated thoroughly.[23] However, usually soundness is not directly expressed because a truth predicate is not available. Therefore proof theorists confine themselves to the uniform reflection scheme

$$\mathrm{Bew}_s(\ulcorner A(\dot{\vec{x}}) \urcorner) \rightarrow A(\vec{x}), \tag{RFN}$$

[20] We could invoke our Desideratum 1. But that comes down to the claim that we reject partial logic because it is not natural according to our taste. Others who are more used to partial logic will disagree. In the context of mathematics at least, the adoption of partial logic means an essential departure from our usual methods of reasoning that one should think twice before giving up classical logic.

[21] See Halbach [10].

[22] See Kreisel and Lévy [20].

[23] See Feferman [5].

which is supposed to express that all theorems of S are true. (The dot above x indicates that this variable is bound from outside in the usual way by formally substituting numerals for the variable x). In the present set-up we can avail ourselves of a truth predicate and we can express soundness by GRFN instead of its surrogate RFN.

The theory CT_0 has been defined above: it contains the base theory and the axioms postulating that the truth predicate commutes with quantifiers and connectives. We define recursively new systems which are obtained by adding the global reflection axiom for the respective system in the style of Turing's and Feferman's progressions.[24] CT_{n+1} is the system CT_n plus the global reflection axiom for CT_n:

$$\forall A \in \mathcal{L}_{\mathrm{T}}(\mathrm{Bew}_{\mathrm{CT}_n}(\ulcorner A \urcorner) \rightarrow \mathrm{T}\ulcorner A \urcorner) \tag{CTR}$$

Since we are dealing with finite progression only and CT_{n+1} extends CT_n only by a single axiom, there is always a canonical provability predicate available and we do not have to deal with the problems of the intensionality of progressions.

CT is defined as the union of all theories $\mathrm{CT}_n (n \in \omega)$.

For the sake of definiteness we consider Peano arithmetic as the base theory and state a few facts about CT built over Peano arithmetic. The observations carry over to many other base theories.

First we compare CT to theories that have been discussed in the literature. To this end we remark that adding all the reflection principles to CT_0 is equivalent to adding the rule

$$\frac{A}{\mathrm{T}\ulcorner A \urcorner} \tag{NEC}$$

to CT_0, where A is any sentence in $\mathcal{L}_{\mathrm{T}}$.

The rule NEC can be derived in CT as follows. If A is derivable in CT_0, then—by the Σ_1-completeness of PA—$\mathrm{Bew}_{\mathrm{CT}_0}(\ulcorner A \urcorner)$ is derivable in PA, and by the global reflection principle for CT_0 we have $\mathrm{T}\ulcorner A \urcorner$. Iterated applications of NEC can the dealt with in a similar way.

Deriving the global reflection principles from NEC is slightly harder; we shall only sketch the proof. CT_0 proves that all induction axioms in $\mathcal{L}_{\mathrm{T}}$ are true because

$$\forall A(v) \in \mathcal{L}_{\mathrm{T}}(\mathrm{T}\ulcorner A(0) \urcorner \wedge \forall x(\mathrm{T}\ulcorner A(\dot{x}) \urcorner \rightarrow \mathrm{T}\ulcorner A(\dot{x}+1) \urcorner) \rightarrow \forall x \mathrm{T}\ulcorner A(\dot{x}) \urcorner)$$

is an instance of the induction scheme and implies that all induction axioms are true. Beyond the induction axioms CT_0 has only finitely many axioms. They can be proved to be true by applying NEC to any of these axioms. Since truth is provably closed under logic, we therefore can prove in CT_0 + NEC that all theorems of CT_0 are true. For the induction step we have to show $\forall A \in \mathcal{L}_{\mathrm{T}}(\mathrm{Bew}_{\mathrm{CT}_n}(\ulcorner A \urcorner) \rightarrow \mathrm{T}\ulcorner \mathrm{T}\ulcorner A \urcorner \urcorner)$ because this implies $\forall A \in \mathcal{L}_{\mathrm{T}}(\mathrm{Bew}_{\mathrm{CT}_{n+1}}(\ulcorner A \urcorner) \rightarrow \mathrm{T}\ulcorner A \urcorner)$. By induction hypothesis we have already $\forall A \in \mathcal{L}_{\mathrm{T}}(\mathrm{Bew}_{\mathrm{CT}_n}(\ulcorner A \urcorner) \rightarrow \mathrm{T}\ulcorner A \urcorner)$ and by one application of NEC and the CT_0-axioms $\forall A \in \mathcal{L}_{\mathrm{T}}(\mathrm{T}\ulcorner \mathrm{Bew}_{\mathrm{CT}_n}(\ulcorner A \urcorner) \urcorner \rightarrow \mathrm{T}\ulcorner \mathrm{T}\ulcorner A \urcorner \urcorner)$. Since CT_0 proves all T-sen-

24 See Turing [33] and Feferman [5].

tences for arithmetical instances we have $\forall A \in \mathcal{L}_{\mathrm{T}}(\mathrm{Bew}_{\mathrm{CT}_n}(\ulcorner A \urcorner) \rightarrow \mathrm{T}\ulcorner \mathrm{T}\ulcorner A \urcorner\urcorner)$ as desired.

Thus the global reflection axioms and NEC are interderivable. This implies that CT is equivalent to the system FS without the converse rule of NEC.[25] That is, if we add

$$\frac{\mathrm{T}\ulcorner A \urcorner}{A}$$

to CT, then we obtain FS. Since it is still an unsolved problem whether this rule can be dropped from FS without any loss, for all we know CT and FS could be equivalent.[26] In fact, it would be nice if the system CT should turn out to be symmetrical, i.e., if the inner and outer logic of FS coincide. If it does not, we would recommend to add the above rule.

Friedman and Sheard have proved the consistency of FS; therefore CT is consistent as well. Models for CT may be obtained by revision semantics in the style of Herzberger.[27]

The iterated global reflection axioms of CT invite an obvious question: Why not iterate the reflection principle into the transfinite in the style of Feferman's transfinite progressions?[28] There is a very good reason for not doing this. The reflection axiom

$$\forall A \in \mathcal{L}_{\mathrm{T}}(\mathrm{Bew}_{\mathrm{CT}}(\ulcorner A \urcorner) \rightarrow \mathrm{T}\ulcorner A \urcorner)$$

for CT is inconsistent with CT.[29] This follows from a result by McGee.[30] He showed that a subsystem of CT is ω-inconsistent. McGee's argument can easily be carried out inside CT, that is, CT proves $\mathrm{Bew}_{\mathrm{CT}}(\ulcorner \exists x \neg A(x) \urcorner$ and $\forall x(\mathrm{Bew}_{\mathrm{CT}}(\ulcorner A(\dot{x}) \urcorner)$ for some formula $A(x)$ of $\mathcal{L}_{\mathrm{T}}$. Together with the global reflection principle for CT the latter implies in CT_0 the truth of $\forall x A(x)$. Thus there is a very good reason for not iterating global reflection into the transfinite.

Sometimes it is thought that the ω-inconsistency of CT and similar systems shows that they are not attractive as axiomatizations of truth. We do not share this view.

CT can be shown to be arithmetically sound, that is, CT does not prove any false arithmetical sentence. So the ω-inconsistency concerns only the part of CT that deals with the truth predicate.

Why would one reject an ω-inconsistent truth theory? Why would one reject CT in particular? One cannot put one's hopes on any particular sentence. For the sentences involved in the ω-inconsistency are circular and truth theories generally disagree on such sentences. So one cannot reject CT because it proves a false sentence. Perhaps one

[25] The system FS ("Friedman–Sheard") was studied under a different name and proved consistent by Friedman and Sheard [9]. See also Halbach [10].

[26] Results by Halbach [10] show that this rule does not contribute to the proof-theoretical strength of FS and that only very special sentences could require this rule for their proof. Further results by Sheard [28], however, showed that this rule is not as weak as it may appear.

[27] See Herzberger [15].

[28] See Feferman [5].

[29] Indeed the uniform reflection principle for CT is already inconsistent with CT.

[30] See [24].

might argue that CT does not have a nice model and that any attractive theory of truth must possess a nice model. To us this line of argument appears questionable. We accept set theory although we cannot prove that there is any nice model for set theory. Because of Gödel's second incompleteness theorem we cannot even prove that set theory has any model. However, there is an important difference between the case of set theory and CT. For set theory does not rule out that there is a nice model of set theory. For instance, set theory does not refute the existence of an inaccessible cardinal number. The truth theory CT, however, is ω-inconsistent, which refutes the existence of a ω-model of CT. Thus one can see from within CT that any model of CT must be nonstandard and that CT is inconsistent with the uniform reflection principle for CT.

Nevertheless we do not think that this makes CT unacceptable. For the semantics of CT are not as weird as it might appear. In fact CT has a very natural semantics. For any subsystem of CT with a finite number of global reflection axioms possesses a nice standard model. Since we can use in any proof only finitely many reflection axioms, at any step of our reasoning we have a nice model. The model is provided by rule-of-revision semantics.[31] A model for CT_n can be obtained by $n + 1$ applications of the revision operator to the standard model of arithmetic. We sketch the procedure: Expand the standard model of arithmetic to the language $\mathcal{L}_{\mathrm{T}}$ by assigning an arbitrary extension S_0 to the truth predicate. The model has the form $(\mathbb{N}, S_0)$, where $\mathbb{N}$ is the standard model of arithmetic and S_0 is the chosen extension of the truth predicate. Given S_n define S_{n+1} in the following way: $S_{n+1} = \{A \in \mathcal{L}_{\mathrm{T}} | (\mathbb{N}, S_n) \models A\}$ (here we identify sentences with their codes), that is, we use the set of all sentences truth in the model $(\mathbb{N}, S_n)$ as the new extension of the truth predicate. This way we obtain models for the theories CT_k.

The problems of revision semantics at limit levels are well known. The problem arises because the set S_ω of sentences that stay in the extension of the truth predicate from some level on is ω-inconsistent.[32] Therefore there is no ω-model for S_ω and the only option that remains is taking S_ω as the new extension of the truth predicate.[33] The ω-inconsistency of CT just reflects the fact that there is no nice limit model at level ω in rule-of-revision semantics. We believe that the axiomatic approach proves superior to the semantical approach based on the standard model. For on the semantical side there is no nice limit model at level ω, while one can simply take the union of all systems CT_n. The consistency of every system CT_n ensures the consistency of the entire system CT.

Therefore at any step in a proof in CT we may affirm that anything we have claimed so far is true: we do affirm it by a global reflection principle. We cannot, however, reflect on this and conclude that all affirmations of the soundness must be sound as well. This would be an additional reflection step that would take us to the global reflection principle for CT itself, which is inconsistent with CT.

We shall now look again at our desiderata and check to what extent they are met by CT. We hope that we have succeeded in describing the axioms of CT as simple and

[31] See Belnap and Gupta [2].
[32] This phenomenon is discussed by Belnap and Gupta [2].
[33] This is basically Herzberger's [15] limit rule.

natural. In particular, the axioms of CT naturally extend the unquestionable axioms T1–T4 to axioms for self-applicative truth.

CT, as it stands, is not compositional. For the reflection axioms CTR are not compositional. But CT can be reformulated with compositional axioms and rules. For the rule NEC surely is compositional if the KF axiom $\forall A \in \mathcal{L}_T(\mathrm{T}\ulcorner \mathrm{T}\ulcorner \dot{A} \urcorner\urcorner \leftrightarrow \mathrm{T}\ulcorner A \urcorner)$ was. KF rejects the compositional axiom C2 for negation, but C2 forms part of the axioms of CT. Thus with respect to the compositionality Desideratum 2 CT scores higher than KF.

The above model-theoretic considerations can be transformed into a proof of the fact that the proof-theoretic strength of CT is the same as of ramified analysis for all finite levels.[34] By comparison KF reaches the strength of ramified analysis up to ε_0. Therefore KF (and a fortiori VF) proves more generalizations than CT.

The real strength of CT lies in Desiderata 4 and 5. CT describes in classical logic a classical notion of truth. We have mentioned above that it is unknown whether

$$\frac{\mathrm{T}\ulcorner A \urcorner}{A}$$

is a derived rule of CT. If it were, the inner and outer logic of CT would be identical. This makes a proof of the hunch that this rule is derivable even more desirable. At any rate we can simply add this rule to CT in order to force the identity of inner and outer logic.[35] In contrast, adding NEC to KF in order to force the inner and outer logic of KF to be identical results in an inconsistent system.

6. CONCLUSION

When certain tenets of deflationism are accepted, one is driven to the axiomatic approach to the notion of truth. And then the question arises how the details of what is from a deflationist perspective the most attractive theory of truth would look like.

This question has hitherto not been given as much attention as it deserves. Deflationists have mostly adopted either Tarski's compositional theory of truth or, more frequently, Tarski's disquotational theory of truth. While this latter theory is simply deductively too weak, there presently exist also serious rivals to Tarski's compositional theory of truth, which are obtained by extending Tarski's compositional theory. In these theories one can prove that certain sentences containing the truth predicate are true. These systems do not obey Tarski's strict distinction between object- and metalanguage. They score much higher on Desideratum 3 than Tarski's compositional theory: they prove more generalizations.

However, one has to pay a price for the gain in expressive and deductive power: Many of these systems like KF and VF no longer describe a classical notion of truth; instead they describe a notion of truth with truth value gaps or gluts.

[34] See Halbach [10].

[35] But if CT + CONEC $\neq$ CT, then the question whether CT + CONEC can be analysed in terms of reflection principles needs to be investigated.

We have focused on a rival theory—CT—that sticks to a classical conception of truth thereby excluding truth value gaps and gluts. This system in many respects looks like a very natural strengthening of Tarski's compositional theory. Nevertheless, as soon as McGee discovered that this theory is ω-inconsistent, it was put aside.

In this chapter, we have argued that this was a hasty judgement. As a theory of truth, CT has much more to be said for it than is commonly appreciated. The effects of the ω-inconsistency are limited to the sphere of the diagonal sentences involving T, where our intuitions about the notion of truth are pretty much of no use anyway. And outside the sphere of these sentences, CT gives us only patently correct results. Moreover, it gives us many of them: CT is proof-theoretically significantly stronger than Tarski's compositional theory. For the moment the system CT (or FS if they are different) seems to be the deflationist's best bet. It is the most successful axiomatic theory of truth that is currently on the table.

REFERENCES

[1] Jody Azzouni. Comments on Shapiro. *Journal of Philosophy*, 96: 541–4, 1999.
[2] Nuel Belnap and Anil Gupta. *The Revision Theory of Truth*. MIT Press, Cambridge, 1993.
[3] Andrea Cantini. A theory of formal truth arithmetically equivalent to ID_1. *Journal of Symbolic Logic*, 55: 244–59, 1990.
[4] ——. *Logical Frameworks for Truth and Abstraction. An Axiomatic Study*, vol. 135 of *Studies in Logic and the Foundations of Mathematics*. Elsevier, Amsterdam, 1996.
[5] Solomon Feferman. Transfinite recursive progressions of axiomatic theories. *Journal of Symbolic Logic*, 27: 259–316, 1962.
[6] ——. Reflecting on incompleteness. *Journal of Symbolic Logic*, 56: 1–49, 1991.
[7] Hartry Field. Deflationist views of meaning and content. *Mind*, 103: 247–85, 1994.
[8] ——. Deflating the conservativeness argument. *Journal of Philosophy*, 96: 533–40, 1999.
[9] Harvey Friedman and Michael Sheard. An axiomatic approach to self-referential truth. *Annals of Pure and Applied Logic*, 33: 1–21, 1987.
[10] Volker Halbach. A system of complete and consistent truth. *Notre Dame Journal of Formal Logic*, 35: 311–27, 1994.
[11] ——. Disquotationalism and infinite conjunctions. *Mind*, 108: 1–22, 1999.
[12] ——. Truth and reduction. *Erkenntnis*, 53: 97–126, 2000.
[13] ——. How innocent is deflationism? *Synthese*, 126: 167–94, 2001.
[14] ——and Leon Horsten. Axiomaticing Kripke's theory of truth. Forthcoming.
[15] Hans G. Herzberger. Notes on naive semantics. *Journal of Philosophical Logic*, 11: 61–102, 1982.
[16] Leon Horsten. Concerning the notion of satisfaction. *Logique et Analyse*, forthcoming.
[17] ——. The semantical paradoxes, the neutrality of truth and the neutrality of the minimalist theory of truth. In P. Cortois, ed., *The Many Problems of Realism*, vol. 3 of *Studies in the General Philosophy of Science*, pp. 173–87. Tilburg University Press, Tilburg, 1995.
[18] Paul Horwich. *Truth*. Oxford University Press, Oxford, second edn, 1998, first edn 1990.
[19] Jeffrey Ketland. Deflationism and Tarski's paradise. *Mind*, 108: 69–94, 1999.

[20] Georg Kreisel and Azriel Lévy. Reflection principles and their use for establishing the complexity of axiomatic systems. *Zeitschrift für mathematische Logik und Grundlagen der Mathematik*, 14: 97–142, 1968.

[21] Michael Kremer. Kripke and the logic of truth. *Journal of Philosophical Logic*, 17: 225–78, 1988.

[22] Saul Kripke. Outline of a theory of truth. *Journal of Philosophy*, 72: 690–712, 1975. Reprinted in [23].

[23] Robert L. Martin, ed. *Recent Essays on Truth and the Liar Paradox*. Clarendon Press and Oxford University Press, Oxford and New York, 1984.

[24] Vann McGee. How truthlike can a predicate be? A negative result. *Journal of Philosophical Logic*, 14: 399–410, 1985.

[25] ——. Maximal consistent sets of instances of Tarski's schema (T). *Journal of Philosophical Logic*, 21: 235–41, 1992.

[26] William Reinhardt. Some remarks on extending and interpreting theories with a partial predicate for truth. *Journal of Philosophical Logic*, 15: 219–51, 1986.

[27] Stewart Shapiro. Proof and truth: Through thick and thin. *Journal of Philosophy*, 95: 493–521, 1998.

[28] Michael Sheard. Weak and strong theories of truth. *Studia Logica*, 68: 89–101, 2001.

[29] ——. Truth, probability, and naive criteria. In Volker Halbach and Leon Horsten, eds, *Principles of Truth*. Dr. Hänsel-Hohenhausen, Frankfurt-am-Main, 2002.

[30] Scott Soames. *Understanding Truth*. Oxford University Press, New York and Oxford, 1999.

[31] Alfred Tarski. Der Wahrheitsbegriff in den formalisierten Sprachen. *Studia Philosophica*, 1: 261–405, 1935. Reprinted as "The Concept of Truth in Formalized Languages" in [32], pp. 152–278; page references are given for the translation.

[32] ——. The concept of truth in formalized languages. In *Logic, Semantics, Metamathematics*, pp. 152–278. Clarendon Press, Oxford, 1956.

[33] Alan Turing. Systems of logic based on ordinals. *Proceedings of the London Mathematical Society*, 45: 161–228, 1939.

13

Naive Truth and Sophisticated Logic

Alan Weir

1. INTRODUCTION

Deflationists hold that all there is to the concept of 'true', as it occurs in ordinary English (or the less ordinary contexts of philosophical discussion) is its satisfaction of the Tarskian T-schema:

s is true iff p

in which substituends for s name substituends for p. Where we name sentences by using quotation marks we get the standard disquotational instances such as

"Tarski was Scottish" is true iff Tarski was Scottish.

According to deflationists, there is no need to add any more metaphysical meat to the concept of truth. There is no need to view truth as a substantive property which sentences (or propositions) can have, a property which stands in need of theoretical explication in metaphysics. On the contrary, the concept of truth is metaphysically neutral. The minimal constraints placed on the concept by the Tarskian schema completely determine the meaning of the notion. The entire utility of the concept is given by its uses in enabling us to state generalities—every sentence is either true or false, for example—which would otherwise require for their expression infinitely long sentences or else generalisation over problematic entities such as propositions.

Clearly such a position has attractions, at least for those with a taste for a certain kind of ontological economy. But there is an obvious and, for some, fatal problem at the heart of deflationism. The deflationist theory concerns not some artificial ersatz notion but the use of 'true' in English, and cognate notions in other natural languages. Such languages provide the resources for generating paradox from the notion of truth by means, for example, of self-referential terms:

This sentence is not true

(the Strong Liar) or by more indirect means:

Calum: Orla's next sentence is true

My thanks to Hartry Field and an anonymous referee for very helpful comments on this material.

Orla: Calum's last sentence is untrue.

At least they do if the Tarskian schema, which the deflationist takes to be constitutive of the notion of truth, applies to the uses of 'true' in those sentences. If not, deflationism is only a partial theory, at best, of truth. If so, then, the argument goes, the Liar paradox shows that deflationism is incoherent.

Deflationists undoubtedly were far too complacent about this problem, at least until recently. One typical response, I noted in 'Ultra-maximalist Minimalism!' (Weir, 1996), was to take the notion of truth to be captured by a maximal consistent set of instances of the unrestricted Tarskian schema, that is a set of instances which is consistent but is not a proper sub-set of any other consistent set of instances.[1] But this response is torpedoed, I claimed in that article, by Vann McGee's demonstration (McGee, 1992) that there are infinitely many pairwise incompatible such sets—for each consistent set of sentences there is a maximal consistent set of T-sentences which entails all members of the set. None of these maximal consistent sets is recursively axiomatisable and the only sentences common to all such sets are ungrounded sentences such as vacuous 'I am true' truth-teller sentences τ: True$|\tau|$.[2]

A more nuanced response plays off maximality against further constraints on truth, all the constraints together taken to be constitutive (or partly constitutive) of the notion. But adding restrictions beyond satisfaction of the T-schema is surely contrary to the spirit of a minimalist or deflationary conception of truth. All sensible theories place some weight on the T-schema. If the deflationist says that the truth predicate is fixed by some pay-off between satisfaction of the T-schema and satisfying constraint X, this is not a deflationary theory of truth—it is an X-factor theory of truth.

For this reason, I argued, McGee's ingenious argument sinks 'maximalist minimalism' without trace. None the less I urged on deflationists an escape route. McGee's argument assumes a background of classical logic; in particular, he assumes that the biconditional which features in the T-schema and in the sentences which torpedo the unwary deflationist satisfies the usual principles, such as associativity and commutativity. We have, for example,

$$P \leftrightarrow (Q \leftrightarrow R) \dashv\vdash (P \leftrightarrow Q) \leftrightarrow R$$

$$P \leftrightarrow Q \dashv\vdash Q \leftrightarrow P$$

with the single turnstile representing derivability.

The crucial sentences in his argument are sentences α of the form True$|\alpha| \leftrightarrow$ P (for consistent P). For suppose our overall theory θ is such that for any one-place open sentence φx there is a sentence β such that:

$$\theta \vdash \beta \leftrightarrow \varphi|\beta|$$[3]

[1] This seems to be one of Horwich's responses (1990, p. 42) though he also seems to be tempted by the more nuanced approach considered next. See Weir (1996, p. 11 fn. 2).

[2] Here |P| is a metalinguistic parameter functioning as a representation of an arithmetical term which canonically stands for the number which is the Gödel code of the sentence represented by the parameter P.

[3] Gödel's diagonalisation lemma shows this result is provable for theories with a certain fairly weak arithmetical strength.

(Metaphorically speaking, these sentences "say of themselves", relative to θ and a coding of sentences, that they have the property φ.) Then for any one-place open sentence of the form (True$|x| \leftrightarrow P$) we can find a sentence α such that

$$\theta \vdash \alpha \leftrightarrow (\text{True}|\alpha| \leftrightarrow \text{P})$$

Associativity and commutativity of $\leftrightarrow$ yield:

$$\theta \vdash (\text{True}|\alpha| \leftrightarrow \alpha) \leftrightarrow \text{P}$$

and if we have the T-schema instance (True$|\alpha| \leftrightarrow \alpha$) as one of our axioms in θ, we can prove P, an arbitrary consistent sentence. A widely accepted set-theoretic principle[4] enables us to expand this result to show that for any consistent set of sentences Δ, there is a maximal consistent set of T-sentences which, along with θ, entails all of Δ.

In response, I suggested the deflationist could focus on the naive inference rules:

$$\frac{\text{True}|\alpha|}{\alpha} \qquad \frac{\alpha}{\text{True }|\alpha|}$$

rather than the Tarskian biconditionals. (Call these TE and TI respectively, for truth elimination and truth introduction.) Arguably these rules are what we implicitly grasp when we grasp the concept of truth, at least if the deflationist is correct in thinking that truth is essentially just a device for disquotation, for moving back and forth between assertions about named sentences and the assertions which the sentences thus named express. Moreover inductive theories of truth such as Kripke's (1975) and Martin and Woodruff's (1975) have shown us how to construct models in which each truth ascription True$|\alpha|$ and the sentence α it ascribes truth to are 'equalised' in the sense of each taking the same semantic value: either determinately true, determinately false or neither.[5] In such models, both the two disquotational rules above are unrestrictedly sound, on any sensible conception of soundness of rules and validity. Inferring True$|\alpha|$ from α or vice versa always leads us from true premisses to true conclusions and backward from false conclusions to false premisses.

However, a problem with this approach is that if, emboldened by the equalisation result in inductive theories of truth, we adopt the naive truth rules, we will have to abandon the classical logic which we 'learn at our mother's knee' (cf. McGee, 1991, p. 100). At any rate, this will be so on the assumption, which I make throughout, that we can create self-referential Liar sentences, for instance by Gödelian diagonalisation techniques which yield:

$$\vdash \lambda \leftrightarrow \sim\text{True}|\lambda|$$

(If we lack the formal means to do this then our formal language does not capture an important feature of the natural languages in which the semantic concepts we are investigating occur, that is the phenomenon of 'self-referentiality'.)

[4] Zorn's lemma, equivalent (in the usual framework) to the Axiom of Choice, a heavily used mathematical principle.

[5] This way of characterising the three values in a three-valued logic is, though, contentious.

Using the well-known Lemmon-style proof architecture (Lemmon, 1965), we get:

1	(1) True$\|\lambda\|$	Hypothesis
1	(2) λ	1 TE
—	(3) $\lambda \leftrightarrow \sim\text{True}\|\lambda\|$	Given
1	(4) $\sim\text{True}\|\lambda\|$	2,3 $\leftrightarrow$E
1	(5) $\bot$	1,4 $\sim$E
—	(6) $\sim\text{True}\|\lambda\|$	5, $\sim$I
—	(7) λ	3,6 $\leftrightarrow$ E
—	(8) True$\|\lambda\|$	7 TI
—	(9) $\bot$	6,8 $\sim$E.

This shows that the package of naive rules, self-reference (diagonalisation) and full classical logic is inconsistent, and indeed trivial ($\sim$E allows us to conclude anything in place of $\bot$, classically).

I suggested in Weir (1996), though, that what our mothers, even perhaps these days our fathers, impart to us are classical operational rules—introduction and elimination rules for example. The structural rules needed to generate the architecture of classical proof systems from these operational rules are technical artefacts, for the most part, artefacts constructed by classical logicians for their own purposes. These purposes may well not serve the interest of thinking and reasoning rationally about truth in general.

Perhaps, then, abandonment of classical structural rules will enable us to retain both the classical operational rules and the naive theory of truth; ideally we should be able to reason entirely classically in 'safe' areas, such as, we hope, arithmetic and standard set theory. We would like, that is, 'classical recapture' of these important theories. I suggested programmatically that we restrict Cut, which is a generalisation of transitivity of entailment—

If $A \models B$ and $B \models C$ then $A \models C$

in order to combine classical operational logic with unrestricted use of the naive truth rules.

Suppose, though, that once we have done so we get a nice 'neo-classical' conception of entailment which does the job we want, i.e. is non-trivial and is such that for all sentences α we have

$\text{True}|\alpha| \dashv\models \alpha$,

the turnstiles representing the notion of entailment in question. What could be more natural than to introduce into the object language a conditional which encapsulates this notion of entailment in the sense that the Deduction Theorem:

$\Delta, A \models B$ iff $\Delta \models A \rightarrow B$

holds (at least where Δ is empty)?

For the Deduction Theorem equates an entailment relation between A and B with the logical truth of the conditional $A \rightarrow B$. (Classically, it holds even for the extensional material conditional $A \rightarrow B \equiv_{df.} \sim A \vee B$.) If one believes, as most do, that the extensional conditional is a poor approximation to natural language indicative 'if... then', if one thinks further that 'if... then' expresses some form of implication and so contains some modal or non-extensional element, then the Deduction Theorem will approach the status of a requirement on any adequate account of logic for a language containing a genuine conditional.[6] But granted the Deduction Theorem, we will have

$$\models \text{True}|\alpha| \leftrightarrow \alpha.$$

and now we are back to the Tarskian biconditionals again.

I did not baulk at this idea though, suggesting that a non-classical conditional might do just this job, though I did not attempt to develop an account of such a conditional, or indeed of the non-classical logic I had in mind, in that short article. In subsequent work I have had no such paper-sparing, rain-forest-saving inhibitions and have tried to develop a 'neo-classical logic' suitable not only for naive truth but also for naive set theory (Weir, 1998b, 1999). Furthermore, Hartry Field (2003a) has developed a non-classical logic and conditional in which the set of all instances of the Tarskian schema is consistent (even where the resources for diagonalisation are present). His theory of truth is a rich, ingenious combination of inductive and revision-theoretic elements.

However, Field's conditional does not validate the rule of conditional introduction $\rightarrow$I:

Δ, A	(1)B	Given
Δ	(2)A $\rightarrow$ B	1, $\rightarrow$ I

or the Deduction Theorem. For anyone sympathetic to the estimate of the importance of the Deduction Theorem given above, this is quite a serious drawback. After all, the fact that all instances of (True |A| * A) are theorems of some system is not in itself very interesting—suppose, for example, the * operator was such that P*Q is equivalent to $(P \rightarrow P) \vee Q$. I suggest such a schema is of greater interest the more accurately the conditional represents, in the object language, the entailment relation of the language. If the argument above is right, to do this adequately one needs at least the deduction theorem in the form: $A \models B$ iff $\models A \rightarrow B$, and this is a form of $\rightarrow$ I. Moreover, in so far as one's approach to non-classical logics is to try to cleave to the classical operational rules but fiddle with the structural rules, the failure of such a simple and obvious introduction rule as $\rightarrow$ I is worrying.

Neither of these are fatal defects—for one thing, the distinction between operational and structural rules is not clear-cut and can be effected in different ways in different proof architectures. But these worries do provide motivation for trying a different approach, one in which (a) we retain all the Tarskian biconditionals (and the naive rules for truth) but (b) we simultaneously retain $\rightarrow$ I and the Deduction Theorem. By retaining $\rightarrow$ I, our approach respects the idea that we retain classical logic at the operational level, all amendments taking place in the structural rules. If we have the Deduction Theorem, as a meta-theorem about the system, that makes the

[6] See, e.g., Read (1988) §2.3.

conditional more like the natural language 'if... then', assuming the latter expresses some notion of implication. And if we have all the Tarskian biconditionals as theorems of our system, the deflationist has a powerful answer to McGee's objection. She now has no need to look for additional criteria for winnowing out the good from the bad maximal consistent sets of T-sentences, criteria which could not be effectively decidable and which would anyway undermine the whole minimalistic import of the deflationist project. Return to a fully naive notion of truth embracing the unrestricted T-schema and deflationism is back in business.

Thus in this paper I will attempt to achieve both goals (a) and (b) above. That is, I will attempt to construct a system which includes the naive rules for truth, has all the Tarskian biconditionals as theorems and where, furthermore, the conditional obeys $\rightarrow$ I and the Deduction Theorem. In addition it should yield classical recapture: it should licence the full classical structural rules in 'safe' areas such as arithmetic or the tamer shores of set theory. In §2 I will informally explain and motivate the conception of logic which forms the background framework to my approach to the paradoxes. The particular focus here is on the right way to implement non-classical restrictions applicable when one moves beyond the cosy world of determinate propositions in which classical logic holds sway. However, this general framework does not cohere all that well with the inductive theory of truth which provides us, from within a classical metatheoretic framework, with the equalisation result. Accordingly in §3, I modify this framework somewhat in order to handle the case of deflationary but inductive theories of truth meeting the unrestricted Tarskian schema. The discussion in both these sections should be accessible, I hope, to everyone with the basic background in logic to be able to follow the recent philosophical debate on deflationism. For those with an appetite for more detail, Appendices 1 and 2 supply it. Finally, in §4 I conclude with an assessment of the philosophical upshot of the results of §§2 and 3.

2. THE 'NEO-CLASSICAL' FRAMEWORK

The general 'neo-classical' logical framework I wish to bring to bear on the problem of the Liar is, I have argued, suitable for handling not only the naive conception of truth, embodied in the naive rules and the class of all instances of the Tarskian schema, but also the naive notion of set. Perhaps the simplest formulation of the latter theory consists in firstly the set of all instances of the (generalised) comprehension schema:

$$\exists y \forall x (x \in y \leftrightarrow \varphi x)$$

(in which y may occur in φ), and secondly the axiom of extensionality:

$$\forall x \forall y (\forall z (z \in x \leftrightarrow z \in y) \rightarrow x = y)$$

One motivation for seeking to save naive set theory from its apparent demise at the hands of the paradoxes is that the conventional rejection of naive set theory generates further paradox in the metatheory, so long at any rate as one is in the business of making general and systematic pronouncements on the semantics and interpretation of the theory (see Weir, 1998a). Clearly if we are to revive the theory, the non-classical logic one develops it in should be weak enough so that the combination of theory and logic is non-trivial. Indeed in my view the naive theory should be consistent in that logical framework (here I differ from the dialetheists). On the other hand, the logic should have sufficient strength to generate, together with the naive theory, the standard mathematics we know, love, and seem to need, in science. Achieving both these goals together is no easy matter.

We must, then, try to avoid 'Russell's Revenge', deeper or more complex set-theoretic paradoxes surfacing in the metatheory.[7] For, as we shall see, inductive theories of truth work with multi-valued semantics. Appeal to third (fourth, fifth, ε_0th or whatever) values, however, will simply generate set-theoretic versions of strengthened Liars. For example, supposing 1 and ½ are our chosen truth and gap values, sentences such as:

$$\sigma\colon\ v(|\sigma|) \neq 1 \mathbin{\&} v(|\sigma|) \neq \tfrac{1}{2}$$

which say, roughly, 'I am neither determinately true nor gappy' will lead to paradox if having value 1 is supposed to coincide with the notion of truth, and having value 0 with falsity, at least in the precise, set-theoretic sector of the language. For this reason we should assume in our (closed) semantics for naive set theory that there are only two values, true and false. Bivalence will not thereby follow since we may not, should not, indeed, have the law of excluded middle in the logic. But how do we know what the correct logic is? Rather than blindly leaping from the steep cliffs of classical logic cum ZFC set theory into the murky void beyond, hoping to land on a coherent alternative, we can attempt to approximate the non-classical theory in a classical setting. That is, from within *classical* logic and *standard* set theory, we try to develop a non-standard semantics and logic in which the non-classical theory—the naive theory of truth, for example—is sound but in which standard theorems are still provable. If we can do this, if we can show the naive theory consistent relative to the consistency of our standard theory, that gives some, albeit fallible, assurance that when one finally throws away the crutch of standard theory, the logic embraced, having survived the test of the approximation, will prove a coherent framework.

With this goal in view, I proposed to work with the strong Kleene/Lukasiewicz three-valued semantics for the operators &, $\vee$ $\sim$, $\forall$ and $\exists$ whilst accepting that this multi-valued semantics is but an approximation. It is for use in a 'test situation' in which we try out logical ideas in the hope of finding the right, or a right, logic for naive semantics and set theory. We need, in addition to the semantics for the operators of the language, to provide an account of the entailment relation suitable for interpreted languages in which, as in this case, not all wffs are determinate. My suggestion is:

> A set of wffs X neo-classically entails a set Y (written $X \models_{NC} Y$) iff:
> (a) For any wff C in Y, in any acceptable valuation v in which all wffs in X are true[8] but all in Y but C are false, C is true in v

[7] For Russell himself was a victim of revenge attacks by the set-theoretic paradoxes, as was argued many years ago by Frederic Fitch in connection with type theory: Fitch (1952) p. v.

[8] When discussing 'true' and 'false' in connection with model-theoretic semantics I am talking of truth-in-a-model or valuation and likewise falsity (that is truth of negation) in a valuation or model,

(b) For any wff P in X, in any acceptable valuation v in which all wffs in Y are false but all in X but P are true, P is false in v

where the acceptable valuations are defined relative to a designated valuation @ which is to be thought of as representing the 'actual' world. Valuation v is acceptable iff every atom which has a truth value, i.e. is non-gappy, in the actual situation @ has a truth value in v (perhaps the opposite one).[9]

A little motivation: one theme here is that falsity-preservation 'upwards' is as important as truth-preservation downward. That is, in the special case of 'singular' inference, that is an inference with one premiss P and one conclusion C, not only must C be true in every valuation in which P is but P must be false in every valuation in which C is false. A second motivating idea is that in non-singular inferences with many premisses or many conclusions generalising that two-way account for singular inferences in the obvious way yields too restrictive an account of entailment. The obvious generalisation is that a set of premisses entails a set of conclusions iff:

(i) in no model are all the premisses true but no conclusion true and
(ii) in no model are all the conclusions false but no premiss false.

But on the strong Kleene semantics for $\vee$ and $\sim$ this would rule out disjunctive syllogism, since if A is gappy and B false we can have $A \vee B$ gappy, $\sim A$ gappy but B false.[10]

Good riddance to disjunctive syllogism, a relevantist might say.[11] But consider &I. On many semantics for &—not just the classical bivalent semantics but also the Kleene rules—the &I rule has the property that if the conclusion is false but one of the two premisses is true, the other is false. This matches, arguably, our linguistic behaviour towards such inferences: if we accept A but reject A&B, we will also reject B. Generalising this idea, if one rejects the conclusion of an inference but accepts all premisses but P, it is incumbent on one to reject P, mere agnosticism is insufficient. Carrying this over to the semantic sphere we get the clause that in a genuine entailment with a false conclusion,[12] if all premisses but P are true then P must be false, a clause which disjunctive syllogism satisfies.

The structural constraints are specified in terms of the determinacy or otherwise of key sentences. The determinacy operator Det P could be defined in a number of ways, perhaps best by $\sim(P \leftrightarrow \sim P)$. On a suitable definition of the conditional (more on this below) this wff will come out as false when P is indeterminate (or at least simply

and not ordinary disquotational truth. The notion of 'truth in a model' is closer to 'determinate truth', a notion which certainly comes apart from that of truth. But rather than write 'true in valuation v' each time, I will leave this relativisation implicit.

[9] The idea here is a fairly classical one, namely that an atomic sentence which is actually indeterminate (at least in non-mathematical cases) expresses no single proposition, whereas an actually determinate sentence expresses a single determinate proposition which has a definite truth value in any possible circumstance.

[10] A similar point holds in the truth-preservation direction with respect to the multiple conclusion inference from B to the conclusion pair $\sim$A, (A&B), with B true and A gappy.

[11] At least if the disjunction operator in question is also supposed to satisfy $\vee$I.

[12] I will focus on the more common format of single conclusion logic from now on.

indeterminate, anyway) and true otherwise. This notion of determinacy can be iterated. Det P is itself determinate if ∼ (Det P ↔ ∼ Det P) holds, we can represent this by Det²P, otherwise Det P is indeterminate; and so on.[13] In the formal implementation of these ideas, the chosen 'actual' valuation @ generates a set of axioms AXDET (which thus has to be thought of as taking @ as parameter) such that AXDET is a set of wffs of the form Det P or ∼ Det Q which are true in all acceptable models.

In Weir (1998b) I set out a system of propositional logic which is sound and complete with respect to this neo-classical notion of entailment. Some further details are given in Appendix 1. For our purposes, a key consideration will be the treatment of the conditional, since a main goal of the whole approach is to have all the Tarskian biconditionals come out (determinately) true, indeed have all of them valid in all models which satisfy the naive rules for truth.

A further goal of the current approach is to interpret the conditional so that it can plausibly be seen as an object language representation of neo-classical entailment itself. Since in the case of singular rules the neo-classical account requires truth-preservation from premiss to conclusion, and falsity preservation from conclusion to premiss, but also permits inferences from an indeterminate (in every acceptable model) premiss to a similarly indeterminate conclusion, the truth-table for an extensional representation of such an entailment notion should take the broadly Łukasiewiczian form:[14]

		Q		
	P→Q	T	Gap	F
	T	T	?	F
P	Gap	T	T	?
	F	T	T	T

What should the value be in the two remaining cases? Since the inference from a true premiss to a gappy conclusion fails to be truth-preserving and so is not neo-classically sound and since similarly an inference from a gappy premiss to a false conclusion fails to preserve falsity upwards, this suggests the correct value in each case should be false, generating a bivalent conditional, bivalent in the sense that no conditional is gappy. On the other hand, gappy conditionals are needed if we are to represent higher-order indeterminacy, if the sentence (P ↔ ∼ P) is itself, on occasion, to be indeterminate. Indeterminate conditionals, indeed, are needed to handle the Curry paradox since sentences of the form γ: True|γ| ← ⊥ cannot non-paradoxically

[13] In Weir (1999) where the formal language in question is infinitary, this hierarchy is extended into the transfinite.

[14] Cf. J. Łukasiewicz (1920), Łukasiewicz and A. Tarski (1930). The Łukasiewicz and strong Kleene three-valued systems diverge over the conditionals: see S. C. Kleene (1952) p. 334.

be treated as either determinately true or determinately false. So this suggests a non-bivalent conditional in which the remaining cases are assigned the value Gap.[15]

In Weir (1998b) I opted for a non-bivalent form of the conditional whilst in Weir (1999) I worked with the bivalent interpretation, without, unfortunately, recording this switch. My preference now would be to go for a 'belt and braces' job, that is to accept only rules which are sound under *both* interpretations. The following rules meet this requirement. Firstly $\rightarrow$ I:

X,P	(1) Q	Given
Y_i	(2.i) Det R_i	Given, $\forall R_i \in X$
$X, \bigcup_{i \in I} Y_i$	(3) P $\rightarrow$ Q	1 [2.i] $\rightarrow$ I

subject to the condition that $X \cap \bigcup_{i \in I} Y_i = \emptyset$. (Det R, remember, is $\sim(R \leftrightarrow \sim R)$.) Next, $\rightarrow$ E:

X	(1) P $\rightarrow$ Q	Given
Y	(2) P	Given
Z_i	(3.i) Det R_i	$\forall R_i \in X \cap Y$
$X, Y, \bigcup_{i \in I} Z_i$	(4) Q	1,2 [3.i] $\rightarrow$ E

where we also lay down also the disjointness condition: $\bigcup_{i \in I} Z_i \cap (X \cup Y) = \emptyset$.[16] The two conditional rules are sound in the sense that they preserve neo-classical entailment (proof: Appendix 1).

It may seem that these rules represent a restriction on the classical operational rules for the conditional, but this is an illusion engendered by the use of sequent proof architectures. Sequent systems of proof are best seen as 'higher-order' in the sense that they 'comment' on what is derivable in some presumed underlying system. Thus sequent (1) in the $\rightarrow$ E rule represents the derivability, in some more basic system, of the succeedent P $\rightarrow$ Q from the assumptions X. If that system has a natural deduction architecture, then the $\rightarrow$ E rule in Gentzen-Prawitz format[17] would take some such form as:

X	Y	Z_1	...	Z_n
...	...	...		...
P $\rightarrow$ Q	P	*Det* R_1	—	*Det* R_n
	Q			

where the italicised premisses are required for any $R_i \in X \cap Y$.

In this format it can be seen more clearly that the one step inference from P $\rightarrow$ Q, P to Q is being accepted as unrestrictedly correct. What we have are global restrictions on proof, in particular on generalised transitivity. Though the single step inference

[15] Though it does not force gappiness. As remarked, if the metalogic is not classical one might admit only two truth values, equate falsity with non-truth but not affirm excluded middle. This way one might still demur from saying of an arbitrary sentence that it is either true or false.

[16] This disjointness requirement can be weakened to a slightly more complex form. See Weir (1998b) p. 247.

[17] For a very clear presentation of Gentzen's system as developed by Prawitz, see Tennant (1978).

where $X = \{P \rightarrow Q\}$ and $Y = \{P\}$ is always correct, the result of applying $\rightarrow$ E as the final step of a longer derivation may not yield a proof of the conclusion from the overall premisses. Each step in the resulting 'quasi-proof' would be correct but if the global determinacy constraint is not met then $X,Y \vdash Q$ fails even though $X \vdash P \rightarrow Q, Y \vdash P$ and $P, P \rightarrow Q \vdash Q$. That is, generalised transitivity fails.

However, natural deduction formulations, with their tree architecture, though more perspicuous in terms of revealing proof structure, can become very cumbersome and unmanageable in complex proofs where the branches of the tree tend to burst across pages. For this reason, I will continue to use the sequent system formulation in which the global structural restrictions, most notably on transitivity, are built into the rules for the operators themselves.

To handle naive set theory in the form given above, we need, of course, to extend our propositional system to full predicate logic with identity. But little alteration is needed to the quantifier rules in the neo-classical framework. Essentially, only a modification of $\exists$E in line with the structural constraints imposed on $\vee$E together with a restriction on identity elimination parallel to the restriction on $\rightarrow$ E (see Appendix 1).

Wff φ is defined to be neo-classically provable from X iff it is provable using the above rules from assumptions which belong either to X or to the axioms among which are included in AXDET. In deciding which sentences belong to AXDET, I urged a bold attitude: adopt a set which is maximally consistent in the sense that it is (neo-classically) consistent but adding any new wff Det P or $\sim$ Det Q induces inconsistency. If the language of number theory is a fully determinate sector, that is, for any P in this language, Det P $\in$ AXDET, then full classical reasoning is legitimate in this area. If the language of set theory with quantifiers restricted to the first inaccessible in the well-founded cumulative hierarchy is a determinate sector, once again classical structural, as well as operational rules, are legitimate here too. In this way, we get a smooth classical recapture; the neo-classical framework does not restrict the standard inferential practices of working mathematicians.

Now generalised comprehension allows unrestricted inductive definitions (negative as well as positive—compare the standard account in Moschovakis, 1974). We can take, for example, as an assumption for $\exists$E the following instance of the comprehension axiom shorn of initial $\exists y$ (skipping a lot of detail, definition of ordered pairs, assignment functions and so forth):

$$\begin{aligned}\langle\varphi, \sigma\rangle \in s \leftrightarrow\ & \varphi = \ulcorner t_1 \in t_2 \urcorner \,\&\, \sigma(t_1) \in \sigma(t_2) \vee \\ & \varphi = \ulcorner t_1 = t_2 \urcorner \,\&\, \sigma(t_1) = \sigma(t_2) \vee \\ & \varphi = \ulcorner \psi \,\&\, \theta \urcorner \,\&\, \langle\psi,\sigma\rangle \in s \,\&\, \langle\theta,\sigma\rangle \in s \vee \\ & \varphi = \ulcorner \sim\psi \urcorner \,\&\, \langle\psi,\sigma\rangle \notin s \vee \\ & \varphi = \ulcorner \psi \rightarrow \theta \urcorner \,\&\, (\langle\psi,\sigma\rangle \in s \rightarrow \langle\theta,\sigma\rangle \in s) \vee \\ & \varphi = \ulcorner \forall x\psi \urcorner \,\&\, \forall\alpha, \langle\psi x, \sigma(x/\alpha)\rangle \in s.\end{aligned}$$

and prove the existence of a set satisfying the definition of s (note the negative clause covering $\sim \psi$). Thus $\ulcorner\langle\varphi,\sigma\rangle \in s\urcorner$ reads as $\ulcorner$ assignment σ satisfies wff $\varphi\urcorner$.

Our goal will be to prove, neo-classically, every instance of

$$\langle|\varphi|,\sigma\rangle \in \mathbf{s} \leftrightarrow \varphi(\sigma(x_1), \ldots \sigma(x_n)).$$

The right hand side represents the result of substituting $\sigma(x_i)$ for each free variable x_i in φ. As a special case we will want to derive the T theorem:

$$\vdash \forall\sigma\langle|\varphi|,\sigma\rangle \in \mathbf{s} \leftrightarrow \varphi.$$

In other words, defining truth as 'satisfaction by every assignment', we will want to prove every instance of $\ulcorner|\varphi|$ is true iff $\varphi\urcorner$.

An outline of how this might be accomplished[18] is given in Weir (1999). Granted that we are able to prove a standard diagonalisation lemma, we will also have a proof of a Liar sentence λ satisfying:

$$\lambda \dashv\vdash \forall\sigma\langle|\lambda|, \sigma\rangle \notin S$$

whence, by $\rightarrow$I and &I we have the theorem L:

$$\vdash \lambda \leftrightarrow \forall\sigma\langle|\lambda|, \sigma\rangle \notin S$$

in which λ is provably equivalent to our formalisation of $\ulcorner|\lambda|$ is not true $\urcorner$.

How are contradiction and triviality avoided when we put together the L Theorem and the Tarskian T theorem for λ? The determinacy restrictions on wffs which occur in the antecedents of both major and minor premiss of $\sim$E block the obvious proof ('Contrap. and 'Trans.' are contraposition and transitivity of $\rightarrow$ rules—see Appendix 1):

1	(1) λ	Hyp(othesis).
—	(2) $\lambda \leftrightarrow \forall\sigma\langle|\lambda|, \sigma\rangle \notin S$	L Theorem
—	(3) $\forall\sigma\langle|\lambda|,\sigma\rangle \in \mathbf{s} \leftrightarrow \lambda$	T Theorem
—	(4) $\forall\sigma\langle|\lambda|,\sigma\rangle \notin \mathbf{s} \leftrightarrow \sim\lambda$	3 Contrap.
—	(5) $\lambda \leftrightarrow \sim\lambda$	2,4 Trans.
1	(6) $\sim\lambda$	1,5 $\leftrightarrow$ E[19]
7	(7) Det λ	Hyp.
1,7	(8) $\bot$	1,6 [7] $\sim$ E
7	(9) $\sim\lambda$	8, $\sim$ I
7	(10) λ	5,9 $\leftrightarrow$E
11	(11) Det Det λ	Hyp.
7,11	(12) $\bot$	9,10, [11] $\sim$ E

The classical proof of $\lambda \leftrightarrow \sim\lambda$ is correct neo-classically but the extension of this to a proof of absurdity is transformed neo-classically into a proof of the inconsistency of the combination of the claim that the Liar is determinate and that it is determinately determinate. And we can live with that.

Of course this in no way amounts to a soundness proof for the system as a whole. Merely blocking one route to contradiction or triviality does not show there are no

[18] But for an infinitary language; indeed a 'naively' infinitary language in which expressions can be Big, can have the length of an ordinal whose cardinality is that of the (naive) universe as a whole.

[19] Strictly, $\rightarrow$E plus &E.

other, perhaps more complex, proofs of absurdity, or of any arbitrary wff. It might seem that our goal should be a relative consistency proof, a proof that the theory of naive sets in neo-classical logic is consistent (or non-trivial) if theory T in classical logic is, where T is a theory we are pretty sure is consistent, such as ZFC. There are such proofs from within standard classical set theory of the non-triviality of naive set theory in certain paraconsistent logics, though in my view, the logics in question are far too weak to yield genuine classical recapture.[20]

Moreover even this is insufficient: we should aim for full semantic closure and absolute consistency proofs—for a soundness proof of theory T from within theory T, in this case a proof of the consistency of naive set theory plus neo-classical logic given within naive set theory in neo-classical logic. This is far from a trivial matter, at least if the theory is indeed non-trivial. Of course, even if we come up with such a proof, this gives no Cartesian guarantee of soundness. Just as a liar could assert a series of lies and follow it with an avowal that she has spoken only the truth, so too any trivial system will include a proof of its own non-triviality. But a soundness proof from within an even *stronger* system is no better off, indeed worse off in lacking the sort of internal stability a semantically closed (in the above sense) theory has: it is rather like someone making a series of claims followed up by the avowal that not everything she has said is true. Rather than a relative consistency proof of the form

$$T \vdash \mathrm{Con}(T) \rightarrow \mathrm{Con}(T^*)$$

where T* is stronger than T (e.g. T is ZFC and T* adds to it the generalised continuum hypothesis), we have in effect the case where T* is *weaker* than T. Such a result is of no epistemological or philosophical importance.

So, at any rate, I argued in Weir (1998a, especially §8). At some stage we have to take off our classical armbands and swim unaided in the neo-classical sea (where we might discover we were swimming unaided all along, the armbands being insufficiently inflated). All that being said, there is still value in venturing out the harbour a little with our armbands on and trying out a few moves to give us confidence before going right out into the open sea. There is value in a relative consistency proof from within standard ZFC set theory of an extension of that theory to include a naive truth theory, even if not the full semantic and logical theory needed for semantic closure. In the next section, then, I will show how a fragment of the fully naive picture—the naive disquotational or deflationary theory of truth—can be shown, in a classical metalanguage and standard set theory, to be coherent in the setting of a variant of the above neo-classical logic taken in conjunction with an inductive theory of truth.

3. APPLYING THE NEO-CLASSICAL FRAMEWORK TO INDUCTIVE TRUTH

Inductive theories of truth apply to languages in which predicates are interpreted by assigning to them not simply extensions but rather a pair consisting of the *positive* extension, the items the predicate determinately applies to and the *negative* extension,

[20] See Weir (2004).

the items to which the predicate determinately does not apply. These two extensions must be exclusive but need not exhaust the domain. So F may neither be determinately true of, nor determinately false of, an item α in the domain. Given such a language L we expand it to a language L^+ by adding a truth predicate True. If *I* is an interpretation of L, we generate from it a series of valuations which assign truth (or, for convenience, 1), falsity (0) or gap (say ½) to each open sentence, relative to an assignment to the variables. Each valuation in the series extends the interpretation of the truth predicate given in the previous valuation and then re-evaluates all sentences of the language according to the fixed rules for the logical operators. Typically we start with a valuation v_0 in which True is given an empty interpretation, that is its positive extension is identical with its negative extension which is identical with the empty set.

The 'engine' which generates the series of valuations is the notion of the 'jump' operation J(x) which applies to valuations. We let valuation v_{n+1} be $J(v_n)$, which means that in $J(v_n)$ we assign to the positive extension of True all codes or names of sentences which come out true in v_n and to its negative extension all items which are not names of sentences and also all codes of sentences false in v_n. We then re-evaluate all the complex sentences of the language given this new interpretation of all the atoms True(x) which are predications of True. This process can be extended into the transfinite. The idea is that we gradually fill out the positive and negative extensions of True.

The crucial property in an inductive theory of truth is the property of monotonicity. Define the ordering on valuations $v \leq u$ to mean that every sentence true in v is true in u and every sentence false in v is false in u (leaving assignments implicit just now). In other words, u may render determinate a sentence which is indeterminate in v but it will never change the truth value of a determinate sentence in v. To call the jump operator monotonic means that if $v \leq u$ then $J(v) \leq J(u)$. In that case, simple cardinality considerations show that at some point in our series we will reach a 'fixed point', v^*, at which $J(v^*) = v^*$. If the language is countably infinite, for example, then the series cannot keep generating new extensions of True into uncountable ordinals; there are not enough sentences to go round. But when $J(v^*) = v^*$ it follows that the positive extension of True in v^* is just the set of true sentences of v^*, its negative extension the set of false sentences in v^* (plus the non-sentences). We get the equalisation of True $|\alpha|$ and α mentioned at the outset: both sentences of such a pair are true or else both are false or else both are gappy.

Now the jump operator is monotonic in the strong Kleene interpretation of &, $\vee$ $\sim$, $\forall$ and $\exists$. The essential reason here is that no conjunction (disjunction, negation, universal or existential generalisation) will flip from true to false or vice versa if we change the truth value of an indeterminate conjunct (disjunct, negate, instance) to a determinate value. These operators are in a derivative sense monotonic. More precisely, let f^O be the extension of an assignment function f from a monotonic language L to one which contains an operator O which expresses a truth-function τ. Then τ is monotonic just in case if $f \leq g$ then $f^O \leq g^O$. The Łukasiewiczian $\rightarrow$ is, however, non-monotonic. For instance, if f assigns ½ to both P and Q, then $f^{\rightarrow}(P \rightarrow Q) = 1$ but if g extends f by assigning 1 to P and 0 to Q then $g^{\rightarrow}$ flips the truth value of $P \rightarrow Q$ from 1 to 0. Thus neo-classical logic, with its Łukasiewiczian conditional, is unsuitable, as it stands, as a framework for a theory of truth in the Kripke, Martin/Woodruff inductive tradition.

Hartry Field's response to this problem (Field, 2003a) is to nest the monotonic Kripkean construction inside a more general recursion with the property that conditional sentences—which are given a non-truth-functional semantics[21]—can oscillate in truth value, with arbitrarily long period, as one ascends the outer hierarchy. However, as has been remarked, the deduction theorem and standard →I fail for Field's conditional. Therefore I follow a different course, also introducing a non-truth-functional conditional but with the aim of preserving monotonicity and thereby standard(ish) →I together with the Deduction Theorem, and thus the link between the conditional and entailment. I will call the logic KN logic ('Kripke-naive', or 'Kleene-naive' perhaps).

The key feature of the KN system is the set of constraints on the assignments of truth value for → laid out in the following table:

		Q		
	$P \rightarrow Q$	1	½	0
	1	1	1/½	0
P	½	1	1/½	1/½
	0	1	1	1

So → has a non-truth-functional semantics, not an unusual feature of a conditional which purports to encapsulate, in some way, entailment. The criterion for 'choosing' between 1 and ½ (determinate truth and gappiness)[22] in the three non-functional cases is best explained after setting out the particular account of a model suitable for KN logic.

We start in fairly standard Kripkean fashion. A KN model M is a pair |D,I| where D is an infinite domain of individuals and *I* assigns to each unary predicate F of language L a pair of subsets of D, $\langle I(F)^+, I(F)^- \rangle$ with $I(F)^+ \cap I(F)^- = \emptyset$, this pair being the positive and negative extension of F. Interpretation *I* similarly assigns pairwise disjoint positive and negative extensions to binary relations, each extension itself being a subset of D^2 and so on for more general relational terms, if there are such in L; it further assigns to each individual constant a member of D and to each function term a fully defined function over D. The construction could be extended to second-order logic, free logic (so that partially defined functions could be accommodated) and so forth, but for simplicity let us stop there.

I assume, though, for purposes of generating self-referential sentences through diagonalisation, that language L contains the wherewithal to develop an arithmetic theory of sufficient strength for that purpose. For example, contains a predicate N,

[21] But this aspect is dropped in Field (2003b).

[22] At the cost of some additional complexity, we could let these three cases vary between 1, ½ and 0, but I will refrain here from incurring that extra cost.

constant term 0, function terms S, $+$ and $\times$ from which, by iteration, we can develop numerical terms and so on. I assume further that the sub-structure of each admissible model M restricted to the arithmetic sub-language (and so with domain the extension of N) is a standard model of arithmetic. I will use, loosely, the meta-theoretic notation $\varphi|A|$ for a predication in which φ is applied to sentence A via some arithmetical term $|A|$ which stands for the Gödel code of A under some chosen system of coding. Granted our assumption about models having a standard model of arithmetic as sub-structures, each such term $|A|$ stands for the same sentence (via our chosen coding) in each model.

Next we turn to valuation functions generated from models; again this is standard for the most part. There is an initial valuation v_0 based on model M of language L. Relativised to an assignment σ which maps the free variables into D (I will leave this implicit when convenient), v_0^σ assigns the truth value true, which we have chosen to identify with the number 1, to Fa if $I_\sigma(\mathbf{a}) \in I(\mathrm{F})^+$, assigns the false value 0 if $I_\sigma(\mathbf{a}) \in I(F)^-$, otherwise assigns the gap $\frac{1}{2}$. The clauses for relational atomic predications are the obvious generalisations. We extend the valuation to L^+ which adds the truth predicate 'True' to L, by stipulating that v_0^σ assigns the value $\frac{1}{2}$ to True x, for all σ, leaving True totally undefined in the initial valuation. The recursive clauses for &, $\vee$, $\sim$, $\forall$, and $\exists$ are the standard strong Kleene ones with universal and existential quantification generalised conjunctive and disjunctive functions. So, for example, $v_0^\sigma(\forall x\varphi x) = 1$ if $v_0^{\sigma'}(\varphi x) = 1$ for all x-variants σ' of σ, $v_0^\sigma(\forall x\varphi x) = 0$ if for at least one x-variant $v_0^{\sigma'}(\varphi x) = 0$, $\forall x\varphi x$ takes value $\frac{1}{2}$ otherwise.

Now we must turn to the conditional. The idea here is to define our notion of entailment for the full language using as a basis a broader, more coarse-grained, notion of entailment which ignores conditionals. So consider a Kleene semantics for L^+ in which all conditional sentences are treated as atoms. That is, every conditional open sentence is assigned, in such 'unconditional' interpretations, a positive and negative extension and evaluated like any other atom; the only structure which registers logically in unconditional models and valuations is that given by &, $\vee$, $\sim$, $\forall$ and $\exists$. Generate fixed points in the usual Kripkean fashion. Then define a notion of unconditional entailment exactly as in neo-classical entailment but restricted to singular inferences and to all unconditional fixed point valuations ("ufpvs").[23] That is, P u-entails Q (written P $\Vdash$ Q) iff

for all ufpvs u, if $u(\mathrm{P}) = 1$ then $u(\mathrm{Q}) = 1$ and if $u(\mathrm{Q}) = 0$ then $u(\mathrm{P}) = 0$.

Note that since we are considering only singular entailments, this is equivalent to what in Appendix 1 I call a 'minimax' notion of entailment: for all ufpvs u, $u(\mathrm{P}) \leq u(\mathrm{Q})$.

For the KN semantics proper, we no longer treat conditionals as atoms so we extend the Kleene semantics for unconditional valuations above by adding a recursive clause for $\rightarrow$ as follows.

[23] I will reserve the letter 'u', with subscripts, as a variable ranging over unconditional valuations only, with v, with subscripts and superscripts as necessary, ranging over KN valuations.

(*i*) $v^\sigma(P \rightarrow Q) = 0$ iff $v^\sigma(P) = 1$ and $v^\sigma(Q) = 0$;
(*ii*) $v^\sigma(P \rightarrow Q) = 1$ if $v^\sigma(P) = 0$ or $v^\sigma(Q) = 1$;
In the other three cases,
(*iii*) $v^\sigma(P \rightarrow Q) = 1$ if $P \Vdash Q$;
(*iv*) $v^\sigma(P \rightarrow Q) = \frac{1}{2}$ otherwise.

The jump operation is the standard Kripkean one. KN valuation $v_\alpha + 1$ is generated from M just as v_0 is except that the positive extension of True is the set of all codes of sentences which take value 1 (relative to all assignments) in v_α, the negative extension is the set of all codes of falsehoods in v_α plus all the members of D which are not codes. At limit levels, the positive extension is the union of all previous positive extensions, likewise for the negative extension of True.

We can then prove (Appendix 2) a monotonicity theorem (strictly a corollary to a monotonicity result) as follows.

MONOTONICITY THEOREM: Every valuation extends all earlier valuations based on the same model.

We say that valuation v_γ extends v_δ just in case when $v_\delta(P) = 1$ then $v_\gamma(P) = 1$ and when $v_\delta(P) = 0$ then $v_\gamma(P) = 0$, for all sentences P.

By the usual cardinality argument, there is a fixed point v_λ at which True |A| and A are 'equalised' each taking the same value (1, ½ or 0) just as in ufpvs. At these, all Tarskian biconditionals take value 1. These fixed point KN valuations are the important ones for the semantics. Neo-classically, the acceptable valuations are the variants of the 'actual' valuation @. We combine this idea with that of a fixed point KN valuation to get a notion of admissible valuation: fixed points generated from variants of some chosen actual model, where a variant never turns a determinate sentence into a gappy one.

KN entailment is therefore defined over the admissible valuations just as in the neo-classical case except the case of singular inferences between 'everywhere gappy' sentences A and B. That is, where A and B take value ½ in all admissible valuations, A neo-classically entails B, $A \models_{NC} B$. Both the truth-preservation and falsity-preservation upwards clauses are satisfied. For KN entailment, however (which I will represent by the double turnstile alone) we add the 'Gap' clause:

$A \models B$ only if $A \Vdash B$.[24]

That is, KN entailment collapses into unconditional entailment in the singular case. In the KN case, even if A and B take value ½ in all KN fixed point valuations, we do not have $A \models B$ unless $A \Vdash B$ and this can easily fail.

[24] Granted that $\models$ is defined by the conjunction of the neo-classical definition plus this clause, the other direction follows from the fact that each KN fixed point valuation is also an unconditional fixed point valuation. This also entails that in the admissible valuations, $A \rightarrow B$ always takes value ½ where A has value 1 and B ½ or where A has value ½ and B 0; thus the only non-functionality at the fixed points is in the middle value for the conditional: $\frac{1}{2} \rightarrow \frac{1}{2}$.

Take, for example, two Curry-style sentences:

C_1: True$|C_1| \rightarrow \sim$ True$|\lambda|$
C_2: True$|C_2| \rightarrow \perp$

where λ is a Liar sentence gappy in every ufpv. Since, for each conditional, C_1 and C_2, there is a ufpv in which it, and thereby the corresponding truth ascription True $|C_1|$ or True $|C_2|$ respectively, takes value 1, we have neither True $|C_1| \Vdash \sim$True$|\lambda|$ nor True $|C_2| \Vdash \perp$. From this we can calculate that both C_1 and C_2 take the value $\frac{1}{2}$ in any KN fixed point valuation. Hence both sentences do not violate either of the neo-classical clauses of truth-preservation downwards and falsity-preservation upwards. None the less $C_1 \models C_2$ fails because there is a ufpv in which C_1 takes the value 1 and C_2 does not.

What sort of proof theory is adequate to the KN logic? To ensure soundness, we do need to make some changes to the neo-classical system. Firstly, every sequent must have an antecedent, empty antecedents are not allowed. This is not an unusual or counter-intuitive feature. However, it does have consequences for the discharge rules such as $\sim$ I or $\rightarrow$ I. Thus in the special case of applications of $\sim$ I in which we have only one premiss, the rule is amended to:

P	(1) $\perp$	Given
A_1, A_2	(2) $\sim$ P	1 $\sim$ I

where A_1 and A_2 are any two distinct axioms. In this way, the Gap clause for $\models$ in the case of singular inferences does not 'bite' in this case.[25] As a consequence, we need to redefine theoremhood: theorems are wffs derivable from at least two axioms. For simplicity I add all wffs of the form $(A \rightarrow A)$ as axioms and use the truth constant symbol T, in a representation of the antecedent of a sequent, to indicate the presence of two distinct axioms. For tidiness we can also add a contraction rule:

X, T P $\rightarrow$ P	(1) C	Given
X, T	(2) C	1 Contr.

We must also note an inadequacy in our definition of determinacy—Det P $\equiv_{df.} \sim (P \leftrightarrow \sim P)$. For on the KN interpretation of the conditional, if P is an atom of L then P could be assigned $\frac{1}{2}$ in a KN valuation v yet $(P \leftrightarrow \sim P)$ could have value $\frac{1}{2}$ not 1, if $P \dashv\Vdash \sim P$ fails. Only a radical form of indeterminacy, that held by sentences gappy in all ufpvs, is expressed by '$\sim$ Det'. This is an unavoidable limitation of the KN system, given its monotonicity. For example, the situation is even worse if we define determinacy in terms of excluded middle: Det P $\equiv_{df.} (P \vee \sim P)$ for then for no P, not even a Liar sentence, is Det P ever determinately false.

What of the conditional rules? The $\rightarrow$ I rule is available unrestricted only in the basic form:

A	(1) B	Given
T	(2) $A \rightarrow B$	1 $\rightarrow$ I.

[25] See Appendix 2 for further details.

For a more general form we need some restrictions:

X,P	(1) Q	Given
Y	(2) Det P	Given
Z	(3) Det Q	Given
X, Y, Z	(3) $P \rightarrow Q$	1, 2, 3 $\rightarrow$ I,

i.e. both consequent and antecedent must be determinate (granted the overall assumptions of the proof) if we are to apply $\rightarrow$I in the context of other assumptions. (In natural deduction format, this amounts to a global determinacy requirement in applications of $\rightarrow$I which extend a non-trivial proof.)

For $\rightarrow$E, we can use the neo-classical version

X	(1) $P \rightarrow Q$	Given
Y	(2) P	Given
Z_i	(3.i) Det R_i	$\forall R_i \in X \cap Y$
X, Y, $\bigcup_{i \in I} Z_i$	(4) Q	1,2 [3.i] $\rightarrow$ E

with the same disjointness condition: $\bigcup_{i \in I} Z_i \cap (X \cup Y) = \emptyset$. This system of rules is provably sound relative to KN entailment (see Appendix 2).

The result is still a fairly powerful logic. In particular, we achieve 'classical recapture'. For if P is any sentence which has a determinate value in all models, then Det P can be treated as an axiom. Hence if $\sim (P \leftrightarrow \sim P)$ is axiomatic for all wffs in a subsector S of L^+ then we can use classical reasoning completely unrestrictedly in S. We can use the KN-sound Expansion rule:

X	(1) P	Given
X, Y	(2) P	1 Exp.

to add in axioms, e.g. wffs of the form $A \rightarrow A$, in order to ensure there never are less than two antecedents in a sequent. Classical $\rightarrow$ E and $\rightarrow$ E, $\vee$ E, $\sim$ E and $\exists$E are all licit since the determinacy clauses are available as axioms. It is reasonable to assume that regimentations of, for example, ZFC or of branches of mathematical physics should each be treated as parts of just such a determinate sub-sector S. Therefore we achieve classical recapture in KN logic just as with neo-classical logic and mathematicians and physicists can be cleared to carry on reasoning classically.[26]

What meaning can we attach, though, to the KN conditional? Roughly speaking, the above interpretation of $\rightarrow$ imposes on it a classical reading, when we deal with a purely determinate sub-sector of language where there are no gaps. Once, however, we stray beyond that region, $A \rightarrow B$ represents 'minimax' entailment, a notion which ignores all but the basic structural properties of &, $\vee$ and $\sim$ and their quantifier generalisations. In these indeterminate realms, the logical power of the conditional is reduced (and iterations of $\rightarrow$ become, in those contexts, irrelevant). It is thereby a

[26] Not that they would pay the least bit of attention if philosophers told them not to, for the most part anyway. This is a sociological factor which has probably been essential for the development of mathematics and science—Bishop Berkeley did not stop them in their tracks—but also a potentially worrying sign of intellectual complacency.

less accurate representation of 'if... then' interpreted as some kind of entailment conditional but not hopelessly inaccurate because it does, at least, sustain the basic version of the Deduction Theorem and $\rightarrow$I[27] (as well as validating a substantial range of standard reasoning, including all the minimax principles).

Moreover we can add the naive truth rules. In fact (see Appendix 2) I will add a stronger substitution rule Sub for which the naive truth rules are special cases, one which generates the unrestricted inter-derivability of True |A| and A thereby validating the naive truth rules. But intersubstitution of True |A| and A *inside* formulae is restricted to occurrences which are not in the scope of $\rightarrow$, which are in 'extensional' position, as I shall say. It has to be conceded that the failure of full substitutivity of True |A| for A and vice versa is a drawback of the KN system. It is, though, only to be expected given the non-extensionality of $\rightarrow$.[28]

Finally, from the naive truth rules we can derive each instance of the Tarskian biconditionals, for any wff $A \in L^+$, paradoxical or not:

1	(1) True |A|	Given
1	(2) A	Sub
T	(3) True |A| $\rightarrow$ A	2 $\rightarrow$ I
4	(4) A	Given
4	(5) True |A|	4 Sub
T	(6) A $\rightarrow$ True|A|	5 $\rightarrow$ I
T	(7) True|A| $\leftrightarrow$ A	3, 6 &I, Contr.

4. PHILOSOPHICAL UPSHOT

How closely does the KN theory approximate the goal of a successful naive semantical theory? We have a theory in which True |A| and A are intersubstitutable in all extensional contexts and in which all instances of the Tarskian schema, including paradoxical instances, are derivable. Paradoxical sentences are handled via determinacy restrictions. The system is sound, relative to standard metatheory, and contains a conditional which satisfies the simple form of the Deduction Theorem:

$$A \models B \text{ iff } \models A \rightarrow B$$

What of McGee's argument for the equivalence of any consistent set of sentences with a consistent set of T-sentences? This is indeed blocked, in the KN semantics, by the failure of associativity for $\rightarrow$. Suppose, for simplicity, M actually *is* (rather than is merely interderivable with) a "biconditionalised" Curry sentence of the form:

$$\text{True}|M| \leftrightarrow P$$

[27] More generally we have X, A $\models$ B iff X $\models$ A $\rightarrow$ B, if Det A and Det B are both axiomatic.

[28] Moreover in any determinate sub-sector of our language, we can ignore $\rightarrow$ sentences and work purely with the 'material' conditional $\sim A \vee B$ which will be subject to the classical rules for the conditional. Full substitutivity is, of course, licit in this arrow-free determinate sub-sector.

(for consistent P). We have in our KN system the T theorem:

$$\vdash \text{True}|\text{M}| \leftrightarrow (\text{True}|\text{M}| \leftrightarrow \text{P})$$

By soundness, this sentence is true in all admissible valuations. Suppose, for example, P is a sentence of L false in KN initial valuation v_0 and in some ufpvs; then the value of True|M| ↔ (True|M| ↔ P) in v_0 computes as $\frac{1}{2} \leftrightarrow (\frac{1}{2} \leftrightarrow 0)$. Since P takes the value 0 in some ufpvs but True|M| can take all three values in ufpvs, the right hand biconditional computes as $\frac{1}{2}$ according to the KN rule for →. So the overall value in v_0 is $\frac{1}{2} \leftrightarrow \frac{1}{2}$, which computes finally as 1, since the left hand side and the right hand side have the same value in all ufpvs.

On the other hand,

$$(\text{True}|\text{M}| \leftrightarrow \text{True}|\text{M}|) \leftrightarrow \text{P}$$

computes as $(\frac{1}{2} \leftrightarrow \frac{1}{2}) \leftrightarrow 0) = 1 \leftrightarrow 0 = 0$ (the left-hand side evaluating to 1 since $u(\text{True}|\text{M}|) \leq u(\text{True}|\text{M}|)$ in every ufpv). Hence associativity fails and the proof of arbitrary P is blocked (since the system is sound).

It is true that the KN system incorporates some pretty artificial features, the artificial definition of theoremhood, the complications in the ∼I and →I rules for example. The marriage of KN logic and inductive theories of truth is not a smooth or entirely successful one. As to which partner is to blame: well, I blame inductive theories of truth; but then I would, wouldn't I? The reason being that any theoretical account of a naive truth-predicate which is developed in classical set theory in classical logic for a semantically open language is, from the perspective of the naive set theorist, bound to differ significantly from a non-classical theory for a notion of truth which is definable, such a theorist claims, in a semantically closed naive theory. One reason for thinking that the 'classically naive', as it were, theory is less satisfactory is the tendency, to say the least, for inductive theories of truth to generate revenge Liars.

This problem arises when we focus on the concepts—determinate truth and determinate falsity, as it may be—which are introduced as part of the solution to the semantic paradoxes. If the semantics of the proposed theory cannot deal with those new concepts, we are no further forward. We have tried to get a systematic theory of one key semantic concept, namely truth, which occurs in our informal philosophical thinking, but in doing so we incur a debt to produce a similar theory for any further semantics concepts—truth in a set-theoretic model, say—we use to solve the original Liar. If we cannot do so, or can only do so by producing a theory as susceptible to paradox as the notion of truth itself, we seem to have made little, if any, progress. Such points are made forcefully, and justifiably in my view, by dialetheists such as Graham Priest (see Priest (1987) §1.5; see also Weir (1998a), Section 8, pp. 777–84).

But on the present approach—KN logic plus an inductive theory of truth—the notion of indeterminacy appealed to in the metatheory cannot even be expressed adequately in the object language. The wff $\sim(\text{P} \leftrightarrow \sim\text{P})$, as we have seen, does not always take value 0 when P takes the gap value $\frac{1}{2}$. The problem is general: no monotonic operator can express determinacy. In a language with indeterminate sentences, for at least some such sentences P (the determinately indeterminate ones), Det P should take value 0 when P is neither 1 nor 0 and should take value 1 when P does. Thus in a Kripkean inductive hierarchy, if P took value $\frac{1}{2}$ at level α, whence Det P takes value 0, then if P's value becomes determinately 1 at $\alpha + 1$, Det P would flip value from 0 to 1.

Is it possible, then, to give a systematic, coherent and paradox-free semantics for the language of this current paper? It may be suggested that a full regimentation would include ZFC as the set theory, with the logic of the language being KN logic; classical reasoning would be legitimate, however, when not using the truth predicate or at any rate when reasoning about ZFC sets. But paradox would re-emerge with respect to a sentence such as ρ: $v(|\rho| \neq 1)$ if we had the equivalent of the Tarskian biconditionals for $v(|A| = 1)$—

$$v(|A| = 1) \leftrightarrow A$$

—for all A (or even all A in the fully determinate set-theoretic sub-sector). Of course, assuming ZFC is consistent (classically) we cannot have all these biconditionals. This is just Tarski's theorem on the undefinability of truth in classical languages (and logics).[29] We have invited back to the feast the ghost of the Tarskian hierarchy.

What this shows, in my view, is that a fully satisfactory solution to the paradoxes, including revenge Liars, cannot be achieved without a fully satisfactory resolution of the set-theoretic paradoxes and this can only be achieved if we manage to construct a semantically closed set theory. We need not just a closed theory of truth-in-L in L, we need a closed theory of satisfaction-in-a-model-of-L, also in L. This requires us to adopt not only a naive theory of truth but also a naive theory of sets, and here again, of course, one must restrict classical logic if one is to avoid triviality. Failing this, we will always be susceptible either to revenge Liars, or to declaring inexpressible some concepts (used in the analysis of paradox) one is manifestly able to express; or else finally lapsing into a nihilistic denial that any satisfactory systematic theory can be given of the semantics of language. One is left whistling in the Wittgensteinian wind.

One way forward, if one wishes to avoid these three unhappy outcomes, is to give a relative consistency proof—relative to standard set theory and classical logic—for naive set theory. This has been done by, for example, Brady (1989) and Restall (1992). In my view, however, their systems are far too weak to be suitable for carrying out standard mathematics or formal semantics (Weir, 2004).

One can rework the current account of truth to yield a naive theory of properties, by giving a parallel inductive account of an instantiation relation ε. We have a naive property in the individual domain for every open sentence of the language (in fact we can just let the naive properties be those wffs). We set $x\varepsilon y$ to $\frac{1}{2}$ in each initial valuation and change it to 1 (0), in valuation $\alpha + 1$, relative to assignment σ, if $v_\alpha(\varphi_{\sigma(y)}x) = 1(0)$ where $\sigma(y)$ is the wff $\varphi_{\sigma(y)}$, with the usual rule at limits. This renders true a naive comprehension principle:

$$\exists x \forall y (y \ \varepsilon \ x \leftrightarrow \varphi x)$$

[29] Note that 'undefinability' here is used in a technical sense: there is no predicate of the language co-extensional, in any model, with the set of codes of true sentences in the model. It is not that 'truth' must be taken as primitive according to some semantic notion of primitiveness.

at each fixed point (indeed with a little twiddling one can validate generalised comprehension). But adding to this a reasonable extensionality principle, incorporating something even approximating to the standard notion of identity, is a very much more difficult matter indeed, certainly if one wishes to work in a background framework of classical logic and standard set theory.

None the less producing an adequate theory of truth-in-L in L, one which can cope with entailment biconditionals as well as non-conditional operators, is a significant step forward even when L is itself not semantically closed with respect to all its semantic concepts. This is the step I have attempted to make in this paper. If successful, it provides grounds for thinking that the logical framework can accommodate a fully naive, semantically closed theory without inconsistency and, more emphatically, shows that deflationists have nothing to fear from the semantic paradoxes.

APPENDIX 1

NEO-CLASSICAL SOUNDNESS

One class of rules which are unproblematically sound neo-classically is the class of 'Minimax' rules, that is to say rules which never permit (in sequent proof architectures) the minimum value of the premiss succeedent to be greater than the maximum value of the conclusion succeedent on the natural ordering $1 > \frac{1}{2} > 0$. But certain minimax unsound rules, such as $\sim$E and $\vee$E have the property that every application, considered as a one-step proof in its own right, is neo-classically correct. However, for these rules, generalised transitivity fails: the overall premisses may fail to entail neo-classically the overall conclusion in longer proofs constructed using applications of these rules. The solution is to hold on to the minimax unsound but neo-classically correct *operational* rules and change the *structural* rules by adding determinacy restrictions to such minimax unsound rules (with a parallel restriction in the predicate calculus case for the $\exists$E rule).

For $\sim$E, the amended rule is:

X	(1) P	Given
Y	(2) $\sim$P	Given
$Z_i,\ i \in I$	(3.*i*) Det Q	Given, $\forall Q \in X \cap Y$
$X, Y, \bigcup_{i \in I} Z_i$	(3) C	1,2, [3.*i*, $i \in I$], $\sim$E

Here $\ulcorner X, Y \urcorner$ abbreviates $X \cup Y$, $\ulcorner X, P \urcorner$ abbreviates $X \cup \{P\}$, and it is required that $\bigcup_{i \in I} Z_i \cap (X \cup Y) = \emptyset$. In general I will omit the index set I where it is clear from the context what it is and bracket the determinacy premiss line numbers (i.e. in this example the premisses 3.*i*) by '[' and ']' as above.

For $\vee$E, we need to restrict the standard sequent natural deduction rule to:

X	(1) $P \vee Q$	Given
Y,P	(2) C	Given
Z,Q	(3) C	Given
$W_i,\ i \in I$	(4.*i*) Det R	Given, $\forall R \in (X \cap (Y \cup Z))$
$X, Y, Z, \bigcup_{i \in I} W_i$	(5) C	1,2,3 [4.*i*, $i \in I$], $\vee$E

We require also that $\bigcup_{i\in I} W_i \cap (X \cup Y \cup Z) = \emptyset$.

In Weir (1998b) I proved the soundness and completeness of the neo-classical (propositional) system built up using minimax rules and standard introduction and elimination rules (for &, ∨ and ∼) with those two amendments. Here is the soundness lemma for ∨E, that is the proof that the rule preserves neo-classical correctness: if each of the premiss sequents at lines (1), (2), (3) and the (4.*i*) is neo-classically correct—the sequent antecedents neo-classically entail the corresponding succeedent—then the conclusion sequent at (5) is correct too.

PROOF: (i) Truth preservation: this is much as in the classical case. Suppose all the given input sequents are entailments and that all of X,Y,Z, $\bigcup_{i\in I} W_i$, are true in admissible valuation v. Indeed all we need is the truth of all of X,Y,Z. Then by line 1, $P \vee Q$ is true in v, so one or other disjunct is. Whichever is the case, line 2 or else line 3 establishes that C is true in v.

(ii) Falsity preservation (upwards): suppose that C is false in v and all of X, Y,Z, $\bigcup_{i\in I} W_i$ are true in v but A. Since $\bigcup_{i\in I} W_i \cap (X \cup Y \cup Z) = \emptyset$, A cannot be a member of a W_i set else all of X, Y,Z are true contradicting, by part (i) above, the falsity of C. If $A \in (X \cap (Y \cup Z))$ then since all of the W_i are true, by the 4.*i* determinacy premisses, A has a determinate truth value in v; since it is not true, it must be false as required. If $A \notin (X \cap (Y \cup Z))$ then either (a) all of X are true in v or else (b) all of $Y \cup Z$ are.

> Case (a): by the correctness of line (1) $P \vee Q$ is true in v hence one of the disjuncts is, suppose without loss of generality that it is P. By the correctness of line (2) in the rule above, $A \in Y$ and is false.
>
> Case (b) By the correctness of lines (2) and (3) both P and Q are false in v hence so is $P \vee Q$. By the correctness of line (1), $A \in X$ and is false in v. ❑

As for the conditional rules, they are:

→I:

X,P	(1) Q	Given
Y_i	(2.*i*) Det R_i	Given, $\forall R_i \in X$
X, $\bigcup_{i\in I} Y_i$	(3) $P \rightarrow Q$	1 [2.*i*]→ I

subject to the condition that $X \cap \bigcup_{i\in I} Y_i = \emptyset$ and

X	(1) $P \rightarrow Q$	Given
Y	(2) P	Given
Z_i	(3.*i*) Det R_i	$\forall R_i \in X \cap Y$
X, Y, $\bigcup_{i\in I} Z_i$	(4) Q	1,2 [3.*i*] →E

where we also lay down also the disjointness condition: $\bigcup_{i\in I} Z_i \cap (X \cup Y) = \emptyset$. For the soundness proof the more difficult cases to consider are the falsity-preservation clauses:

(a) Falsity-preservation →I, non-bivalent interpretation: suppose $P \rightarrow Q$ is false in valuation v and all of X, $\bigcup_{i\in I} Y_i$ but A are true there. Then P is true at v and Q is false at v. By IH (induction hypothesis) applied to line (1), A is false at v as required.

(b) Falsity-preservation $\rightarrow$I, bivalent interpretation: suppose $P \rightarrow Q$ is false in valuation v and all of X, $\bigcup_{i \in I} Y_i$ but A are true there. $A \notin \bigcup_{i \in I} Y_i$ else, by the disjointness condition, all of X are true there and hence, by the correctness of line (1), given by IH, and the semantics for $\rightarrow$, so is $P \rightarrow Q$. Hence all members of X, including A, are determinate in v. But A cannot be true, else all members of X are true, hence $P \rightarrow Q$ is true; so A is false as required.

(c) Falsity preservation $\rightarrow$E, non-bivalent interpretation: suppose Q is false and all of X, Y, $\bigcup_{i \in I} Z_i$ but A are true. $A \notin \bigcup_{i \in I} Z_i$ else by the disjointness condition all of X, Y are true whence, by the correctness of lines (1) and (2) and the semantics for $\rightarrow$, Q is true. Hence $A \in X \cup Y$ and if it belongs to $X \cap Y$, it is true or false. But by the reasoning of the previous sentence it cannot be true, and so is false as required. If A belongs to X only then P is true, Q false so $P \rightarrow Q$ is false, whence by the correctness of line (1), A is false. Similarly if $A \in Y$, P is false since $P \rightarrow Q$ is true and Q is false; hence A is false as required.

(d) Falsity preservation $\rightarrow$E, bivalent interpretation: suppose Q is false and all of X, Y, $\bigcup_{i \in I} Z_i$ but A are true. If P is false in the valuation then by the correctness of line (2), $A \in Y$ and is false. If P is either true or gappy, then by the bivalent semantics for $\rightarrow$, $P \rightarrow Q$ is false and so $A \in X$ and is false by line (1). ❑

Further principles which are neo-classically correct include contraposition and permutation which we can add as basic principles.

Contraposition:

X	(1) $P \rightarrow Q$	Given
X	(2) $\sim Q \rightarrow \sim P$	1, Contrap.

Permutation:

X	(1) $P \rightarrow (Q \rightarrow R)$	Given
X	(2) $Q \rightarrow (P \rightarrow R)$	1, Perm.

Transitivity holds for the non-bivalent conditional but for the bivalent one we have only the restricted form:

X	(1) $P \rightarrow Q$	Given
Y	(2) $Q \rightarrow R$	Given
Z_i	(3.*i*) Det A_i	$\forall A_i \in X \cap Y$
X, Y, $\bigcup_{i \in I} Z_i$	(4) $P \rightarrow R$	1,2 [3.*i*] Trans.

which is thus, on the 'belts and braces' principle of using only rules sound on both interpretations, the form we use.

The generalisation to predicate logic is fairly straightforward, the only non-classical case being $\exists$E which is amended in an analogous way to $\vee$E:

X	(1) $\exists x \varphi x$	Given
Y, $\varphi x/\mathbf{t}$	(2) C	Given
Z_i	(3.*i*) Det P	Given for $P \in X \cap Y$
X, Y, $\bigcup_{i \in I} Z_i$	(4) C	

As with $\vee$E, we have the disjointness constraint that $\bigcup_{i \in I} Z_i \cap (X \cup Y) = \emptyset$ and of course in premiss (2) the usual constraints on the parameter $\mathbf{t}$, which must also not occur in φ.

As to identity, in Weir (1999), I used a second-order framework in which $x = y$ was defined by $\forall F(Fx \rightarrow Fy)$. The neo-classical framework validates, under this definition,[31] standard =I and a restricted =E (with the usual disjointness condition):

—	(1) $\mathbf{t} = \mathbf{t}$	Axiom = I
X	(1) $\mathbf{t} = \mathbf{u}$	Given
Y	(2) $\varphi x/\mathbf{t}$	Given
Z_i	(3.i) Det A	$A_i \in X \cap Y$
$X, Y, \bigcup_{i \in I} Z_i$	(4) $\varphi x/\mathbf{u}$	$1, 2[3._i, i \in I] = E$

APPENDIX 2

Moving from the neo-classical framework to the KN semantics, we need to prove that the jump operator on this semantics has the Kripkean monotonicity property that where $\alpha \geq \beta$, the KN valuation v_α extends all earlier valuations if valuation v_β does. Valuation v_γ extends v_δ just in case when $v_\delta(P) = 1$ then $v_\gamma(P) = 1$ and when $v_\delta(P) = 0$ then $v_\gamma(P) = 0$, for all sentences P. We prove this by a double induction on the stage of the valuation[32] and on sentence complexity.

MONOTONICITY THEOREM: Every valuation extends all earlier valuations based on the same model.

PROOF: Take any KN model M and consider the hierarchy of all valuations based on it. Suppose (IH_1) that for all $\beta < \alpha$ and all $\gamma < \beta$, v_β extends valuation v_γ. To prove: v_α extends each earlier valuation v_β. We prove this by an inner induction (inductive hypothesis: IH_2) on sentence complexity. For atoms and sentences without $\rightarrow$ as the dominant operator, the monotonicity property is demonstrated in the usual way. Thus the only atoms which may change value at v_α^σ (i.e. in valuation v_α relative to assignment to variables σ) are truth ascriptions of the form True x. But if $\sigma(x)$ is not a code of a sentence then True x is false relative to σ in every valuation. And True |A| cannot go from truth to untruth or falsity to non-falsity else, at earlier valuations v_β and v_γ, A will have itself gone from truth to gap or falsity or from falsity to gap or truth, contrary to IH_1. Similarly v_α extends earlier valuations on conjunctions, disjunctions, and quantifications, given that it does so on their constituents, because these operators are monotonic, they never change in determinate truth value when an indeterminately valued constituent changes.

For the conditional, we argue firstly that if $v_\beta(A \rightarrow B) = 0$, for an earlier β, then $v_\beta(A) = 1$ and $v_\beta(B) = 0$. By IH_2, $v_\alpha(A) = 1$ and $v_\alpha(B) = 0$ so $v_\alpha(A \rightarrow B) = 0$. In the other case, if $v_\beta(A \rightarrow B) = 1$ then one possibility is that either $v_\beta(A) = 0$ or $v_\beta(B) = 1$ in which case IH_2 yields $v_\alpha(A) = 0$ or $v_\alpha(B) = 1$ whence $v_\alpha(A \rightarrow B) = 1$. The other possibility is that $v_\beta(A) \neq 0$ and $v_\beta(B) \neq 1$ and A $\Vdash$ B. Then $v_\alpha(A \rightarrow B) = 1$ unless $v_\alpha(A) = 1$ and $v_\alpha(B) = 0$. But

LEMMA: If A $\Vdash$ B then we cannot have $v(A) = 1$ and $v(B) = 0$ for any KN valuation v. (Corollary: if A $\Vdash$ B then A $\rightarrow$ B takes value 1 in each KN valuation.)

[31] And given the usual second-order comprehension axioms, or else the use of λ terms and λ abstraction.

[32] From now on valuations are KN valuations except where otherwise noted.

PROOF: Suppose for reduction, $v(A) = 1$ and $v(B) = 0$. Any KN valuation v is itself, in effect, an unconditional Kripkean valuation, since the clauses for the operators other than the conditional are standard. To get the unconditional valuation u_v simply assign to each conditional, treated now as an atom, the truth value which v assigns it (more fully a truth value relativised to an assignment to variables) leaving the assignment to all the other atoms as in v. An induction on wff complexity, purely in terms of the operators other than $\rightarrow$, shows this unconditional valuation agrees with v on all wffs. Hence $u_v(A) = 1$ and $u_v(B) = 0$. This unconditional valuation u_v can be expanded to a fixed point u_κ at which, by monotonicity, $u_\kappa(A) = 1$ and $u_\kappa(B) = 0$. But this contradicts $A \Vdash B$. ❑

Thus $v_\alpha(A \rightarrow B) = 1$ as required. ❑

Note that by the above Corollary, all Tarskian conditionals, conditionals of the form $\text{True}|A| \rightarrow A$ or $A \rightarrow \text{True}|A|$, take value 1 in every KN valuation since True|A| and A always take the same value in every ufpv.

By the usual cardinality argument, there is a fixed point v_λ at which True|A| and A are 'equalised' each taking the same value (1, ½ or 0) just as in ufpvs and at which, as we have seen, all Tarskian biconditionals take value 1. These fixed point KN valuations are the key ones, the ones in terms of which we will define entailment. Neo-classically, the acceptable valuations are the variants of the 'actual' valuation @. We can combine this idea what that of a fixed point KN valuation to get the notion of admissible valuation we need.

First we need to select an arbitrary model M as the 'actual' model. Each model, it has been stipulated, contains as a sub-structure a standard model of arithmetic. (More generally, one might choose for @ a model with a standard model for ZFC as a sub-structure.) Variants of M will each contain isomorphic copies of the standard numbers, with the successor, addition and multiplication functions defined over them, as their interpretation of N, 0, S, + and ×. Moreover, where $\mathbf{t}_1, \ldots \mathbf{t}_n$ are any closed terms and R is an n-ary relation, $R\mathbf{t}_1, \ldots \mathbf{t}_n$ is gappy in any variant model M′ only if gappy in M. The admissible valuations are then all the fixed point KN valuations based on variants of M.

We then define entailment in terms of the admissible KN valuations exactly as in the neo-classical case except for a weakening of the relation in the case of singular inferences among 'everywhere gappy' sentences. For KN entailment we introduce a third 'Gap' clause to rule out some of those entailments, in particular, we required in the case of singular arguments (one premiss, one conclusion) that $A \models B$ only if $A \Vdash B$.

To make this work, we need to require that every sequent has a non-empty set of antecedents; to make this work in turn, we need some rather artificial amendments to the discharge rules and the notion of theoremhood.

If we turn to the minimax rules including the singular I and E rules &E, ∨I and their predicate correlates ∀E and ∃I, things are pretty straightforward. Thus for ∀E, soundness is provable for the case of a multi-antecedent conclusion sequent just as in the neo-classical case. The singular case is:

P	(1) $\forall x\varphi x$	Given
P	(2) $\varphi x/\mathbf{t}$	1, ∀E.

Suppose, then, line (1) is correct, that is to say $P \models \forall x\varphi x$ that is $P \Vdash \forall x\varphi x$. Consider an arbitrary admissible model M, ufpv u defined on M and assignment σ. Suppose $u_\sigma(P) = i (i = 1 \text{ or } 1/2 \text{ or } 0)$. By the correctness of line (1), $u_\sigma(\forall x\varphi x) \geq i$ whence, by the semantics for ∀, for every x-variant $\sigma[x/\alpha]$ of σ, (i.e. agreeing with σ except, at most, in its assignment of α to x) we have $u_\sigma[x/\alpha](\varphi x) \geq i$. Since $u_\sigma(\varphi x/\mathbf{t}) = u_\sigma[x/\beta](\varphi x)$ where β is the referent in M of closed term $\mathbf{t}$, $u_\sigma(\varphi x/\mathbf{t}) \geq i$ as required. ❑

For multi-premiss sequent rules &I and ∨E things are almost as straightforward. Soundness for both rules is exactly as in the neo-classical case except when the conclusion sequent has only one premiss (since if P ⊩ Q then P ⊨ Q as noted in fn. 24). Given the ban on null premiss sequents, this is only possible, for &I, in the following situation:

P	(1) Q	Given
P	(2) R	Given
P	(3) Q & R	1,2 &I

We need to show P ⊩ (Q & R). But this is direct from the semantics for & given our hypotheses that P ⊩ Q and P ⊩ R. (The case of ∀I is similar.) For ∨E, a singular conclusion sequent is possible only in the following case:

P	(1) Q ∨ R	Given
Q	(2) C	Given
R	(3) C	Given
P	(4) C	1,2,3 ∨E

with P distinct both from Q and R. For, given the neo-classical determinacy restriction on wffs occurring in the assumptions both of major and minor premiss, if P also occurred as an antecedent in lines (2) or (3) the determinacy constraint requires an additional premiss sequent of the form X ⇒ ∼ (P ↔ ∼ P). Moreover the members of X must be distinct from P, given the disjointness clause in the determinacy restriction. So looking at the only possible form of the rule with singular conclusion, P ⊩ C is fairly direct from the semantics for ∨, since the correctness of (1), (2) and (3) gives us $u(\mathrm{P}) \leq u(\mathrm{Q} \vee \mathrm{R})$, $u(\mathrm{Q}) \leq u(\mathrm{C})$ and $u(\mathrm{R}) \leq u(\mathrm{C})$, with $u(\mathrm{Q} \vee \mathrm{R}) = \max[u(\mathrm{Q}), u(\mathrm{C})]$. This generalises straightforwardly to the ∃E case where we have $\mathrm{P} \Rightarrow \exists x\varphi x$ and $\varphi x/\mathbf{a} \Rightarrow \mathrm{C}$. Note that though both these rules are discharge rules, given that no premiss sequent has an empty antecedent, the same is true of the conclusion sequent.

If we can assume that we are dealing with a perfectly determinate range of individuals, for example, if each M contains only the natural numbers, =E can be simplified in KN logic to its classical form, minus the determinacy restrictions. So KN will be stronger than neo-classical logic, in this respect.

Our basic structural rules, namely the Reflexivity axiom schema:

X	(1) P	Refl. (P ∈ X)

and Expansion:

X	(1) P	Given
X,Y	(2) P	1 Exp.

survive unscathed in the neo-classical form, the former by dint of the reflexivity of ⊩, in the case where X = {P}. For Expansion, truth-preservation and falsity preservation are trivial and the gap clause is inoperative in the only non-trivial case, where Y is not a subset of (non-empty) X.

Turning to the negation introduction and elimination rules, no changes are needed in ∼E since the case of a singular conclusion sequent is ruled out by the determinacy restriction on antecedents occurring in both premisses. But when we turn to the ∼I rule, a discharge rule which can reduce the number of antecedents to zero, we need to make changes. First of all we need to specify how to interpret ⊥. We cannot interpret it as false in all unconditional valuations since no wff (not itself a logical constant) has that property; rather ⊥ is false in all admissible models. We could use any wff of the form ∼(A → A) to play the role. Now we can leave the standard rule untouched[33] so long as there are at least two additional assumptions that is, where the rule is:

X, P	(1) $\bot$	Given
X	(2) $\sim$P	1 $\sim$ I

X must have at least two members. If X is a singleton the rule takes the form:

Q, P	(1) $\bot$	Given
Q, A $\rightarrow$ A	(2) $\sim$P	1 $\sim$ I

where Q $\neq$ {A $\rightarrow$ A}. And when X is empty, the rule takes the form:

P	(1) $\bot$	Given
A $\rightarrow$ A, B $\rightarrow$ B	(2) $\sim$P	1 $\sim$ I

where A and B are two distinct wffs. In this way, the gap clause never 'bites' in $\sim$I. The notion of theoremhood, in the KN logic, therefore, has to be: φ is a theorem iff for some A, B, we have that A $\rightarrow$ A, B $\rightarrow$ B $\vdash \varphi$ is provable.

Now we get to the main action, the conditional rules. As remarked, the $\rightarrow$I rule is available unrestricted only in the basic form:

A	(1) B	Given
T	(2) A $\rightarrow$ B	1 $\rightarrow$I

(with the convention given above that T stands for two separate axioms). This rule is sound.

PROOF: Since the conclusion sequent has two antecedent premisses, the criterion for correctness is the neo-classical one. If the two axioms in T are true in admissible valuation v (which, of course, they are) then A $\rightarrow$ B must be true in v, which it is. For, by the correctness of line (1), A $\Vdash$ B, so A $\rightarrow$ B is true in every admissible valuation by the Corollary above. For this reason, the falsity-preservation clause is trivial. ❑

As to the more general $\rightarrow$ I

X,P	(1) Q	Given
Y	(2) Det P	Given
Z	(3) Det Q	Given
X, Y, Z	(3) P $\rightarrow$ Q	1, 2, 3 $\rightarrow$ I

where X $\cap$ (Y $\cup$ Z) = Ø, this too is sound:

PROOF: If X is empty then P $\rightarrow$ Q is true in all admissible models, by the argument for the soundness of the basic form of $\rightarrow$ I, hence Y, Z $\models$ P $\rightarrow$ Q by expansion. If X is non-empty we cannot have X $\cup$ Y $\cup$ Z a singleton set by the disjointness requirement (and the requirement that there be no null antecedent sequents) so the gap clause is not activated. So we consider the remaining case in which X $\cup$ Y $\cup$ Z is a plural set and X is non-empty.

In the truth-preservation direction, if all of X, Y, Z are true in v, then neither P nor Q take value $\frac{1}{2}$ in v. Since the correctness of (1) rules out v(P) = 1 and v(Q) = 0, one of the other three classical cases obtains and hence P $\rightarrow$ Q is true in v. In the other direction, if P $\rightarrow$ Q is false in v then v(P) = 1 and v(Q) = 0; if all of X, Y, Z but A are true in v then by the correctness of (1), A $\in$ X and is false in v as required. ❑

[33] And its classical variant with X $\Rightarrow$ P as the conclusion from premiss sequent X, $\sim$P $\Rightarrow \bot$.

Turning now to $\rightarrow$ E:

X	(1) $P \rightarrow Q$	Given
Y	(2) P	Given
Z_i	(3.*i*) Det R_i	$\forall R_i \in X \cap Y$
$X, Y, \bigcup_{i \in I} Z_i$	(4) Q	1,2 [3.*i*] $\rightarrow$ E

with the disjointness condition: $\bigcup_{i \in I} Z_i \cap (X \cup Y) = \emptyset$, this neo-classical form of the rule remains sound in the KN semantics. Since neither X nor Y can be empty, the gap clause in $\models$ is never applicable since if $X = Y = \{A\}$ then we need as an additional premiss Det A and the antecedent of that premiss sequent must be distinct from A (by the disjointness clause).

We also have to drop, in the general case, the principles of transitivity, contraposition and permutation as these are no longer valid. Thus let A, B, C be gappy sentences with no unconditional entailments among them (three distinct gappy conditionals, say): then computing the value of

$$(A \rightarrow B) \rightarrow ((B \rightarrow C) \rightarrow (A \rightarrow C))$$

we get $(\frac{1}{2} \rightarrow \frac{1}{2}) \rightarrow ((\frac{1}{2} \rightarrow \frac{1}{2}) \rightarrow \frac{1}{2} \rightarrow \frac{1}{2}))$ which computes as $\frac{1}{2} \rightarrow (\frac{1}{2} \rightarrow \frac{1}{2})$ (since no minimax entailment holds among the component conditionals) so $\frac{1}{2} \rightarrow \frac{1}{2}$ so $\frac{1}{2}$. However, in the special case where $A \rightarrow B$ and $B \rightarrow C$ are both axioms, $A \rightarrow C$ is logically true: if the value of A in v is 0 or that of B is 1, whence C is 1, then $A \rightarrow C$ has value 1 in v, and similarly if the value of B (hence A) is 0 or C is 1 then the value of $A \rightarrow C$ is 1. The only other possibility compatible with the axiomatic status of $A \rightarrow B$ and $B \rightarrow C$ is that $A \Vdash B$ and $B \Vdash C$ in which case $A \Vdash C$. So we could add as a further rule, that if $\vdash A \rightarrow B$ and $\vdash B \rightarrow C$ then $\vdash A \rightarrow C$. Similarly contraposition in the form if $\vdash A \rightarrow B$ then $\vdash \sim B \rightarrow \sim A$ is sound.

What of substitutivity in our KN semantics? Let $\varphi[A]$ represent ambiguously the result of substituting some occurrences of A in φ by True|A| or some of True|A| by A. Unrestricted substitutivity in all contexts fails. For example, consider the inference:

1	(1) $\text{True}|A \rightarrow B| \rightarrow C$	Hyp.
1	(2) $(A \rightarrow B) \rightarrow C$	[1 Sub]*.

for atomic A, B, C. The first line is sound regardless of the truth value of $\text{True}|A \rightarrow B| \rightarrow C$. But for the soundness of line (2), the gap clause for $\models$ requires that $\text{True}|A \rightarrow B| \rightarrow C \Vdash (A \rightarrow B) \rightarrow C$. But since conditionals can take any value one likes in ufpvs, this is false. There is a ufpv in which $\text{True}|A \rightarrow B| \rightarrow C$ takes the value 1, for example, but in which $(A \rightarrow B) \rightarrow C$ has the value 0.

But a more restricted substitutivity principle is sound. Let an extensional frame for a wff φ be any conditional-free sentence F such that φ results from F by applying a substitution function f in which open sentences are substituted in F for primitive predicates, including, as 0-place predicates, propositional letters. A does not occur in the scope of $\rightarrow$ in φ iff there is an extensional frame F for φ in which A is one of the substituends for a primitive predicate. Where such an F and function f exists for φ, with A the image of a primitive predicate in F, say that A is in extensional position in φ. For such a φ and A we have the following:

LEMMA II: If there is an extensional frame F for φ in which A is in extensional position then in *any* ufpv, φ and $\varphi[A/\text{True}|A|]$ (that is the result of substituting True|A| for some or all occurrences of A in φ) have the same truth value relative to each assignment to variables. Similarly φ and $\varphi[\text{True}|A|/A]$ have the same truth value in any ufpv, if True|A| is in extensional position in φ.

PROOF: By induction on the minimum complexity of a frame for φ with A in extensional position. The base clause follows from the fact that A and True|A| have the same value in every ufpv. The inductive steps are routine. Thus if φ is $\forall x \psi x$ then (where $A \neq \forall x \psi x$: that case is a base clause one) there is a conditional-free sentence, $\forall x \theta x$ and substitution function f such that $f(\forall x \theta x)$, that is $\forall x(f(\theta x)) = \forall x \psi x$. The open sentence θx is thus an extensional frame for ψx in which A is in extensional position. By inductive hypothesis, since there is a frame of lower complexity than $\forall x \psi x$ for ψx, it follows that for any ufpv u and assignment σ', $u_{\sigma'}(\psi x) = u_{\sigma'}(\psi x[A/\text{True}|A|])$ from which it follows in turn that for every σ, $u_\sigma(\forall x \psi x) = u_\sigma(\forall x \psi x[A/\text{True}|A|])$. ❑

Hence substitution for a formula in extensional position is KN sound:

SUBSTITUTION THEOREM: If A is in extensional position in φ, i.e. not in the scope of $\rightarrow$, then if $X \models \varphi$, $X \models \varphi[A]$.

PROOF: This is pretty much immediate from the fact that φ and $\varphi[A]$ have the same value in any ufpv and any admissible valuation is also a ufpv. ❑

REFERENCES

Brady, Ross (1989): 'The Non-Triviality of Dialectical Set Theory' in G. Priest, R. Routley and J. Norman (eds.), *Paraconsistent Logic: Essays on the Inconsistent* (Munich: Philosophia Verlag).

Field, Hartry (2003a): 'A Revenge-Immune Solution to the Semantic Paradoxes', *Journal of Philosophical Logic* 32.

—— (2003b): 'The Consistency of the naïve(?) theory of properties', in Godehard Link (ed.) *One Hundred Years of Russell's Paradox: Logical Philosophy Then and Now* (Walter de Gruyter).

Fitch, F. (1952): *Symbolic Logic* (New York: The Ronald Press Company).

Horwich, Paul (1990): *Truth* (Oxford: Blackwell).

Kleene, Stephen C (1952): *Introduction to Metamathematics* (Amsterdam: North Holland).

Kripke, Saul (1975): 'Outline of a Theory of Truth' in R. Martin (ed.) (1975) pp. 53–82.

Lemmon, E. J. (1965): *Beginning Logic* (London: Nelson).

Łukasiewicz, Jan (1920): 'O logice trójwartosciowej', *Ruch Filozoficzny*, (Lwów) 5, pp. 169–71.

—— and Tarski, Alfred (1930): 'Untersuchungen über den Aussagenkalkül', *Comptes Rendus des séances de la Société des Sciences et des Lettres de Varsovie* 23, pp. 30–50.

Martin, Robert L. (1975): *Recent Essays on Truth and the Liar Paradox* (Oxford: Clarendon Press).

—— and Woodruff, Peter W. (1975): "On Representing 'True-in-L' in L" in R. Martin (ed.) 1975, pp. 47–52.

McGee, Vann (1991): *Truth, Vagueness and Paradox* (Indianapolis: Hackett).

—— (1992): 'Maximal Consistent Sets of Instances of Tarski's Schema (T)', *Journal of Philosophical Logic* 21, 235–41.

Moschovakis, Y. (1974): *Elementary Induction on Abstract Structures*. (Amsterdam: North Holland).

Priest, Graham (1987): *In Contradiction* (Dordrecht: Nijhoff).

Read, Stephen (1988): *Relevant Logic* (Oxford: Blackwell).

Restall, Greg (1992): 'A Note on Naïve Set Theory in LP', *Notre Dame Journal of Formal Logic*, 33, pp. 422–32.

Tennant, Neil (1978): *Natural Logic* (Edinburgh: Edinburgh University Press).

Weir, Alan (1996): 'Ultra-maximalist Minimalism!': *Analysis* 56 pp. 10–22.
—— (1998a) 'Naïve Set Theory is Innocent!' *Mind* 107 October 1998. pp. 763–98.
—— (1998b): 'Naïve Set Theory, Paraconsistency and Indeterminacy I'. *Logique et Analyse* pp. 161–3 pp. 219–66.
—— (1999): 'Naïve Set Theory, Paraconsistency and Indeterminacy II'. *Logique et Analyse,* pp. 167–8, pp. 283–40.
—— (2004): 'There are no True Contradictions', in JC Beall and G. Priest (eds.) *The Law of Non-Contradiction* (Oxford: Oxford University Press).

14

Anaphorically Unrestricted Quantifiers and Paradoxes

Jody Azzouni

1.

In two earlier papers, Azzouni (2001) and Azzouni (2004c), I offer a new deflationist approach to the logic of truth, *anaphorically unrestricted quantifiers*; but in those papers I deliberately set aside any discussion of the paradoxes. Simmons (1999), however, has argued that deflationist approaches to truth *must* take account of the paradoxes and, further, that there are great obstacles to their so doing. In this paper, I take issue with Simmons by challenging the purported data his attack is based on: I deny there are any purposes served by truthtalk in the vernacular that require impredicative approaches to the logic of truth; thus I deny the need for an approach to the logic of truth that allows the *expressibility* of paradoxical, and more generally, (certain sorts of) ungrounded, statements. Along the way to this conclusion, I argue that the best way to approach truthtalk in the vernacular is by a formal regimentation (of that discourse) designed to capture the logical role of the truth predicate (as it occurs in English), but not (certain) additional properties that the vernacular truth predicate seems to have.

2.

Let us start with Tarski's (1932, pp. 187–8) famous Convention T, an adequacy condition he placed on any truth theory (complications in Tarski's adequacy condition not germaine to the topic of this paper are omitted, and his formulation is modified accordingly):

CONVENTION T. *A formally correct definition of the symbol "Tr", formulated in the metalanguage, will be called* an adequate definition of truth *if it has the following consequence:*

My thanks to Bradley Armour-Garb and to Mark Richard for comments and suggestions on an earlier version of this that helped change it into a later version of this. Also, thanks are due to the students in my truth seminar, spring 2003, for similar reasons.

(α) *all sentences which are obtained from the expression "x ε Tr if and only if p" by substituting for the symbol "x" a . . . name of any sentence of the language in question and for the symbol "p" the expression which forms the translation of this sentence into the metalanguage.*

This constraint arises from Tarski's discussion of the failure of a "semantical definition" for truth in colloquial language (§1). He writes there (p. 155):

As a starting-point certain sentences of a special kind present themselves which could serve as partial definitions of the truth of a sentence or more correctly as explanations of various concrete turns of speech of the type "*x* is a true sentence". The general scheme of this kind of sentence can be depicted in the following way:
(2) *x is a true sentence if and only if p.*

Tarski explains (2) thus (pp. 155–6):

In order to obtain concrete definitions we substitute in the place of the symbol "*p*" in this scheme any sentence, and in the place of "*x*" any individual name of this sentence.

This begins a more than seventy-year-long fetish with "Tarski biconditionals", despite Tarski's explicit description of Convention T as *only* an "adequacy condition", and the biconditionals as mere "explanations of various concrete turns of speech of the type '*x* is a true sentence'." The (nearly exclusive) focus on "T-sentences" allows a mischaracterization of Tarski's theory: that it is—or is close to, anyway—a redundancy theory of truth,[1] and the mistaken view that a theory of truth adequate to all our uses of "true" can be built *solely* upon the constraint that such a theory have Tarski biconditionals as consequences.[2]

An obsession with Tarski biconditionals can also lead to the belief that *they* are the key, conceptually, to truth. Thus Wright (1992, p. 13) describes a deflationist position as assuming of the truth predicate that:

At least as far as what we may call the basic case is concerned, when the truth predicate is applied to an exhibited declarative sentence, its content is wholly fixed by the principle that

"P" is true if and only if P.

He continues (p. 14):

Deflationists recognize, of course, that something more needs to be said to account for the role of the predicate as attached to a singular term .. or as it occurs in quantification over its primary bearers. . . . Such uses of the truth predicate are, however, to be explained in terms of the basic case . . .[3]

[1] *I* won't name names, but Kirkham (1992, p. 185) writes of a "common but reckless tendency to identify Tarski's theory with F. P. Ramsey's redundancy theory".

[2] Thus Horwich (1998). Soames (1999, p. 68) writes: "In fact, Tarski regarded the truth and assertibility of all instances of schema T to be not merely a necessary condition for T to be a truth predicate for L but a sufficient condition as well." I don't know of any textual evidence that unequivocally supports this claim. Soames (1999) not only attributes the view to Tarski, but seems committed to a propositional version of it himself. [After the completion of this paper, I learned of a forthcoming paper of Douglas Patterson's which masterfully discusses the issue of whether Tarski saw the condition as necessary.]

[3] Although Wright, here, describes a view of truth he does not hold, he does retain *these* claims for *his* "Minimalism." The centrality of the Tarski biconditionals for the meaning/significance of truth is associated by nearly all recent authors with what is called "deflationism", "minimalism", and "disquotationalism". See, e.g., Horwich (1998), Field (1994), Gupta (1993), Simmons (1999),

But this will not work for at least *two* reasons. First, a mere list of Tarski biconditionals is *unsurveyable*. Without some device of explicit (or implicit) generality—something that indicates how the infinite list of sentences is generated, such a list can not be comprehended.[4] The *second* reason is linked to the first. For Tarski biconditionals to fix the truth values of blind ascriptions,[5] they must be semantically connected to a device of generality: objectual quantifiers ranging over propositions or sentences, sentential substitutional quantifiers (hereafter, *SS-quantifiers*), etc.; and when such devices are introduced (in the right way), Tarski biconditionals (if they show up at all!) emerge as *theorems*. To say this much *is not* to say that Tarski biconditionals are not appropriate as adequacy conditions on a theory of truth;[6] it is to say that any analysis of truth that starts with Tarski biconditionals is *backwards*. The right first step is to determine what the truth predicate is *used for*, and to read off of *that* constraints on the truth idiom.[7]

This naturally brings us to the second truth paradigm, one often entangled with the deflationist view—as described above—but nevertheless quite distinguishable. It *originates* in Quine (1970), and is taken up by Leeds (1978), Putnam (1978), and others: a truth idiom is needed *only* because of blind truth-ascription. On this view, Wright's basic case is *not* the significant use of truthtalk—not its raison d'être, anyway. Instead we start with a blind truth-ascription, such as "what he said is true", and (this is one way to go) note that (Putnam (1978), p. 15) "if we had a meta-language with infinite conjunctions and infinite disjunctions ... [and if] we wanted to say 'what he said was true' ... we could say:[8]

Armour-Garb and Beall (2001). My (anaphoric) quantificational deflationist rejects this purported centrality of the Tarski biconditionals, as I will show in due course.

[4] For example: Quotation names for sentences arise by sandwiching sentences between quotes. In turn, a Tarski biconditional is generated by flanking a biconditional with a quote-name of a sentence followed by the phrase "is true" on its left side, and the sentence named on its right. This description is (pretty explicitly) metalinguistic: it describes how to construct such Tarski biconditionals for any sentence, and it *quantifies* over sentences and their parts to do so. One can try to avoid linking an understanding of the infinite list of Tarski biconditionals to possession of some generalizing device or other, by invoking an (unanalyzed) notion of a disposition to assent to such biconditionals. Since one needs a generalizing device *anyway* to handle a large class of truth ascriptions (see the second reason immediately following), it is hard to motivate invoking dispositions this way. In any case, one *should not* irresponsibly (stipulatively) introduce dispositions to solve issues about how we do and do not grasp our semantic notions. See Collins (2002), esp. pp. 669–73, for an interesting and detailed discussion of the drawbacks of the dispositional approach.

[5] *Blind truth ascriptions* are ones which do not exhibit (via quote names) the sentences they ascribe truth or falsity to: "(9) is false", "Everything Newton wrote is true", etc.

[6] Although—for the record—they are *not*: truth ascriptions can be made to sentences of other languages even without the presence (or possibility) of translation; such a (transcendent) truth idiom cannot be constrained in its operation by Tarski biconditionals. A full discussion of this issue is not germaine to the current discussion, and so, for the most part, I am leaving the details aside. See my (2001) and my (2004c).

[7] Notice that here and in the foregoing, I have deliberately switched from "truth *predicate*" to "truth *idiom*": as I will show, the needs truthtalk satisfies can be handled by idioms other than truth predicates.

[8] I assume, on Putnam's behalf, on Wright's—earlier (and on behalf of myself, later)—that quasi-quote conventions are in force rather than (as typographically appears) ordinary quotation. The reader should presume such conventions (where needed) in what follows.

(1) [He said 'P_1' & P_1] or [He said 'P_2' & P_2] or. . . . "

But we can not use infinite disjunctions and conjunctions. "So," (Putnam (1978), p. 15) "we look for a finite expression equivalent to (1)":

(2) For some *x* he said *x* & *x* is true

is equivalent to (1) provided for each i ($i = 1, 2, 3, \ldots$)

(3) "P_i" is true if and only if P_i.

On this view, Tarski biconditionals are *not* a self-ratifying constraint on truth, something that analytically or a priori follows from our notion of truth; rather, T-sentences, far from being the paradigmatic or central use of "true", are merely the technical by-product of the transmogrification of an (infinitely demanding) ink-consuming device into a modest *predicate*.

Putnam's argument, presumably, is not supposed to establish that the truth predicate is the *only* finitary device that can substitute in blind truth-ascriptions for infinite conjunctions and disjunctions; that clearly is not the case. In moving from (1) to (2), one particular syntactic decision ("regimentation", if you will—see section 4) among other options has been enacted: As "[He said 'P_1' & P_1] . . . " stands, we have quote-names of sentences *and* the sentences themselves. Reworking (1) into something finite via quantifiers calls for anaphora, but this can be done in one of *three* ways. One can turn all the occurrences of "P_1," "P_2," . . . , into nominal contexts: this is Putnam's route, which calls for a predicate ("true") and names to appear in those contexts where "P_1", "P_2", . . . , stand alone; that is, it involves nominalizing apparent sentential contexts. *Or*, one can treat all occurrences of "P_1," "P_2," . . . , as occurring in sentential contexts (including the context, "He said 'P_1' "): this is the strategy of Grover et al. (1975), which takes nominal contexts, what otherwise look like predicates followed by quote-names of sentences, as composed of sentences and sentential operators instead; lastly, we can leave the apparent presence of both nominal and sentential contexts untouched by quantifying into those contexts *simultaneously*.

Leave the intriguing third option aside for a moment, and focus on the second. *If* SS-quantifiers occur in natural languages—something I think unlikely—and if all contexts which seem to involve predication and names of sentences are taken to involve sentence operators instead, then a truth *predicate* is *redundant*.[9]

So why *do* natural languages handle truth—at least as far as surface syntax is concerned—predicationally rather than sententially? Soames (1999, p. 34) notes that, in *English*, although we can generalize from "John's mom said that John solved the problem," or "Bill's mom said that Bill solved the problem," or "Harry's mom said

[9] Given equality, SS-quantifiers which quantify into quotation-contexts, *and* objectual quantifiers, we can define "T" like so: "$(x)(Tx \leftrightarrow_{\text{def}} (\exists p)(p \;\&\; \text{“}p\text{”} = x))$," where "(x)" is an objectual quantifier ranging over the substitution class of "$(\exists p)$," a substitutional quantifier. We can do so *without* the objectual quantifiers more directly like so: "$(p)(T\text{“}p\text{”} \leftrightarrow_{\text{def}} p)$." But what do we want "T" for? Also, not only is the truth predicate redundant, but the Tarski biconditionals governing it are *unnecessary* to understand the concepts needed to implement blind truth-ascriptions. We have already got everything we need to grasp *that* from the notion of *generality* with respect to assenting and dissenting from (groups of) sentences. (More on this later.)

that Harry solved the problem," . . . , etc., to "Some man's mom said that he solved the problem," we can't generalize from "1 = 1 although no one can prove 1 = 1," or "1 = 2 although no one can prove 1 = 2," or, . . . , etc., with every sentence, to "Some sentence although no one can prove it." We have to say: Some sentence is true, although no one can prove it is true.[10]

But *why*? Soames writes (1999, p. 34): "Since quantifier phrases like these are noun phrases in English, neither they nor the pronouns they bind can occupy the position of sentences in English." Two points, I think, are worth making.

First, Soames' remark involves an implicit (and easily overlooked) constraint. It is *logically possible* for quantifiers to simultaneously bind prosentences *as well as* pronouns. What stops this in natural languages is that, in such languages, anaphora will not cross syntactic borders. Much of the complexity of "true" (indeed, I dare say, that a *predicate* "true" in English exists *at all*)—is due to this constraint; an example of the complexity that arises when a predicate "T" is introduced, for example, is that we cannot express a Tarski-biconditional *generalization* to govern it like so: "$(p)(Tp \leftrightarrow p)$."[11] Proponents of prosentential truth also accept the anaphoric constraint.

Second: Soames' considerations (which I am otherwise swayed by) make the presence of a truth *predicate* in English a parochial fact about *English* (and other natural languages): because quantifier phrases are noun phrases, we need a predicate that employs pronouns to generalize over sentences. One can ask *why* natural languages are so structured, and the answer, though no doubt fascinating, sheds no light on the primary question facing us: what are the *purely* logical requirements for a device to facilitate the expression of blind truth ascriptions?

3.

The points made in Section 2 show several things. I will start by stressing one of them again: Tarski biconditionals are not needed as an adequacy condition, as the possibility of an SS approach to truth reveals.[12] A truth *predicate* is needed exactly for and only for the reasons Quine originally gave: semantic descent and ascent. If we characterize a set of sentences using a predicate, and want to assent to them, we need a device that takes us from a *description of them* to an *assertion of them* (or vice versa); we need, that is, to navigate the use/mention divide. But SS-quantifiers quantify into sentential contexts, and so, given them, and *given the assumption that descriptions of sentences are (despite appearances) contexts that can be treated as sentential ones*, no such use/mention navigating device (no truth predicate) is called for.

[10] I take it that other natural languages are analogous on this point.

[11] Most react to this sentence as Kirkham (1992, p. 130) does: " . . . it seems . . . as if the p is being used as two different kind of variables within the same formula. . . . " This *intuitive* repulsion to the needed generalization is *merely* the manifestation of the bar in English against anaphora crossing syntactic boundaries.

[12] "But we can *define* such a predicate using SS-quantifiers, and given certain forms of quotation." That misses the point.

This point about SS-quantifiers (I surmise) has been overlooked for several reasons. First, it is often mistakenly assumed that SS-quantifiers presuppose the concept of truth—that is, to put the objection crisply—in giving the semantic conditions for those quantifiers, talk of *truth* is required; e.g.: "$(\exists p)p$ iff there is a substitution-instance S so that S is true." But, of course, the appearance of "true" in the above formulation of the "truth conditions" for substitutional quantification is an eliminable one: "$(\exists p)p$ iff there is a substitution-instance S so that S." Indeed, the (informally stated) quantifier appearing in this second characterization of the "truth conditions" for "$(\exists p)p$" can itself be taken to be substitutional.[13] The semantics of an SS-quantifier, being a *quantifier*, must be given via a quantifier (or something equivalent to a quantifier in logical strength), the same as with any other logical item: connectives, etc.—this benign circularity of the semantic conditions for logical idioms is unavoidable in any case—but a *truth predicate* need not come into the semantics of the SS-quantifier at all.

Another reason for overlooking that SS-quantifiers make the truth predicate unnecessary may be that it is common for deflationists to treat such quantifiers as "short for"—in some sense—infinite conjunctions and disjunctions (of the sentences of the language the quantifiers take as their substitution-instances). The force of Gupta's (1993) polemic against deflationism turns on this construal of SS-quantifiers—and his assumption is a fair one, given the philosophers he targets; the same point holds of the objections found in Simmons (1999). Some motivation for this infinite-disjunction-and-conjunction-construal of SS-quantifiers is due to the previously noted centrality of the Tarski biconditionals on typical deflationist views; and so, given such a motivation, one will hardly notice that once SS-quantifiers are in place, the truth predicate is *otiose*. But, of course, there is no need to read substitutional quantifiers in this infinitary way instead of more naturally as genuine generalizing devices (although as accompanied with substitution-classes of terms rather than accompanied with domains of objects).

Although Gupta's (1993) polemic turns on denying generality to SS-quantifiers when interpreted as infinitary conjunctions and disjunctions, neither his attack, nor that in Simmons (1999), is intended solely against the deflationist who, in particular, (a) takes the Tarski biconditionals as central to our concept of truth, and (b) takes SS-quantifiers to be infinitary disjunctions and conjunctions. Rather, it seems to be a presupposition of both Gupta and Simmons that the deflationary motive *behind* these two technical assumptions—that truth is just a device to facilitate blind truth ascription—is one that *requires* assumptions (a) and (b). That "true" is just a device to facilitate blind ascription is one claim; that (a) and (b) both hold is a *second* claim; it is important to realize that the first claim does *not* imply the second.

I have just described one insight yielded by the discussion in section 2. Here is another. If *sentential* substitutional quantifiers enable blind ascriptions, quantifiers (anaphorically unrestricted quantifiers—*AU quantifiers*, hereon) which can bind

[13] Qualification: This works subject to one or another way of surmounting the objection I shortly bring against SS-quantifiers. "*AU-quantifiers*"—to be described soon—can (quite cleanly) occur in semantic characterizations of themselves.

prosentences and pronouns *simultaneously* will do even better at enabling blind ascriptions. This is because replacing the truth *predicate* with SS-quantifiers blocks anaphora between truth *assertions* and nominal contexts. To make sense of "what John said is true", one treats "John-said" as a *sentence* operator rather than as a predicate: all occurrence of the variable "x" in "$(\exists x)$(John-said$x$ & x)" are prosententialized. Transforming all apparently predicational contexts into sentential ones enables us to handle blind truth-ascriptions, regardless of the description used to pick out the set of sentences one wants to ascribe truth or falsity to. But there is a problem if one wants to combine descriptions of sentences (and truth ascriptions to those sentences) with descriptions of other objects. For example, consider "Any sentence which is purple is true if and only if some rock is also purple." The natural way to construe this is: "$(x)(\mathrm{P}x \rightarrow x) \leftrightarrow (\exists y)(\mathrm{R}y \ \& \ \mathrm{P}y)$"; but to capture this using SS-quantifiers requires that we treat the first occurrence of "P" as a sentential operator, and the second as a predicate. And this points to the fact—rather overwhelmingly obvious about ordinary language—that we can (in principle) apply any description (that we apply to objects of any sort) to sentences *too*, and go on to ascribe truth or falsity to sentences fitting that description.

The only other option (if we want to keep to an SS-approach) is to introduce quote-names and quantify *into* these. That is, we treat descriptive contexts as predicational, but tuck within them (technically, within the "quote-names" appearing within such predicational contexts) a sentential context that sentential quantifiers can bind variables within. If "P" stands for "is on the blackboard in room 201", then "$(\exists p)(\mathrm{P}`p' \ \& \ p)$" is the claim that some sentence on that blackboard is true, and its truth-value status depends on the results of substitutions (of the substitution-instances of the SS-quantifier) for all its variables within and without quotes.[14]

Quantifying into quotes is supposed to circumvent the obstacle of directly linking nominal devices (e.g., names) with sentences (i.e., those very sentences—or variables standing for them) via SS-quantifiers. Unfortunately, allowing quantifiers to bind prosentences inside and outside quotation is not an ideal blend of use and mention with respect to singular-term blind-ascriptions, if we allow ourselves the use of ordinary (nonquotational) names, as well as quantifiers that bind such contexts. Consider the context: "P'John is running'," and consider the identity: " 'John is running' = (1)." We'd like the draw the conclusion: "P(1)." But how? The substitutional quantifier binds the context the sentence "John is running" appears in: within, that is, the context of "P'–'," but a (nominal) quantifier that binds the context of "(1)" binds the context of "P–," a different matter entirely.

Notice the problem. It is not that the (linguistic) resources to express "P(1)" are missing on this approach: if there are both ordinary constants and quote-names, then singular ascriptions using either proper names or quote-names can be written down. The problem is that there should be inference rules from quantified expressions to singular ascriptions of all kinds, and vice versa, and it is hard to see what these rules can be if the quantifiers are SS-ones.

[14] See Grover et al. (1973) and (1975).

One solution is to introduce *two* sets of variables, nominal ones and SS-ones. We can then state the same generalization with either kind of variable, and choose an appropriate form of the generalization—using either nominal or SS-quantifiers—depending on which inferences we intend to use the generalization in. But, although this can be done, it is awkward.

Let us admit it: What are needed are quantifiers (Π, Σ) that simultaneously govern nominal *and* sentential contexts, and instead of all the sentential substitutional *trickery*, why not just directly introduce such things? Indeed, such AU-quantifiers have surprisingly natural and tractable proof and model theories.[15] For current purposes, we need only note the neat expressive power of AU-quantifiers: To write "Every sentence on the blackboard is true" with such quantifiers, we write "$(\Pi x)(Bx \rightarrow x)$"; to write "The conjunction of two sentences is true iff each sentence is true" with such quantifiers, we write: "$(\Pi x)(\Pi y)(\Pi z)(z = Cxy \rightarrow (z \leftrightarrow (x \,\&\, y)))$." Notice that replacing SS-quantifiers with AU-quantifiers preserves the deflationist's insights because the latter also provides a generalizing device for blind ascription that makes a truth predicate unnecessary.

4.

There is yet another point to milk from section 2; but it really requires a new section (which I have just given it). We can explain why AU-quantifiers don't appear in ordinary languages, namely, for reasons *extrinsic* to blind ascriptive needs: the confusion that such quantifiers would lead to. Missing neat devices (e.g., variables) to ease complex cross-linking, anaphora must be kept to a minimum in natural languages.[16]

Armour-Garb and Beall (2001, p. 601) describe liar's paradoxes as "semantic spandrels" ("spandrel" here is adopted from Gould and Lewontin (1978)); they are sentences "which arise as by-products of introducing 'true' into a language with the underlying grammatical rules that exist in English. . . . " Despite the Lamarckian evolution of natural languages, there are *many* (traditional) evolutionary lessons applicable to those languages. One is the engineering point that evolutionary structures are usually jerry-built on structures already in place due to a sequence of quite different (and historically successive) reasons.[17] This is why linguistic devices from the vernacular often have properties that are, given their current functional roles, irrelevant.[18] And, despite the importance of the empirical study of the syntax and semantics

[15] See Azzouni (2001). Pertinent to the topic of this paper is that the tractable model and proof theories I mentioned are predicative ones: an interpreted language is assumed, and the apparatus of AU-quantification is defined over it.

[16] Uniform convergence is very difficult for novice calculus students because of the quantifier interchange involved, and *that* is difficult because natural languages do not equip ordinary speakers to handle complicated cases of anaphora.

[17] Lamarckian evolution allows (at least in principle) the ditching of previous structures altogether, and starting anew. But there is great inertia in the evolution of ordinary language.

[18] The analogy with artificial design versus evolved design is exact. Despite the subtlety of any evolved structure, there is always the extreme likelihood that aspects of it are useless or even pernicious (given its current niche), that something else, designed from scratch, could do the job much *better*. An

of natural languages, this is why old-fashioned *regimentation* (in something like the Quinean sense) is still of interest.

A regimentation, as I understand it, of a designated section of ordinary language *replaces* that designated section with a (piece of) engineered artificial language, not in the sense of giving speakers a different language to (as a practical matter) use, or speak in, but, more narrowly, as supplying *normative constraints* on inferences, and other logical matters, that speakers *should* acknowledge on the basis of statements they have committed themselves to.[19] The model for regimentation, that is, is very close to how highly developed branches of mathematics are used to correct the nonprofessional's computations (in arithmetic, say, or probability). What is claimed is not (and cannot be) that the ordinary person *really means* to carry out calculations of such and such a sort—and that, as an empirical matter, the rigor introduced in the development of a mathematical field makes the ordinary person's intentions explicit. No such empirical study (of the ordinary person's "intentions") is carried out by mathematicians; and when psychologists do study how the ordinary person computes, what is found instead is that the dispositions of the ordinary person usually deviate sharply from the mathematized approach to a subject area.[20] Rather, rigorous mathematics constrains more informal mathematical practice by serving as a corrective when disputes arise.

Regimentation as philosophers/logicians have engaged in it, is (as I have said) similar. The purpose is (a) to systematically present sentential vehicles with inferential properties that are computationally transparent and tractable, and to supply a mathematically tractable semantic theory for such items. (For example, languages governed by the first-order predicate calculus have mechanically recognizable derivation rules, and the semantics for such languages are well-understood.[21]); and (b) to use results about such systematically presented sentential vehicles—*if they are attractive and clear enough*—as the final court of appeal with respect to logical issues surrounding the ordinary-language statements the regimentation concerns. The above italicized rider is crucial: regimentations can come and go: they certainly do not constrain decisions, say, about what logically follows from what, if their dictates are (for one reason or another) particularly controversial—for example, if important functional roles that idioms in ordinary language implement are ones the regimented proxies of those idioms are incapable of sustaining. Thus, the use in regimentations of, for example, first-order classical languages, is (1) for technical reasons: our superior facility in being

example is (alas) our *brains*—with respect to number crunching, but not only that, I am sorry to say—in contrast to the current crop of computers.

[19] The reader should not over-rate my invocation of normativity via the word itself, and via the locution "should". I say more shortly, but I need to stress—early on—that what is "normative" about regimentation is only that we use it to *stipulate,* for example, that "such-and-such" (from the vernacular) means "***", where what "such-and-such" means in the vernacular is either unclear or clear enough—but we prefer it to mean something somewhat *different.* "Stipulate", I also want to stress, is the right word to describe in what sense a regimentation trumps the dictates of the vernacular it regiments.

[20] See Dehaene (1997) for some examples of this.

[21] Consistent models for such languages are not, generally, mechanically recognizable; but there are many mathematical results about them that give us a fairly good grip on their properties.

able to use them (draw inferences within them and prove properties of them), and (2) because they adequately replicate the functions and roles of idioms in ordinary language that we want to keep.

It is easy to confuse regimentation with an empirical study of natural languages. Under such a misapprehension, one may presume that if a regimented idiom operates the way an idiom in a natural language does (as far as we can tell), then the syntax and semantics of the regimented idiom may be (provisionally, and more or less) attributed to the natural language idiom. This is naive:[22] the idioms of invented languages can suggest empirical hypotheses about empirical idioms which we can then go on to try to vindicate the presence of. But the purpose of regimentation is different: It is, as I have said, a *normative practice.* (a) The regimenter determines the needs that an ordinary language idiom **O** satisfies in ordinary language. Success in fulfilling these needs may turn only on a subset of the properties that such an idiom has. Or, it may be that—from a technical point of view—the best way to implement those needs is via a device that shares no properties with **O**. It can also turn out that **O** serves two or more roles, and that these are—again from an engineering point of view—best segregated, so that some of the uses **O** is put to are ignored (given certain purposes). (b) The regimenter coins logical devices with mathematically transparent semantic properties to satisfy those needs. "Mathematically transparent" only means that the properties of such designed devices are matters determinable by pure mathematics: there is no empirical issue of what properties they "truly" have. (c) (and it is here the normative element in regimentation is explicit) The logical properties of such coined devices *trump* the empirically determined properties of the original items in natural languages *in some cases.* For example, some of the apparently semantic intuitions of ordinary speakers about an idiom may be ignored—e.g., certain implications speakers ordinarily presume are disallowed; or certain implications speakers ordinarily do not presume on, are taken to be implications of (some of) the sentences (such idioms appear in).[23]

Before focusing specifically on the regimentation of "true", some jargon is appropriate: When an idiom (or sentence) is regimented, I will describe the result as a *proxy* of the original idiom or sentence in natural language.

Turning to the vernacular "true", I have already claimed that the role of that idiom in the vernacular is part of a package deal the function of which, and the only function of which (that we need concern ourselves with), is to handle blind truth-ascription.[24]

[22] It is, I claim, as naïve as it would be to *assume* that how helicopters hover sheds light on how hummingbirds hover.

[23] Notice a sharp methodological difference with other approaches. Some philosophers of language attempt to explain away certain intuitions—describing them, for example, as "performance errors" or as a matter of "pragmatics" and not "semantics". This *may* be appropriate if one is truly designing a theory about the idioms of natural languages (which—given the formal tools nearly all philosophers of language automatically help themselves to—*cannot be* how to construe what they are up to); but the regimenter's aims are different: the regimenter recognizes that natural language idioms can involve all sorts of linguistic practices that give rise to intuitions that are, strictly speaking, irrelevant to the functions that the idioms in question have been discovered to have, and that are ones that should be preserved in the regimentation.

[24] I have not argued for this here: I've only cited Quine (1970) as an authority on the matter. But I *have* indicated in my (2001) and my (2004c) how the giving of "truth conditions" for

I have also already suggested that the introduction of a *truth predicate* for these purposes is an accident of linguistic history: because anaphora is not handled in ordinary language by *variables* but rather by a cacaphony of heterogeneous devices that make it forbiddingly complicated to introduce anaphora between sentential and nominal positions. From this fact, yet another spandrel emerges: the (intuitive) centrality of Tarski biconditionals. The AU-quantifier—like the SS-quantifier—does not need Tarski biconditionals in order to facilitate blind ascriptions. This is because an AU-quantifier, binding a free-standing variable, can simultaneously bind a variable occurring within a complex description. Automatically, what we assent to (in uttering, say, "$(x)(Px \rightarrow x)$") is anything that falls under "P". This blind ascriptive task is implemented by the standard role of a quantifier. But a truth predicate, being a predicate, must be axiomatically fixed in what is taken to fall under it (otherwise what falls under "P" need not fall under "T"—even if it *should*); its "domain", as it were, must be axiomatically specified. In itself, that is no big deal. Unfortunately, however, because what falls under such a predicate cannot be given by a description,[25] it must be done on a sentence-by-sentence basis: thus the unnatural list-like quality of the set of Tarski biconditionals.[26]

I have, so far, applied "spandrel" to the presence of a truth *predicate* in ordinary language, to handle semantic ascent and descent; I have also, as a result, applied "spandrel" to the intuitive centrality of Tarski biconditionals to our notion of truth. I now want to claim one additional set of spandrels exist in ordinary language. These are sentences which need not appear *at all* [27] in our regimentations of the ordinary language. Before explicitly discussing what sentences I have in mind, I should first make a methodological point, and introduce some terminology. When an idiom is regimented, it can be that its scope is narrowed in such a way that (certain) sentences within which that idiom appears (in the vernacular) are not replicable in the regimented language: no proxies of them appear in the regimentation. Such sentences have an interesting twilight status: since they are present in the vernacular, they—let's say—may be uttered by speakers on certain occasions. But (and here the normativity of regimentation again manifests itself), we nevertheless regard such sentences as

idioms— as it is done in Tarski-style approaches—is only a matter of blind ascription. I claim (but will not show here) that all uses of "true" in the vernacular are similar. In particular, "true" is *not* central to giving a theory of "meaning" for a language—except insofar as blind truth ascriptions are needed for this purpose. There may also be other (e.g., rhetorical) purposes that "true" is put to that I take the regimenter as free to ignore. I cannot get further into this now.

[25] If we could describe all truths as, say, those statements which will be ultimately ratified by Science, then we could coin a predicate S, and use *it* as our truth predicate. See my (2000), Part II, §7, and my (2004a), chapter 2, for why no such predicate can play this role for us.

[26] By contrast, to axiomatize AU-quantifiers, one can imitate the axiomatizations of ordinary quantifiers. See Azzouni (2001).

[27] The intuitive *centrality* of Tarski biconditionals, so I claim, is a spandrel due to the fact that the role satisfied by AU-quantifiers in our regimentation is one satisfied in natural languages by a truth predicate that *needs* to be fixed by such biconditionals to what it applies to. But I am hardly denying that Tarski biconditionals *themselves*—the sentences, I mean—are an (eliminable) spandrel. For a predicate satisfying those biconditionals is certainly definable in AU-languages (under certain conditions). Not so for the set of sentences I go on to discuss next.

failures of a sort; we do not regard speakers as having successfully uttered something. We can say, in fact, that speakers have failed to express a *proposition*.

This use of "proposition" is a purely technical one. Denying that a sentence of the vernacular "expresses a proposition"—in this sense—does not mean that the sentence is taken to be meaningless *in the vernacular*. Presumably, what is successfully expressed in the vernacular is not meaningless; and indeed, there still remains the empirical question to be answered about the semantic (and syntactic) properties of what has been expressed in the vernacular. But if it has been determined that, given the roles of the idioms appearing in that sentence, resources allowing the construction of its proxy need not be included in the regimentation, we see the question about the semantic and syntactic properties of the sentence (in the vernacular) as only an empirical question *about the vernacular*; we do not see it as a question that *we* have to answer in order to determine (say) what the implications of what we should have (normatively speaking) claimed or not claimed about something; from *that* point of view, we have failed to express a proposition at all (in this technical sense)—and so (from this point of view), we can be taken to have uttered something no better than a meaningless noise. I should stress this: given the semantic purposes we have determined certain idioms in the vernacular (and therefore the sentences in the vernacular containing those idioms) to have, we have determined that a certain subset of those sentences can be left out of account; proxies for them need not appear in our regimentation. This analysis and the corresponding notion of "proposition" that I have offered here will be put to specific use with respect to truth shortly.[28]

5.

As I have already mentioned, my treatment of AU-quantifiers is predicative: the sentences in the domain of such quantifiers do not explicitly include themselves. This makes natural a predicative AU-*hierarchy* which handles the regimentation of iterations of the use of "true" in the vernacular, e.g., "Every sentence in Box A is true", where Box A contains the single sentence, " 'John is running', is true". The AU-hierarchy is similar to the Tarskian one—at least in so far as both handle this class of

[28] One other point should be made now: since the notion of "failing to express a proposition"—as I construe it—operates at the interface between the vernacular and its regimentation, adapting such a regimentation (and its proprietary notion of proposition) need not require the adoption of truth-value gaps, three-valued logic, or anything like that in the regimentation, nor does it require attributing truth-value gaps, three-valued logic, or anything like that to the sentences of the vernacular—not, at least, on the grounds that certain sentences of the vernacular fail to express a proposition in this proprietary sense. Instead the class of what is (grammatically speaking) expressible in the vernacular is ***deliberately mismatched*** with the class of what is (grammatically speaking) expressible in the regimentation of that vernacular. If the claim were instead that the regimentation was an (admittedly idealized) ***empirical model*** of the vernacular (see, e.g., Gupta (1982), pp. 177–9)—and that the sentences in it were supposed to replicate the semantic properties of sentences from the vernacular, things would be different: we would ***have to*** introduce truth-value gaps, three-valued logic, or something to that effect.

truth ascriptions in pretty much the same way.[29] Do we need anything *more* to capture the truth-ascriptive practices of ordinary language (that we *want* to capture)?[30]

My answer is a (tentative) "*No*", and I will spend the remainder of the chapter motivating this answer. Kripke (1975, esp. pp. 57–63) has raised several powerful objections against predicative approaches to truth—his objections are specifically directed to what he describes as an "orthodox approach".[31] Apart from this, there are other motivations in the literature, prior to Kripke's (1975) watershed article, and after, for analyzing truth ascriptive practices in the vernacular via a non-predicative approach to truth. I am not, of course, impugning the substantial mathematical interest such approaches have—the issue is their *philosophical value*.

Before undertaking this, I must first waylay a potential misunderstanding: the predicative approach to AU-quantification *does not* rule out self-reference. As Anderson (1970, especially pp. 8–11) points out,[32] one cannot, in any case, stipulate the elimination of self-reference from languages, formal or otherwise. And the predicative AU-hierarchy *does not*. Apart from the fact that self-reference can be present in the given language that AU-quantifiers are defined *on*—in the sense that the language of AU-quantification itself may be codable in such a language, nothing prevents the presence of *other* quantifiers defined on the language along with AU-quantifiers (or already existing within it) that directly allow self-reference.[33] So the issue is not whether an approach to AU-quantifiers that rules out self-reference suffices for truth ascriptive practices in the vernacular; the issue is whether the predicative approach to AU-quantifiers suffices for truth ascriptive practices in the vernacular *worth retaining*.

This raises a related point. Truth predicates are ubiquitous in formal work. That is, the presence (or absence) of predicates obeying Tarski biconditionals can be used to prove important facts about formal systems (e.g., undecidability of non-monadic first-order logic). There is no obvious link between such technical predicates and the

[29] However: the AU-hierarchy is much simpler, mathematically speaking, than the Tarskian hierarchy. Kripke (1975, pp. 60–1) raises the technical issue of the transfinite iteration of the Tarskian hierarchy; such iteration is sensitive to exactly how previous truth predicates are coded into truth predicates at limit ordinals. I do not know the current status of the problem, but in any case, it *does not* arise for the AU-hierarchy because, unlike in the Tarski hierarchy, truth ascription has been separated from a characterization of the syntax of the sentences truth is ascribed to. For the motivation for this, see Azzouni (2001).

[30] This is *not* the technical question of whether impredicative approaches to AU-quantifiers are available; of course they are: Kripke and Gupta/Herzberger approaches to the truth predicate can be pretty easily adapted to quantifiers and, in particular, to AU-quantifiers. The question is a different one: is there substantial evidence that such impredicative approaches are needed *at all*, given the needs of truth ascriptive practices in ordinary language?

[31] Kripke (1975, p. 58, fn. 9) writes: "By an 'orthodox approach', I mean any approach that works within classical quantification theory and requires all predicates to be totally defined on the range of the variables..."—but the objections so raised easily apply to predicative versions of the AU-approach.

[32] Also see Kripke (1975), p. 58, fn. 9.

[33] As it has been repeatedly noted, many examples of self-reference are benign in that the logical resources they are based on need not give rise to either paradox or, more broadly, truth-value ungroundedness, e.g.: "This sentence has five words." These sorts of examples, of course, do not involve truth ascription, and do not need regimentation by AU-quantifiers.

tools needed for blind ascription in ordinary languages. It may *look* this way to those who centralize Tarski biconditionals; but all *that* link guarantees is that under certain circumstances the truth idiom used for blind ascriptions and these technical predicates will prove co-extensive over certain (restricted) domains of discourse. That the result is not conservative when the truth predicate is added to PA, for example, and allowed within the inductive schema, shows nothing about the truth idiom *needed for blind ascription*. That is, even if (which I doubt—see Azzouni (1999)) such a truth predicate must be treated as indicating a "substantive property", *that is* insufficient to show that the truth idiom, as needed for blind ascription, indicates such a thing. This is because the two idioms may differ in the other conditions placed upon them: any condition placed upon the truth predicate, as it appears in a formal context, must be independently justified (with respect to the role of the truth idiom for blind ascription) before conclusions about truth—as it is needed for blind ascription—can be drawn.

Let us turn now to possible motivations for impredicative approaches to truth. One motivation arises from the appearance that natural languages have of being "semantically complete". The particular form the concern takes in the context of our truth-ascription practices is our ability, as it were, to ascribe truth or falsity to certain (large) classes of sentences in our language—for example, *every* sentence (including, of course) the very sentence so ascribing truth or falsity. One issue is whether, in fact, the vernacular *really does* allow such a thing. This question can be left aside: if the language gives the appearance that it allows such an ability, it may do so for reasons that force it to be inconsistent;[34] but in any case that is, of course, an empirical question about the vernacular. From the regimentalist's point of view, the important question is: Do we need a capacity to ascribe truth and falsity to, say, *any* class of sentences *whatsoever*?

One may think to read such a need off the practice of blind ascription because one could think: *any* description (of a set of sentences) may be impounded to characterize a set of sentences we want to ascribe truth or falsity to. But this is too general a characterization of the function of blind ascription. What is at issue—especially since we already know that allowing the devices that enable blind truth-ascription to operate impredicatively will lead to paradox—is whether a predicative approach to such a device, e.g., a predicative AU-hierarchy, leads to an inability to express proxies for sentences in the vernacular that speakers *really need*. As I said, I am going to (tentatively) claim that the answer is "No".[35] My answer is tentative because what has to be done is to look at a number of cases of specific sorts of blind truth-ascriptions that can be made in the vernacular, but that seem problematical (if one adopts a predicative approach to truth ascriptions) and show their unimportance. I stress again that the mere fact that a sort of (impredicative) blind ascription exists

[34] There are *very* good reasons to think natural languages *are* inconsistent: see my 2004(b).

[35] Gupta (1982, p. 229) writes of such sentences—not just paradoxical ones, but other various sorts of "ungrounded sentences" such as truth-tellers—that "... from the ordinary viewpoint these are the 'don't care' cases...." I will dwell on this important insight shortly.

in the vernacular is no argument—by itself—that regimentation need take account of it.[36]

To start: It may be thought that semantic characterizations, complete in this sense, of the "truth conditions" of *all* the sentences in a language (including the very sentences *in* the semantic characterization) are especially valuable. It may be thought so, but not by me. If an empirical characterization of the semantic properties of natural languages is at issue, it is hard to see why it is required that such semantic properties be characterized within the language itself.[37] And if the issue is the semantic characterizations of the regimentations constructed for the normative purposes I have stressed in this paper, again, it is hard to see why global (self-referential) semantic characterizations should be required.[38]

Another motivation for impredicative approaches to truth ascription also arises from a direct concern with the vernacular. This is the idea that the presence of paradox calls for an *explanation*: there is something to diagnose here, something to discover about natural language that explains why paradoxes can arise or what they (really) are due to.[39]

It is unclear what a successful diagnosis is supposed to look like in this context. The resolution of a "paradox" (when they are to be had) takes the following form: (a) it is parsed as a contradictory set of assumptions, and (b) one of those assumptions is a hitherto unrecognized false principle that must now be rejected. Unfortunately, something like this—which is reasonable *given an antecedent subject matter that the assumptions are about*—can impel the thought (in this context) that diagnosing paradoxes is simply teasing out an assumption to be exhibited as rejected by a reductio. And this, in turn, leads to something weird. Consider the sentence: (1) (1) is false. Imagine the following (purported) presupposition: (1) *refers to* "(1) is false," and consider the following argument.

(a) (1) refers to "(1) is false."	Assumption.
(b) (1) is true if and only if (1) is false.	{use of standard Liar reasoning}
(c) (1) doesn't refer to "(1) is false."	Reductio on (a) and (b).[40]

[36] What motivates impredicative approaches in set theory, for example, is their value given attempts to induce set-theoretical proxies of classical mathematical objects (see, Kleene 1971, e.g., p. 42–3, for an accessible discussion of this). So, similarly, one wants to examine the specifics of truth-ascription practices in order to see if there are motivations *in that practice* for impredicative truth ascriptions. This is what I go on to do.

[37] After all, every other science allows itself to extend natural language in whatever way it needs to ply its trade. Why should semantics be different?

[38] The worry may be: *We'll never finish*. After all, we would also like a semantic characterization of the (meta)language in which the semantic characterization is carried out. OK, that can be supplied too; but why must everything be done at once? The thought of hierarchies of semantic principles seems to panic some, but that is hardly an *argument*.

[39] The suggestion that semantic paradoxes are open to "diagnosis" seems to have originated with Chihara (1979). Of course, he was introducing a bit of jargon (which subsequently caught on) for something philosophers were previously clearly engaged in—as he admits.

[40] I explored this "solution" to paradoxes in my (1991). This is not to suggest I motivated it by means of a reductio.

Or, consider *this* presupposition: (1) is either true or false. Again we find:

(a) (1) is either true or false.	Assumption.
(b) (1) is true if and only if (1) is false.	{use of standard Liar reasoning}
(c) (1) is neither true nor false.	Reductio on (a) and (b).

I am *not* claiming that one or another solution to the paradox that might be offered will not be interesting, or will not be something we might eventually adapt; rather, the claim is that the intuitions generated by ordinary uses of reductio ad absurdum give the impression that there is something to explain about paradoxes, and that when an assumption that leads to the paradox is rejected, we have indeed explained how the paradox arises (as opposed to the very different methodological suggestion that nothing has been *explained*—that is the wrong model—rather, we are exploring whether the "rejected" assumption is one we can or should live without).[41]

Again, it is important to separate the project of regimentation from the empirical study of language, and both of these from the project of determining the principles governing a subject matter. In the third case, a "paradox", an inconsistency in the set of principles governing a subject matter involves (we presume) a mistake *on our part*: we have wrongly formulated the principles governing that subject matter, and we must find out which one(s) should be rejected. Reductio ad absurdum only indicates that the principles, *as a group*, are problematical, and not which ones should be rejected. The (and this is where diagnosis, properly, arises) latter is determined by our understanding and study of the subject matter in question. Regimentation is a different matter entirely. Here, as I have said before, we are out to construct idioms that replicate functions of ordinary language items (that we want to retain), and it is a matter of sheer mathematics which ones have which properties. Again, there is

[41] In pointing out that such reductios are uninformative—beyond, of course, their exhibiting the *inconsistency* of a set of sentences—I am *not* suggesting that philosophers generally do not realize this (for Quine and Popper, for example, this very insight is a joint substantial plank of their respective approaches to philosophy of science): more specifically, the most common attitude towards semantic paradoxes is that there are many approaches and that one must delicately evaluate the vices of competing systems; see, e.g., Feferman (1982). Indeed, much earlier, Martin (1970) writes: "A solution [to the Liar] consists in convincing ourselves that at least one of the assumptions that led to the contradiction is after all not so plausible. Obviously if our own move in trying to remove the plausibility of a particular assumption is to treat the argument to contradiction as a *reductio*, as though it proves that the assumption in question is false, we have failed entirely." He adds: "What is wanted, ideally, is the uncovering, the making explicit, of some rulelike features of our language which when considered carefully have the effect of blocking at least one of the assumptions of the argument; if not actually showing an assumption to be false, at least casting doubt upon it." Martin, near as I can tell, does not reveal what tools we are to use to *empirically determine* that the targeted assumption is *not* operative among speakers.

The reader may be wondering why I bother to make this point if philosophers generally *are* aware that such reductios are uninformative. Well, as we shall see, they are aware in *some* contexts but not in others. I will allude to two examples now: One motivation Herzberger (1982) offers for the (otherwise purely mathematical) study of how the truth-value revision process he uses gives rise to cycles among pathological sentences is the diagnostic one (see p. 135, in particular). For reasons I give momentarily, it is hard to see how any diagnostic aim can be satisfied in this way. For a criticism of a second example from the revisionary literature, see my (1995). Cases similar to these are discussed later in this paper.

nothing to diagnose; inconsistency is sheerly a (mathematical) fact about certain formal systems. Lastly, there is the empirical question which syntactic (and semantic) principles are actually in use among speakers of a natural language. Here too there is nothing to diagnose because if the principles speakers use are shown (empirically) to be inconsistent, *then it just follows that the principles speakers use are inconsistent.* We can go on to explain *why* an inconsistent set of principles are so used, e.g., what it is about the evolution of language use among speakers that caused them to converge upon an inconsistent set of principles, and how they could retain such a set of principles *despite* an official norm *against* inconsistency; but *that* does not involve diagnosis in the sense that Martin or Chihara have in mind. Rather, it seems, from the foregoing, that nothing involving diagnosis (in their sense) exists.

Let us turn to the objections Kripke offers against "orthodox approaches", objections, if sustained, that apply to the predicative AU-approach as well. Here is the first: Regimenting the vernacular via predicative AU-quantifiers, like regimentation via the standard Tarski hierarchy, seems to impose subscripted idioms (truth predicates or AU-quantifiers), each with its own level.[42] Kripke (1975, pp. 58–60) writes:

> [This approach takes] the ordinary notion of truth [to be] systematically ambiguous: "level" in a particular occurrence is determined by the context of the utterance and the intentions of the speaker. The notion of differing truth predicates, each with its own level, seems to correspond to the following intuitive idea.... First, we make various utterances, such as "snow is white", which do not involve the notion of truth. We then attribute truth values to these, using a predicate "true_1".... We can then form a predicate "true_2", and so on. We may assume that, on each occasion of utterance, when a given speaker uses the word "true", he attaches an implicit subscript to it, which increases as... he goes higher and higher in his own Tarski hierarchy.

Kripke goes on to say:

> [T]his picture seems unfaithful to the facts. If someone makes an utterance [such as "Most (i.e., a majority) of Nixon's assertions about Watergate are false"]... he does *not* attach a subscript, explicit or implicit, to his utterance of "false" which determines "the level of language" on which he speaks.... [The problem is that o]rdinarily... a speaker *has no way of knowing the "levels" of Nixon's relevant utterances*.... The idea that a statement such as (4) ["All of Nixon's utterances about Watergate are false"] should, in its normal uses, have a "level" is intuitively convincing. It is... equally intuitively obvious that the "level" of (4) should not depend on the form of (4) alone (as would be the case if "false"—or, perhaps, "utterance"—were assigned explicit subscripts), nor should it be assigned in advance by the speaker, but rather its level should depend on the empirical facts about what Nixon has uttered.

This objection misses its target if the hierarchy is supposed to be a regimentation. For then it is not required that the ordinary truth predicate, say, have subscripts. All that is required is that a regimentation that subscripts truth predicates, and locates proxies of ordinary language sentences (on the basis of those subscripts) in the hierarchy, be the best artificial approach (known to date) for facilitating truth ascriptions. So, in particular, speakers need not be taken to have any intentions whatsoever about the location of their truth ascriptions in a hierarchy; and it can, of

[42] The "ground floor" AU-quantifiers regiment truth ascriptions to sets of sentences which themselves do not involve truth attributions. The next level includes the first collection of sentences plus truth (and falsity) attributions to sentences (and groups of such) in the first collection. And so on.

course, be an empirical matter what level the proxy of an ordinary sentence is assigned in the Tarski hierarchy, and one based (of course) on what sentences that sentence is about.

Since I am imposing a regimentation analysis of predicative approaches, it may be that—strictly speaking—this objection, put this way, does not apply to how *Kripke* understands the relationship between, say, the Tarskian hierarchy approach and the vernacular. *So let us assume* that applying the Tarskian hierarchy to the vernacular *does* require that a speaker's truth ascriptions—in the vernacular—use subscripted truth predicate as Kripke describes it; let us suppose that the Tarskian approach is not a regimentation in the sense of section 4, but rather more: an (idealized) model of the vernacular.[43] But (again) why *should* this imply that speakers need to have intentions about where the sentences they have uttered are located in the (vernacular) hierarchy? That speakers generally do not know what level their truth ascriptions have should hardly be surprising given that such a level depends on what sentences they are attributing truth or falsity to (and blind truth ascriptions are often—usually, I should think—to sentences we do not know a lot about). There does not seem to be any reason to require that the speaker (or anyone, for that matter) must know what level that is. That this means, in some sense, the speaker does not know exactly which truth predicate he or she is using, is not objectionable; indeed, on this view, such typical ignorance on the part of speakers might be used to explain why subscripts *do not* appear appended to truth predicates in the vernacular.[44]

Kripke's second objection is far more important. As he (1975, p. 60) points out (and he is, I think, the first to point this out), there are examples of truth ascriptions *in the vernacular* which seem to resist a predicative approach, and which, nevertheless, it is very natural to treat as *successful* in the sense that such truth ascriptions are (intuitively) assigned truth values despite our inability to order them in a predicative structure.[45]

Kripke's example is the pair of statements uttered by Dean and Nixon respectively:

(4) All of Nixon's utterances about Watergate are false.
(5) Everything Dean says about Watergate is false.

[43] I have to say, though, that the formal tools used in the Tarskian, Kripkean, and for that matter, in *all* the approaches taken in this literature, are not ones that have been (or, I think, can be) justified, *if one is actually engaged in an empirical study of natural languages.*

[44] Actually, there does not seem to be any reason to expect a speaker to *even know* that his or her use of the vernacular "true" possesses subscripts. There is a great deal of empirical evidence that how (natural language) sentences are represented in users' minds involves all sorts of items that such speakers have no introspective access to. See, e.g., Chomsky (1986). Although, in this case, the actual subscript could not be represented in the speaker's mind, surely something could be represented there that indicated that the truth predicate used by the speaker has a higher subscript than the sentences characterized by the appropriately related complex description. Such a representation would presume that the sequence of levels generated must be grounded (if the truth ascription is to be successful). But this point, rather than sustaining Kripke's first objection, brings us directly to his second.

[45] In a sense, all the forthcoming examples are generalizations of "All Cretans are liars"; this statement, recall, is paradoxical iff every *other* statement uttered by a Cretan is false. Otherwise we are quite willing to treat this statement as *unremarkably* false.

Both speakers—somewhat megalomaniacally—want to include all of each other's statements within the scope of their quantifiers—and this makes location of either statement in a predicative hierarchy perilous. Unfortunately, the hope of simply ruling out such claims as unsuccessful (as not expressing propositions, in the sense of section 4) seems to founder on the naturalness of assigning both (4) and (5) truth values under certain empirical circumstances. Imagine (as Kripke suggests) Dean has uttered at least one true statement about Watergate (other than (4)); then on these grounds alone, we take (5) to be false. *And* if everything else Nixon ever said about Watergate is false, then (4) (we naturally think) is *true*.[46]

Another neat example is due to Gupta (1982, p. 210). He introduces his example with the significant remark: "There are types of reasoning that we allow in everyday discourse . . . ".

A says:
(a1) Two plus two is three. (false)
(a2) Snow is always black. (false)
(a3) Everything B says is true. (-)
(a4) Ten is a prime number. (false)
(a5) Something B says is not true. (-)

B says:
(b1) One plus one is two. (true)
(b2) My name is B. (true)
(b3) Snow is sometimes white. (true)
(b4) At most one thing A says is true. (-)

Gupta points out that it is very natural to reason as follows: Since (a3) and (a5) contradict each other, (b4) is true. Therefore (a3) is true and (a5) is false.

The importance of these examples for *our* purposes is this.[47] Even if one finds the project of studying *paradoxical* sentences of no interest—at least when it comes to evaluating our blind-ascription needs in the vernacular—and even if one thinks our ability (in the vernacular) to construct paradoxical sentences *does not* show anything significant about the adequacy of predicative approaches to truth ascriptions, even if, that is, one is comfortable leaving paradoxical sentences out of one's regimentation of our truth-ascription practices, and even if, in doing so, one concedes that it is an empirical matter out of the speaker's hands whether the truth ascription a speaker makes *does* express a paradox or not, these examples pose a problem precisely because they are *not* examples of paradoxes: they are cases of blind ascription which we are intuitively inclined to treat as successful (in the sense that truth values—truth *or* falsity) are assigned to all the sentences in question. This seems to show not only that it is an empirical matter, out of the hands of speakers, whether their truth ascriptions *are* successful or not (this is the motivation for Kripke's oft-repeated assertion that such truth ascriptions should be "allowed to find their own level"), but, more importantly,

[46] As Kripke also points out, it is easy to change the empirical circumstances to reverse the truth values for (4) and (5); it is also easy to construct other sorts of examples.

[47] Kripke and Gupta have *different* purposes, of course. Kripke (1975) takes his examples to show that a predicative approach to truth will not work. Gupta (1982) takes his example(s) to illustrate sorts of reasoning in the vernacular that Kripke's approach has trouble accommodating.

that any regimentation of truth ascription which leaves us without resources for directly replicating non-predicative kinds of reasoning is one which fails to capture a large class of blind truth-ascriptions which speakers routinely make (since, after all, one can assume that speakers routinely utter successful truth ascriptions that under other empirical circumstances would have proven paradoxical, and thus which resist predicative treatment).[48]

Just because truth ascriptions of speakers can go sour in ways speakers cannot anticipate, *does not mean* that the ways such sentences do go sour need be captured by regimentation. After all, the common response to paradoxes (when presented at parties during, say, the course of ordinary chatter) is to move on (after, perhaps, a barely polite laugh or two). There is *no* evidence that ordinary speakers *do* anything when faced with sentences that *are* paradoxical or otherwise truth-value defective (e.g., truth-tellers) that shows that there is something special about their reasoning with such items that needs to be captured by regimentation. The ordinary person's practice of ignoring such sentences can be reasonably imitated by the regimentalist (that is, by treating such sentences as failing to express propositions, in the proprietary sense of section 4).[49]

It is that under certain empirical circumstances a sentence that resists predicative treatment *is nevertheless assigned specific truth values* that causes a problem. But what is important is not the mere fact that speakers naturally assign truth values to such sentences; the critical issue is whether the fact that they do so is significant to our blind ascriptive practices.

There is an important consideration that suggests that it *is not* significant. Recall the point made earlier about attempts to "diagnose" paradoxes. The logical principles we have imbibed along with our language are ones it is natural for us to employ *anywhere we can.*[50] And what this means is that even with sentences that, strictly speaking, we have no genuine need for (given the purposes our truth-ascribing practices satisfy), we may find ourselves with logical intuitions resulting from the (rote) application of those principles.

Consider the lying Cretan again.[51] We *can* reason our way a priori to the empirical claim that some Cretan or other must have lied; for in this way we avoid paradox. Ordinary speakers carefully restrain their otherwise exuberant application of logical principles, such as reductio ad absurdum, precisely because such principles otherwise lead to the assignment of truth values to empirical claims where no such inferences are (empirically) justified. But the only difference bertween this example and the ones

[48] A technical point. Predicative (or hierarchical) approaches, as I understand them, assign levels to sentences based only on which sentences they refer to and quantify over. (4) and (5) are immune to a level-assignment on these grounds alone. Kripke's approach is to assign such sentences "levels" (stages at which they are assigned truth values) based on in addition the *truth values* assigned to the sentences they refer to and quantify over.

[49] Again, this is *not* to exclude the purely empirical study of establishing what it is about the semantic rules that *actually governs* natural languages and that allows such sentences into the vernacular in the first place.

[50] That is, our logical principles are topic-neutral. One reason is confirmation holism. I intend to take this up in some detail at a later time.

[51] Recall fn. 45.

Kripke and Gupta offer, is that since none of the claims made in the latter examples are in danger of leading to empirical refutation (because they are ungrounded!), we are willing to rest with the intuitive assignment of truth values dictated by those principles, even though the kind of reasoning involved *differs in no significant way, logically speaking, from the (unjustifiable) inference to the existence of a lying Cretan.*

And *this* shows that the reasoning exhibited in examples such as Kripke's and Gupta's *is not* evidentially admissible in the evaluation of the adequacy of predicative approaches to truth ascription in the vernacular. Since these are the only sorts of examples that anyone has ever offered to show that reasoning in the vernacular about "ungrounded" sentences can lead to successful truth-value attributions, I draw the conclusion that the regimenter can ignore impredicative truth attributions altogether. Although it is an empirical matter—out of the speaker's hands—whether, inadvertently, one of these has been uttered, characterizing such sentences (distinguishing impredicative from predicative uses of the truth predicate in the vernacular) can be carried out without having to engage in Kripke or Gupta/Herzberger style constructions, because the distinction, although semantic, does not turn on the assignment of truth-values.[52]

[52] There is another objection that can be made to these approaches, but since it is not as central to the topic of this chapter, I will make it in this footnote. Crucial to the intuitions elicited by the Kripke/Gupta examples is not just what truth values *are* assigned to such sentences but *how* we reason ourselves *to* these truth values. Although Kripke's formal construction supplies the right truth values for the examples he discusses, and although Gupta's formal construction supplies the right truth values for the examples *he* discusses, neither approach assigns such truth values in anything like the way ordinary reasoning does it: neither step-by-step reasoning from sentences at lower levels to higher levels (as in Kripke's approach) is at work—as Gupta's examples show—nor is revisionary reasoning present, as Gupta's approach requires. Despite both philosophers (admittedly, with hedging on Kripke's part) treating their formal techniques as capturing, in some sense, the informal notion of truth itself (as opposed to a formal analogue which is, at best, extensionally equivalent), this would not be an insurmountable problem if such approaches did assign the *same* truth values to pathological sentences as ordinary intuition does. Unfortunately, all such approaches breed *artifacts* because of how their impredicative models are constructed: sentences, that is, are given truth values at variance to ordinary intuition—for example, sentences ordinary intuition regards as pathological are treated as stably true or false (in the Gupta-Herzberger approach). (See my (1995) for some details on this.) This is good evidence that what is involved in the intuitive assignment of truth values in the kinds of "circular reasoning" examples given by Kripke and Gupta is the extension of ordinary practices of reasoning, and not something more drastic—such as a "revision concept of truth".

Another indication of this very same point is that both Kripke's and Gupta/Herzberger's approach sort sentences according to their sort of pathology ("paradoxical", "intrinsically paradoxical" ...). They *do not* illuminate or even indicate what sort of reasoning may be appropriately applied to such sentences—thus they ratify the "don't care" attitude taken towards them by practitioners in the vernacular. (See fn. 35.)

I hope no reader mistakenly thinks I am suggesting that this faults *in any way* the examples of self-referential reasoning that arise in technical areas; these are not examples of blind truth ascription that require nonpredicative approaches to truth ascription: these are syntactic results based on the existence (or not) of certain sorts of predicates in certain systems. Even in the cases of Gödel's theorem, which is often popularly described as a proof that there are true sentences which are not provable, what is going on is a proof (via self-reference) of the syntactic incompleteness of a certain class of formal systems; and, subject to the co-referentiality of (some of) the terms in these systems, the attribution of truth to sentences derivable in some of these formal systems but not in others. (See Azzouni 1994, Part II, §7, for details on this.)

More vaguely put (but still rhetorically compelling) objections to hierarchy approaches occur in the literature regularly. Echoing this now-traditional source of discomfort, Simmons (1999, p. 475) writes:

> . . . the English predicate "true" is divided into infinitely many distinct predicates, and English itself is stratified into a hierarchy of distinct languages. This seems, as Russell once put it, "harsh and highly artificial".

To some extent, this concern may be due to the view that hierarchy views require attributing to competent speakers an appreciation of the location of sentences in the hierarchy. If, as I have argued, such views *do not* require any such thing, then the mere fact that the truth predicate in English does not intuitively seem to be scattered amongst a hierarchy of languages is no objection to these approaches—nor, of course, is their apparent harsh and artificial quality. Another source of the ill-ease quoted above may be, as we have seen before, the clash of seriously different *projects*: A genuine empirical study of ordinary language on the one hand versus regimentation on the other.

5.

In a sense there is nothing simpler than the (simple) liar's paradox: it can be presented to a child—and understood. And, in a sense, there is nothing simpler (as well) about how reductio ad absurdum can snooker us into "solutions" of such a thing. (The intense but naïve delight one feels when first thinking, for example, "That's it!—not *every* sentence is true or false.") But, really, the "diagnosis" is this: *there is nothing to diagnose*. Certain languages—most likely our natural ones—allow *ineliminable* inconsistent sentences, via syntactic and referential principles which are not at all hard to understand. If there were a simple way to replace such languages with ones which *do not* imply such contradictions—to change their syntactic or referential principles in some way—and yet have a resulting language as expressive as natural languages (at least with respect to those parts of natural language being modeled), we would do so immediately. This would not be a diagnosis of *anything*: the intuitive gloss on reductio ad absurdum that, using it, one unearths a false assumption about a subject-matter, is just *wrong*. Rather, we would have discovered the (mathematical) existence of such a language. We could then regiment our own language in it: proxy (some of) the sentences of the vernacular in that artificial discovery, and leave for another time the difficult and subtle empirical question of whether our natural languages are, in some way, like this artificial discovery, or whether, as they appear, natural languages are simply inconsistent. Unfortunately, no such desirable artificial language exists.[53]

[53] Apart from all the work exploring what sorts of languages—that allow various sorts of self-reference—are possible, there is almost a proof of this fact, the existence of which can be recognized via the very common criticism offered to solutions of paradoxes which impose contextual levels on paradoxical sentences, e.g., Parsons (1974) or Burge (1979), so that such a sentence (on a use) fails to say of itself (on that use) that it is false but only succeeds in saying of some other use (of that sentence) that *it* is false: this is that such an approach fails to allow the paradoxical sentence to say what is intended. But, of course, if it were to do *that*, it would still be paradoxical.

Luckily, we can circumscribe those cases of truth ascription that we need—regiment them in a predicative hierarchy, and discard the rest. The fact that it is an empirical question whether certain (chancy) sentences we have uttered *are* ones that can be so regimented, and thus treated as successfully expressing a proposition, or not, is yet one more fact of life that we had better accommodate ourselves to.[54]

REFERENCES

Anderson, A. R. (1970). St. Paul's epistle to Titus. In *The paradox of the liar*, ed. R. L. Martin, 1–11. New Haven: Yale University Press.

Armour-Garb, B. and J. C. Beall (2001). Can deflationists be dialetheists? *J. Philos. Logic* 30(6): 593–608.

Azzouni, J. (1991). A simple axiomatizable theory of truth. *Notre Dame Journal of Formal Logic* 32(3): 458–93.

——(1994). *Metaphysical myths, mathematical practice: the ontology and epistemology of the exact sciences*. Cambridge: Cambridge University Press.

——(1995). Review of "The liar speaks the truth". *Mind* 104(413): 222–5.

——(1999). Comments on Shapiro. J. *Philos.* 97: 541–4.

——(2000). *Knowledge and reference in empirical science*. London: Routledge.

——(2001). Truth via anaphorically unrestricted quantifiers. *J. Philos. Logic* 30: 329–54.

——(2004a). *Deflating existential commitment: A case for nominalism*. Oxford: Oxford University Press.

——(2004b). The strengthened liar, the expressive strength of natural languages, and regimentation. *The Philosophical Forum*. 34(3&4): 329–50.

——(2004c). Tarski, Quine, and the transcendence of the vernacular "true". *Synthese* 142: 273–88.

Burge, T. (1979). Semantical paradox. *J. Philos.* 76:169–98. Reprinted in *Recent essays on truth and the liar paradox* (1984), ed. Robert L. Martin, 83–117. Oxford: Oxford University Press.

Chihara, C. (1979). The semantic paradoxes: a diagnostic investigation. *Philos. Review* 88: 590–618.

Chomsky, N. (1986). *Knowledge of language: Its nature, origin, and use*. New York: Praeger.

Collins, J. (2002). On the proposed exhaustion of truth. *Dialogue* XLI: 653–79.

Dehaene, S. (1997). *The number sense*. Oxford: Oxford University Press.

Feferman, S. (1982). Towards useful type-free theories, I. *JSL* 49(1): 75–111. Reprinted in *Recent essays on truth and the liar paradox* (1984), ed. Robert L. Martin, 237–87. Oxford: Oxford University Press.

Field, H. (1994). Deflationist views of meaning and content. Mind 103(41): 249–85.

Gould, S. J. and R. C. Lewontin (1978). The spandrels of San Marco and the Panglossian paradigm: A critique of the adaptionist programme. *Proc. Roy. Soc. London* 205: 581–98.

Grover, D. L. and N. D. Belnap (1973). Quantifying in and out of quotes. In *A prosentential theory of truth* (1992), 244–75. Princeton, NJ: Princeton University Press.

——, J. L. Camp, and N. D. Belnap (1975). A prosentential theory of truth. In *A prosentential theory of truth* (1992), 70–120. Princeton, NJ: Princeton University Press.

[54] We would have to live with it regardless of our approach to paradoxes—this is one of the most important lessons of Kripke (1975).

Gupta, A. (1982). Truth and paradox. *J. Philos. Logic* 11: 1–60. Reprinted in *Recent essays on truth and the liar paradox* (1984), ed. Robert L. Martin, 175–235. Oxford: Oxford University Press. Citations are to the reprint.

—— (1993). A critique of deflationism. *Philosophical Topics* 21/2: 57–81. Reprinted in *Truth* (1999), eds. S. Blackburn and K. Simmons, 282–307. Citations are to the reprint.

Herzberger, Hans (1982). Notes on naïve semantics. *J. Philos. Logic* 11: 61–102. Reprinted in *Recent essays on truth and the liar paradox* (1984), ed. Robert L. Martin, 133–74. Oxford: Oxford University Press. Citations are to the reprint.

Horwich, P. (1998). *Truth*, 2nd ed. Oxford: Oxford University Press.

Kirkham, R. L. (1992). *Theories of truth*. Cambridge, MA: The MIT Press.

Kleene, S. C. (1971). *Introduction to metamathematics*. Amsterdam: North-Holland Publishing Company.

Kripke, S. (1975). Outline of a theory of truth. *J. Philos.* 72: 690–716. Reprinted in *Recent essays on truth and the liar paradox* (1984), ed. Robert L. Martin, 53–81. Oxford: Oxford University Press. Citations are to the reprint.

Leeds, S. (1978). Theories of reference and truth. *Erkenntnis* 13: 111–29.

Martin, R. L. (1970). A category solution to the liar. In *The paradox of the liar* (1970), ed. Robert L. Martin, 91–120. New Haven: Yale University Press.

Parsons, C. (1974). The liar paradox. *J. Philos. Logic* 3: 381–412. Reprinted in *Recent essays on truth and the liar paradox* (1984), ed. Robert L. Martin, 9–45. Oxford: Oxford University Press.

Patterson, Douglas (forthcoming). Tarski on the necessity reading of convention T. *Synthese*.

Putnam, H. (1978). Meaning and knowledge. In *Meaning and the moral sciences*, 1–80. London: Routledge and Kegan Paul.

Quine, W. V. (1970). *Philosophy of logic*. Englewood Cliffs, NJ: Prentice Hall.

Simmons, K. (1999). Deflationary truth and the liar. *J. Philos. Logic* 28(5): 455–88.

Soames, S. (1999). *Understanding truth*. Oxford: Oxford University Press.

Tarski, A. (1932). The concept of truth in formalized languages. In *Logic, semantics, metamathematics* (1983), ed. John Corcoran. Indianapolis, Indiana: Hackett Publishing Company, Inc.

Wright, C. (1992). *Truth and objectivity*. Oxford: Blackwell.

Index